LOUISIANA

The History of an American State

LOUISIANA

The History of an American State

ANNE CAMPBELL

&

WILSON A. MARSTON

CLAIRMONT PRESS

Montgomery, Alabama

AUTHORS

ANNE CAMPBELL is a faculty member at the LSU Laboratory School, serving as a master teacher and a middle school team leader. She has taught social studies in Louisiana for more than twenty years, in East Baton Rouge and Bossier parishes. She has presented a number of workshops throughout the state as a member of the Louisiana Writing Project. She worked with the committee of teachers to develop the Louisiana Social Studies Standards. She has also served as a curriculum writer for both state and local projects. Ms. Campbell earned a B.A. and an M.Ed. from Northwestern State University and has completed additional postgraduate work at Louisiana Tech and Louisiana State University.

WILSON A. MARSTON is a native Louisianian. He was born and raised in Baton Rouge, where he attended public schools and Louisiana State University. He taught in grades 4-8 in the East Baton Rouge Parish school system for twelve years. After completing his doctorate at the University of Virginia, he returned to LSU as an assistant professor in the College of Education. Dr. Marston teaches courses in elementary/middle school social studies, with emphasis on integrated thematic instruction and creative thinking, and teaches and advises in gifted education.

Editor-in-Chief: Ralph M. Holmes

Editor: Kathleen K. Conway

Associate Editor: Billie Holmes

Design: Robin McDonald

Photo Research: Robin McDonald
                Marie Martin

Prepress production: Photographics, Inc., Birmingham, Alabama

ISBN: 1-56733-985-9   Second Printing   Printed in the U.S.A.

TO THE STUDENTS

YOU ARE A PART of the story of Louisiana, and Louisiana is a part of the story of the world. You can add to this story in a positive way. Your actions and your attitude affect everyone who plays a role in the ongoing story of Louisiana. You will create the future of Louisiana. This account of the past and present will lead you there.

The events that tell the history of Louisiana include the horror of war, social conflict, and difficult economic times. Other experiences brought change and progress. Louisiana's history is complex and unique. The rich heritage of Louisiana includes a fascinating variety of people. You will learn about mysterious cultures of the time before recorded history as well as the many groups who came to Louisiana in the hundreds of years since those ancient civilizations. The land itself helped create the history of Louisiana. The natural environment continues to add a special element to life today. The need to protect that environment will affect the future.

The information in this book will help you study geography, history, economics, and civics. You will learn about Louisiana as you study these elements of social studies. You will explore, research, think, analyze, evaluate, and communicate as you learn more about your state. The story of Louisiana continues with you.

Above: This painting by William Woodward shows Jackson Square in New Orleans at the end of the nineteenth century. Cover: Bayou Teche as it appeared in 1870, painted by Meyer Straus. Page i: Ladies leaving the Opera House in New Orleans by Paul Poincy. Page ii-iii: A view of New Orleans from the west bank in 1841. Page iv-v: This statue of Louisiana's first state governor, William C. C. Claiborne, by Adolph A. Weinman, can be seen at the Old Mint in New Orleans. This plaster model was used to make the finished statue that now stands in the State Capitol in Baton Rouge.

TABLE OF CONTENTS

Top: *The honeybee is the state insect of Louisiana.* **Above:** *The unusually patterned Catahoula leopard dog is our state dog.*

Top: The alligator is Louisiana's state reptile. *Above:* The crawfish is our state crustacean.

CHAPTER ONE

LOUISIANA'S CULTURE: FAMILIES AND FESTIVALS

Louisianians are . . . a fun loving people, and newcomers to the state rapidly learn to enjoy those amusements that the natives of the state have enjoyed for generations.

— Edwin A. Davis, noted Louisiana historian, 1959

WHEN ALISON MOVED FROM TUCSON to Baton Rouge, she left behind the brown desert she knew and came to the green landscape of Louisiana. As she traveled across the Atchafalaya (a CHAF a li a) Basin on I-10, she was amazed at all the water under the raised highway. She looked out the window, watching for alligators. Her friends in Arizona had teased her by saying her poodle would be eaten by the alligators in her new backyard.

Baton Rouge was like Tucson in many ways. Alison spotted familiar fast-food restaurants, several ten-screen movie complexes, and a nice mall just a few blocks from her new home. But she also noticed differences. The family's new house looked like an Acadian cottage instead of a Spanish adobe casa. Their Arizona yard had cactus and rocks, but blooming azaleas surrounded her new house. Snack counters at Baton Rouge gas stations sold Cajun Boudin instead of the cinnamon churro she ate in Arizona.

New Orleans' Mardi Gras is the most famous of Louisiana's many festivals. These masks are worn by revellers on 'Fat Tuesday.'

Terms: cultural diffusion, culture, Protestant, jazz, blues, cultural anthropologist, fais-do-do, zydeco, gospel music, spirituals, gumbo, jambalaya, Mardi Gras, region, upland South, urban, rural, ethnic group, lowland South, free people of color

People: Acadians, Anglos, Creoles, Isleños

Places: Sportsman's Paradise region, Crossroads region, Cajun Country region, Plantation Country region, Greater New Orleans region

Opposite page: Religion is an important element of Louisiana culture. Reverend John Harris, shown here, is a Baptist minister in St. Mary Parish.

At her new middle school, Alison discovered that she would study Louisiana in her social studies class. At the open house, Alison's teacher offered her parents a copy of the newest state tour guide. He showed them the festival calendar and suggested that they might enjoy seeing Louisiana this way.

Alison's class project became her visits to the festivals. After a year in Louisiana, she had seen much of her new state. She had a huge collection of festival T-shirts and had even learned to eat boiled crawfish. Alison had learned much about her new home and its culture. She continued a long tradition of **cultural diffusion** (the spreading of one's own culture) when she invited her classmates to a party where she served her favorite Arizona foods along with some of her new Louisiana favorites.

ELEMENTS OF CULTURE

According to the *National Geographic*, a group's **culture** defines its way of life and its own view of itself and other groups. The elements of a culture include religion, music, food, clothing, language, architecture, art, literature, games, and sports. All of these elements combine to create the interesting culture of Louisiana. They add to and enhance the quality of life for the state's citizens. Often, these elements are the basis for one of the many festivals in the state.

RELIGION

The first European religion in Louisiana was Roman Catholic because the French and then the Spanish controlled the colony. At the time, both were Catholic countries. After the Louisiana Purchase in 1803, members of various **Protestant** (Christian non-Catholic) religions moved into the territory. Methodists, Baptists, and Presbyterians were later joined by other Protestant groups such as the Lutherans, who were often German immigrants. Members of the Jewish faith have come to Louisiana at various times. More recent immigrants have brought Buddhism and Islam into Louisiana.

MUSIC

New Orleans is the birthplace of jazz. **Jazz** is a kind of music with strong rhythms and much syncopation (accents in unexpected places), often improvised. Brass bands and piano players helped create this new sound. Jazz has spread across the planet, an ambassador for Louisiana culture. In New Orleans, jazz funerals for musicians feature marching groups called second lines. The music of contemporary jazz greats like the Marsalis family owes much to the music of earlier artists. Al Hirt's trumpet and Pete Fountain's clarinet entertain both tourists and locals with exciting jazz.

The **blues** is also a link to the past. This music style is based on black folk music, especially on the chants of the black workers on the plantations. Those rhythms were memories of their African culture and made the slaves' lives and the work more bearable. The instruments most associated with blues music are the guitar and the harmonica. Later, when horns were added and the tempo changed, the new style was known as *rhythm and blues*.

In the 1930s, a **cultural anthropologist** (a scientist who studies human cultures) toured the United States collecting folk music. The blues music Alan Lomax recorded in Louisiana is now part of the Smithsonian's Folkways Collection. One of those he recorded was a Shreveport musician named Huddie Ledbetter, better known as Leadbelly. A statue of this artist now stands in downtown Shreveport.

A very young Cajun musician is sharing his culture with the world. Hunter Hayes recorded his first CD at the age of five. Playing his accordion and singing in French, Hunter has entertained national television audiences. He plays with a Cajun band, which features fiddles, the triangle, and the accordion. The Cajuns, who are descended from the Acadians, learned to play the accordion from the Germans who moved into southwest Louisiana in the 1880s.

The early Cajuns often held dance parties at their rural homes. Entire families came, and the young children were put on blanket pallets in the bedroom. They were told to go to sleep, which in French is *fais-do-do* (fay doh doh). This became the name of these dance parties, and today the term **fais-do-do** refers to a Cajun dance.

Zydeco (ZI de koh) is the special music of French-speaking African Americans of South Louisiana. It is much like Cajun music; the song is sung in French and played on an accordion. An added instrument, the rub board, is used for rhythm.

Country music is part of the heritage of North Louisiana. In the days before television, when people gathered for entertainment, musicians brought their instruments. Their string bands usually included a guitar, a fiddle, and a mandolin. This traditional southern country music developed into *bluegrass* music and then into modern country music. This heritage continues with a state fiddling championship held each year at Marthaville in Natchitoches (NAK a tosh) Parish.

Country music and blues were adapted to become *rock and roll*. Rock and roll started in New Orleans as early as the 1940s. Antoine "Fats" Domino and Little Richard recorded 1950s rock-and-roll hits. A young musician named Elvis Presley performed his new music in

Storytellers and local musicians, such as accordianist Ophe J. Romero of the Romero Brothers, entertain visitors every day under the Evangeline Oak in St. Martinville.

the Municipal Auditorium in Shreveport before he gained national fame. Jerry Lee Lewis left Ferriday in Concordia Parish to become a piano-pounding rock-and-roll star. The Beatles and the Rolling Stones listened to Louisiana musicians as they developed their own style. The Neville Brothers and many other musicians continue Louisiana's contribution to rock and roll.

Many early rock-and-roll musicians started out singing **gospel music**. Gospel is church music that blends elements of folk music, **spirituals** (the sacred folk songs of African Americans), hymns, and popular music. You can hear gospel music in churches throughout Louisiana every Sunday morning. Songs sung in African-American churches preserve the old spirituals and add contemporary music. Rural churches in North Louisiana feature gospel quartets.

More formal classical music also contributes to the musical sound of Louisiana. Orchestras have created musical culture since colonial days. Young musicians today continue this tradition as they audition for the Louisiana Youth Orchestra in Baton Rouge.

Community brass bands were popular at the turn of the century. Today high school bands perform concerts and provide the marching bands for local parades. Music continues to add a tempo to life everywhere in Louisiana.

FOOD

Newcomers and visitors to Louisiana usually comment on the music and the food. Louisiana food is considered one of the best elements of the culture, although some find the spices a little too hot! The food of Louisiana has spread across the world in recent years, with Cajun restaurants in places like Williamsburg, Virginia.

The food most identified with the state is actually the Cajun and Creole food of South Louisiana. Until recently, residents of North Louisiana ate more like their neighbors in East Texas and Mississippi. For many years, crawfish were not considered food anywhere outside of Cajun country. People north of Alexandria were more likely to eat fried chicken or barbecue. Fish fries featuring catfish took the place of crawfish boils. Today, boiled crawfish is served throughout the state.

Do You Remember?
1. What was the first European religion in Louisiana?
2. Where is the birthplace of jazz?
3. What is a fais-do-do?

Dickie and Cynthia Breaux, of the Cafe des Amis in Breaux Bridge, specialize in Cajun cuisine. Dishes like gumbo, jambalaya, boudin, and crawfish etouffee have become popular across the country.

People first organized their lives around the seasons and only later developed the formal calendar. Their earliest festivals celebrated a successful harvest. These celebrations are part of cultures around the world. In Louisiana, the harvest festivals have expanded into year-round fun.

The more than four hundred Louisiana festivals showcase the local food and music. The fall festivals begin Labor Day weekend. These late August and early September celebrations signal the end of summer.

AUGUST AND SEPTEMBER

On the Gulf Coast at Morgan City, the Shrimp Festival celebration began more than sixty years ago. The blessing of the shrimp fleet combines a religious rite and a social occasion. This is a common feature of Louisiana culture. Not long ago, to honor a new source of income for St. Mary Parish, the festival planners expanded its title to the Shrimp and Petroleum Festival. But the solemn ceremony with the priest blessing the pennant-decorated shrimp boats is still the highlight of the weekend. Carnival rides signal the festive side of the event. As you can guess, the featured food is shrimp, any way you like it.

The Frog Festival began in Acadia Parish more than twenty-five years ago. Rayne calls itself the "Frog Capital of the World," and huge frog murals decorate the entrance to the town. Visitors to the festival can eat frog legs and watch frog-jumping contests.

On the same weekend in nearby Plaisance in St. Landry Parish, zydeco music has created a different kind of festival. Crowds of music lovers gather at this party and dance for hours as famous bands and newcomers play the upbeat music.

Dancing and music also invite everyone to enjoy the French heritage at Festivals Acadiens (a KA di en). Every year, more than 100,000 people join the fun in Lafayette. Cultural preservation combines with a good time for the locals and their international visitors. Experienced elders demonstrate traditional crafts to young beginners. The alligator skinning always draws a large crowd.

Alligators are the focus of an entire festival in St. Charles Parish — at the Boutte Alligator Festival. After years of selling only the valuable alligator hides, trappers now have a market for the meat too. This is the place to go if you want to try fried alligator or alligator sauce picante.

Sweet foods are part of the Sugar Cane Festival in New Iberia. The huge fair serves as a pause before the hectic time of the actual harvest, or *cane grinding* as it is called. As one of the state's oldest festivals, this celebration offers dancing, music, food, and carnival rides. A Bayou Teche (BI you tesh) boat parade and a street parade entertain the crowds. Cooking contests and livestock shows bring many competitors to the festival.

Above: *The rub board is a featured instrument at the Southwest Louisiana Zydeco Festival in Plaisance.* **Opposite page:** *Lively Cajun music is just one aspect of the Festivals Acadiens, a celebration of Cajun culture.*

OCTOBER AND NOVEMBER

Shreveport, the largest city in North Louisiana, celebrates the arts in the fall. The Red River Revel is held along the banks of the Red River in the downtown area. This art show and sale features the works of artists who compete for prizes at the festival. Music and food of the region add to the week-long party. A special feature of the Revel introduces children to art and artists.

Another salute to the arts is held in Hammond. Southeast Louisiana State University sponsors Fanfare, held throughout the month of October. This program displays the culture of the region and introduces new cultural experiences. The fine arts, including theater and literature, are featured.

In Acadia Parish, the heart of Cajun country, Robert's Cove is home to some people of German heritage. The residents there have recently begun to celebrate the traditional German OktoberFest. The publicity poster says *Wilkommen*, the German word for welcome. And that welcome is an invitation to share German bands, German singing, and German foods.

Along the Texas border, Zwolle (za WA lee) in Sabine Parish recognizes its ties to Spanish and Native American cultures. The Tamale Festival highlights the special food that combines these two legacies. A parade and street dance entertain the community.

Located in the rice-growing prairie region, Crowley recognizes the economic importance of rice. This Acadia Parish town calls its festival the International Rice Festival. Visitors from other countries now join neighbors at this harvest celebration, which was begun in 1939. A school holiday highlights the importance of this local tradition.

Another of the older festivals in the state has been held in Opelousas (op e LOO sas) in St. Landry Parish for more than fifty years. Begun to celebrate the harvest of the locally grown Louisiana yam, that favorite food is still featured at the Yambilee Festival. Children can enter a contest in which they create yam-i-nals, yams decorated to look like animals.

Abbeville in Vermilion Parish has recently added an unusual title to the list of Louisiana festivals. The Giant Omelette Festival has an interesting history. Legend has it that an innkeeper in a small French village made a fine omelette for Napoleon. The emperor liked it so much that he directed the people from the village to bring all the eggs they could find. The giant omelette made from the eggs fed his entire army. The tradition continues today, with French villages making huge omelettes to feed the poor at Easter. Abbeville joined an organization called the Confrerie, an international association that celebrates French culture and tradition, including the tradition of the giant omelette. More than five thousand eggs go into the giant omelette in Abbeville. The chefs always add hot sauce to give it a Cajun flavor.

The central Louisiana town of Colfax in Grant Parish salutes another Louisiana crop — the pecan. Delicious sweets made with pecans are sold along with handmade crafts. The Louisiana Pecan Festival offers a glimpse of country life in the past. A country store offers old-fashioned items like home-ground cornmeal and homemade jellies. Cultural diffusion, however, is responsible for the alligator on a stick to be found at this North Louisiana festival.

Many of Louisiana's festivals celebrate local foods. The Pecan Festival in Colfax (above), and the Tamale Festival in Zwolle (opposite, above and below), are just two of many examples.

DECEMBER

During the Christmas Festival of Lights, Natchitoches fills its riverbank with Christmas lights and its streets with visitors. The first Saturday in December is the day for parades, food, and music. A fireworks display is the highlight of the evening; then the historic town is filled with the lights of the season.

A unique Christmas celebration occurs in St. James Parish. Bonfires burn on the lower Mississippi levee on Christmas Eve. Family groups and organizations take part in the tradition of building wooden structures. They create replicas of houses and steamboats or just erect the more basic

This wooden Christmas tree in St. James Parish will be set ablaze as part of a tradition that dates back to the late 1800s.

shape, which looks like the framework for a tepee. This preparation is done about a month ahead, so the willow logs will dry and burn easily.

The Christmas Festival of Lights in Natchitoches features more than 250,000 colored lights and over 70 displays.

JANUARY AND FEBRUARY

A new celebration involves the descendants of a long-established cultural group. The French and African-American heritage combined in colonial Louisiana as part of the Creole culture. In Natchitoches Parish, the St. Augustine Historical Society invites relatives and friends from across the United States to gather and recognize their culture. At the Creole Heritage Day Celebration, traditional skills are demonstrated, such as making filé powder for gumbo from the leaves of the sassafras tree. **Gumbo** is a traditional Louisiana dish, a hearty Creole soup made of seafood, chicken, okra, and other vegetables.

The Red Bud Festival in Vivian in Caddo Parish offers southern hospitality, crafts, and food to guests. The masses of hot pink blooms on the town's favorite trees are a joyful announcement of this festival. A parade brings out the town as they head for the carnival and rodeo.

Do You Remember?
1. What Louisiana town claims the title "Frog Capital of the World"?
2. Where does the Sugar Cane Festival take place?
3. What seasonal festival does Natchitoches host?

MARCH AND APRIL

Baton Rouge and New Orleans both celebrate St. Patrick's Day with parades. The wearing of the green honors the Irish heritage of Louisiana. Following Louisiana tradition, float riders throw trinkets to the waiting crowd.

Above: Ponchatoula claims to be the "strawberry capital of the world." *Right:* The New Orleans Jazz and Heritage Festival features thousands of musicians. *Opposite, above and below:* The Crawfish Festival in Breaux Bridge features Cajun music, food, and crawfish races.

The Strawberry Festival draws huge crowds to Ponchatoula (pon cha TOO la). The strawberries grown in Tangipahoa (tan ji pa HO) Parish are eagerly awaited each year. Buying and eating berries are a favorite activity at the festival, along with the music and regional foods.

The New Orleans Jazz and Heritage Festival brings more visitors to Louisiana than any celebration except Mardi Gras. More than a half million people come to see the thousands of musicians who perform every style of music. For ten days, the fairgrounds are filled with people, music, food, and dancing.

MAY

The well-known Crawfish Festival is held in Breaux Bridge. Fewer than 10,000 people live in this St. Martin Parish town, but in May more than 100,000 visitors show up to eat crawfish and dance to the chank-a-chank music. *Chank-a-chank* is the music of the Cajun bands who sing in French. This party first started in 1959, and the state legislature has proclaimed Breaux Bridge as the "Crawfish Capital of the World."

Fisher hosts Sawmill Days. This tiny town in Sabine Parish invites everyone to see how a lumber town looked at the turn of the century. The old company store and theater are examples of how a company-owned town was organized. As at many other Louisiana festivals, visitors enjoy the folk crafts and regional food. Here you might buy a sock doll or some mayhaw jelly.

Baton Rouge sponsors several festivals, including a Blues Festival in the fall. In May, it is Fest for All that brings everyone to the tree-shaded North Boulevard downtown. Art, food, and music are features of this popular event. The organizers spotlight local artists and invite participants from other states. Children's hands-on activities add to the fun.

Just south of Baton Rouge in Ascension Parish, Gonzales holds the Jambalaya Festival to determine the jambalaya champion of the state. The cooking is done outside in huge pots, and most of the contestants are men. **Jambalaya** — a spicy dish of rice and meat — is considered a basic dish in Cajun kitchens. An example of cultural diffusion, it was developed from a Spanish dish called *paella*. This adaptation came about during the colonial period, when the Acadians came to Spanish Louisiana.

JUNE AND JULY

You can buy a hand-sized fried peach pie in Ruston during the Peach Festival. The sweet peaches that grow in the nearby orchards are a Louisiana treat. Visitors come to this Lincoln Parish town to buy the peaches and stay for the parade and arts and crafts show.

Blueberries have recently become a commercial crop in DeSoto Parish, and the residents of Mansfield created a celebration for their community. The Blueberry Festival offers elements of country life in northwest Louisiana, including good barbecue and good country music. A wood-chopping contest is a reminder of an important skill of the past.

The Folklife Center at Northwestern State University in Natchitoches was established to preserve information about Louisiana's cultural elements. In July, the university sponsors the Folklife Festival. Visitors and participants can escape the hot Louisiana summer as they enjoy this indoor event. The gathering bridges the distance between nineteenth-century folkways and the Internet. You can watch the Isleños mend a fishing net or use a computer to find information about an ancestor.

Above: This man is carving decoys at the Folklife Festival in Natchitoches. Opposite, above: Visitors can test their lumberjack skills at Sawmill Days in Fisher. Opposite below: Local crafters display their wares at Baton Rouge's Fest for All.

MARDI GRAS

Louisiana's biggest celebration is, of course, **Mardi Gras**. The tradition began in Europe and was brought to Louisiana by the first French explorers. An eighteenth-century Mardi Gras parade was described as a group of men ringing cow bells in the streets of New Orleans. Today, more than a half million people line the streets for the more than fifty parades held in the city.

Mardi Gras is the festive time before the solemn religious season of Lent. The forty days of Lent are part of the Christian religion, especially in the Roman Catholic Church. Lent begins on Ash Wednesday, and Mardi Gras Day is the day before. *Mardi Gras* means "Fat Tuesday."

In Louisiana, however, the celebration of Mardi Gras begins on January 6, also known as Twelfth Night. Parties, balls, street dances, and parades fill South Louisiana. Mardi Gras parades have long been a part of the culture of Lafayette, Morgan City, New Roads, and Thibodaux.

Above: *People crowd streets and balconies to watch the colorful and elaborate floats that are a trademark of New Orleans's Mardi Gras parades.* **Right:** *The colorful king cake is a Mardi Gras tradition.*

The traditional country version of Mardi Gras takes place in Basile, Church Point, Eunice, and Mamou. This piece of the prairie Cajun culture had almost been lost until, in the 1950s, an appreciation for the importance of cultural customs developed.

The traditional celebration is described as "running the Mardi Gras" *(le courir de Mardi Gras)*. Masked riders on horseback go from house to house collecting food for the community feast. The riders entertain with singing and dancing as they go. Part of the tradition requires the participants to catch live chickens on the farms they visit. The chickens later become part of the gumbo.

Mardi Gras celebrations have even spread to the Protestant cities of North Louisiana. Because this area has few Catholics, the celebration holds little religious significance. Their neighbors in South Louisiana say the North Louisiana cities simply could not resist the fun.

Riders from Mamou (above) are ready to take part in "le courrir de Mardi Gras." The capuchons (tall pointed hats) and masks (above right) are part of their costume.

Do You Remember?
1. What town hosts the Louisiana Strawberry Festival?
2. What special name did the Louisiana legislature give Breaux Bridge?
3. Where might you find the cook-off to determine the jambalaya champion of Louisiana?

CULTURAL REGIONS

Visiting the state's many festivals is one way to study the elements of Louisiana's culture. A map shows these elements in a different way. The Louisiana Department of Culture, Recreation, and Tourism divides the state into five regions: Sportman's Paradise, Crossroads, Cajun Country, Plantation Country, and Greater New Orleans. A **region** is an area defined by similar features, which usually include common climate, landforms, and economic or recreational opportunities. In this case, each of the five regions has unique cultural ties that makes it different in some ways from the rest of the state.

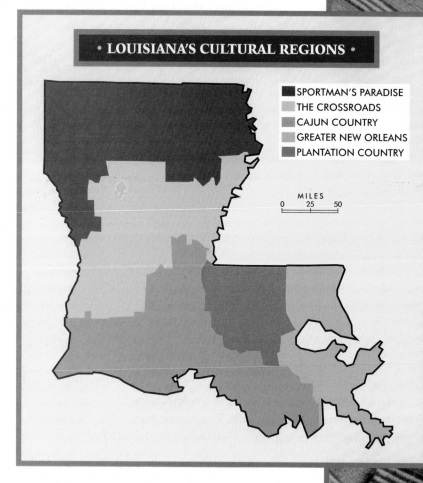

· LOUISIANA'S CULTURAL REGIONS ·

- SPORTMAN'S PARADISE
- THE CROSSROADS
- CAJUN COUNTRY
- GREATER NEW ORLEANS
- PLANTATION COUNTRY

MILES
0   25   50

The Acadians who came to live in south Louisiana did most of their own spinning and weaving. These antique blankets from the late 1800s and early 1900s are examples of their skill.

Above: Shreveport is the state's third-largest city. ***Above right:*** The lakes in the Sportsman's Paradise region are a popular destination for anglers and other outdoors enthusiasts.

SPORTSMAN'S PARADISE REGION

This region's label was chosen because of the many lakes, rolling hills, and forests in northern Louisiana that offer abundant outdoor recreation for residents and visitors. Fishing and hunting have been a part of life here for generations. Bass fishing tournaments are big business on the lakes of the region. Newer sports like water-skiing and power-boat racing add a different kind of excitement.

North Louisiana has more in common with the neighboring states of Mississippi, Alabama, and Georgia than with South Louisiana. A cultural anthropologist uses the term **upland South** to describe the characteristics of this region. Early settlers came from other southern states.

Left: Monroe, on the banks of the Ouachita River, is the commercial center of northeast Louisiana.

BEN LILLY,
STRONGMAN OF MOREHOUSE PARISH

The Louisiana Folklife Program collected stories from Louisiana's different cultures and has published them in Swapping Stories. *The following story, taken from this book, describes the famous hunter Ben Lilly. It was recorded by C. Renee Harvison from James B. Rider, who was a writer about outdoor life for the Bastrop Enterprise.*

Ben Lilly, around Mer Rouge, was always entertaining people. He was supposedly a tremendously strong man. People that have been witnesses to the things he did according to what's been written on him, he once stood on the sidewalks of Mer Rouge and got in a barrel. And without touching the barrel, just flat-footed, jumped out of the barrel onto the sidewalk.

They said it was many times that he could pick up a hundred pound steel anvil from the ground and just extend it out at arm's length and just hold it there.

They said that he once picked up a five-hundred-pound bale of cotton and walked off with it.

Lilly made his own knives. He once said that, he showed a knife to a fellow one time out West and said that he had killed, in so-called hand-to-

hand combat, six bears with this knife. He held it up and showed that he had stabbed those bears to death. They weren't all black bears. One or two were supposed to be grizzlies. Pretty tough customers.

Ben Lilly would not do any kind of work on Sunday, no matter what. If his cows got out, he wouldn't let anybody herd those cows up. They might stay lost for days. On Monday morning he'd go hunt them, but not on Sunday. He read his Bible on Sunday. He tried to adhere to the Bible as near as he could.

AUDIENCE MEMBER: Mr. Rider, I have heard that he organized a hunting expedition for Roosevelt. For President Roosevelt. Is that true? Have you found that to be true in your research?

JAMES B. RIDER: That was Theodore Roosevelt. Teddy Roosevelt. Roosevelt came down to Tensas Parish, around Transylvania down there, and he wanted to kill a bear. So they hired Ben to come over with his dogs to run bear. And he hunted with Teddy.

AUDIENCE MEMBER: And I've also been told, since I'm a Mer Rouge resident, and because so many people enjoy talking about Ben Lilly, that he had such a keen sense of smell and keen sense of hearing, they say he was more animal than human. But he could be a gentleman when the occasion arose. Didn't they say something about how he could lay on the ground and tell you how the grass was growing, he had such a keen sense of smell?

JAMES B. RIDER: He said that. He told that. He was, like you were talking about, he was a gentle man, too. When he did come back to Mer Rouge on one of his hunts, he'd play with the children. He just spent a lot of time playing with children, no matter whose they were.

He had all kind of idiosyncrasies. He believed if you got wet, naturally out in the rain, that nothing would happen to you if you just kept wearing your clothes till they dried. You might get sick if you took them off and took a bath and dried off real good and put on dry clothes. You'd probably get sick. So what he did, he'd even go to bed with his wet clothes on. If he come in wet, and he wanted to go to bed, he'd

President Theodore Roosevelt enjoyed hunting, camping, and fishing. After he left the presidency, he went to Africa on a hunting and collecting tour.

just crawl in bed and pull the covers up and sleep wet. He had a belief, he stuck with it.

AUDIENCE MEMBER: They say he believed in bathing. He'd even bathe in the snow!

JAMES B. RIDER: One time, him and another fellow had been out in the woods for a long time. They hadn't taken a bath in months. They decided they'd take a bath. Ben said, Let's take a bath.

This guy said, Well, you know, it's about thirty degrees. Only thing they had was this stream to take a bath in. He'd heard that Ben didn't mind. He'd pull of his clothes and wade on in, start taking a bath. This guy didn't want to do that. So Ben took his bath in that cold water. It didn't make him any matter. It was just like when he was tracking a bear or cougar. He'd pull off everything but his pants. He'd take his rifle and knife and take off. No food, no nothing. He might hunt two days without a bite to eat. Sometimes when he'd eat, he would just go out in somebody's corn field and pull two ears of corn.

The heritage of the people of this region is Anglo-Saxon or Celtic, meaning their ancestors were English, Scottish, or Irish.

The northwest section of the region has Shreveport-Bossier City as its **urban** (city) area. These two cities are in different parishes and are separated by the Red River, but they blend together into one urban culture. Museums and theaters expand the region's culture beyond the Sportsman's Paradise image.

In northeast Louisiana, the urban center is Monroe-West Monroe. These cities are joined by a bridge across the Ouachita (WASH i taw) River, and both are in Ouachita Parish. Northeast Louisiana State University provides a cultural focus for the community.

CROSSROADS REGION

The region called the Crossroads covers the center of the state and merges the cultures of North and South Louisiana. The urban center is Alexandria-Pineville. Like Shreveport and Bossier City, these cities are on the banks of the Red River. Both are in Rapides Parish.

In this region, small towns like Cheneyville and Winnfield feature main street stores and churches. In the **rural** (country) areas, some people still live on farms and continue their traditions. Weathered old barns symbolize these rural roots.

Opposite page, above and below: Cheneyville, in Rapides Parish, is typical of the small towns in the Crossroads region. *Above:* Alexandria is the parish seat of Rapides Parish and at the geographical center of Louisiana. *Left:* Weathered old barns, like this one in Natchitoches Parish, symbolize the rural roots of the Crossroads region.

Top: *A scenic bayou winds through the Cajun town of Bordelonville.* **Above:** *Cajun Country's Catholic heritage is reflected in churches like St. Peter's in Bordelonville.*

CAJUN COUNTRY REGION

Small towns fewer than ten miles apart show the change from the crossroads of North Louisiana culture to the Cajun heritage. The two towns of Bordelonville and Acme in Avoyelles Parish reveal these differences. Bordelonville is filled with Cajun French Catholics, and Acme, just across the Red River, was settled by Anglo-Protestants.

In the 1990s, the two towns shared their lifestyles in a special program. Bordelonville invited the people from Acme to a *cochin de lait*, a Cajun pig roast. Later, the Bordelonville residents attended a concert of gospel music singing in Acme.

Cajun Country itself spreads over a triangle in southwest Louisiana. Within this region, the culture can be further divided into prairie Cajun and wetlands Cajun. The National Park Service Center features the prairie culture in Eunice (Acadia Parish) and the wetlands culture in Thibodaux (Lafourche Parish). On the prairie, the Cajun culture centered on agriculture and livestock, while the wetlands Cajuns were fish-

ers and trappers. This life continues today, but new economic developments such as the oil industry have brought cultural changes.

Urban centers in Cajun Country include Houma, Lafayette, Morgan City, and Thibodaux.

Although American fast-food restaurants are now common in these cities, some of the customers still speak Cajun French. Many of those customers work in the oil industry instead of in the traditional occupations of their fathers.

The lifestyle of the Acadians in southern Louisiana in the early 1800s is preserved at Acadian Village in Lafayette (above left and top) and at the Longfellow-Evangeline State Commemorative Area in St. Martinville (above).

PLANTATION COUNTRY REGION

Old plantation homes, live oak trees, and Spanish moss are the common symbols of this region. As its name suggests, this region has more plantation homes than any other place in the South. And, like cultural regions everywhere, there is much more to life here than the expectations suggest.

Life reaches from the past toward the future in this area along the Mississippi River. The cultural mix includes the conflicts of that past and the struggle for a better tomorrow. Today, people have begun to look for the cultural heritage of all who live in the region, not just the heritage of those who lived in the big house on the plantation.

Baton Rouge is the urban center of this region. The state's capital city has a mix of people and lifestyles that mirrors the state. Every ethnic group living in Louisiana today is represented in Baton Rouge.

Right: Bocage Plantation house in Darrow was built in 1801. *Above:* Ormond Plantation house in Destrehan dates from the late 1790s.

GREATER NEW ORLEANS REGION

The city of New Orleans often seems like another world to visitors, even those from other parts of Louisiana. It is often described as "cosmopolitan," an American city that is more like a European one. A busy port on the Mississippi River exists alongside an exotic historic district. A walk through the French Quarter reminds the tourist of Louisiana's past.

The largest city in the state is sometimes described as having more in common with the Caribbean and South America than with the rest of the United States. The relaxed atmosphere of the tropics replaces the bustle of Boston.

OTHER REGIONAL LABELS

Cultural regions are not mandatory boundaries on a map. Unlike the parish lines that are set by law, regions can change and can have different labels. People of many backgrounds live in each area of the state, and variations can be found in every community.

Some people describe the state as North Louisiana, South Louisiana, and New Orleans. Others say that South Louisiana should be divided into New Orleans, Acadiana, and the Florida Parishes. The part of the state in "the toe of the boot" is called the Florida Parishes because it was once part of the colony of West Florida. This region was settled by people more like their neighbors in North Louisiana than those in New Orleans and Acadiana.

Whatever regional divisions are used, it is important to know that the cultural histories of North Louisiana and South Louisiana have been very different. These differences are no longer as great as they once were, but they still affect social, political, and economic interactions.

*Above: The ornamental fences are a feature of the Garden District of New Orleans, originally a strictly "American" section. **Opposite:** The French Quarter, famed for its "lacey" balconies, is New Orleans's greatest attraction.*

Do You Remember?

1. Why is North Louisiana referred to as a Sportsman's Paradise?
2. What is the urban center of the Crossroads region?
3. What economic development has brought change to the Cajun Country region?

LOCAL MUSEUMS

Local museums around the state display elements of Louisiana's culture, past and present.

In New Roads in Pointe Coupee Parish, a historic house dating from the French colonial days of Louisiana is the museum and tourist center. The building was built around 1750 and was once part of Parlange Plantation.

The building was constructed in the style called "Louisiana Creole." That is, it was built of cypress timbers sawed by hand into 3 - by 10-inch timbers, which were held in place with large wooden pegs. This construction style was also used by the French in Canada. The space between the timbers was filled with *bousillage*, a combination of mud and moss.

Today, the house displays many cultural elements of French Louisiana. A loom is still used to weave cotton just as it did more than 150 years ago. Baskets woven by early settlers and their Indian neighbors decorate the rooms.

Louisiana has many other museums, both large and small. The state museums include the Cabildo in New Orleans and the Louisiana State Exhibit Building in Shreveport. Local museums include the Ford Museum in Homer, Claiborne Parish; the W. H. Tupper Museum in Jennings, Jefferson Davis Parish; and the West Baton Rouge Parish Museum in Port Allen.

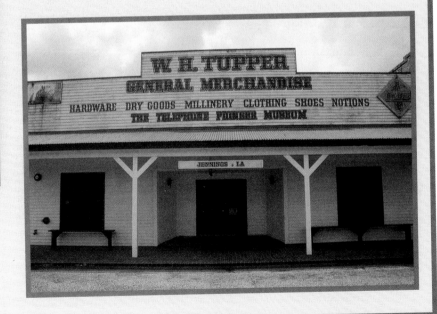

Above: Parlange Plantation in New Roads is a National Historic Landmark. ***Right:*** A 1940s rural general store is now a museum in Jennings.

ETHNIC GROUPS

Louisiana has a great diversity of people. Their cultural backgrounds have blended into the fascinating mix that is Louisiana today. The cultural differences in the state come from the different ethnic backgrounds of its citizens. An **ethnic group** is a group of people who have strong feelings of belonging and who share common traditions, beliefs, and patterns of living that include language, religion, customs, and food. The people of Louisiana are much more diverse than some tourists expect to meet.

ACADIANS

French Canadians migrated to Louisiana in the eighteenth century. When the English gained control of the Canadian province of Acadia (now called Nova Scotia), they forced the French to leave. This exile became an important episode in the history of Louisiana. The French-speaking Acadian farmers made their way to the bayous and prairies, developing the region of Acadiana. In fact, the word *Cajun* came from the French pronunciation of the word *Acadianne*, meaning "people of Acadia."

On the map, twenty-two parishes form this triangle of Cajun culture. The many descendants of the first **Acadians** who migrated to Louisiana proudly preserve their language and their customs. Today, people outside Louisiana recognize elements of Cajun culture because of the spread of Cajun food and music.

ANGLOS

Parts of the state continue the **Anglo** culture developed in the English colonies on the eastern coast of the United States. This English-speaking heritage includes the Scots-Irish, who migrated to Louisiana and established farms in the hill country of North Louisiana. The culture here is described as upland South, the accent is southern, and the religion is Protestant.

The low-lying lands along the rivers were perfect for the establishment of plantations. Anglos from other southern states and from New England settled in this area, and the plantation culture that developed is described as **lowland South**. This lowland South culture existed along the Mississippi River, as well as along the Red and the Ouachita rivers in the northern part of the state. Some differences in customs, speech patterns, and religion are still seen between the upland South and lowland South cultures.

Louisiana's people are a blend of many ethnic groups. Norbert LeBlanc is a Cajun alligator hunter and fisherman.

AFRICAN AMERICANS

The African-American population came to Louisiana in several different ways. The first slaves brought to colonial Louisiana came from West Africa. One of Louisiana's most famous foods — gumbo — is a gift from these Wolof and Bambara people. The word itself means "okra," a vegetable used in the soup.

Other slaves were brought from the French colonies of the West Indies. They brought features of their African culture as well new features that had developed in the West Indies. These slaves spoke French in a dialect known as Creole.

Not all people of African heritage in Louisiana were slaves. Those who were free during the years of slavery were called **free people of color**, or *gens de couleur libre*. Communities of the descendants of this cultural group thrive in several sections of the state today. They consider themselves **Creoles**, referring to their connection to the days when Louisiana was a colony. The term referred to those who were born in the Louisiana colony instead of in Europe or Africa.

Spencer Frank and a younger member of the Frank Family prepare for a performance at the Louisiana Folklife Festival.

St. Landry Parish is the home of several large Creole communities. They continue to speak French, as their ancestors did during colonial times. Zydeco music, with its French lyrics, is one of their contributions to world culture.

GERMANS

Germans also immigrated to Louisiana during the early colonial years. However, they did not retain their language and soon blended with the dominant French culture. More Germans arrived in the nineteenth century. A group of these German farm families settled in Acadia Parish and created the community of Robert's Cove. Their grandchildren continue to preserve elements of their German heritage. On December 6, a procession celebrating the religious feast of St. Nicholas goes from house to house.

ITALIANS

The Italians were another large group of immigrants in the nineteenth century. These new arrivals became farmers, raising vegetables and strawberries. Outside of New Orleans, the largest group of their descendants live in Independence in Tangipahoa Parish.

The Italians contributed an interesting custom known as St. Joseph's Altar to Louisiana culture. The altar is a thank you for blessings of the past year. The altars are set up sometimes in homes and sometimes in the church. Brought from Sicily, the tradition includes a feast for friends and strangers. Each visitor is given a dried fava bean for good luck until the next year.

HISPANICS

The oldest and best preserved Hispanic culture in Louisiana is the group of people who still refer to themselves as **Isleños** (is LAY nyos). The word means "islanders." These people are descended from Canary Islanders who were brought to Louisiana when it was a Spanish colony. They live in St. Bernard Parish, where their ancestors settled in the eighteenth century. Some Isleños can still speak the Spanish dialect and sing the songs of those first settlers. Those songs are called *decimas*, ten-stanza narrative songs. Some of the songs tell of the difficulties the first Isleños faced in the Louisiana colony; others tell of Spanish knights who lived centuries ago.

The Hispanic community around Zwolle in Sabine Parish traces its ancestry to the Spanish colony of Texas. In the twentieth century, an influential Cuban community developed in New Orleans after Castro's revolution drove them from Cuba. The most recent Hispanic immigrants have come from Mexico.

Present-day Isleños (left to right) Emily Vega, Bertin Esteves, and Dorothy Benge display traditional fiesta dress at the annual Isleño fiesta in St. Bernard.

Derek Medford of the Coushatta Tribe of Louisiana is dressed for a traditional tribal dance.

NATIVE AMERICANS

The descendants of the region's earliest residents have land and tribal headquarters in several parts of the state. The Chitimacha, Choctaw, Coushatta, Tunica-Biloxi, and Houma are the primary tribes remaining in Louisiana.

OTHER ETHNIC GROUPS

The Gulf Coast has offered refuge to many groups of immigrants. Croatians came from the coast of the Adriatic Sea with their sailing skills and developed the oyster industry in the state. Their descendants live in Plaquemines (PLAK mins) Parish. They share this region with Filipino immigrants who were shrimpers. The most recent arrivals to become part of the culture of the wetlands are the Vietnamese. Communities of Vietnamese fishermen now dot Louisiana's coastline.

Chinese immigrants came to Louisiana as laborers during the nineteenth century. Some of them worked on plantations, while others became involved in the shrimp drying industry along the coast. Chinese communities thrive in Louisiana's cities today. As tolerance for cultural differences has increased, the Chinese now share part of their New Year's tradition with their neighbors. The Lion Dance is a popular sight in Baton Rouge and New Orleans.

A community of Czechs in Rapides Parish continues to preserve their customs. They gather annually to share elements of their culture with each other and with visitors. In Livingston Parish, a Hungarian community still thrives near Albany. Other cultures have contributed to Louisiana's diversity, including Arabs, Greeks, and natives of India.

FAMILIES

Culture is preserved not only by regions and communities but also by families. Often, they come together to share their heritage and pass it along. The tradition of family reunions continues and grows in Louisiana today. In the small North Louisiana town of Dubach in Lincoln Parish, the Colvin family reunion has been held annually since the beginning of this century. Relatives gather from across the United States to share food and memories. They also visit the family cemetery to honor past generations.

You and your family also contribute to the unique culture of Louisiana. The traditions of the past combine with the customs of today. Your music, food, clothing, language, games, and sports blend into the cultural picture of our state.

Do You Remember?
1. How did the word *Cajun* originate?
2. Which ethnic group settled the lowland South?
3. Louisiana Italians give thanks for the year's blessings with what special altar?
4. Which ethnic group developed the state's oyster industry?

Vietnamese immigrants have settled along Louisiana's Gulf Coast. Here, Tran Phu of Delcamber mends a shrimp net.

SUMMARY

Louisiana boasts a rich cultural heritage, blending the traditions and celebrations of its diverse people. Giving thanks for the harvest while sampling regional foods and music is enjoyed at many festivals held throughout the year. Seasonal holidays and religious occasions add more reasons to celebrate. Louisiana's many festivals bring together the essence of each cultural region.

Louisiana can be divided into five cultural regions: Sportsman's Paradise, Crossroads, Cajun Country, Plantation Country, and Greater New Orleans. Cultural characteristics for each region are defined by history, ethnic customs, and geography. These different cultural histories affect social, political, and economic interactions in each region.

CHAPTER · REVIEW

Reviewing People, Places, and Terms

Define, identify, or explain the importance of each of the following.

1. blues
2. cultural anthropologist
3. cultural diffusion
4. culture
5. ethnic group
6. fais-do-do
7. free people of color
8. gospel music
9. gumbo
10. jambalaya
11. jazz
12. lowland South
13. Mardi Gras
14. Protestant
15. region
16. rural
17. spirituals
18. upland South
19. urban
20. zydeco

Understanding the Facts

1. Name at least five elements of culture.
2. What musical instruments are found in a typical Cajun band?
3. What type of food is commonly associated with Louisiana?
4. What occasions did early festivals celebrate?
5. Why did the Shrimp Festival in Morgan City add "petroleum" to the title of its celebration?
6. Where is the Red River Revel celebrated? What is the occasion?
7. Name two large New Orleans festivals that bring together people from around the world.
8. What is the purpose of Mardi Gras? What does the phrase mean?
9. Name the five cultural regions of Louisiana.
10. Name at least five ethnic groups who have settled in Louisiana.

Developing Critical Thinking

1. Study a complete list of Louisiana festivals. Which months have more festivals? Why do you think that is so?
2. What cultural characteristics separate North Louisiana, South Louisiana, and New Orleans?
3. How do families preserve culture?

Using Your Skills

1. Make a special-interest map of some of the Louisiana festivals mentioned in this chapter. Mark each location with a symbol representing the festival. Create a legend that identifies your symbols.
2. Make a chart showing five elements of culture. List examples of each of these elements that you have observed in your community.

Special Projects

1. Visit a festival or interview someone who has visited one of the festivals mentioned in the chapter. Prepare a short report on the festival to share with your classmates.
2. Use a Louisiana tour guide to identify a museum close to your community. Read the description and visit the museum to identify elements of culture. Write a persuasive letter convincing a friend to visit this museum.
3. Many towns and tourist areas in Louisiana have their own *home page* on the Internet, where interested persons throughout the world can learn about an area's attractions. If you have access to the Internet, investigate one of these home pages and share with classmates the types of information found there.

1. How does the story of Morehouse Parish's Ben Lilly compare with stories about other legendary frontiersmen, such as Davy Crockett and Daniel Boone?
2. What parts of this story are probably exaggerated? Why would the storyteller do this?
3. Why would Teddy Roosevelt want to hunt with Ben Lilly?

Louisiana Lagniappe

- Louisiana musicians still achieve fame in the world of country music. Kix Brooks of the country duo Brooks and Dunn is from Shreveport.
- Egg knocking is an Easter custom in Marksville in Avoyelles Parish. Children of the community compete by tapping each other's eggs. The owner of the last unbroken egg is declared the winner.
- Folktale stories of the *Loup Garou*, or Cajun werewolf, have entertained South Louisiana residents for generations. "The Loup Garou will get you if you don't watch out" was often used to encourage good behavior.
- A popular radio and stage show of the 1950s was the "Louisiana Hayride," based in Shreveport. Most country artists wanted to perform on the Hayride stage and at the Grand Ole Opry in Nashville, Tennessee.

• BUILDING SKILLS: USING YOUR TEXTBOOK •

Being able to properly use your textbook is an important skill. Your textbook has two parts: the narrative, which tells the story of the state of Louisiana, and the visual information, which makes the narrative come alive. The visual information — photographs, illustrations, maps, charts, and captions — is an important part of the study of the history of Louisiana.

The narrative is divided into sections by headings. The major headings are large, bold, centered, and underlined. Lower-level headings are set in bold capital letters and bold italic letters. These headings are like an outline; they help organize the information in the chapter. If you scan the headings before you begin to read, you may better understand the plan of the chapter.

Look over the terms, people, and places listed in the Chapter Preview before you begin reading. If you do not know the meaning of some of the terms, locate them in the glossary at the back of the book or in a dictionary. The terms appear in bold type the first time they appear in the narrative and are often defined there.

Once you begin to read the chapter, read the narrative straight through and answer the questions labeled Do You Remember? These questions will help you check your understanding of what you have read. After you have read the narrative, study the photographs and their captions and any maps and charts in the chapter. Photographs help you visualize some of the people, places, and events in the chapter. The captions may point out important information about the photograph or provide more information. Maps and charts summarize information provided in the chapter.

Try This! To help you make use of these suggestions, complete these activities.

1. Prepare an outline of Chapter 1 using the headings in the chapter.
2. Look at the maps in the chapter. What information do the maps provide? How do they help you understand the narrative?
3. Find two captions that provide information not in the narrative. What is that information?
4. Find and list the photographs that illustrate the cultural region in which you live. Choose your favorite photograph from the list. Why did you choose that photograph?

Be sure to follow these suggestions as you read the rest of the chapters in the textbook.

CHAPTER TWO

LOUISIANA'S GEOGRAPHY: RIVERS AND REGIONS

One will soon discover that few states of the Union possess a greater diversity of surface, soil, climate, scenery, and products than Louisiana. And certain it is that no state has a more varied and interesting population.
— Samuel H. Lockett, from his *Louisiana as It Is*: A Geographical and Topographical Description of the State, 1873

WHEN YOU NEED TO KNOW where you are or how to get to another place, you use a map. A **map** shows the direction from one place to another and indicates the distance between those locations. As you move around in your **environment** (surroundings), your mind stores information like an internal video camera. Every time you move from one place to another, you use this information — your mental map. The first person who described that mental image to someone else might have sketched in the dirt with a stick, becoming the first *cartographer* or mapmaker.

The science of **cartography** or mapmaking has come a long way since the first map was scratched in the dirt. Today's maps use satellite information for accuracy. Computers relay the information through a system called GIS, the Geographic Information Service. Because this new technology is so important, the Louisiana state legislature created the Louisiana Geographic Information Systems Council to develop the use of GIS in Louisiana. The maps developed from this new technology make it easier to plan hurricane evacuation routes, study coastal erosion, and select the best location for a new business. Louisiana's present and future needs can be analyzed with more information than has ever been available before.

Bayou Lafourche, called "the longest Main Street in the world," is seen here as it flows through Thibodaux.

Because sailors needed to know and explain how to get around on our planet, a system of measurement was gradually developed based on their expanding knowledge. The system uses a network of imaginary intersecting lines that circle the globe. Location and distance are stated using this system of latitude and longitude.

Lines of **latitude**, also called *parallels* because they run parallel to the equator, measure a location's distance north or south of the equator. Lines of **longitude**, also called *meridians*, run from the North Pole to the South Pole. They measure how far east or west a location is from the Prime Meridian, the arbitrary starting point at Greenwich, England. You could describe the Prime Meridian as the place where time begins, because the counting of the hours of each day begins there.

Today, GIS uses a high-tech system to measure latitude and longitude. Its specialized images reveal new information about Louisiana. For example, maps of the artificial reefs created off the Gulf Coast show details of the entire coastline. The Global Positioning System enables a user to determine latitude and longitude by bouncing a signal off a satellite. The coordinates give the *absolute location*, the exact spot on the earth's surface where a place is found.

Louisiana's location lies between 28 degrees, 55 minutes and 33 degrees north latitude and between 89 degrees and 92 degrees west longitude. Louisiana shares approximately the same latitude with North Africa, the Middle East, and the Indian subcontinent. The longitude lines through Louisiana also pass through parts of Mexico, El Salvador, Honduras, and through Ontario, Manitoba, and the Northwest Territories of Canada. Because time is based on longitude, those places are in the same time zone as Louisiana. A *time zone* is one of twenty-four divisions of the earth's surface used for measuring time. Each division marks the approximate distance that the earth rotates in one hour. Louisiana is in the Central Time Zone.

If a cartographer drew a north-south line through the center of the United States, Louisiana would lie just east of that line. Twenty-four states lie east of Louisiana, and twenty-five lie west of westernmost Louisiana. Louisiana joins other coastal states to form the southeastern United States. To be further south in the United States, you would have to be in Texas, Florida, or Hawaii. Our neighbor Texas is the only state that is both north and south of Louisiana.

In a comparison of the physical size of the fifty states, Louisiana ranks thirty-first, with an area of 48,523 square miles. Like eggs in a carton, a dozen Louisianas would fit into Alaska, but it would take forty-eight Rhode Islands to fill Louisiana.

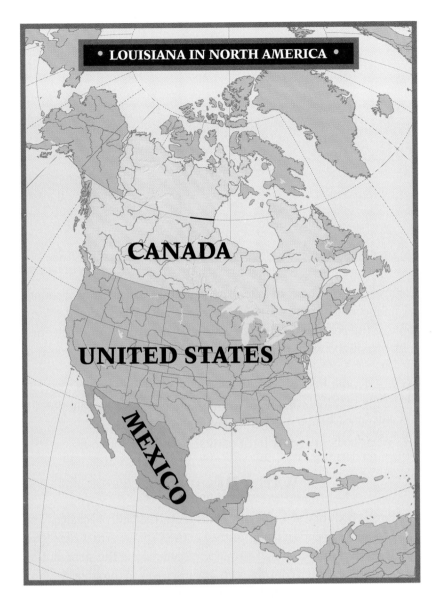

· LOUISIANA IN NORTH AMERICA ·

CANADA

UNITED STATES

MEXICO

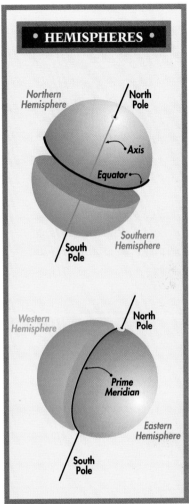

· HEMISPHERES ·

Northern Hemisphere

North Pole

Axis

Equator

South Pole

Southern Hemisphere

Western Hemisphere

North Pole

Prime Meridian

Eastern Hemisphere

South Pole

BOUNDARIES

The system of latitude and longitude is also used to mark boundaries. Parallels and meridians mark one or more of the political borders between states. For example, one of the boundaries between Mississippi and Louisiana is set at about the 31st parallel north. The boundary between Arkansas and Louisiana is at about the 33rd parallel north. The 94th meridian west separates Louisiana and Texas.

Several waterways form the other, natural boundaries of Louisiana. The Mississippi River shapes the upper boundary between Louisiana and Mississippi, and the Pearl River forms the lower boundary. The Gulf of Mexico marks Louisiana's southern boundary. The Sabine River and its reservoir, Toledo Bend, act as the boundary between Louisiana and Texas.

The Toledo Bend Reservoir on the Sabine River is the largest manmade lake in Louisiana.

Changes in these bodies of water have made the exact location of boundary lines confusing and sometimes controversial. Waterways also form some of the political boundaries within the state, sometimes creating controversies between **parishes** (the political divisions in the state).

Do You Remember?

1. What is the starting point for measuring latitude? longitude?
2. Name the states that border Louisiana.
3. What bodies of water form natural boundaries for Louisiana?

WATER RESOURCES

The largest body of water affecting Louisiana is the Gulf of Mexico. The Mississippi River ends its long journey in the Gulf's warm waters. Not only does the Gulf serve as the southern boundary of the state, but its wide continental shelf contributes many resources to the state. Seafood and petroleum found there have brought wealth to Louisiana.

Water is not only the dominant feature of Louisiana's environment, but it has also shaped the state's physical landscape. The Mississippi River and the changes it has gone through over the ages formed the terrain of the state.

Louisiana has almost 5,000 miles of navigable rivers, bayous, creeks, and canals. (**Navigable** means the water is deep enough for safe travel by boat.) One waterway near the coast is part of a system of protected water routes from the Atlantic Ocean to the Gulf of Mexico. The Gulf Intracoastal Waterway extends from Apalachee Bay in Florida's Panhandle to Brownsville, Texas. For more than 1,100 miles, the system takes advantage of rivers, bays, coastal sounds, and canals to provide a safe channel for shippers, fishing boats, and pleasure craft. Part of that shipping passage is a canal paralleling Louisiana's Gulf Coast.

RIVERS

The Mississippi River has had many names, emphasizing its importance and its many roles in the history of North America. The "great river," as its name *Messipi* meant in the language of the Algonquin, serves not only as a key boundary but also as an important trade route. Some French explorers used the name it had already been given, but others gave it new names to honor saints or important people in France. The Spanish knew it as the Rio del Espiritu Santo, the "river of the Holy

Above: The Mississippi River, shown here at New Orleans, drains at least part of thirty-one states. *Opposite, below:* The Mississippi is an important "highway" for transporting goods.

Spirit." "The basin of the Mississippi is the body of the nation," begins Mark Twain's *Life on the Mississippi*, his account of his river experiences. Later, twentieth-century writer John Gunter called it the "Nile of America" to emphasize its importance in American history.

The story of Louisiana cannot be told without the Mississippi representing both the stage and a main character. The Mississippi River area covers more than 1,245,000 square miles, draining at least part of thirty-one states. The Mississippi funnels 375 billion gallons of water through Louisiana each day. That process also brings 256 million tons of sediment down the river each year.

LIFE ON THE MISSISSIPPI BY MARK TWAIN

Mark Twain said before he began his training to become a river pilot on the Mississippi, "I supposed that all a pilot had to do was to keep his boat in the river, and I did not consider that would be much of a trick since it was so wide." He soon discovered he had underestimated the mighty river and the skill he would need. His account in his book Life on the Mississippi *describes the mental maps he had to learn.*

At the end of what seemed a tedious while, I had managed to pack my head full of islands, towns, bars, "points," and bends; and a curiously inanimate mass of lumber it was, too. However, inasmuch as I could shut my eyes and reel off a good long string of these names without leaving out more than ten miles of river in every fifty, I began to feel that I could take a boat down to New Orleans if I could make her skip those little gaps. But of course my complacency could hardly get started enough to lift my nose a trifle into the air, before Mr. Bixby would think of something to fetch it down again. One day he turned on me suddenly with this settler:

"What is the shape of Walnut Bend?"

He might as well have asked me my grandmother's opinion of protoplasm. I reflected respectfully, and then said I didn't know it had any particular shape. My gun-powdery chief went off with a bang,

Mark Twain's Life on the Mississippi *describes his experiences training to become a Mississippi River pilot.*

of course, and then went on loading and firing until he was out of adjectives.

I had learned long ago that he only carried just so many rounds of ammunition, and was sure to subside into a very placable and even remorseful old smooth-bore as soon as they were all gone. That word "old" is merely affectionate; he was not more than thirty-four. I waited. By and by he said:

"My boy, you've got to know the shape of the river perfectly. It is all there is left to steer by on a very dark night. Everything else is blotted out and gone. But mind you, it hasn't the same shape in the night that it has in the daytime."

"How on earth am I ever going to learn it, then?"

"How do you follow a hall at home in the dark? Because you know the shape of it. You can't see it."

"Do you mean to say that I've got to know all the million trifling variations of shape in the banks of this interminable river as well as I know the shape of the front hall at home?"

"On my honor, you've got to know them better than any man ever did know the shapes of the halls in his own house."

"I wish I was dead!"

"Now I don't want to discourage you, but —"

"Well, pile it on me; I might as well have it now as another time."

seems to be a solid, straight wall (you knowing very well that in reality there is a curve there), and that wall falls back and makes way for you. Then there's your gray mist. You take a night when there's one of these grisly, drizzly, gray mists, and then there isn't any particular shape to a shore. A gray mist would tangle the head of the oldest man that ever lived. Well, then different kinds of moonlight change the shape of the river in different ways. You see —"

"Oh, don't say any more, please! Have I got to learn the shape of the river according to all these five hundred thousand different ways? If I tried to carry all that cargo in my head it would make me stoop-shouldered."

"No! You only learn the shape of the river; and you learn it with such absolute certainty that you can always steer by the shape that's in your head, and never mind the one that's before your eyes."

"Very well, I'll try it; but, after I have learned it, can I depend on it? Will it keep the same form and not go fooling around?"

Before Mr Bixby could answer, Mr. W. came in to the watch, and he said:

"Bixby, you'll have to look out for President's Island, and all that country clear away up above the Old Hen and Chickens. The banks are caving and the shape of the shore's changing like everything. Why, you wouldn't know the point above 40. You can go up inside the old sycamore snag, now."

So that question was answered. Here were leagues of shore changing shape. My spirits were down in the mud again. Two things seemed pretty apparent to me. One was, that in order to be a pilot, a man has got to learn more than any one man ought to be allowed to know; and the other was, that he must learn it all over again in a different way every *twenty-four hours*.

Source: From *Life on the Mississippi* by Samuel L. Clemens, pp.70-77. Copyright 1874, 1875 by H. O. Houghton & Company; 1883, 1899, 1903 by Samuel L. Clemens; 1911 by Clara Gabrilowitsch. New York and London: Harper & Brothers.

"You see, this has got to be learned; there isn't any getting around it. A clear starlight night throws such heavy shadows that, if you didn't know the shape of a shore perfectly, you would claw away from every bunk of timber, because you would take the black shadow of it for a solid cape; and you see you would be getting scared to death every fifteen minutes by the watch. You would be fifty yards from shore all the time when you ought to be within fifty feet of it. You can't see a snag in one of those shadows, but you know exactly where it is, and the shape of the river tells you when you are coming to it. Then there's your pitch-dark night; the river is a very different shape on a pitch-dark night from what it is on a starlight night. All shores seem to be straight lines, then, and mighty dim ones, too; and you'd run them for straight lines, only you know better. You boldly drive your boat right into what

The second largest river drainage area in Louisiana is the Red River. It rises in the high, cold plains of eastern New Mexico, where fly-fishing enthusiasts angle for trout. The river ends its journey in Avoyelles Parish, where commercial fishing boats harvest catfish with their hoopnets. The Ouachita River begins as a mountain stream in the Arkansas mountains of the same name. In Catahoula Parish, the Little River and the Tensas River join the Ouachita to form the Black River. The Black River then flows into the Red River, which in turn connects with the Atchafalaya.

The name *Atchafalaya* is based on the Choctaw words *hache*, meaning "river," and *falaia*, meaning "long." This river has been altered more in recent years than any other Louisiana river. First, the river was cleared

Above: *The Atchafalaya River gets much of its water from the Red and Mississippi rivers.*
Right: *The Ouachita River begins in the Ouachita Mountains of Arkansas.*

Cypress trees grow in the shallow waters of Lake Bistineau, an example of a raft lake. Raft lakes are created when massive logjams block the flow of a river.

of logs and other debris in the 1830s, which increased the flow of the water. Then, Captain Henry Shreve, a self-taught engineer, created a shortcut for steamboats on the Mississippi at Turnbull's Bend, diverting water from the Red River into the Atchafalaya. Later, when Shreve cleared the Red River of its logjam, an even greater volume of water flowed down the Atchafalaya. Today the Red River flows into the Atchafalaya River, which also gets 30 percent of the water volume of the Mississippi River.

The Pearl River begins in east-central Mississippi and flows to Lake Borgne. After forming part of the boundary between Louisiana and Mississippi, the river divides into the East and West Pearl rivers. The area between the two branches is a prized natural habitat, Honey Island Swamp.

The Calcasieu (KAL ka shoo) River begins in the hills of Vernon Parish, east of Leesville. In 1926, a deepwater channel was dug to improve navigation and connect Lake Charles to the Gulf of Mexico. Because of these improvements, Lake Charles is now the third largest port in Louisiana. The Gulf Intracoastal Waterway canal connects the Calcasieu with the Sabine River to the west.

The Sabine River is a key element in the geography and history of both Louisiana and Texas. It rises in the uplands of east Texas, then it turns south to form the boundary between the two states. Joining in a major project in 1967, Louisiana and Texas engineered a giant reservoir, Toledo Bend. As the largest manmade lake in Louisiana and the tenth largest in the United States, Toledo Bend covers 186,000 acres. It provides hydroelectric power, a water supply, and great fishing and boating.

LAKES

Toledo Bend is just one of many reservoirs engineered to alter the natural drainage of Louisiana's waterways. You can go fishing or water-skiing on other reservoirs such as Lake D'Arbonne in Union Parish, Lake Claiborne in Claiborne Parish, Sibley Lake in Natchitoches Parish, or Lake Chicot in Evangeline Parish.

The largest natural lake (625 square miles) in Louisiana is Lake Pontchartrain. Thousands of vehicles cross the lake every day by way of a 24-mile-long causeway bridge. Lake Pontchartrain is just 10 to 16 feet deep, a tidal lagoon connecting to the Gulf of Mexico by a narrow passage, the Rigolets (RIG uh lees). Because of that connection with the Gulf, the water in Lake Pontchartrain is *brackish*, a mixture of sea water and fresh water. Lake Maurepas is another large lagoonal lake just to the west of Lake Pontchartrain.

The rivers of Louisiana have created many lakes. *Cutoff lakes* are formed as the bending, meandering rivers seek shorter, straighter courses through flat terrain. These lakes are also called *oxbow lakes*, because the shape reminded early settlers of the bow-shaped harnesses worn by their oxen. False River in Pointe Coupee Parish, Lake Bruin in Tensas Parish, and Larto Lake in Catahoula Parish are cutoff lakes. One interesting cutoff lake in Natchitoches charms the many tourists who visit there. This 39-mile-long lake was formed when the Red River took a shortcut and left the town without a river. The scenic attraction is called Cane River Lake, although it is a little confusing to call it both a river and a lake. Perhaps because it had first been a river, the name stuck.

The Red River created another kind of lake — *raft lakes*. Huge log-jams or rafts of logs blocked the flow of the river. One nineteenth-century explorer described the raft as "a matted mass of tree tops and trunks, weeds and canes, with cottonwood and willow trees growing on its surface." The mass of debris acted like a dam, and the swampy areas filled with water, forming lakes. Two of the raft lakes are Caddo Lake in Caddo Parish and Lake Bistineau in Bossier and Webster parishes. These two scenic lakes feature the cypress trees and Spanish moss that create the romantic Louisiana portraits recognized around the world.

Marsh lakes form where the high ridges called "chenieres" (sha NEER) slow the rivers' progress to the Gulf of Mexico. The chenier ridges also protect these lakes from salt water encroachment. White Lake in Vermilion Parish, Grand Lake in Cameron Parish, and Calcasieu Lake in Calcasieu Parish are all marsh lakes.

Lake St. Joseph (right) at Newellton and Lake Bruin (above) at Lake Bruin State Park are examples of cutoff lakes, formed when the Mississippi River changed direction. Cane River Lake (opposite below, at Natchitoches) is a cutoff lake formed from an old stretch of the Red River. Early settlers called lakes such these oxbow lakes.

BAYOUS

No other waterway name is more associated with Louisiana than **bayou**. In fact, one of the state's most popular slogans is "Louisiana, The Bayou State." But it is hard to find someone who can give you an exact definition, because so many kinds of streams in Louisiana are called bayous.

The word *bayou* comes from the Choctaw language and means "creek." The early French called bayous "the sleeping water." Some bayous are very small and sluggish, and others can send flood waters rushing out of their banks. Some are tributaries that flow into a larger body of water, and others are *distributaries*, which flow out of a larger body of water. Some are miles long and deep enough for navigation, and some are less than a mile long and shallow enough to wade across.

Hundreds of bayous thread across the landscape of Louisiana, with interesting names hinting of stories and legends. Some of the most well-known bayous were once channels of the Mississippi River. Bayou Lafourche, called "the longest Main Street in the world," has been the center of life for the people whose houses line this water-road. Bayou Teche offered a navigation route for steamboats traveling to St. Martinville, home of the legendary Evangeline.

Top: Bayou Robert, in the Atchafalaya Basin, is a perfect picture of "sleeping water." **Above:** Bayou Teche was once used by steamboats traveling to St. Martinville.

Do You Remember?

1. What is the purpose of the Gulf Intracoastal Waterway?
2. Name the largest manmade lake in Louisiana.
3. How did raft lakes get their name?

NATURAL REGIONS

The variety in Louisiana's natural environment often surprises travelers. Depending on where you are in the state, you can listen to a rushing waterfall, photograph a flowering prairie, wade in a clear and sandy-bottomed creek, climb to a rocky hilltop, or hike an ancient trail worn between straight-sided bluffs. You can also pole your pirogue (a canoelike boat) through a swamp or explore the marsh in an airboat.

Observing this change of scenery as you explore the natural world is the basis of geography. **Geography** investigates place and space; that is, it is the study of our planet's natural features, climate, resources, and population. Studying the physical geography of a place includes identifying, classifying, and analyzing regions. Dividing an area into regions makes it easier to study and understand a place. The natural regions of an area are defined and classified according to the relief, soil, vegetation, and climate.

Geographers divide the United States into eight natural regions. Louisiana is in the Gulf Coastal Plain, an area on the coastal edge of the continent, with a low elevation. **Elevation** refers to the height of a place above sea level, and **relief** is the difference between the highest and lowest elevation in a given area. Louisiana's elevation ranges from about 4 feet below sea level in New Orleans to 535 feet above sea level at Driskill Mountain near Arcadia in Bienville Parish.

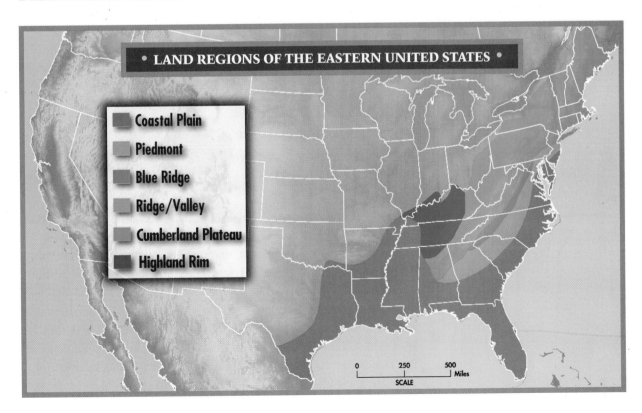

LAND REGIONS OF THE EASTERN UNITED STATES

- Coastal Plain
- Piedmont
- Blue Ridge
- Ridge/Valley
- Cumberland Plateau
- Highland Rim

0   250   500 Miles
SCALE

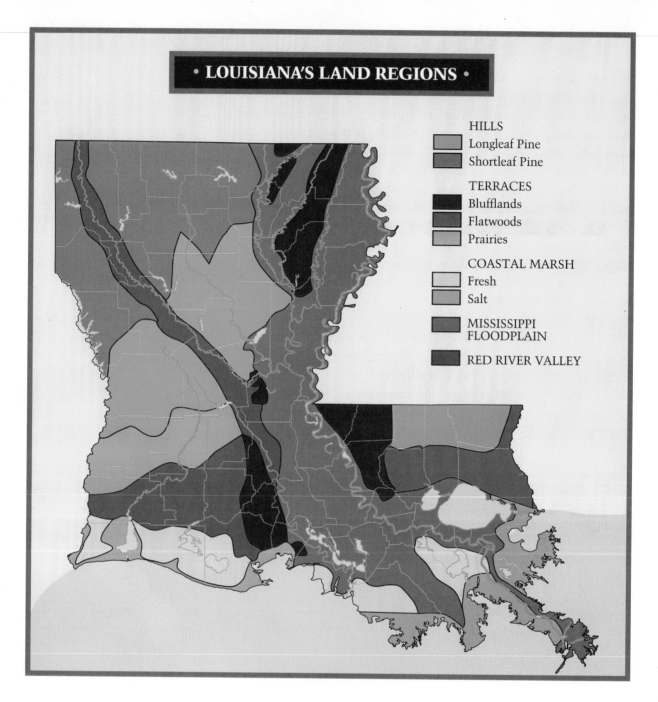

• LOUISIANA'S LAND REGIONS •

HILLS
Longleaf Pine
Shortleaf Pine

TERRACES
Blufflands
Flatwoods
Prairies

COASTAL MARSH
Fresh
Salt

MISSISSIPPI FLOODPLAIN

RED RIVER VALLEY

Samuel Lockett, an engineer, mapped Louisiana's elevation and relief. This professor from the Louisiana State Seminary and Military Academy (now Louisiana State University) traveled around the state off and on from 1869 to 1874 studying the elevation, relief, drainage, and vegetation. His analysis and organization of the state's natural regions are still used today. Lockett's early survey of Louisiana identified five major natural regions. These are the Mississippi Floodplain, the Terraces, the Marsh, the Red River Valley, and the Hills.

MISSISSIPPI FLOODPLAIN REGION

A *floodplain* is the level land along a river that is subject to flooding. The Mississippi Floodplain region parallels the Mississippi River in the eastern part of the state. The soil in this region is **alluvial**, meaning it was deposited by a river. As a result, the soil is very fertile and produces abundant natural vegetation as well as valuable agricultural crops. The Mississippi Floodplain region is divided into three parts: the Natural Levee, the Swamp, and the Passes.

The soil in the Mississippi Floodplain region is very fertile and produces valuable agricultural crops. Cotton is one of the crops grown in the alluvial soil of Madison Parish.

The Natural Levee

Natural levees are the natural riverbanks built over time by flooding. The levees lie within one hundred feet of the river and cover an area about five miles wide. Only about ten to fifteen feet high, the levees are not naturally high enough to keep the river from flooding. Manmade levees that parallel the natural levees were built to try to keep the river inside its banks.

The trees that grow on the sandy batture (the slope between the top of the levee and the river) are usually willows, cottonwoods, and sycamores. These are the trees that can tolerate periodic flooding. Out of the reach of the floodwaters grow hardwood forests of oak, magnolia, hickory, pecan, and sweet gum. A **hardwood** tree is a broadleaf, deciduous tree that sheds its leaves in winter. These hardwoods are sometimes called second-bottom forests (trees in the swamp are called first-bottom forests). In earlier times, the Natural Levee area often had a canebrake of switch cane, but most of this vegetation is now gone.

The Swamp

Beyond the Natural Levee area is the lowest part of the river basin, the Swamp. One of the definitions for **swamp** is "a seasonally flooded forest." Much of the city of New Orleans was built in the drained swamp of the Mississippi Floodplain, and other towns, such as Boutte, are also built on former swamp land.

The swampy image of cypress trees sharing their muddy home with lurking alligators is what tourists expect to find in Louisiana. They may not be disappointed because small swamps do exist in some of our cities, since even small bodies of water can have a swamp ecosystem. (An **ecosystem** is a community of organisms — plants, animals, bacteria, and so on — and its environment that function as a unit in nature.) Cypress and tupelo gum trees thrive in the water-soaked swamp. They are frequently adorned with Spanish moss. Many people assume that this plant is an unwelcome, tree-killing parasite. Actually, Spanish moss is a member of the bromeliad family and gets its nourishment from the air, not the tree.

The Passes

The Passes are the routes the Mississippi River takes to merge with the Gulf of Mexico. The area is also called a *delta* because the triangle-shaped mouth of the river is similar to the Greek letter *delta*. (The word *delta* is also used to talk about the entire lower Mississippi River Valley.) The region's appearance has given it yet another name. Because it looks like the foot of a monster-sized bird from the air, it is sometimes called the "birdsfoot delta" of the Mississippi River.

At the **estuary** (the place where the river meets the sea), the water changes from fresh to salt water and the land shifts as the Passes change. The vegetation here is mostly marsh grasses, which can survive the unstable ecosystem.

Near the mouth of the river, strange little islands called *mudlumps* come and go. These temporary landforms are built by the interaction of escaping marsh gas and sediment. These islands often develop rapidly, sometimes as much as four feet a day, but they rarely last more than about fifteen years.

Mississippi Floodplain swamps, like this one in Terrebonne Parish, may be the home of alligators and other aquatic life.

TERRACES REGION

The Terraces region contains the old Mississippi floodplains. These ancient structures were the old channels of the river, formed when the river changed its course to the Gulf of Mexico after each ice age.

If you imagine that this part of the land was once natural levees and low swamps, you can picture its **topography**, its physical features. The three divisions of the Terraces region are the Blufflands, the Prairies, and the Flatwoods.

The Blufflands

The Blufflands, the old natural levees, are the highest part of the Terraces region. A wind-deposited soil called *loess* built up the old levees even higher. This fine silt erodes easily, leaving almost vertical slopes on the high bluffs. A good place to see these eroded bluffs is in West Feliciana Parish.

In the Blufflands, beautiful upland forests showcase the state flower— the magnolia — when it blooms in the summer. In addition to the glossy-leafed magnolia trees, dogwood, holly, ash, and oak fill these woods. Along the forest floor are oak leaf hydrangea, green mosses, and ferns.

Blufflands pastures, like this one, can be found in West Feliciana Parish near St. Francisville.

The Prairies

Old river channels also formed the Prairies, another part of the Terraces region. But unlike the Blufflands, the Prairies are as flat as a giant table top. This part of Louisiana looks more like the midwestern United States. When farmers from that part of the country moved to Louisiana, they thought of home. In Calcasieu Parish, they named a town "Iowa," to honor that prairie state.

Two million acres of the Louisiana Prairies were once covered with grasses and wildflowers. Some of the most common plants were broom sedge and bluestem sedge, water grass and switch grass — all growing for as far as the eye could see. A nineteenth-century traveler said that the lush grasses were so tall they brushed the stirrups on his horse's saddle.

Because this tall grass looked like rippling water, the early settlers described the area in terms that usually refer to places near the sea. Narrow extensions of forests in the Prairies were called "points," a grove of trees around a group of houses was called an "island," and small prairies were called "coves." Settlements in the Prairies region were given names like Roberts Cove.

The Flatwoods

If you can imagine that same prairie covered with a forest, you can picture the Flatwoods area. Trees rarely grow in the prairies because of the hard clay just below the topsoil. The soil of the Flatwoods region, however, drains better and allows trees to grow. This area was covered with a mixed pine and hardwood forest and with wire grass and palmetto. Early settlers called the Flatwoods region the "pineywoods." There are still many pine forests in this area, along with many small towns.

Top: This cow pasture in the Prairies area looks a lot like the midwestern United States.
Above: The soil of the Flatwoods area encourages the growth of pine forests like this one near Hammond.

The coastal marshlands are covered by a variety of marsh grasses that grow in the muck and fertile peat soil.

MARSH REGION

The Marsh region lies along Louisiana's Gulf Coast. A **marsh** is a wet, treeless prairie covered with water and grasses. People sometimes confuse the terms *marsh* and *swamp*. Besides not having trees, the marsh is found only along the coast. The U.S. Department of the Interior identifies 2.5 million acres of Louisiana as marshland.

The only part of the Marsh region where people live is along the chenier ridges. The word *chenier* means "places of the oak" in French, and live oak trees draped with Spanish moss rise from the flat, wet marshland nearby. The ridges were once part of the beach along the Gulf of Mexico, and as a result the soil is composed of shells and sand. That sandy soil and a slight elevation allow just enough drainage for

the trees to grow. The live oak trees battle the fierce windstorms and lean — twisted and gnarled — above the marsh grass.

This marsh grass grows in the muck and peat soil, which is very fertile. The Marsh region also gets abundant rainfall during a very long growing season. This richness provides a banquet for the state's largest group of tourists — the migratory birds who return annually to enjoy the hospitality of the marsh. The naturalists who count the birds in the spring and fall have identified more than 180 species, ranging from Canadian geese to tiny hummingbirds.

The Marsh region is also the transition zone between the land and the ocean. The part of the region closest to the Gulf of Mexico is the salt marsh, whose waters are brackish. The saltwater vegetation includes such plants as salt grass, cord grass, black rush, and the mangle bush or mangrove. Where the ecosystem changes to freshwater marsh, plants such

The marsh in Sabine National Wildlife Refuge in Calcasieu Parish is a winter home to many migratory waterfowl.

as rosseau (rozo) cane, cattail, iris, and three corner grass appear. The freshwater marsh vegetation cannot grow in the salt water. The encroachment of salt water into the freshwater marsh endangers the habitat of many species of wildlife that cannot survive on salt marsh plants.

A natural geological feature of the salt marsh is the **salt domes**. These formations are layers of rock that have folded upward, rising above the surface. They hold mineral treasures: sulphur, petroleum, and salt. The most significant domes are called the Five Islands because they are high places in the otherwise marshy land. The islands, found between New Iberia and Morgan City, are Avery Island, Weeks Island, Jefferson Island, Cote Blanche, and Belle Isle.

The 2,500 acres of Avery Island rise 150 feet above the marsh. The island is famous for its Tabasco factory, which located there to take advantage of the available salt. Weeks Island is used to store petroleum, part of the reserve supply maintained by the U.S. Department of Energy. Jefferson Island was the site of a major accident in 1980. An offshore oil rig accidentally drilled into the salt mine. Lake Peigneur flowed into the dome, which partially collapsed. Amazingly, no one was killed. The salt dome Belle Isle is 25 miles from Cote Blanche and cannot be reached by road.

Above: *The peppers from Avery Island are turned into a hot, savory sauce.* ***Left:*** *Lake Peigneur was the site of a major oil rig accident in 1980.*

RED RIVER VALLEY REGION

The Red River Valley region spreads on either side of the Red River as it flows from the northwestern corner of the state to central Louisiana. The region is similar to the Mississippi Floodplain; it has a single stream with natural levees and low-lying areas. The elevation and relief are consistently low, compared to the hills surrounding the region.

The fertile red soil comes from the Permian Basin in Oklahoma and Texas and has spread over the valley as sediment. The natural vegetation in the Red River Valley is bottomland forest, which can live through periodic floods. These forests include such trees as willow, cottonwood, sweet gum, and sycamore. The region also contains some first-bottom swamp forest with cypress, tupelo gum, and swamp oak.

Above: The French were early settlers along the Red River, shown here near Natchitoches.
Right: The soil of the Red River Valley is very fertile.

HILLS REGION

The Hills region covers much of the upper portion of Louisiana, as well as the toe of the boot. It is the highest region with the roughest terrain. Geologists (scientists who study the origin, history, and structure of the earth) explain the Hills by referring to rock formations. The raised uplands and ridges are called **wolds**. Erosion has worn down the surrounding rock, leaving the wolds.

A major part of the Hills is the Sabine Uplift, also called the Dolet Hills. (An *uplift* is a raised area of rock folded upward.) Two ridges that are part of this uplifted rock are the Nacogdoches Wold and the Kisatchie Wold, which were named for the places where they begin. Driskill Mountain, Louisiana's high point, is part of the Kisatchie Wold.

The soil of the Hills region is old, infertile, and usually a reddish color because of its iron content. The Hills are a poor place for farming. However, pine trees grow well in this soil, and much of the region is now planted in tree farms.

Pine forests are also part of the natural vegetation of the Hills. The pines usually grow alongside hardwood trees, such as oak, hickory, ash, sweet gum, and pecan. In other parts of the Hills, there are longleaf pine forests where the tall, majestic trees grow unencumbered by other trees or underbrush.

Do You Remember?
1. Why are areas divided into regions?
2. What is the difference between a swamp and a marsh?
3. What mineral resources are found at the Five Islands?

Above left: *Tree farms abound in the Hills region.* **Above:** *Lake Claiborne provides a place for rest or recreation.*

KISATCHIE NATIONAL FOREST

In 1917, a young teacher traveled twenty miles in a mule-drawn wagon to reach her school in Natchitoches Parish. She passed through forests of longleaf pine, accented in the spring by wild magnolia, azalea, and dogwood. Along the way, she glimpsed quail, wild turkey, coyote, cottontail rabbit, and white-tailed deer. She later described her trip, ". . . over rolling hills, through mile after mile of majestic longleaf pine. I was in heaven."

Caroline Dormon's passionate description of this beautiful wilderness persuaded Congress to create the Kisatchie National Forest in 1930. The Kisatchie is the only national forest in Louisiana. If you follow Caroline Dormon's footsteps today, you can see the natural beauty that her efforts preserved.

The entire Kisatchie National Forest totals more than 600,000 acres, has six separate districts, and covers parts of seven different parishes. The Kisatchie Hills Wilderness area covers 8,700 acres of some of the steepest and most rugged terrain in Louisiana. The area includes ridges and sandstone bluffs.

Along the Wild Azalea National Trail in the early spring, you will see the pink blooms that give this trail its name. This 31-mile-long trail winds through pine forests, where some of the trees are marked as nesting trees for endangered birds. The Longleaf Scenic Byway is a 17-mile auto tour that is one of the most scenic drives in Louisiana. The Sugar Cane National Trail mixes nature with history as it passes by an old sugar cane mill.

Near Saline, in Bienville Parish, is Briarwood, the former home of Caroline Dormon. Today it is a nature preserve, where visitors can see many beautiful wildflowers in the gardens established by Miss Dorman. Schoolchildren who visit Briarwood and the Kisatchie National Forest benefit from Caroline Dormon's vision.

Above: *The Kisatchie Hills contains some of the steepest and most rugged terrain in the state.* **Left:** *Many tourists enjoy the beautiful drive along the Longleaf Scenic Byway.*

CLIMATE

Natural regions are sometimes identified by their climate. People often confuse weather and climate. **Weather** measures the immediate conditions of the atmosphere: temperature, precipitation, and wind. **Climate** is the average weather of an area over a long period of time, such as 25-30 years. The daily television news gives a weather report, not a climate report.

The major influences on Louisiana's climate are its closeness to the Gulf of Mexico, its distance from the equator, and its position on the North American continent. Based on its climatic differences, Louisiana has only two regions — North Louisiana and South Louisiana — and the five natural land regions fit into these two climatic regions.

Louisiana has a *humid subtropical* climate. This means the summers are just as hot as a tropical climate, a fact that surprises no one who has spent much time outdoors in August! It is the winter freezes that cause Louisiana to be classified as subtropical. However, the winter season does have days of warmer temperatures too. Much of the warm air and moisture that create this humid subtropical climate are the result of high pressure systems — called Bermuda highs — that approach Louisiana from Florida and carry huge amounts of moisture.

Another factor influencing Louisiana's climate is its location in the path of other high pressure systems that generally move from west to east across the North American continent. Louisiana lies on the east side of these continental air masses. Canadian air masses bring cold, dry air from the northwest; Sonoran air masses bring hot, dry air from Mexico. Because there are no mountains to stop them, these continental air masses hit Louisiana full strength and flow uninterrupted across the state.

Temperature, precipitation, and wind are the atmospheric conditions used to describe climate.

TEMPERATURE

Interestingly, and surprisingly to some, it is North Louisiana that has the highest and the lowest temperatures. That is because this area is too far from the Gulf of Mexico to benefit from its influence. The highest temperature ever recorded, 114°F (Fahrenheit), occurred on August 10, 1936, in Bossier Parish at Plain Dealing. Fewer than fifty miles away, Minden in Webster Parish recorded the state's lowest temperature of -16°F on February 15, 1899.

Heat and moisture from the Gulf of Mexico frequently produce thunderstorms in the summer months. Here is one forming over Six Mile Lake near Morgan City.

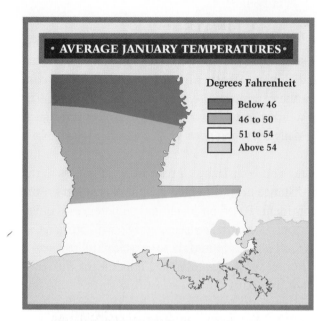

·AVERAGE JANUARY TEMPERATURES·

Degrees Fahrenheit

Below 46
46 to 50
51 to 54
Above 54

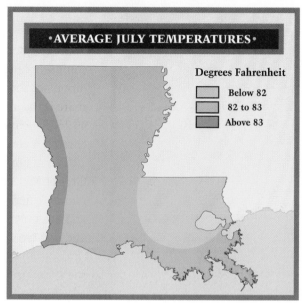

·AVERAGE JULY TEMPERATURES·

Degrees Fahrenheit

Below 82
82 to 83
Above 83

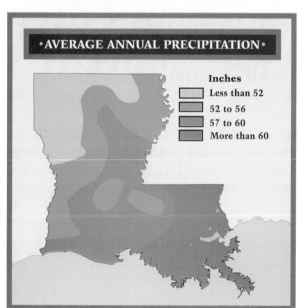

·AVERAGE ANNUAL PRECIPITATION·

Inches

Less than 52
52 to 56
57 to 60
More than 60

The greatest temperature variations occur in northwest Louisiana. Both the annual and the daily range of temperature are greater here, a result of the continental air masses that blast hot air or cold air into this part of the state. In July, the average temperatures range from 73°F to 93°F; January's average temperatures range between 32°F and 55°F.

PRECIPITATION

Precipitation means any form of water — liquid or solid — that falls from the atmosphere and reaches the ground. Rain is the most frequent type of precipitation in Lousiana, with occasional summer hail storms. In winter, sleet is more common than the rare snowfall.

The heat creates the summer rain of July and August in South Louisiana. This rain is *convectional*; that is, it is caused by the heating of the ground. The winter rainy season of December and January results from moist Gulf air masses rising over cold Canadian air masses. That same collision of air causes winter rain in North Louisiana. However, the summer rain in North Louisiana is much less predictable.

The average annual precipitation increases from the northwest to the southeast. Caddo Parish has an annual average rainfall of 48 inches, while Washington Parish has 70 inches.

In most Louisiana winters, there is little or no measurable snowfall. In 1895, a snowstorm covered all of the state — except the northwest.

That was unusual because it generally snows more frequently near the Arkansas line. In 1899, snow covered all of Louisiana, even the mouth of the Mississippi. Rayne in Acadia Parish got a record 24 inches from that storm.

WIND

It is wind that causes the most traumatic weather assaults on Louisiana. Two kinds of windstorms bring danger and destruction to the state each year.

Hurricanes

One type of severe windstorm originates over tropical ocean waters. When the wind speed of the storm reaches 74 miles per hour, it becomes a **hurricane**. The hurricane winds rotate around a calm center or *eye* and get their energy from the warm, moist air. That tremendous energy, bringing such destruction, is equal to the electric energy used by the United States in a year!

The hurricane attacks the coastline with high winds and the high water of storm surges. These walls of water, pushed inland by the fierce winds, are sometimes more than ten feet high. When high tide coincides with the storm surge, the walls of water may be twenty feet high. Torrential rain is blown by the wind, and flood damage can reach millions of dollars. Sometimes the hurricane winds spawn tornadoes, which do even more damage.

The greatest risk for hurricanes is during September, but hurricane season runs from June to October. Between 1890 and 1990, Louisiana experienced more than twenty-four hurricanes. Hurricane Audrey killed more people in Louisiana than any other hurricane

·THE PATHS OF HURRICANES·

Scale Number or Class	Kilometer/Hour	Miles/Hour	Storm Surge Meters	Feet	Reported Damage
1	119-153	74-95	1.2-1.5	4.0-4.9	Minimal
2	154-177	96-110	1.6-2.4	5.0-7.9	Moderate
3	178-209	111-130	2.5-3.6	8.0-11.9	Extensive
4	210-250	131-155	3.7-5.4	12.0-18.0	Extreme
5	greater than 250	greater than 155	greater than 5.4	greater than 18.0	Catastrophic

· SAFFIR-SIMPSON HURRICANE SCALE ·

in the twentieth century. That deadly storm hit Cameron Parish on June 28, 1957, and killed more than four hundred people. An unusual hurricane, Betsy, hit the mouth of the Mississippi in 1965 and traveled up the river to Baton Rouge, killing fifty-eight people along the way. In August 1992, Hurricane Andrew hit the Southeast and caused more than $25 billion in damage, $2.4 billion of damage in Louisiana alone, making it the costliest hurricane in United States history.

· FUJITA INTENSITY SCALE FOR TORNADOES ·

Rating	Miles/Hour	Expected Damage
F-0	40-72	Light: Loose Debris
F-1	73-112	Moderate: Broken Windows and Doors
F-2	113-157	Considerable: Trees Broken
F-3	158-206	Severe: Outer Walls Collapse
F-4	207-260	Devastating: Structure Damage
F-5	261-318	Incredible

Tornadoes

The second kind of windstorm that threatens Louisiana gives little warning. This is the vicious and unpredictable **tornado**, the notorious funnel-shaped cloud. If atmospheric conditions are right, a tornado can develop in five or ten minutes.

Weather radar and computer technology can spot the tornado, but often there is not enough time to get out of its way. The path of the tornado is usually erratic, making safety

Tornadoes sometimes strike without warning. Here is a funnel cloud forming in the summer sky.

precautions even more difficult. The dangerous storm moves forward at about 50 miles per hour and is usually about 100 yards wide. Inside the funnel cloud, the winds are circling at speeds up to 500 miles per hour. These high winds move counterclockwise around a low pressure center. The extreme low pressure center is particularly dangerous and causes most of the damage.

CLIMATE AND AGRICULTURE

When we talk about the climate and the weather, we are usually thinking about our own safety and comfort. But of even greater significance is the effect of climate and weather on the natural environment. Louisiana's humid subtropical climate results in a growing season that ranges from 210 days in north-central Louisiana to more than 290 days near the Passes. Only about once every seven years does a severe freeze occur at the mouth of the river, killing the citrus trees. But because the growers have a ready market for premium fruit, they are willing to lose the trees and replant.

Sugar cane is a major crop in the southern part of Louisiana. Here is a field of sugar cane in Avoyelles Parish.

Another crop that is the pride of Louisiana producers is the strawberry. Louisiana's early spring gives Tangipahoa Parish strawberry growers an advantage over northern competitors. After 90 days, their crop is ready to sell. The first ripe berries to reach the market are from the fields of Louisiana.

Sugar cane is a plant native to the tropics; in its natural state, sugar cane has a two-year growing season. But farmers can cultivate the cane for harvest with a minimum growing season of 250 days. Only in the southern part of the state is the growing season long enough for sugar cane. If you drive south from Cheneyville in Rapides Parish, you will see where the cotton fields end and the sugar cane fields begin.

Do You Remember?
1. What type of climate does Louisiana have?
2. What part of Louisiana gets hotter in the summer?
3. When is hurricane season?

PEOPLE AND THE ENVIRONMENT

Over the years, people have gradually changed Louisiana's environment. Those changes have had both positive and negative results.

FLOOD CONTROL

The many descriptions given to the Mississippi River indicate the conflicting relationship between people and their natural environment. We call it everything from the "father of waters" and the "great artery of the continent" to the "unruly neighbor of the farmers" and the "raging killer of small towns." The battle to decide who is conquered and who is the conqueror continues unceasingly.

The efforts to control the river have become increasingly complex, and they often contradict each other. Flood-control efforts in other areas of the United States are affecting coastal erosion and contributing to the loss of **wetlands** (swamps, marsh, and other areas that have a natural supply of water and are covered or soaked with water at least part of the year). The U.S. Army Corps of Engineers estimates that Louisiana loses at least thirty-five square miles of land each year. This erosion includes the loss of **barrier islands**, sea islands that protect the wetlands, estuaries, and bays from the direct impact of ocean waves.

The French made the first efforts to control the mighty Mississippi in 1717. Many flood-control structures were built over the next two hundred years, but it took the flood of 1927 to get the federal government involved in a comprehensive program of flood control. That frightening flood drove a half million people from their homes. Congress had established a Mississippi River Commission in 1879; its work was expanded after the Great Flood. The U.S. Army developed the Corps of Engineers, which was given the task of overseeing the drainage of the United States. This now includes a system of locks, dams, reservoirs, canals, and levees — all intended to control the huge funnel that is the Mississippi River Basin.

An important part of the flood-control system is the Bonnet Carre Structure, which was built in 1935 to protect the city of New Orleans. This concrete structure is nearly 8,000 feet long and has an electric crane to open or close its 350 bays. The spillway has been opened several times to save the city of New Orleans from flooding.

Another part of the flood-control system is the Old River Control Structure, completed in 1963. It was built at the point where the Red River enters the Mississippi and diverts the Red River into the Atchafalaya. At the same time, the Old River Control Structure had to prevent the Mississippi River from changing course and heading to the Gulf of Mexico through the Atchafalaya River.

The Old River Control Structure was built by the U.S. Army Corps of Engineers to control flooding, and prevent the Mississippi from changing course.

This screech owl on Little Pecan Island is a beneficiary of the efforts to conserve Louisiana's coastal habitats.

CONSERVATION

Conservation is the careful management of a natural resource to prevent its destruction. In an attempt to balance the conflict between people and nature, groups such as the Nature Conservancy have tried to protect endangered habitats like the 800 acres near Abita Springs that contains old-growth longleaf pine and dozens of rare plants. The Nature Conser-vancy's first successful project was the Honey Island Swamp, 70,000 acres between the East and West Pearl rivers.

Another important natural setting, the Bluebonnet Swamp, is part of the park system of the city of Baton Rouge. This balanced ecosystem survives in the center of urban life. In another effort, a group from Southeastern Louisiana University is working at Turtle Cove Research Station to replant cypress trees in the Pass Manchac swamp.

The rich network of wetlands in Louisiana is now the focus of conservation efforts by both private and government agencies. In 1989, a series of gates was built by the U.S. Wildlife and Fisheries Department to help control the salinity (saltiness) of the marsh. This experiment has helped maintain the brackish water that is essential for the life cycle of shrimp, an important part of the seafood industry in Louisiana. Another effort to maintain the delicate balance of the marsh involves attempts to stop erosion. Families in some Louisiana towns donate their Christmas trees to become part of a Christmas tree fence helping to keep the marsh safe.

Not all human intervention with the environment is planned or successful. Louisiana's environment is full of mistakes and accidents. One expensive and frustrating example is the water hyacinth. It is said to have been brought to the 1884 Cotton Exposition in New Orleans because it was a beautiful, exotic plant. It quickly spread, depriving fish of needed oxygen and clogging the waterways. Another plant, the Chinese tallow tree, has created a tremendous problem in the Atchafalaya Basin. In 1992, Hurricane Andrew flattened the trees in the swamp forest, and the tallow trees have taken over. These trees are not a food source for any bird or animal, and they prevent natural vegetation from returning to the area.

An animal that is also a relative newcomer to the natural environment of Louisiana is the **nutria**, a rodent that lives near water. Brought from South America to Avery Island, they supposedly escaped during a hurricane and made themselves at home in the marsh. These animals have now spread across the southern part of the state, becoming a nuisance. While they have been a source of revenue for trappers, they have also become a problem. The nutria eat the vegetation that protects the freshwater marsh, allowing salt water to move into the delicate ecosystem. Even regular trapping has not brought the nutria under control.

Lately, they have begun to invade the drainage canals in urban areas like Jefferson Parish. They eat the vegetation along the drainage ditches, causing erosion. The most recent plan to deal with the nutria is to encourage its use as food.

Zero tolerance is demanded for the latest threat, the zebra mussel. After hitching a ride by ship to the Great Lakes, these tiny mollusks are migrating down the Mississippi, clogging water systems as they come.

Even in the twenty-first century, the physical environment and the space around us must be understood and appreciated. As anthropologist Nicholas Spitzer has remarked, "The land is still where people toil to give shape to beliefs, desires, and dreams. The search must increase for a balance between nature and technology that will keep the Louisiana landscape a desirable place to live."

Some waterways, like this small bayou, have been completely clogged by the water hyacinth.

Do You Remember?
1. Why was the Bonnet Carre Spillway built?
2. Name three things that have had a negative affect on Louisiana's natural environment.

SUMMARY

Louisiana is located in the southeastern United States, along the Gulf of Mexico. Its neighbors are Mississippi, Arkansas, and Texas. Rivers form three of Louisiana's natural boundaries: the Mississippi and the Pearl rivers on the east and the Sabine River on the west. Louisiana's other important waterways are its bayous and lakes. The state has almost five thousand miles of navigable rivers, bayous, creeks, and canals.

Louisiana has been divided into five natural regions: the Mississippi Floodplain region, the Terraces region, the Marsh region, the Red River Valley region, and the Hills region. These regions are characterized by differences in their relief, soil, and vegetation.

Louisiana's climate is classified as humid subtropical. The southern part of the state has milder temperatures because of the influence of the Gulf of Mexico. The growing season is also longer in the south, where the winter freezes come later. Most of the precipitation in Louisiana falls in the form of rain, and the state is subject to occasional hurricanes and tornadoes.

People have affected Louisiana's environment in both negative and positive ways. Flood control and efforts to expand agriculture and industry have brought major changes. Fortunately, people are beginning to realize the dangers to the environment and are taking steps to protect and improve the Louisiana landscape.

CHAPTER · REVIEW

Reviewing People, Places, and Terms

Define, identify, or explain the importance of each of the following.

1. barrier island
2. bayou
3. climate
4. conservation
5. environment
6. estuary
7. geography
8. hurricane
9. latitude
10. longitude
11. map
12. parish
13. precipitation
14. relief
15. topography
16. tornado
17. weather
18. wetlands

Understanding the Facts

1. What is GIS? What is its function?
2. What is a time zone? In what time zone does Louisiana lie?
3. From what river was Toledo Bend created?
4. What is Louisiana's largest natural lake?
5. How were cutoff lakes created?
6. Name the five natural regions of Louisiana.
7. What are the three parts of the Mississippi Floodplain region?
8. What part of the Terraces region has loess soil that erodes easily?
9. What part of the Terraces region was once covered with grasses?
10. Why is the Hills region not good for farming?
11. What purpose does the Old River Structure serve?

Developing Critical Thinking

1. How have increased knowledge and increased technology influenced our interactions with our physical world?
2. How have human beings unintentionally created problems in Louisiana's environment?
3. Why is the disappearance of the Louisiana wetlands a focus of state and national government and private conservation groups?

Using Your Skills

1. Using a map of Louisiana, name one parish that is found in each of the five natural regions.
2. Identify the parishes that border the Mississippi River.
3. Using the map of Louisiana, identify five towns that are in the area of Louisiana that gets the most rainfall.

Special Projects

1. Using your research skills and an outline map, identify and label the location of at least one state or federal park found in each of the five natural regions of the state.
2. Choose a natural region of Louisiana other than where you live. Make a list of the reasons why you would want to visit that region, and write a summary of things you might do and see in this region.

Making Connections

1. Why did Mark Twain's mental map of the Mississippi River have to change so often?
2. Why was it so important for a river pilot to have such accurate knowledge of the Mississippi River?
3. Research to find out whether there are any river pilots still operating on the Mississippi River today.

- Hiking to the top of Louisiana's highest point, Driskill Mountain, would be like walking from one end of a football field to the other and turning around and going back 78 yards. The scientific classification for a mountain requires an elevation of 10,000 feet, but apparently an early Louisiana pioneer decided that the highest place he could find deserved to be called a mountain.
- On April 12, 1973, during a major flood, the Old River Structure almost gave way. If the river had won the struggle, the Mississippi would have headed down the shorter route to the Gulf.
- The U.S. National Weather Service started naming hurricanes in 1953, using women's names. In 1979, men's names were included. If a hurricane causes significant damage, the name is retired from the list and is not used again.
- Live oak trees in Louisiana have their own club, the Live Oak Society. Member trees must be at least one hundred years old. The president of the Society each year is actually a tree.
- A detailed map of Louisiana made in 1866 illustrates all of the plantations, towns, and landings along the Mississippi River, as well as mileage points. The beautiful, hand-drawn map is on display at Washington University in St. Louis, Missouri, where the map was made.
- The migratory bird path passing through Louisiana is known as the Mississippi Flyway.

• BUILDING SKILLS: READING MAPS •

Maps are one of the most helpful and frequently used social studies tools. Knowing how to read and interpret maps is important to your understanding of Louisiana's past and present. Follow these steps to develop your map skills.

1. Decide what is shown on the map. Most maps have a title and a legend. The *title* tells you what the map is illustrating. It may be the major cities in the state or the location of various natural resources. The *legend* explains what the symbols and colors used in the map represent. The legend may indicate the symbols for types of roads, size of listed cities, landmarks, or special attractions. Look at the map on page 51. What is the title of this map? Find a map in this textbook that includes a legend. What do the symbols represent?

2. Use the scale to help you determine the distance between cities or other points. The *scale* of a map uses a certain measurement for a set number of miles. Many maps show distance in both miles and kilometers. The scale is different for each map. Use a road map to determine the distance between Lake Charles and Shreveport and between Bossier City and Baton Rouge.

3. Understand latitude and longitude. Latitude and longitude lines pinpoint the exact location of a place on our planet. Find a map that displays latitude and longitude lines. Which longitude and latitude lines pass through Louisiana?

4. Use the grid system and the index of cities and towns to locate places quickly. Large maps are prepared using grids much like graph paper. Letters are used along one axis of the map and numbers along the other axis. The letters and numbers give each grid box on the map an "address." Each entry in the map index has an address, such as B-6, that identifies the grid box where that city or town is located. On a map of Louisiana, make a list of all the cities that are located in the C-4 grid box.

5. Maps often contain other useful information. Using a map of Louisiana, make a list of the other types of information contained on the map.

Try This! Using a grid system, create a map that shows your class's seating arrangement. Be sure to include a "student index" and a legend.

CHAPTER THREE

LOUISIANA'S RESOURCES: ECONOMICS AND ENVIRONMENT

Feast or famine, boom or bust, rags or riches: The Louisiana economy seldom, if ever, has known a middle ground.
— John Wilds, Charles Dufour, and Walter Cowen,
Louisiana Yesterday and Today

SUPPOSE YOU HAVE A DOLLAR BILL IN YOUR POCKET. That dollar has probably passed through the hands of thousands of people. You and every person who touched that dollar bill and the choices each one of you made about how to use it are all part of the economic system of Louisiana. The **economy** is a community's system of producing, distributing, and consuming goods and services. No matter where people live, they are part of an economic system. For that reason, it is important for you to understand how you fit into Louisiana's economic system.

Refineries such as this one process Louisiana's mineral resources into gasoline and chemicals. The field of sugar cane in front represents one of Louisiana's most important cash crops.

ECONOMIC SYSTEMS

Communities develop economic systems to meet their economic needs and wants. All people have the same basic needs—food, clothing, and shelter. But people's wants — things that they would like to have to make their lives more comfortable — are almost unlimited. Both people's needs and wants are satisfied through the goods and services the economy produces. **Goods** are physical items such as food, clothing, cars, and houses. **Services** are activities people do for a fee and include such things as medical treatment, education, equipment and car repairs, haircuts, and concerts. The person who buys or uses goods or services is called a **consumer**; the person or organization that makes or provides the goods or services is called a **producer**.

SCARCITY AND CHOICES

While consumers' needs and wants are unlimited, the resources needed to satisfy them are not. Resources include natural resources, human resources, and capital resources. A **natural resource** is a gift of nature, part of the natural environment. The term **human resources** refers to the people who produce the goods and provide the services. **Capital resources** are the money and property — factories, tools, bridges, machines, and other items — that are used to produce goods and services. Because these resources are limited, they are said to be scarce. **Scarcity**, a basic fact of any economy, means that people need and want more than the available resources can provide. The unlimited needs and wants of people must be balanced with the limited resources in the world.

The scarcity of resources means that choices must be made. Choosing how to use the resources is what an economic system is all about. In the economic system that exists in the United States, individuals, businesses, and communities make choices.

Each choice is an opportunity, with both a benefit and a cost. For example, let's assume that you go to the mall with $25. You could choose to buy a shirt you need or two CDs you want. Let's also assume that you choose to buy the shirt. The opportunity *benefit* is whatever you gain — in this case, the shirt. Your opportunity *cost* is whatever you give up by not buying it; in the example, that would be the two CDs.

Opportunity benefits and costs also apply to other types of choices, such as allocating resources, using time, or opening a business. The opportunity cost for those types of choices is the value of the alternative that is *not* chosen. For example, when you graduate from high school, your choices might include getting a job, joining the military, or going to college. The choice you make is your opportunity benefit. According to economists (those who study the economy), your *second* choice is your opportunity cost.

INTERDEPENDENCE

The first economic systems were simple trade arrangements involving basic items. Today's economic systems overlap and are **interdependent**. That is, the businesses and industries in an economy rely on each other and on other economies to succeed. Advances in communication and transportation have resulted in trade arrangements that are worldwide. For example, oil refined in Louisiana becomes a chemical, which becomes plastic, which is used to make a toy in China. The toy is shipped to Germany, where it becomes a gift for a child. Even fresh produce has become part of the global economy. A Louisiana grocery store might carry tomatoes grown locally and those grown in Spain.

How successful an economy is depends in part upon its resources. What two types of resources are illustrated in this photograph?

LOUISIANA'S ECONOMIC HISTORY

The European nations sought colonies in the New World to increase their power and wealth. This early tobacco factory was one example of the cash crops found in the New World.

The first economic system in Louisiana was based on **barter** (trading goods and services without money). The Native Americans had a thriving trade economy. Tribes traded goods with each other and later with Europeans. The economy that the European settlers developed in Louisiana was based on agriculture and commerce (the buying and selling of goods).

By the eighteenth century, Louisiana's colonial economy was governed by the theory of **mercantilism**. Under mercantilism, a government strictly controlled its resources and its markets in order to acquire wealth (gold and silver). The government used that wealth to build up its military forces and become even more powerful. To do all this, the government had to have a "favorable balance of trade." In other words, the government had to sell more of its goods to other countries than it bought from other countries. The government expected its New World colonies to provide raw materials and crops to the mother country. Colonies were also expected to buy goods only from the mother country.

Mercantilism, however, never worked well in Louisiana. Louisiana was first a colony of France and then of Spain. Both of these countries expected to find gold and silver or some other valuable products here.

But Louisiana did not have the easily extracted minerals nor enough people for an effective mercantile economy. The colony cost its mother country more than the mother country ever gained from operating it.

Finally, the colonists changed the economy to meet *their* needs rather than those of their European owners. Colonial Louisiana developed a frontier exchange economy. The colonists trapped for furs, made their own goods, grew their own crops, and traded with their neighbors. Some of those neighbors were colonies owned by other European countries. Sometimes this trade with the other colonies was considered illegal by the mother country and was called **smuggling**. The colonists, however, believed the smuggling was necessary for their survival.

By the time Louisiana's colonial period ended with the Louisiana Purchase, growing crops had become profitable. The earliest crops that were grown for sale were tobacco and indigo; cotton and sugar cane became important later. New Orleans developed into a major port for North America. A visitor in 1801 described the city on the Mississippi as "the grand mart of business, the Alexandria of America."

Indigo, which was used to produce a blue dye, was one of Louisiana's early cash crops. This early engraving shows how indigo was processed.

In the early years of statehood, Louisiana continued its agricultural economy. The economy boomed in the twenty years before the Civil War, but the end of the war brought great economic suffering. The state struggled economically until after World War II.

The war changed the economies of the world, and Louisiana felt those effects. After World War II, advances in technology brought new agricultural equipment that required less manual labor; many workers left the farms. New industries that had developed as part of the war effort survived and grew after the war ended.

But economic change had come to Louisiana even before World War II. Louisiana's vast forests were cut beginning about 1880. By 1920, most of the old-growth trees were gone. Unfortunately, most of the profits from this activity were made by out-of-state companies, not the people of Louisiana.

Another resource — oil — became valuable in the early twentieth century. This new oil (also called *petroleum*) industry began to change Louisiana's economic base. The demands for oil during World War II combined with the changes in agriculture to give the state a new economic direction.

Louisiana's economy today is based on the production of minerals: oil, natural gas, sulphur, salt, and lignite. Petroleum refining and the related chemical plants provide a large segment of the state's economic base. The forestry industry adds pulp, plywood, and paper making. **Agribusiness** (farming as a large-scale business operation) includes both crops and food processing. Louisiana's many waterways are home to commercial fishing, shipbuilding, shipping, and international trade.

The twenty-first century brings even more changes. Louisiana's economy must become more diverse (varied) to adapt to a changing world. Jobs that did not even exist twenty-five years ago require new skills. The state must develop its human resources to meet this demand. Choices made today about the use of capital resources may affect fu-

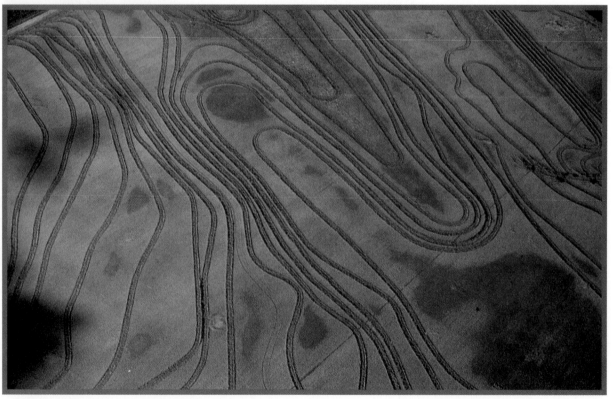

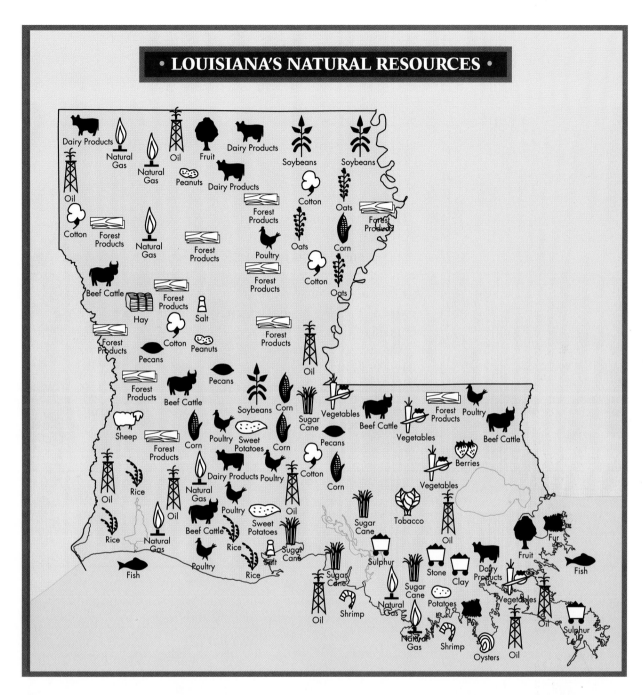

• LOUISIANA'S NATURAL RESOURCES •

ture economic growth. Finally, Louisiana must manage its abundant natural resources wisely to not only provide for economic needs but also preserve the environment.

Do You Remember?

1. What is a barter system?
2. Why did the early colonists smuggle goods into Louisiana?
3. In Louisiana, what early crops were grown for sale?

Opposite page, above: Petroleum refining and related chemical plants provide a large segment of the state's economic base.

Opposite page, below: There are over 500,000 acres of land in Louisiana on which rice is grown.

NATURAL RESOURCES

Natural resources are gifts of nature — air, water, soil. Louisiana's economy is largely based on its abundant natural resources.

The rich soil of Louisiana has provided bountiful harvests since the Indians first planted corn. Agricultural production, however, has shifted from the small farms and plantations of the past to today's huge agribusiness systems. Fewer people work in agriculture, but the amount of crops grown has not decreased. Louisiana ranks second in the United States in the production of sugar cane and sweet potatoes. Rice, cotton, and soybeans are also important crops.

The fertile soil and good climate also provide the right conditions for raising cattle. Herds of beef cattle range in pastures around the state. Some dairy farms continue as family farms, although they are a smaller part of today's economy.

An abundant water supply is an economic asset for Louisiana. Surface water and aquifers (underground rock formations where water collects) supply water for agriculture, industry, and human use. Waterways also provide transportation and recreation.

The water, soil, and air combine to create a bountiful natural environment. This environment provides many resources to supply human needs. These resources can be grouped as either mineral resources or biological resources.

Above: Sugar cane, seen growing here in Terrebonne Parish, is the principal source of sugar. **Right:** Herds of cattle roam the pastures of West Feliciana Parish.

MINERAL RESOURCES

Mineral resources are inorganic (not living) substances that occur naturally in the earth. Louisiana's mineral resources are an important element of the state's economy. They are, however, **nonrenewable**; that is, these resources are not replaced by nature once they are extracted from the environment.

Oil, natural gas, salt, sulphur, and lignite are some of the mineral resources found in Louisiana. The state also has deposits of sand, gravel, and limestone. These mineral resources are used in the construction industry.

Oil

Plants that decayed millions of years ago created the oil that today satisfies much of the world's energy needs. Louisiana contains more than 10 percent of the known oil reserves in the United States. Even more oil waits beneath the floor of the Gulf of Mexico. These deposits have made Louisiana the third largest oil producer in the United States.

The twentieth century began with the drilling of Louisiana's first oil well. A wooden derrick held that drilling rig in Jennings in Acadia Parish in 1901. The drill bit struck oil some 1,800 feet beneath the surface. More oil was located in Caddo Parish. It was in Caddo Lake that the industry's first offshore drilling took place. A valuable deposit of oil existed beneath the lake. Another large deposit was found in Claiborne Parish. Soon hundreds of oil derricks hinted at the possible riches across Louisiana. But those early years of oil exploration were based more on hunch than on geology; sometimes the landowner got a dry hole instead of an oil royalty check.

The richest recent discovery was the Tuscalousa Trend in South Louisiana, found in the 1970s. During the oil boom of that decade, many people realized their dream of getting rich quickly. The crash of oil prices in the 1980s changed their luck.

Coastal Louisiana has provided oil for many years. The oil deposits also lie offshore, beneath the floor of the Gulf of Mexico. Geologists discovered this oil by using sound waves to produce three-dimensional images of the earth's crust. The first platform in the Gulf was built in 1947.

Today, new techniques allow more efficient and deeper drilling. Drillers have even revisited some of the earlier sites and found more oil.

Large refineries process this "black gold" for hundreds of uses. More than fifteen refineries in Louisiana produce enough gasoline each year to fill 800 million automobile gas tanks. Jets fly around the world using fuel refined in Louisiana. Chemicals refined from oil create an almost unlimited list of other products.

This Texaco offshore oil platform is located in the Gulf of Mexico.

Natural Gas

The natural gas deposits in Louisiana are even larger than the oil deposits. More than a quarter of the nation's supply of natural gas comes from Louisiana. The natural gas is moved throughout the country by pipelines.

During the early days of the oil rush, natural gas was considered a nuisance and burned at the well sites. In 1917, however, a process was developed that converted natural gas into a substance called *carbon black*. Carbon black is used in making tires, carbon paper, ink, and other products. The large Monroe natural gas field, which had been discovered in 1907, became very valuable.

Later, natural gas was used as a fuel for homes and industry. The clean, efficient fuel is still in widespread use. Thanks to advances in technology, natural gas can even be used instead of gasoline as fuel in some vehicles. Entergy, a Louisiana utility company, has been using natural gas in its trucks since the mid-1980s.

Salt

Salt is essential to the diet of both humans and animals. The first people to use the salt in Louisiana were Native Americans. They found animals licking the soil where the salt had made its way to the surface. The Indians used the salt recovered from these *salt licks* in trade. Later, people used salt as a form of money.

During the Civil War, an underground salt deposit was discovered on Avery Island. This underground deposit was almost pure rock salt. The salt was a valuable asset to the Confederacy during the war years. Other salt deposits have been discovered, some of which are more than 50,000 feet deep and a least a mile across! Salt in these deep deposits is recovered by mining it.

Most of us think of salt as a seasoning or as a way to preserve food. But much of the Louisiana salt is used to make chemicals. Those chemicals are then used to make other products. One major product made from Louisiana salt is polyvinyl chloride, from which PVC pipe is made. While PVC pipe is mainly used for plumbing, it has also become very popular for making outdoor furniture.

Above: *Avery Island is a huge salt dome. Louisiana leads the nation in salt production.* ***Left:*** *Salt is being loaded onto a barge for shipment.*

Sulphur

Sulphur is a mineral that is today used to make matches, gunpowder, medicine, plastic, paper, battery acid, and fungicide. The Louisiana Petroleum and Coal Oil Company made the first major discovery of sulphur in Louisiana in 1869. The discovery was known as "Sulphur Mine" and was called the "richest 50 acres in the world." The town of Sulphur in Calcasieu Parish developed around this industry. Port Sulphur in Plaquemines Parish also owes its name to sulphur mining. The town was built as a model community for the employees of Freeport Sulphur who worked at Grande Ecaille.

At the end of the nineteenth century, Dr. Herman Frasch developed a technique, now known as the **Frasch process**, to use superheated steam to melt sulphur and force it to the surface. As a result, sulphur mining boomed.

After a troubled start, Sulphur Mine was, by 1904, producing enough sulphur to meet all the needs of the United States. At its peak, Sulphur Mine had 660 wells in operation. But the mine was played out and shut down in 1924. Sulphur Mine reopened briefly from 1966 to 1970.

Other deposits of sulphur have been discovered in salt domes and along the Gulf of Mexico coast. Today, sulphur mining is focused in the Gulf of Mexico. The second-largest sulphur deposit in the United

States — Main Pass Block 299 — began producing in 1993 and is expected to last thirty years.

This lignite surface mine is located in the Dolet Hills near Mansfield.

Lignite

Lignite is a soft, brownish-black coal that, because of its high water content, burns poorly. Although it is the lowest-quality coal, Louisiana lignite gained in importance in the 1970s. After a shortage of imported oil occurred, the United States government encouraged the use of other sources of energy. The coal deposits in Louisiana are burned to supply energy. In fact, lignite fuels the Dolet Hills Power Station near Mansfield.

The lignite deposits in Louisiana lie in the Dolet Hills, mostly in DeSoto Parish. Two commercial mining operations began in the 1980s and continue today. These surface-mining operations produce more than a million tons of lignite each year.

Do You Remember?

1. What percentage of the oil reserves in the United States is found in Louisiana?
2. What is carbon black?
3. What Louisiana natural resource is used in the manufacture of PVC pipes?

BIOLOGICAL RESOURCES

Biological resources are plants and animals, also called *flora* and *fauna* by scientists. Biological resources are **renewable**; that is, they replenish themselves in time.

One unusual form of vegetation that once was an economic resource for Louisiana is Spanish moss. The plant, gathered from live oak and cypress trees, was sold as stuffing for mattresses and furniture. The early Model T Fords even had seats stuffed with Louisiana Spanish moss. The most recent use for the moss is to make bedding for minnow farms. Gathering moss for sale, however, has almost disappeared as an economic activity in Louisiana.

Forests

Money may not grow on trees, but trees can certainly bring money to the economy. Trees are Louisiana's second-largest income producer. Almost half of Louisiana — over 13.9 million acres — is covered in forests. Trees are sold from the forests of fifty-eight parishes.

More than 90 percent of the trees cut are pine, and more than 75 percent of those pine trees are cut for **pulpwood**. These smaller, softer trees are shredded into pulp, which is made into paper. Over 3.6 million cords of pine trees are cut for pulpwood each year. That pulpwood would make enough paper to print over a billion copies of the Sunday *New York Times*.

Large trees cut for lumber are called *sawtimber*. More than one billion board feet of timber are cut from these trees, enough to build over 150,000 houses. Most of the sawtimber is also pine, although some sawtimber is cut from hardwood trees such as oak. The hardwood sawtimber is used for specialty products such as furniture and wall paneling.

The forestry-related industry includes paper mills, lumber mills, plywood plants, container board factories, and paper bag manufacturers. Flooring and furniture are also manufactured. Furniture makers are excited about a new source of the beautiful and weathered Louisiana cypress. Most of the huge cypress trees were cut during the lumber boom of the early 1900s. Those slow-growing cypress trees were hundreds of years old. As the huge trees were floated to the mills, some of the logs sank. Cypress does not rot, and those sunken logs are now being recovered from their underwater resting places.

The lumber industry has come under closer regulation since the days when the forests were cut without any thought of replanting. Today, over a hundred million trees are replanted each year.

The Office of Forestry in the Louisiana Department of Agriculture provides assistance with forestry management. That department has also helped start a new industry. More than 150 Christmas tree farms supply this seasonal specialty. Families who want to cut their own trees can now select their favorite from the planted forest.

Most of Louisiana's harvested trees go to make pulpwood. Here pine logs are awaiting shipment on the Red River.

Wildlife

Animals have always helped satisfy people's needs. Louisiana's natural regions provide a habitat for a variety of wildlife. These animals continue to be an economic resource for trappers, and hunting continues to be a tradition throughout the state. Seasons and limits on both activities are set by law and regulated by the state Department of Wildlife and Fisheries.

Louisiana once sold more than a million fur pelts annually. That number has decreased by about 75 percent. Trapping has declined as the demand for furs has dropped. Those animals that are trapped include the muskrat, raccoon, mink, otter, and beaver. Today, however, more nutria are trapped than any other animal.

Hunters in Louisiana continue a generations-old activity as they head outdoors. As a sport, a recreation, a hobby, or a source of food, hunting is a part of Louisiana's economy and generates millions of dollars each year.

The early years of timber cutting and clearing land for crops reduced the forest land. The numbers of forest animals dropped drastically as their habitats were lost. The proper management of game animals (those hunted for sport or food) has increased the animal population in recent years. White-tailed deer have increased to more than a million animals in the state. Other game animals include squirrels and rabbits.

Top: *The brown pelican is Louisiana's state bird.* **Above:** *Although the demand for furs has declined, the racoon is still trapped in Louisiana.*

The largest wild animal in Louisiana is no longer hunted. The black bear is a protected species and considered endangered. The loss of the bear's natural habitat has made it almost extinct. Fortunately, the state has a program to release bears brought here from other states. Radio collars track the bears so they can be protected and observed.

Benjamin Franklin wanted the wild turkey, not the bald eagle, to be the symbol of the United States. Franklin would be pleased at the efforts that have increased the numbers of this native bird in Louisiana. The gobble of the wild turkey is heard in forests throughout the state. Thanks to the management of the Louisiana Department of Wildlife and Fisheries, it is estimated that the number of wild turkeys has increased from 20,000 to more than 90,000.

The wild turkey is classified as a game bird in Louisiana. Other game birds that can be hunted in season are dove and quail. Doves are plenti-

ful, but the number of quail has dropped in recent years. The most plentiful game birds are the migratory waterfowl that pass through Louisiana on their way south for the winter. Millions of ducks and geese cover the marsh during November and December. Ducks are also hunted in the wetlands of North Louisiana, the wood duck being the most plentiful.

The state bird of Louisiana — the brown pelican — was almost lost to future generations. The pesticide that saved Louisiana's cotton industry from the boll weevil earlier in the century almost destroyed the pelicans. DDT harmed the environment in ways that were not known until years after its use. Pelicans exposed to DDT laid fragile eggs that would not hatch into healthy birds. In 1973, DDT was banned, and environmentalists (people who work to protect nature) have worked hard to rescue the brown pelican.

The alligator is also a symbol of Louisiana around the world. The hide of this reptile is valuable and in demand as leather. However, extensive hunting and environmental problems reduced the number of alligators to the endangered level. The states along the Gulf Coast stopped alligator hunting in 1963, and the animal was placed on the federal protected species list. The plan worked.

More than a half million alligators live in Louisiana. In 1981, after eighteen years, alligator hunting resumed under strict rules. In 1995, about 28,000 alligators produced $11.9 million in hides and meat. The state now has alligator farms, which add almost the same dollar value to the economy as trapping the alligators in the wild. The alligator thrives in Louisiana, holding its place in the ecosystem and in the economy.

Top: Salt is being rubbed into this alligator hide to preserve it.
Above: More than a half million alligators live in Louisiana.

One in four people in Louisiana fishes. Some fish for recreation, and others fish for a living. Their equipment ranges from a simple cane pole to huge hoop nets.

The rivers, lakes, and bayous of Louisiana provide freshwater fish such as bream, bass, perch, and catfish. Most of these fish are caught for recreation. The catfish is the main freshwater fish that can be legally caught to sell. The growing demand for catfish led to a new industry — catfish farming. The catfish are raised in ponds.

The popular freshwater crustacean (shellfish) is the crawfish. The swamps of the Atchafalaya River Basin produce millions of pounds of crawfish annually. Crawfish are also raised commercially on crawfish farms. Some rice farmers even produce crawfish as a second crop in their flooded fields.

Fishing in the Gulf of Mexico is a popular activity for local families as well as tourists. Old oil rigs in the Gulf have been converted into artificial reefs and attract thousands of fish and many charter boats.

The Gulf of Mexico provides Louisiana with a generous harvest of seafood. Game fish include speckled trout, redfish, drum, mackerel, blue

Below: Louisiana is a fishing paradise. The Atchafalaya Basin is a popular destination.
Opposite, above: *Many visitors charter boats to take them fishing in the Gulf of Mexico.*
Opposite, below: *These speckled trout will end up on someone's dinner plate.*

marlin, amberjack, grouper, and tarpon. Commercial fishing is allowed for tuna, sea trout, red snapper, and other fish that are headed for the dinner table. Seafood caught off the coast of Louisiana totals 25 percent of the United States catch each year. The largest catch of fish ever taken in one year was almost 2 billion pounds. This is the record for the United States.

Shrimp, oysters, and crabs flavor our gumbos and help fund our economy. More shrimp and oysters come from Louisiana than any other coastal state. Louisiana oysters are even sold in Asian countries.

The biggest contributor to the seafood economy is a fish no one eats. The menhaden, also called the pogy, is used to make pet food and fertilizer. This small sardinelike fish brings millions of dollars into the state each year.

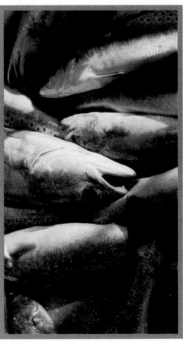

Do You Remember?
1. How are most Louisiana trees used once they are cut down?
2. What is sawtimber?
3. What is the Louisiana state bird?

CAPITAL RESOURCES

Capital resources include buildings and equipment used to produce goods or services. Examples of capital resources in Louisiana are rice mills, sugar refineries, oil refineries, cotton gins, and meat-packing plants. Transportation facilities — bridges, highways, and airports — are also capital resources. More than one hundred airports — large and small — serve Louisiana.

Banks serve the economy by making it possible for producers and consumers to trade, borrow, save, and invest. Banks in Louisiana are regulated by the federal and the state governments.

In recent years, Louisiana banks have grown to meet the demands of people and industry. At first, Louisiana banks were small and could not expand beyond their parish. The first change in banking laws came in 1984 and allowed banks to merge with banks in other parishes. Several large banks in the state bought smaller banks and increased their influence on Louisiana's economy. In 1994, Congress passed a law that allowed large interstate bank mergers. In other words, banking companies can own banks in many states. Today, large national banking companies own a number of Louisiana banks.

Above: This building under construction in Shreveport is a capital resource, which will be used in the production of goods or services. **Opposite page:** *Human resources—people such as this furniture craftsman in Covington—are Louisiana's most valuable resource.*

HUMAN RESOURCES

Human resources are the people who supply the labor — either physical or mental — to produce goods and provide services. In the economic system, they receive wages or salaries for providing this resource. (A *wage* is a set amount paid to an employee for each hour the employee works. A *salary* is a fixed amount paid to an employee at set intervals, such as every week.)

Today's diverse and interdependent economies require new skills and specialization. Productivity and flexibility are important skills that today's employers value. Employees who want to get and keep satisfying, good-paying jobs know that the key to doing so is education and training. Employees who know their jobs well are an asset to the economy.

PROVIDING GOODS AND SERVICES

An economic system uses the available human, natural, and capital resources to produce goods and provide services. Louisiana's economy today produces a wide variety of goods and services.

MANUFACTURING

Louisiana manufactures business telephone systems, light trucks, electrical equipment, pharmaceuticals (medicinal drugs), glass products, automobile batteries, playground equipment, mobile homes, yachts, and clothing as well as several hundred other products. Products made in Louisiana are sold throughout the world.

The chemical industry is a major part of Louisiana's economy. Louisiana ranks second in the United States in the primary production of *petrochemicals*, chemicals made from petroleum. More than one hundred chemical plants in Louisiana produce an almost endless list of products. Fertilizers, plastics, and synthetic rubber are just three of the important goods made from petrochemicals.

The petroleum refineries in Louisiana produce some 15 billion gallons of gasoline each year. Among the state's refineries are those operated by Exxon, Shell, Citgo, Mobile, Marathon, Texaco, and Conoco. These refineries also produce jet fuels, lubricants, and some six hundred other petroleum products.

Fuel from Louisiana's refineries supplies the energy for the many ships built in our state. Some of the largest ships are giant transport ships designed to carry natural gas. Louisiana's shipbuilders also design and build merchant vessels, Coast Guard cutters, barges, tugs, supply boats, fishing vessels, and pleasure craft. Avondale Shipyards on the Mississippi River near New Orleans is the largest shipbuilder in the state.

AEROSPACE AND AVIATION

The United States space program depends on Louisiana workers. At Martin Marietta in New Orleans, more than 2,500 people build fuel tanks for the space shuttles. The National Aeronautics and Space Administration (NASA) also operates an aerospace computer services center in Slidell in St. Tammany Parish. Other aviation-related industries are a Boeing Corporation repair plant in Lake Charles and an aircraft modification plant in Shreveport.

BIOTECHNOLOGY

Scientists are taking Louisiana's economy in a new direction. University researchers are adding new technological knowledge to the study

Geismar, on the Mississippi, is home to this Vulcan Chemicals plant.

PENNINGTON BIOMEDICAL RESEARCH CENTER

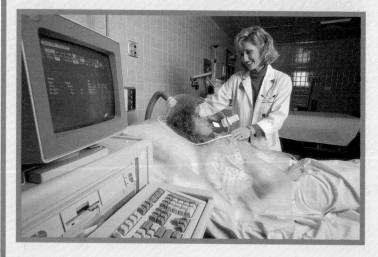

The mission of the Pennington Biomedical Research Center is to promote healthier lives through nutritional research and preventive medicine. Researchers at the Center study the effects of nutrition on such chronic illnesses as heart disease, diabetes, obesity, hypertension, and cancer. More than 1,500 human volunteers assist the researchers each year. The Center shares its research results with such universities as Harvard, Johns Hopkins, Duke, and Columbia.

In 1980, philanthropist Claude B. (Doc) Pennington donated $125 million to Louisiana State University for the establishment of the Center. At the time, this donation represented the largest private gift given to a university by an individual. "Doc" Pennington, a former optometrist and oil man, had been interested in nutrition and health.

The Research Center complex, which opened in 1988, is located in Baton Rouge and covers an area the size of five football fields. The Center contains forty research laboratories and millions of dollars in equipment.

Top: *The Pennington Biomedical Research Center complex covers an area the size of five football fields.* **Above:** *More than 1,500 human volunteers assist the researchers each year.* **Opposite:** *Researchers at the Center study the effects of nutrition on such illnesses as heart disease, obesity, diabetes, and cancer.*

Volunteers who participate in nutrition research agree to eat their meals at the Center, where dieticians and gourmet chefs create healthy recipes based on Louisiana foods. There is another interesting area of research at the Pennington Center. Workers in a special laboratory study volunteers as they sleep. Their research is designed to help people with health problems caused by sleep deprivation.

Research at Pennington Center reaches into the twenty-first century. The National Institute of Health selected Pennington Center to study diabetes and heart disease. The Center has also studied bone and muscle loss during space flight for NASA.

of biology. *Biotechnology* combines biological research with engineering. The Pennington Biomedical Research Center is a leader in Louisiana's growing role in the world of biotechnological research.

TOURISM

One service industry — tourism — is an important part of Louisiana's economy. Tourists visit Louisiana to experience the culture that makes us special. While in Louisiana, they sightsee, eat, shop, fish, hunt, and join the crowds at Mardi Gras. Those travelers spend more than $5.2 billion a year in the state and provide jobs for more than 87,000 workers.

Another service industry that attracts money and people to Louisiana is movie-making. The first movie made in Louisiana was a silent movie, filmed in 1908. More recent films shot here include *Steel Magnolias*, *The Pelican Brief*, *Dead Man Walking*, and *Heaven's Prisoners*. In 1994, more than $37 million was made from feature films, television commercials, and music videos produced in Louisiana. The Louisiana Film Commission is happy to welcome both in-state and out-of-state production companies.

Tourists bring billions of dollars each year into the Louisiana economy. These tourists are at Jean Lafitte National Park.

THE ENVIRONMENT

Regardless of the types of economic activities that people take part in, those activities affect our environment. Today, several federal and state agencies and private organizations examine the environmental effect of economic activities. In 1970, Congress established the **Environmental Protection Agency** (EPA) to direct efforts to protect the environment throughout the United States. The Louisiana legislature established the **Department of Environmental Quality** (DEQ) to provide state protection.

These agencies examine water pollution, solid waste, air quality, hazardous waste, nuclear energy, litter control, recycling, and the wetlands. Their efforts sometimes create a conflict between economic growth and environmental protection. For example, the environmentalists and the oil industry disagree about the danger of oilfield waste.

Environmentalists are also concerned about coastal erosion. **Erosion** is the gradual wearing away of the land by the action of wind or water. Louisiana's marsh is disappearing at a rapid rate. Some people estimate the loss at 25 to 35 square miles a year, down from as much as 40 square miles a year. Coastal residents can point to underwater locations that were once their homes.

Environmentalists are working to protect Louisiana's coastal wetlands from erosion and other threats.

Coastal erosion is partly caused by nature and partly by humans. Geologists say that the coast of Louisiana is gradually sinking, or tilting downward. The overflow from the Mississippi River once added new soil on a regular basis. But human-built levees have blocked this natural process.

Recent efforts to slow the coastline loss are beginning to show results. Stricter regulations about the use of wetlands have helped. Restoration projects have also brought improvements. In 1997 and 1998, a high school student, Joy Yoshina, organized volunteers to help save Louisiana's coast. The group prepared marsh grass seedlings to be planted in the wetlands. Joy, a student at the Louisiana State University Laboratory School at the time, also led a group of volunteers in the annual Beach Sweep. This cleanup program removes the unsightly litter along Louisiana's coastline.

Louisiana's economy has grown from its basic beginnings of barter and trade. Today, Louisiana joins in a worldwide trading economy. Goods from around the world make their way to Louisiana. At the same time, Louisiana products enter the global market.

CONNECTING · WITH · TECHNOLOGY

THE AMERICAN ECONOMY AND COMPUTERS

Suppose that one day all the computers stopped operating. How would this affect the American economy?

Our economy depends on communications, which depend on computers. Telephone companies use computers to route long-distance calls. Without microprocessors (simple computers), cellular phones would not send and receive signals. Practically all newspapers and magazines use computers to set type and control the printing presses. Television and radio stations use computers to handle technical aspects of broadcasting. Even the post office uses computers to determine postage charges and sort the mail.

Most transportation would stop cold without computers. Microprocessors in today's motor vehicles control vital operations. Aircraft use computers to navigate and monitor engineering systems. Airline reservation systems are completely dependent on computers, as are railroad signaling systems and switches. Inside cities, traffic lights would not work without computer-controlled timing devices, nor would subways operate without the computers that control train movements.

Money would flow at a snail's pace if governments, businesses, and banks had to write checks by hand. Banks use computers to keep tabs on customers' accounts and generate monthly statements. Automatic teller machines and credit cards would not work without computers.

The buying and selling of goods would also be hindered. Modern cash registers are connected to computers that read bar codes and tally bills. These machines also keep records of stores' inventory and tell the stores when to reorder.

These are only a *few* of the ways computers keep our economy going. Without them, the economy would fall into chaos.

This interdependence is both positive and negative. Economic growth is a benefit of an expanded market. For example, Louisiana seafood is sold throughout Asia. Shipping from Louisiana's major ports totals about 400 million tons of cargo a year. More than 40 percent of all the grain exported from the United States passes through Louisiana's ports. Over five thousand ocean-going ships arrive at Louisiana ports each year.

Louisiana's offshore port, the **Superport**, is the only facility in the United States capable of handling extremely deep vessels. The Superport was constructed to serve the offshore oil industry and Louisiana's oil refineries. Tankers from around the world dock at this port in the Gulf of Mexico.

However, along with economic growth have come problems. The North American Free Trade Agreement (NAFTA) removed trade restrictions between the United States and other countries in the western hemisphere. Some U.S. companies moved to Mexico or South America to take advantage of cheap labor. For example, Fruit of the Loom closed several Louisiana factories employing thousands of workers. The economic impact was felt throughout those communities.

As Louisiana's economy grows and interacts with other economies in the world, specialization and skill become more important. The state's abundant natural resources provide one aspect for a strong economic system. Investment in capital resources and good education are equally important. Despite the problems, our future demands a strong involvement in the interdependent world economies.

The largest city in Louisiana, New Orleans is a major U.S. port through which millions of tons of cargo flow every year.

Do You Remember?

1. Name three specific capital resources found in Louisiana.
2. Name two important Louisiana service industries.
3. What is the job of the DEQ?

SUMMARY

Louisiana's first economic system involved simple trade with basic items such as furs. Today's economic system goes far beyond the basic resources of the state's early people. Louisiana businesses produce a variety of goods and services.

Natural resources, capital resources, and human resources have all contributed to the development of the state's interdependent economy. Natural resources include nonrenewable mineral resources such as oil, natural gas, salt, sulphur, and lignite. They also include biological resources such as forests, wildlife, and fish. These gifts from nature have added to our state's economic growth. Capital resources are both a contributor to and a byproduct of this economic growth. A skilled workforce provides the human resources needed to produce the economic goods and services.

The interactions of natural, capital, and human resources have led to changes in the environment — both positive and negative. Today, agencies monitor these changes. With proper care, Louisiana's natural resources will be available for future generations.

CHAPTER · REVIEW

Reviewing People, Places, and Terms

Define, identify, or explain the importance of each of the following.

1. agribusiness
2. barter
3. biological resources
4. capital resources
5. consumer
6. DEQ
7. economy
8. erosion
9. EPA
10. Frasch process
11. goods
12. human resources
13. interdependent
14. lignite
15. mercantilism
16. mineral resources
17. natural resources
18. nonrenewable
19. producer
20. pulpwood
21. renewable
22. scarcity
23. services
24. smuggling
25. Superport

Understanding the Facts

1. What is the difference between needs and wants?
2. Explain opportunity benefit and opportunity cost.
3. What is a frontier exchange economy?
4. What are Louisiana's most valuable natural resources?
5. Where was Louisiana's first offshore oil well located?
6. What natural resource is mined using the Frasch method?
7. Where is lignite found in Louisiana?
8. Name three forestry-related industries found in Louisiana.
9. What is a game bird? Give three examples of game birds native to Louisiana.
10. What Louisiana fish is used to make pet food and fertilizer?
11. How do businesses in Louisiana help NASA's space program?
12. What are the major causes of coastal erosion in Louisiana?

Developing Critical Thinking

1. How are goods and services alike? How are they different?
2. Why did early Louisiana Indians use salt as money?
3. Suppose more vehicles (cars, trucks, and so on) were converted from the use of gasoline to natural gas. What effects might this have on Louisiana's economy?

Using Your Skills

1. Using the Yellow Pages of the telephone book, identify the listings of five businesses that rely on Louisiana natural resources. For example, your local service station sells gasoline refined from Louisiana petroleum.
2. Prepare a chart with the following headings: Resource, Location, Uses. Complete the chart by listing Louisiana's major resources, identifying where they can be found, and what the resource is used for.
3. Choose one of the cultural regions of the state and develop a brochure to attract tourists to that region.
4. Read the newspapers for one week and cut out any articles you find concerning controversies about land use. Are any of these controversies in your area?

1. Look through the classified section of a recent newspaper. Find two jobs that involve the manufacture of goods and two jobs that involve providing a service. Write a paragraph explaining which of the jobs you would prefer to have and why.

2. Every time someone tosses a piece of paper to the ground in Louisiana, it costs all of us. The direct cost is, of course, cleaning up the litter. But there are also other costs. Tourists comment that Louisiana's beauty is hidden by all the litter they see in the state. Tourists, as you know, are a major contributor to our economy. How could you help solve Louisiana's litter problem? Plan an antilitter campaign for your community.

3. Identify an environmental problem in your neighborhood, school, or community. Investigate the causes of the problem and find out what individuals, authorities, or agencies are doing to solve the problem.

Making Connections

1. Make a list of ten of your daily activities that are affected in some way by the computer. Compare your list with the lists of your classmates.

2. Write a one-page story entitled "The Day the Computers Shut Down." Share your story with your classmates.

Louisiana Laginappe

- One of the newest and largest oil platforms in the Gulf of Mexico — the Enchilada platform — is 95 feet by 210 feet.
- Sulphur was called *brimstone* and "the stone that burns."
- Some Louisiana ships are built upside down and launched sideways rather than stern first, as is the custom elsewhere.
- The first offshore sulphur mining rig was sunk to create an artificial reef. This reef attracts numerous fish and fishermen. Over sixty rigs have been converted as part of the "Rigs to Reefs" program.
- The lignite found near Shreveport was used at the federal arsenal during the Civil War.
- Most of the dairy farms in Louisiana are found in Caddo, DeSoto, and Washington parishes.
- The Tuscaloosa Trend runs across the state, east-west, just below the central region.
- America's first movie theater opened in New Orleans in 1896.

• BUILDING SKILLS: DECISION MAKING •

You will find it easier to make choices or decisions if you follow a step-by-step process. The steps in the decision-making process are:

1. Identify the problem or the choice to be made.
2. List the different alternatives.
3. Evaluate each alternative.
4. Choose one alternative (in other words, make a decision).
5. Act on your decision.
6. Evaluate your decision or choice.

Try This! Use the steps in the decision-making process to solve the following problem. Describe the actions you would take at each step.

Edward is a high school student with a B+ average. His teachers think that, if he can maintain his grade average, he could earn an academic scholarship to college. He is also on the football team, and the coach thinks he has a chance to get an athletic scholarship. Edward wants a car. He is considering quitting football to take an after-school job. He would work every afternoon from 4:00 p.m. to 9:00 p.m. at minimum wage.

Use the steps listed above to help Edward make a wise decision. Consider his present wants and his future potential. Identify the opportunity benefit and the opportunity cost for each of Edward's alternatives. What decision would *you* make?

CHAPTER FOUR

LOUISIANA'S GOVERNMENT: RIGHTS AND RESPONSIBILITIES

We, the representatives of the people . . . do mutually agree with each other to form ourselves into a free and independent State.
— Preamble of the first Louisiana constitution, 1812

THE GOVERNMENT OF THE STATE OF LOUISIANA has been influenced by its colonial founders, the French and the Spanish. When Louisiana was a Spanish colony, the Spanish government established parishes as geographical divisions of the Catholic Church. These parishes later formed Louisiana's first governmental divisions. Louisiana is the only state to have parishes instead of counties.

Its colonial founders also gave Louisiana a very different view of government than those states that were originally British colonies. Many of the British colonies were founded by people seeking freedom. Those colonists expected to be heard by their government. Louisiana and other colonies founded by the French and the Spanish had a much less participatory government.

The Louisiana State Capitol building, the tallest in the nation, is the seat of government for the state.

Terms: political alliance, constitution, amendment, executive branch, budget, veto, impeachment, legislative branch, bicameral, census, reapportionment, caucus, constituent, bill, lobbying, judicial branch, civil laws, criminal laws, jury, deficit, surplus, taxes, bond, police jury, home rule, open primary

People: governor, lieutenant governor, attorney general, secretary of state, treasurer, speaker of the house, president of the senate

The Louisiana Purchase of 1803 brought the more democratic, United States government to the people of Louisiana. Adjusting to this participatory government deeply affected the developing state. The adjustment changed the ongoing political alliances. (A **political alliance** joins several groups of people to support a political cause or candidate. The alliance includes people with common backgrounds and interests.) Historically, the Acadian Catholics of South Louisiana formed a political alliance based on common goals. The Protestants in North Louisiana also joined together to protect their interests. Residents of New Orleans are usually considered a separate political alliance. The statewide elections in Louisiana have often centered around these three groups.

The French influence on Louisiana government is also seen in the legal system. In a *civil law system*, there are written codes of laws. Judicial decisions are based on these written laws. This idea first began with the Romans and was later used in both Spain and France. When Napoleon had power in France in the early nineteenth century, the civil law system was made even clearer in the Napoleonic Code. On the other hand, decisions in the British *common law system* are based more on *precedents*, the legal decisions made in earlier, similar cases. Louisiana's legal system is often described as the Napoleonic Code. It is actually based only partly on those French laws.

THE STATE CONSTITUTION

The basic framework for Louisiana's government is the state **constitution**. This document explains the broad organization of the government. The state constitution grants power to the government to act in the interest of the people. At the same time, it includes limits to protect the rights of the state's citizens.

Louisiana's present constitution was approved by the voters in 1974; it is the eleventh constitution for the state. No other state has had so many constitutions. Why has the Louisiana constitution been rewritten so many times? It is because each time political power shifted, the new group in control wanted to put in place its ideas of government. But each of the pre-1974 constitutions had been so specific that rewriting the constitution was the only way the new group could bring about the changes it wanted. In addition, constitutional protection is much stronger than writing new laws. Laws can be changed by a simple act of the legislature; a new constitution has to have the approval of the voters.

This was the pattern throughout the nineteenth century. After a major power struggle, the winners would rewrite the constitution for their own benefit. But by the twentieth century, the method for change shifted. Instead of rewriting the constitution, the new group in power added amendments. (An **amendment** corrects or adds to the current constitution.)

The constitution in effect in 1973 had been written in 1921 — and amended 536 times, in so much detail that it filled several volumes. Finally, the voters got tired of having to decide upon so many proposed amendments each year and refused to pass any more. The legislators realized that a new constitution had to be written.

The present Louisiana constitution follows the federal constitution more closely than any of the earlier state constitutions. The bill of rights—the section that guarantees basic rights—is even stronger than the one in the United States Constitution, adding the right to individual dignity and freedom from discrimination. The inclusion of that right is a result of the civil rights struggle of the 1960s. Although the current constitution is more like a framework for government, it is still more specific on some issues than legal scholars think it should be. The purpose of the state constitution is to give a broad structure for government; laws should provide the specific details.

Do You Remember?

1. Is Louisiana law based on a civil law system or a common law system? What is the difference between the two?
2. Why did the state write a new constitution in 1974?

BRANCHES OF GOVERNMENT

Louisiana's constitution organizes the state government around the same framework as the federal government. The powers of the state government are divided among three branches: the executive, the legislative, and the judicial. This arrangement creates a system of *checks and balances* so that each branch can use its powers to protect the rights of the people and prevent the other two branches from becoming too powerful.

Louisiana's legal system is based in part upon the Napoleonic Code, the name given to the written civil laws of France. The code was named after Napoleon Bonaparte, emperor of France in the early 1800s, who helped formulate it.

EXECUTIVE BRANCH

The **executive branch** is responsible for enforcing the laws passed by the legislative branch. The executive branch also operates the state government and administers state services.

The chief executive officer of the state is the **governor**. There are also a number of other elected officials in the executive branch: lieutenant governor, secretary of state, treasurer, attorney general, commissioner of agriculture and forestry, commissioner of insurance, and commissioner of elections.

Governor

The governor of Louisiana must be at least twenty-five years old and a citizen of the United States and Louisiana for at least five years. The governor is elected for a four-year term and can serve two consecutive (back-to-back) terms. The election for governor is held in the odd-numbered year before a presidential election (for example, 2003, 2007, and so on).

The Louisiana constitution gives the governor broad powers. This strong constitutional power comes partly from French and Spanish traditions of a strong central government.

Perhaps one of the governor's most important duties is to prepare and submit operating and capital **budgets** to the legislature. These plans set out how money should be obtained and spent by the state government. In this way, the governor influences the way the state spends its money.

The governor appoints citizens to hundreds of boards and commissions. These appointments give the governor power and influence. The executive branch can also influence the legislative branch through *administration bills*, laws the governor wants passed. Legislators who support the governor introduce these bills in the legislature. Those legislators are called the governor's "floor leaders," because they guide the bills to passage on the floors of the state house and state senate.

The governor also has the authority to call *special sessions* of the legislature to discuss specific subjects. These special sessions are usually called when the governor believes the state has a need that cannot wait until the regular legislative session. In recent years, special sessions have dealt with Medicaid funding problems and the New Orleans land casino.

As part of the system of checks and balances, the governor can **veto** (refuse to approve) bills passed by the legislature. The governor can also use a line-item veto on any part of the budget passed by the legislature. The one piece of legislation that the governor cannot veto is a proposed constitutional amendment. The legislature in turn can override the governor's veto, but it must do so by a two-thirds vote.

The governor has the power to grant a *reprieve*, a delay in carrying out the sentence handed down to a convicted criminal. The governor can also *commute*, or reduce, a prisoner's sentence. The governor's broadest power is the ability to *pardon* a criminal, or officially cancel the criminal's sentence. A pardon board, which is appointed by the governor, is also part of this process.

The governor is commander-in-chief of the state's military force — the National Guard. The Louisiana National Guard is commanded by a general, who is appointed by the governor. The National Guard can

Governor Mike Foster, a motorcycle and outdoor enthusiast, is shown here at his family home, Oaklawn, near Franklin.

The Louisiana Governor's Mansion is one of the most beautiful in the nation.

be called to serve as a military force to keep order. Most often in Louisiana, it serves in emergencies such as hurricanes and floods. In extreme emergencies, the National Guard can be called into national service under orders of the president.

The salary of the governor is not as much as that paid to the heads of large businesses, but the job has other benefits. The governor's mansion and staff, a car and driver, and bodyguards are all provided.

The governor can be removed from office in two ways: impeachment or a recall election. **Impeachment** is the process of charging a public official with wrongdoing while that official is still in office. During an impeachment, the Louisiana house of representatives brings the impeachment charges, and the state senate holds the impeachment trial. The two governors in Louisiana's history who faced impeachment charges were Henry Clay Warmoth during Reconstruction in 1872 and Huey P. Long in 1929. Warmoth was removed from office, but Long was not.

For a *recall election* to be held, organizers must first get a certain number of voters' signatures on a recall petition. To remove a governor by recall, two-thirds of the voters must vote in favor of it. If the governor dies, leaves office, or is removed, the order for filling the vacancy is as follows: lieutenant governor, secretary of state, attorney general, treasurer, senate president, and speaker of the house.

Lieutenant Governor

The office of **lieutenant governor** of the state is similar to the office of vice president of the United States. If the governor is out of the state, the lieutenant governor acts as governor. According to the constitution, if the governor leaves office or is unable to act, the lieutenant governor becomes governor.

The lieutenant governor serves much like a public relations officer for the state. The State Department of Culture, Recreation and Tourism is headed by this elected official.

Attorney General

The **attorney general** heads the state's legal office, the Department of Justice. The attorney general provides opinions on questions of law to all state agencies and other public bodies. The attorney general also has the authority to bring legal action on behalf of the state in civil cases. In the late 1990s, the Louisiana attorney general joined with other states to sue tobacco companies. They wanted to recover some of the money the states had spent for tobacco-related health care.

The Louisiana attorney general also defends Louisiana laws if they are challenged in the federal courts. That might happen if the legislature passes a law that a citizen thinks is a violation of the U.S. Constitution. The attorney general is usually not involved in criminal matters but may become involved at the request of a local district attorney.

Secretary of State

The **secretary of state** is the chief election officer for Louisiana. This means overseeing the preparation of the ballots and announcing the official results of elections.

The secretary of state is also responsible for Louisiana's official records, including publishing the acts and journals of the legislature. The secretary of state is the keeper of the Great Seal of the state of Louisiana, which is used to give official approval to documents. Other records that are filed with the secretary of state's office include articles of incorporation, corporate reports, trademarks and trade names, and registrations for all commissions.

Lieutenant Governor Kathleen Babineaux Blanco of Lafayette is one of only a few female lieutenant governors in the nation. She was first elected to the position in 1995.

As the elected secretary of state, Walter Fox McKeithen of Caldwell Parish is responsible for Louisiana's official records.

All of Louisiana's official records are now preserved at the State Archives Building in Baton Rouge. These records include some of Louisiana's historic legal documents.

Treasurer

The elected head of the Department of the Treasury, the state **treasurer** is custodian of the state's money. As such, the treasurer is required to keep records of the monies received and expenses paid out. State money not needed immediately must be properly invested. The law requires the treasurer to give the governor and the legislature an annual financial report, one month before each regular session of the legislature.

Other Elected Officials

Louisiana voters also elect other statewide officials. The *commissioner of agriculture* oversees soil and water conservation and promotes Louisiana agriculture and forestry. The *commissioner of insurance* must enforce the insurance laws and regulations passed by the legislature. The *commissioner of elections* is responsible for voter registration and elections.

Two state boards have elected members. The five-member Public Service Commission regulates the rates of public utilities such as telephone, electric, natural gas, and water companies. The eleven-member Board of Elementary and Secondary Education (BESE) supervises education in Louisiana and appoints the state superintendent of education. The governor appoints three members of this board.

Do You Remember?

1. What are the three branches of Louisiana's government?
2. Who is the chief executive officer of the state?
3. Who is the chief election officer of the state?

POLITICAL CARTOONS

A *political cartoon* is a drawing that makes a statement about a subject of public interest. It can be about a person, an event, or an important problem. Good cartoons deal with emotions and are a form of protest. They get their message across in a simple and humorous way, usually with few words.

Thomas Nast was one of the earliest and best known American political cartoonists. His cartoons were very dramatic and supportive of the Union during the Civil War. Abraham Lincoln called him the Union's best recruiting sergeant. Nast created several symbols that are used by political cartoonists today, among them the Republican elephant and the Democratic donkey.

In 1884, Joseph Pulitzer's New York *World* became the first newspaper to hire a political cartoonist, Walt McDougall. One of McDougall's cartoons so increased the *World*'s circulation that Pulitzer hired him full time. Political cartooning as a profession was born.

A well-known cartoonist in Louisiana is Walt Handelsman from the *Times-Picayune*. Handelsman was awarded the Pulitzer Prize for Editorial Cartooning in 1997. Other cartoonists known for their caricatures of recent governors are John Chase, "Pap" Dean, and Fred Mulhearn.

Above: *Walt Handelsman is an award-winning political cartoonist for the New Orleans* Times-Picayune. ***Left:*** *Political cartoons make a humorous or sarcastic political statement. What point is being made here?*

*Above: There is a seat for each of the 105 members in the state house of representatives chamber. The state house and state senate chambers are at opposite ends of the capitol lobby. **Oppo-site, above:** The state senate chamber has been the scene of many political debates. **Oppo-site, below:** In 1996, Randy L. Ewing was elected president of the state senate. The senate president is responsible for appointing all senate committees and chairs of committees.*

LEGISLATIVE BRANCH

The **legislative branch** is the law-making body for the state of Louisiana. Like the United States Congress, Louisiana's legislature has two bodies—the house of representatives and the senate. This two-house legislative model is called **bicameral**. (*Camera* is the Latin word for "chamber.") The purpose of the bicameral plan is to limit the power of each group. If one chamber proposes a bill, the other chamber must also approve it for the bill to become law.

The Louisiana legislature has 144 members, the number set by the constitution. There are 39 senators and 105 representatives. Each is elected from a geographic district based on population. One member is elected from each district, and the house and senate districts are not the same.

New districts are redrawn after each United States **census**, the official population count done every ten years. Revising the district lines based on the new population numbers is called **reapportionment**. The 1974 constitution requires that the Louisiana supreme court reapportion voting districts if the legislature does not.

In its 1962 *Baker v. Carr* decision, the U.S. Supreme Court ruled that state legislatures must base their voting districts on population. That decision became known as the "one-man, one-vote ruling." Before that ruling, districts were usually based on land area; in Louisiana, the dis-

tricts had been based on parishes. Rural districts with lower populations had much more influence than districts in cities with greater populations.

State Legislators

Anyone old enough to vote is old enough to be elected to the Louisiana legislature. The candidate must be a registered voter, at least eighteen years old, and a resident of Louisiana at least two years and of the district he or she hopes to represent at least one year. Legislators are elected to four-year terms, and there are no term limits.

Legislators are paid a salary and a per diem supplement. (*Per diem* is Latin for "by the day.") The per diem supplement is paid for each day of the legislative session, including special sessions, and for each day the legislator attends a committee meeting. The legislators also receive travel allowances, expenses for an office in their home districts, and retirement and health benefits.

Legislators with specific interests join together to promote bills that help their common goals. These groups are called **caucuses**. Another term used to describe a group of legislators is *delegation*, which usually indicates a certain geographic region, such as the New Orleans delegation or the Acadiana delegation. Members of the same political party also refer to themselves as a delegation. The Republican delegation has become stronger in the Louisiana legislature in the last twenty-five years.

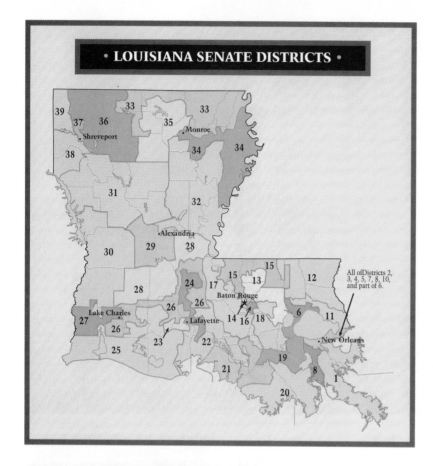

· LOUISIANA SENATE DISTRICTS ·

All ofDistricts 2, 3, 4, 5, 7, 8, 10, and part of 6.

Legislative Sessions

The legislature meets every year. In even-numbered years, the legislature meets for 30 days during a 45-day period. In odd-numbered years, it meets for 60 days over an 85-day period. The sessions can consider any kind of bill, except a tax bill. Tax bills can be passed only in even-numbered years. The legislators propose bills and then take a break to visit their districts to hear from their **constituents** (the people they represent). When they return to the capital, they debate and vote on the bills.

Members of each chamber elect officers to preside over the sessions. The house of representatives elects a **speaker of the house**. In the state senate, the elected leader is called the **president of the senate**. Vice chairs (chairpersons) are also elected and are called the *speaker* and the *president pro tempore*. (This Latin term means "temporary.")

Law Making

It is the job of the legislature to write and approve laws. Proposed laws, called **bills**, may be introduced in either house of the legislature. A bill becomes law only when it is approved in the same form by both the house and the senate and is signed by the governor. An average of about 3,000 bills are introduced in a session. Only about one-third of those bills become laws.

Legislative committees do much of the work on proposed laws. The bills are studied and debated in a committee first. Some of the committees are permanent. These *standing committees* include education, finance,

Much of the real work of the senate is done in committees, such as the Senate Revenue and Fiscal Affairs Committee.

health and welfare, natural resources, environmental quality, insurance, and transportation. The house has sixteen standing committees and the senate has seventeen standing committees. Other committees are temporary, appointed for a special purpose. Committees and committee chairs are appointed by the speaker of the house and the president of the senate. Each legislator serves on at least one committee.

Suppose that a bill is introduced in the senate. It is assigned to a senate committee, either standing or temporary, for discussion and debate. The committee may hold hearings so that interested persons can tell the committee what they think about the bill. After the hearings, the committee members vote either to approve the bill and send it on to the full senate for consideration, to amend the original bill, or to kill it. If the bill is approved by the full senate, it is sent to the house of representatives, where the entire process is repeated. If either house votes no, the bill is dead.

A bill must pass both houses in exactly the same form if it is to become law. If the versions of the bill passed by each house are different, the two versions are sent to a conference committee. The *conference committee* includes members from both the senate and the house who work out the differences. The committee returns the revised bill to both houses for another vote.

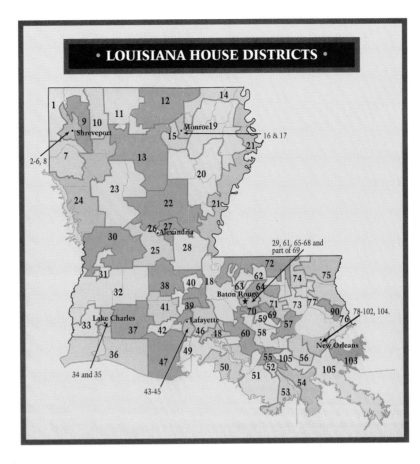

After the legislature passes a bill, it must be delivered to the governor within three days. The governor has ten days (twenty if the legislature is not in session) to act on the bill. The governor may sign the bill into law, veto it, or allow the bill to become law without his signature. The absence of the governor's signature is a way of showing his or her opposition to the bill.

Lobbying

Trying to influence a legislator about a proposed law is called **lobbying**. Every citizen can be a lobbyist. Lobbyists write letters to legislators or visit the legislators at the Capitol. Some lobbyists work as volunteers, while others are paid to speak on behalf of one or more organizations.

The influence of paid lobbyists is part of the political debate in Baton Rouge and in Washington. Laws have been passed to set guidelines and limits on the actions of lobbyists. Paid lobbyists often have large sums of money available from the groups they represent. Using that money to buy influence is illegal.

Most members of the legislature have offices in their home districts in order to maintain close contact with their constituents.

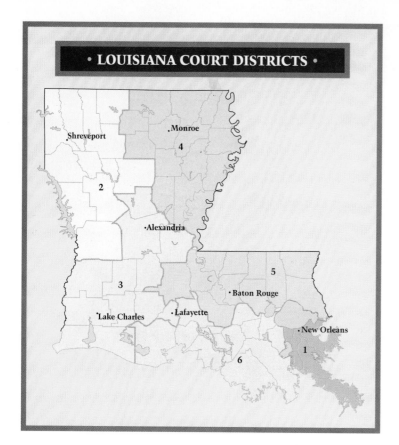

· LOUISIANA COURT DISTRICTS ·

Shreveport · Monroe 4

2

·Alexandria

3

5

·Baton Rouge

·Lake Charles · Lafayette

·New Orleans 1

6

JUDICIAL BRANCH

The **judicial branch** of government consists of the state's courts. The major duty of the courts is to interpret and apply the constitution and laws of the state. As one of the three branches of state government, the courts also act to limit the power of the other two branches. If the legislature passes a law that some citizens consider unconstitutional, the Louisiana supreme court must decide if the law follows the state and federal constitutions. This power of *judicial review* is part of the system of checks and balances.

The judicial branch is also responsible for protecting the rights of the citizens. The constitution states that no one shall be deprived of life, liberty, or property except by *due process of law*, which refers to the fair and specific rules established by courts to protect a person's rights.

Civil and Criminal Law

The laws of the state are divided into two broad categories. **Civil laws** deal with the relationships between and among individual citizens. A civil lawsuit asks the court to settle a dispute between two people or between an individual and a business or government. The legal matter is personal, not affecting all of society. Civil law covers such issues as citizenship, property rights, contracts, marriage, divorce, child custody, and inheritance.

Criminal laws are intended to protect society from the wrongdoing of an individual. The *criminal code* sets out those offenses that are so harmful to society that violations are punished by fines, imprisonment, or even death. Less serious crimes are called *misdemeanors*. Major crimes punishable by imprisonment are called *felonies*; these offenses include murder, armed robbery, theft, rape, kidnapping, assault, and embezzlement. The most serious felony is classified as a *capital crime* and carries the death penalty or life imprisonment. It is the government (federal or state) that brings criminal charges against an individual, and it is in the courts where the guilt or innocence of a person accused of a crime is determined.

Many elected and appointed officials function within the judicial branch of government. Law enforcement officers such as police, sheriffs, and marshals are part of the legal system. Others include district attorneys and clerks of court. A district attorney prosecutes criminal cases in district court. A clerk of court maintains the official records for a parish, much like the secretary of state does for the state.

Louisiana's Court System

The court system in Louisiana has three levels: the Louisiana supreme court, five courts of appeal, and forty-two district courts.

The *district courts* are the main trial courts for the state, hearing both civil and criminal cases. Louisiana is divided into forty-one judicial districts. Each district covers one to three parishes. Because of its large population, Orleans Parish has two district courts, one criminal and one civil. The number of judges in a district is based on population and ranges from one to sixteen. The district judges are elected for six-year terms.

Louisiana's second step in the judicial process is the *court of appeals*. If a person believes the district court did not handle his or her case correctly, the case can be appealed (taken to a higher court for rehearing) to a court of appeals. This procedure is not like a second trial. The appeals court judge reviews the records of the case in the district court and makes a decision based on the records alone. Sometimes attorneys present arguments to the court of appeals, but witnesses do not appear.

The court of appeals is structured into five areas or *circuits*, as they are called. The courts are referred to as the First Circuit, Second Circuit, and so on. Each circuit covers at least three district courts. Each appeals court has at least three judges. The appeals court judges are also elected, but they serve ten-year terms.

The highest court in the state is the Louisiana *supreme court*. Louisiana's supreme court has seven judges elected from specific districts for ten-year terms. This court hears appeals from the lower courts. The supreme court is also required to hear two other types of cases. If a lower court has declared a law unconstitutional, the supreme court must evaluate that decision. If a defendant in a criminal case has been sentenced to death, the case is reviewed by the Louisiana supreme court.

Serving on Juries

Citizens participate in the judicial system as parties to and witnesses for a legal case. But they also serve on juries. A **jury** is a group of citizens chosen to hear evidence on a legal case and to make a decision based on the evidence presented. District court judges appoint a jury commission. The commission draws the names of potential jurors from the lists of registered voters and motor vehicle registrations. Jurors hear evidence and issue verdicts in both civil and criminal trials. Serving on a jury is an important responsibility of any citizen. A person accused of a crime has the right to be tried before a jury of his or her peers.

Both civil and criminal cases are heard in parish courthouses, like this one in Alexandria in Rapides Parish.

Citizens may also serve on a *grand jury*. Twelve citizens serve for six months on a grand jury. These citizens are involved in the first step of legal action against an accused criminal. After listening to the district attorney, it is the grand jury's responsibility to determine if there is enough evidence to *indict* a person (formally charge the person with a crime). A regular trial jury would hear the evidence during the trial. Based on evidence, the grand jury may even ask that the district attorney charge a person with a crime. This action must be approved with a vote of at least nine members.

Another duty of the grand jury is to inspect parish buildings, including examining the conditions of the parish jail. The grand jury would report its findings to the local government.

Do You Remember?
1. What is the major function of the Louisiana legislature?
2. What are the most serious felonies called?
3. Name the three levels of courts in Louisiana.

Homeowners pay property taxes on the value of any real estate they own. However, the homestead exemption excludes a portion of a home's value from taxation. Owners of smaller homes, like this one in Cheneyville, may pay little or no property tax at all.

FINANCING STATE GOVERNMENT

Governments need money for the programs they provide citizens. Louisiana, like other states and the federal government, gets this money in several ways. Planning for the needs of state government starts with a detailed budget.

THE STATE BUDGET

A budget is a plan for receiving and spending money. Each year, the state government estimates how much money (revenue) it will collect for the fiscal year. (A *fiscal year* is a financial year; Louisiana's fiscal year runs from July 1 to June 30.) Once the estimated revenue is known, the state can decide how to distribute it (expenditures) to meet the needs of the state.

The governor prepares both an operating budget and a capital budget. The *operating budget* covers the cost of running the state for a year and includes salaries, equipment, and supplies. The *capital budget* covers capital improvements such as roads, bridges, and buildings. The governor must carefully match revenue and expenditures because the state constitution requires that the budget be balanced. A budget **deficit** means that there were more expenditures than revenue received. A budget **surplus** means that there is revenue left over after budget expenditures are met.

TAXES

Much of the state revenue comes from several kinds of taxes. **Taxes** are amounts charged citizens by their governments (federal, state, and local) to pay for services provided. A *sales tax* is charged on items as they are purchased; it is the largest single source of tax revenue. An *excise tax* is a consumption tax imposed on specific products such as gasoline, alcohol, soft drinks, and cigarettes.

Louisiana also has a *severance tax*, a charge for removing (severing) natural resources from the state. Louisiana's severance tax is imposed on timber and on minerals such as oil, gas, sulphur, and salt.

Individual citizens pay a state *income tax*, which is due on May 15 each year. Business corporations that operate in Louisiana also pay a tax on their income. Other taxes that provide revenue for the state are inheritance taxes and taxes on vehicles. Louisiana has lower *property taxes* than most other states. One reason for this is the *homestead exemption*, which excuses a portion of the value of the home from the property tax. In other words, taxes are paid only if the value of a home is above a certain amount.

Natural resources, such as the timber shown here, that are removed from the land are subject to a severance tax.

OTHER SOURCES OF REVENUE

Louisiana earns a royalty or rent from state-owned land that produces oil or other minerals. The state also receives revenue from fees and interest on the investment of idle funds. Another source of revenue for Louisiana is federal grants, revenue sharing, and matching funds. These funds are usually provided to help the state carry out programs required by Congress. Federal funds must be supplemented with state funds.

The government also borrows money by selling bonds to investors. A **bond** is a document that serves as proof of a long-term debt. The bondholder receives interest at set times and, after a certain number of years, the return of the original investment. Bonds are a way to borrow money for large-scale projects that require more money than the state has available.

Louisiana also has a source of money that is somewhat controversial. The state has joined other states in holding weekly lotteries. A lottery is a legalized form of gambling in which the consumer buys chances to match a series of numbers in the hope of winning a large sum of money. Riverboat casinos also pay special taxes to the state for the privilege of operating a gambling facility. The state receives large sums of money from these sources, but critics say problems make it a bad decision.

LOCAL GOVERNMENT

The level of government with which most Louisianians have the greatest contact is local government. In Louisiana, the units of local government are the parishes, municipalities, and special districts.

PARISH GOVERNMENT

The government division created to provide local government throughout the state is the parish. Louisiana has had its present number of sixty-four parishes since 1912. The parish government and courthouse are located in the town or city known as the *parish seat*. In other states, this town is called the county seat.

During Louisiana's Spanish colonial days, the parish government became known as the **police jury**. A group of citizens was chosen to supervise or police the parish. This group was referred to as a *jury*. Forty-six of Louisiana's parishes still refer to the parish-elected government as the police jury. Today, the police jury has five to fifteen elected members. These members are elected from districts within the parish that are usually called *wards*.

The police jury passes ordinances (local laws) for the parish government. The police jury is also responsible for building and maintaining parish roads and buildings such as the jail and the courthouse. The jury has the authority to raise money for parish expenses through taxes, fees, and bond issues and to grant permission to lay electric lines and pipelines along parish roads.

The police jury appoints the parish registrar of voters and the treasurer. In addition to these positions, each parish has several elected officials established by the state constitution. The *sheriff* is the chief law enforcement officer and tax collector. The *assessor* determines the value of property for tax purposes. The *district attorney* is the chief prosecutor who represents the people in criminal cases. The *clerk of court* maintains the court records and other official records such as marriage licenses. These officials are not under the control of local government; they report only to the voters.

The parish police juries sometimes create special districts to perform a specific service for a local area. The most common special districts include fire protection, levee, and water districts.

The parish courthouse is the seat of government for a parish. This is the DeSoto Parish courthouse in Mansfield.

HOMER

Located in the rolling hills of North Louisiana, Homer is the parish seat of Claiborne Parish. Like several other North Louisiana towns, Homer's name came from Greek history; Homer was a Greek poet who lived around 850 B.C. The town of Homer was established at a time when the ancient Greek civilization was popular among southerners.

The courthouse itself dates from this time. Built in 1861, the Greek Revival structure is surrounded by the town square. White columns support the brick building, which has an exterior staircase. The stairs lead to the second-floor courtroom. The first floor contains parish offices, but the historic building is now too small for all the parish offices. Public records are housed across the square in a newer building.

Claiborne Parish was formed in 1828 from part of Natchitoches Parish. Like many other parishes, Claiborne had other parish seats before Homer. The first was Russellville and then Overton, which was a landing on Bayou Dorcheat. The parish seat was moved to Homer, a new town that soon grew to be larger than the previous parish seats.

During the early years of American government in Louisiana, people traveled long distances to do business at this parish seat. People rode to Homer on horseback and camped in the nearby woods to wait for their turn in court. The first parish business was conducted at the home of

John Murrell, one of the first settlers in the area. The first court in Homer was held in a frame building described in one account as a "cheap shanty."

The present courthouse once had a bell that was rung to announce public assemblies. The old bell rang many times for meetings, as well as to warn of fires and to ring in the new year. That bell is now on display in the nearby Ford Museum. The museum, located in the old hotel on the town square, offers a view of Claiborne Parish in earlier times. One of the exhibits is a pioneer log cabin, built at about the same time as the courthouse. The cabin was moved into the museum to preserve it. The cabin's hand-hewn logs remind us of the skill and work required to survive in early Louisiana.

The Claiborne Parish Library is a recent addition to the government buildings in Homer. The rear of the building faces a wooded area, and an upper-level deck offers a comfortable spot to read. Observant visitors can sometimes see white-tailed deer walking among the trees.

Above: The Claiborne Parish courthouse in Homer is one of only four pre-Civil War courthouses still in use. ***Opposite, below:*** The Ford Museum is located in what was once the Claiborne Hotel.

Top: *The courthouse in Houma is the center of Terrebonne Parish government, a home rule parish.* **Above:** *The West Feliciana Parish government is a police jury.*

Other Government Plans

Louisiana's current constitution grants more power to local governments than did previous constitutions. This power of political subdivisions to govern themselves is known as **home rule**. In other words, parishes and municipalities can manage their own affairs unless specifically prohibited by the state constitution or state law. Some parishes have a *home rule charter*, which allows a community to organize its local government in a form other than the police jury. Parishes that have another form of local government include East Baton Rouge, Jefferson, Lafourche, Orleans, Plaquemines, St. Tammany, St. Charles, St. James, and Terrebonne parishes.

The first move away from the police jury form of government came with the constitution of 1912. The *commission form* of government is similar to the police jury, although the number of commissioners is generally fewer than the number of police jurors. Commissioners are elected from parish wards, and each elected commissioner heads a department of parish government. Plaquemines Parish is the only one operating under a commission plan.

The city of Baton Rouge and East Baton Rouge Parish have a combined government and use the *council form*. Seven council members are elected from districts within the city limits of Baton Rouge, and five are elected from districts outside the city. A mayor-president is elected

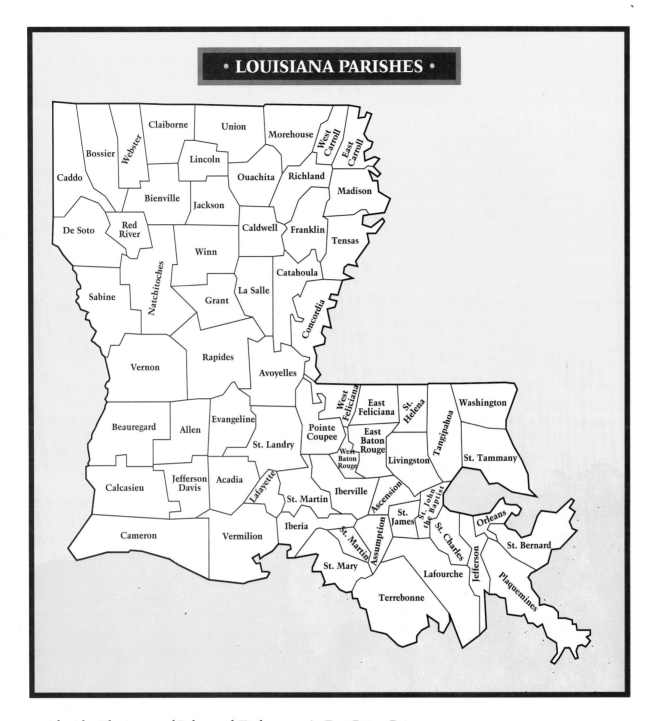

• LOUISIANA PARISHES •

parishwide. The towns of Baker and Zachary are in East Baton Rouge Parish, and their residents have representatives on the city-parish council. The two towns also have their own local governments and mayors.

Orleans Parish and the city of New Orleans have the same political boundaries and share the same government. Council members are elected from districts, and the mayor is elected by all of the voters in Orleans Parish. Jefferson and Terrebonne parishes both use

the *council-president form* of parish government. An elected council carries out legislative functions of the parish government, while the elected president is the chief administrator.

School Boards

Louisiana's local school systems have the same political boundaries as the parishes, except that there are two additional city school districts in Monroe and Bogalusa. A school board is elected from districts based on population, and the members serve four-year concurrent terms. In other words, all school board members are elected at the same time and their terms all end at the same time.

The school boards are separate governmental bodies, which cannot be controlled by other local governments. But they are more closely regulated by the state than the parish and municipal governments. To operate the schools, a local school board can levy and collect taxes and issue bonds. The board appoints a superintendent to supervise the school system.

MUNICIPALITIES

Within the political boundaries of the parishes are municipalities (cities and towns) of different sizes. Some people who live in a parish also live in a municipality, while others live in the rural area of the parish and have no municipal government.

The smallest municipalities are *villages*, with a population from 150 to 999. A village becomes a *town* when the population reaches 1,000. An increase to 5,000 earns the label of *city*. These local governments operate with a commission or a council-manager form of government.

Top: *School districts are separate bodies, which are not controlled by the local government.* **Above:** *Municipalities, such as Gretna, provide such services as police and fire protection to residents.*

Do You Remember?

1. What is the difference between an operating budget and a capital budget?
2. What is an excise tax?
3. How many parishes does Louisiana have?
4. For what purpose might a special district be established?
5. What is a municipality?

POLITICS

The term *politics* refers to the policies, activities, and methods of a government. This includes campaigns, voting, and elections. Generally, people who have similar ideas about government organize into political parties to get their candidates elected and put their policies into effect.

POLITICAL PARTIES

Political parties are an important part of politics. The political party system in the United States developed early in the country's history. The first two political parties formed around Thomas Jefferson and Alexander Hamilton, two men who served in the cabinet of President George Washington and who had very different views on the role of the federal government. Since that time, parties have come and gone, but the United States has, for the most part, a two-party system.

Today, the two major political parties are the Republican party and the Democratic party. More Louisiana voters are registered as Democrats than as Republicans. In recent years, however, many of those Democrats have voted for Republican candidates.

Louisiana voters often vote more by faction than by party. Groups of voters with common interests and goals tend to vote alike. Factions in Louisiana include Catholics, Protestants, Acadians, and African Americans.

VOTING AND ELECTIONS

The Twenty-Sixth Amendment to the U.S. Constitution lowered the voting age from twenty-one to eighteen. This is now the legal age for voting in every state, including Louisiana.

A voter must be a resident of the parish in which he or she is voting. Voters must register at least twenty-four hours before an election. Citizens may register to vote with the registrar of voters at the parish courthouse. They may also register by mail. In 1994, the legislature passed the "motor voter law," which established more locations for voter registration. Today, residents can register to vote at the Office of Motor Vehicles at the same time they are renewing their driver's licenses. A person must vote at least once every four years to stay on the list of qualified voters. A person convicted of a felony or declared mentally incompetent by the court loses his or her right to vote.

The secretary of state and a state board of election supervisors direct election procedures. They establish rules, publish an election manual, and prepare examinations for poll commissioners. A *poll* is the place

Citizens show their interest and involvement in elections in various ways. These homemade signs appeared on a St. Martinville lawn.

Voting machines such as this one in Lafayette provide a fast and accurate way for citizens to vote.

where voting is done, and the commissioners are the officials who supervise the voting. The secretary of state and his or her staff also prepare and certify absentee ballots and voting machine ballots. When the election is over, this officer verifies the vote count and announces the official results.

Louisiana also has an elected commissioner of elections, who works with the parish board of election supervisors to set up the voting precincts. (A voting precinct is a special subdivision of the parish or city set up for election purposes.) The clerk of court of the parish counts the votes and reports the results to the secretary of state.

Statewide elections in Louisiana are held as **open primaries**. Louisiana is the only state to have an open primary election. All candidates — regardless of their political party membership — compete in the first, or primary, election. The two candidates receiving the most votes then have a *runoff election*. The two candidates could be from the same political party or from different political parties.

The open primary law was passed in 1975 to stop the growth of the Republican party in Louisiana. Before this change, each political party had its own primary election, and the party winners faced each other in the general election. The Democratic party had dominated state politics until the 1960s. When the Republican party began to enter candidates in the state races, the Democrats had to choose one candidate to face a Republican opponent. This meant that strong Democratic candidates were often eliminated in the Democratic primary. Democrats intended for the open primary to allow two Democrats to be in the runoff, keeping out the Republicans. However, the plan backfired. In an open primary, a voter can choose any candidate, even if the candidate's political party is different from the voter's. Many Louisiana Democrats began to vote for Republican candidates in the open primary.

CAMPAIGNS

All candidates for public office campaign to sell themselves to the voters. Technology has greatly changed campaign styles from those days when the best way to get votes was to speak directly to the people in the town square. Candidates once walked the streets of the town, going door to door to ask for votes. Now districts are larger, people are busier, and the media (the communications industry) reaches many more people than personal contacts can.

Candidates hire political consultants to run their campaigns. These consultants take advantage of public opinion polls — surveys of a random group of people — to help their candidates. The consultants also plan the television spots and newspaper advertisements. This increased use of the media to campaign means that much more money is needed. Television, radio, and newspaper advertising costs money. Fund-raising is now essential for candidates and political parties.

Concern about campaign financing has increased as more and more money is spent. The Louisiana governor's races are among the most expensive political campaigns in the United States. Campaign finance laws have been passed to limit the amount of money an individual or group can contribute. In addition, candidates must report their campaign spending and contributors' names to a state campaign board.

Do You Remember?

1. Which political party has more members in Louisiana?
2. What is the name given to the place where people vote?
3. What is the purpose of campaign finance laws?

The amount of money spent on political campaigns—and how that money is raised—is of great concern to citizens in Louisiana and the rest of the country.

SUMMARY

Louisiana governmental practices are rooted in the state's rich cultural heritage. French, Spanish, and British traditions blended to form today's government. Louisiana's state constitutions have reflected these cultural and political influences.

Like the federal government, Louisiana has an executive branch, a legislative branch, and a judicial branch. These branches carry the authority to make and enforce laws, as well as settle disputes about these laws. Taxes are the major source of revenue needed to carry out the state governmental programs.

For most of Louisiana's parishes, the government takes the form of a police jury. Local governing bodies oversee the operation of municipalities throughout Louisiana. The state constitution grants local communities — parish or municipality — the power to govern themselves through a home rule charter. The commission plan, the city-parish council, and the council-president plan are the other forms of local government.

Louisiana politics reflects the colorful exchange of culture and interests found in the state. The open primary system allows voters to select the candidates of their choice, regardless of political party affiliation. Campaigns provide the people of Louisiana with promises and entertainment.

CHAPTER · REVIEW

Reviewing People, Places, and Terms

Define, identify, or explain the importance of the following.

1. amendment
2. bicameral
3. bill
4. bond
5. budget
6. caucus
7. census
8. civil law
9. constituent
10. constitution
11. criminal law
12. deficit
13. executive branch
14. governor
15. home rule
16. impeachment
17. judicial branch
18. jury
19. legislative branch
20. lobbying
21. open primary
22. police jury
23. political alliance
24. reapportionment
25. surplus
26. taxes
27. veto

Understanding the Facts

1. Name the three most familiar political alliance groups in Louisiana.
2. What is the purpose of a state constitution?
3. Why has Louisiana had so many different state constitutions?
4. What are the laws called that the governor wants passed?
5. What are the two ways a governor can be removed from office?
6. How many members make up the Louisiana legislature?
7. How often is reapportionment done?
8. Why are committees so important to the legislative process?
9. What is the difference between civil law and criminal law?
10. Name four state revenue sources.
11. What are the three types of local government in Louisiana?
12. What is the legal voting age in Louisiana?

Developing Critical Thinking

1. Why is a constitution so valuable?
2. Why is it important in a democratic society to have a separation of powers among the branches of government?
3. What impact do you think lobbyists have on the actions of the government?

Using Your Skills

1. Prepare a poster that shows (a) the current elected officials in the executive branch, (b) your state senate district and your current senator, and (c) your state house district and your current representative.
2. On a map of Louisiana parishes, locate and label all the parish seats.

Special Projects

1. Part of a legislator's job is to listen to his or her constituents. Identify an issue that is of concern to the people in your district. Write a letter to your state senator or representative expressing your opinion. Be specific.
2. On your eighteenth birthday, you will be eligible to run for the state legislature. Prepare the cam-

paign speech you would give if you decided to do this. Emphasize reasons why your age would be an advantage.

3. Research the history of government in your parish. What is the present parish seat? Were any other towns the parish seat? How many different buildings have served as the courthouse? When was the present courthouse built?

Making Connections

1. Collect three political cartoons from the newspaper. Write a brief interpretation of each cartoon.

2. Draw a political cartoon about a leading state or national politician or political issue. Share the cartoon with classmates.

Louisiana Lagniappe

• New laws take effect on the sixteenth day after the end of a legislative session.

• Some rural parishes built small frame buildings just for the purpose of voting.

• In addition to campaign buttons, political candidates have given away nail files, pocket combs, paper fans, and rulers printed with their names and campaign slogans.

• Louisiana was one of the first states to have electronic voting machines.

• The term *lobbyist* was coined by President Ulysses S. Grant. He used the term to describe the people who waited in the lobby of the hotel hoping to get his attention.

• Cameron is the largest parish in the state in terms of land area.

• It is probable that the flags of more sovereign nations have flown over Louisiana than any other state in the United States.

• Of the eleven members of the Board of Elementary and Secondary Education (BESE), eight are elected and three are appointed.

• BUILDING SKILLS: READING NEWS ARTICLES •

Newspapers are a good way for citizens to keep informed on a wide range of topics — local, national, or international. First, however, you must distinguish a news article from an editorial. Editorials mix facts and opinions and give a newspaper's or a writer's opinion on an issue or event. A news article does not include opinions.

Newspaper articles usually follow a standard format. The *headline* is written in large, bold type with just a few key words. Its purpose is to capture the "heart" of the story and make you want to learn more. The size of the headline type often indicates the story's importance. The *byline* indicates who wrote the story, either an individual or a news service. The *dateline* includes the city and date where the story was filed. The *lead* is the first sentence of the article — the most important. It summarizes the main idea of the article and should tell you the five W's: *who, what, when, where,* and *why.* The *body* contains a more detailed account of the basic facts. The body

often contains quotations and background facts. As you read through the body of the article, you will find fewer and fewer important details.

Look at any daily newspaper and select one of the major stories on the front page. Answer the following questions:

1. From reading just the headline, can you tell why the editors chose to put the article on the front page?

2. Who wrote the story and where was it filed?

3. What are the *who, what, when, where,* and *why* of the story?

4. After reading the article, do you think the headline accurately represented the information in the article?

Try This! Reread this chapter and choose an issue on which to write a news article. Write the article first, then the headline.

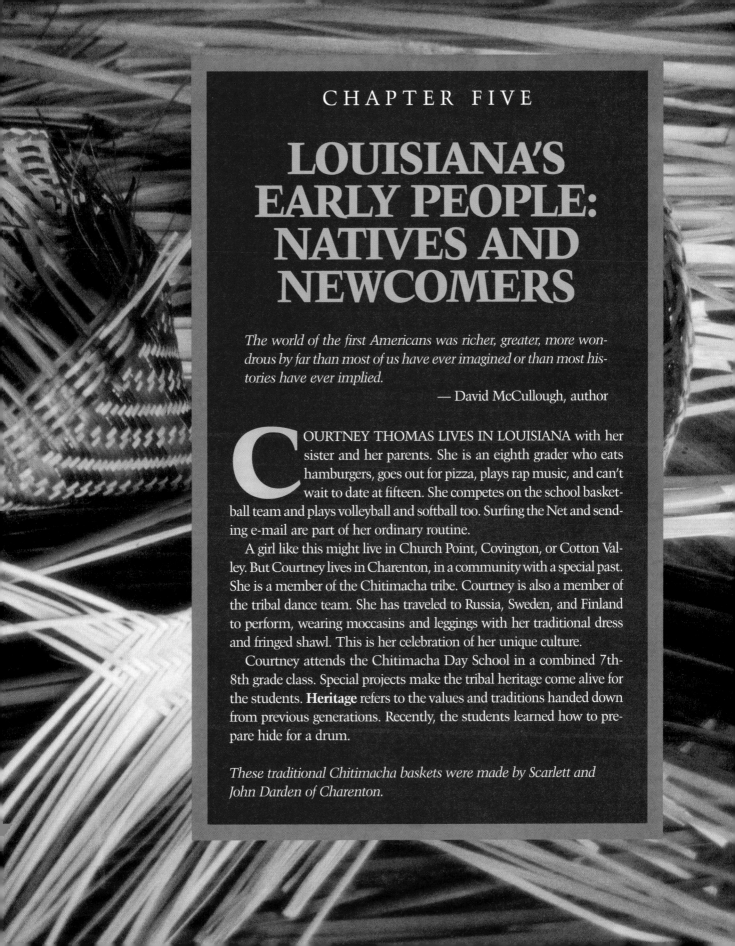

CHAPTER FIVE

LOUISIANA'S EARLY PEOPLE: NATIVES AND NEWCOMERS

The world of the first Americans was richer, greater, more wondrous by far than most of us have ever imagined or than most histories have ever implied.

— David McCullough, author

COURTNEY THOMAS LIVES IN LOUISIANA with her sister and her parents. She is an eighth grader who eats hamburgers, goes out for pizza, plays rap music, and can't wait to date at fifteen. She competes on the school basketball team and plays volleyball and softball too. Surfing the Net and sending e-mail are part of her ordinary routine.

A girl like this might live in Church Point, Covington, or Cotton Valley. But Courtney lives in Charenton, in a community with a special past. She is a member of the Chitimacha tribe. Courtney is also a member of the tribal dance team. She has traveled to Russia, Sweden, and Finland to perform, wearing moccasins and leggings with her traditional dress and fringed shawl. This is her celebration of her unique culture.

Courtney attends the Chitimacha Day School in a combined 7th-8th grade class. Special projects make the tribal heritage come alive for the students. **Heritage** refers to the values and traditions handed down from previous generations. Recently, the students learned how to prepare hide for a drum.

These traditional Chitimacha baskets were made by Scarlett and John Darden of Charenton.

The story of the past for Courtney and her classmates is the story of the earliest people in Louisiana. Their **ancestors** (those people from whom one is descended) lived here long ago, beyond the measure of time. Scientists refer to this as the *prehistoric* period, the time before written or recorded history.

PREHISTORIC CULTURES

Although the first people did not leave written records of their culture, they did leave behind clues about their lives. They left those clues at places where they prepared food, made tools, built shelters, and conducted ceremonies. **Archaeologists** (scientists who study the items left behind by ancient peoples) interpret those clues. Archaeologists even dig through ancient garbage dumps, called **middens**. Their findings explain who left the items, when they were left, and what happened at those places, called *sites*. Scientists have dated (set the age of) some of those sites at thousands of years before any European set foot on the soil of Louisiana.

Archaeologists have separated Louisiana prehistory into four periods. Those time periods are characterized by changes in movement, weapons and tools, food, and religious practices. Changes happened very gradually, and these four periods are just convenient ways to divide prehistory.

PALEO INDIANS

The oldest known Indians in Louisiana date to the Paleo Indian period. (The word *paleo* means "ancient.") About 10,000 B.C., scientists believe, these first people came to North America from Asia on a land bridge that connected what is now Alaska and Siberia. The Paleo Indians traveled in small groups and followed the animals, on which they de-

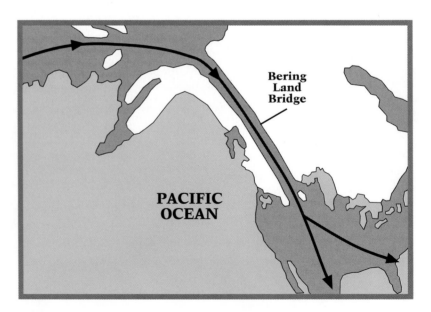

pended for food and clothing. They traveled east and south, gradually spreading over the North American and South American continents.

When these **nomads** (wanderers) reached Louisiana, they found a good hunting area with a dependable source of food. They ate a wide range of animals and plants. People hunted game in small groups using three-inch stone points attached to wooden poles — spears. The hunters used the primitive spears to kill prehistoric elephants, called **mastodons**. The hunters' spear points have been found throughout much of Louisiana — on ridges and hills, at salt domes, and at other places. The rock the Paleo Indians used for the spear points probably came from Arkansas or Texas.

Stone points provide clues that tell us how these people lived. Hunting was the basis of their way of life, and they moved around to find the animals they hunted. They probably made clothing from animal skins and lived in temporary shelters.

Using stone-tipped weapons, Paleo Indians killed mammoth and other large animals. These large hairy elephants were native to the New World until about 6000 B.C.

This campsite was typical of the Meso Indians who relied on gathering natural food and hunting smaller animals after the large game died out.

MESO INDIANS

After about 7500 B.C., the climate changed and some large animals like mastodons began to die out. The Indians hunted smaller animals like deer and rabbit and no longer followed the migrating herds. This lifestyle change signaled a new prehistoric period — the Meso Indians. These people were still nomadic, but they stayed in one place longer.

The Meso Indians ate a wider range of foods. The natural environment provided many species of birds, mammals, fish, clams, reptiles, amphibians, seeds, roots, nuts, and fruits. The people gathered hickory nuts, pecans, acorns, persimmons, huckleberries, and elderberries. They hunted deer, rabbits, raccoons, and squirrels.

The Meso Indians adapted their hunting weapons for this smaller game. For example, they added a throwing stick with weights, called the **atlatl** (at LAT l), to their spears. The weights (banner stones) were made of clay, stone, or shell. These improvements enabled hunters to throw their spears for greater distances and with more power. For this kind of hunting, the spear points were more varied in size and shape, were cruder than the Paleo Indian points, and were made from local stone.

Because they did not move around as much, the Meso Indians built more permanent houses. The structures were covered with branches or thatch and built on posts in the ground. Near these houses the Meso Indians also built **mounds**. The first mounds may have been built as early as 5000 B.C., and those in Louisiana existed by 3000 B.C. These mounds were probably used during special ceremonies, but they were not used for burials.

The Meso Indians made many different kinds of **artifacts,** which are objects left behind by ancient people. These artifacts included shaped and polished stones for bowls and jewelry. They also made baskets, bone needles, awls (tools to make holes in wood or leather), fish hooks, beads, hairpins, tortoise shell rattles, and shell ornaments. Their improved tools included stone axes for chopping down trees.

EARLY NEO INDIANS

One of the things that distinguishes the early Neo Indian period from earlier ones is pottery making. Although pottery shards (broken pieces) have been found elsewhere dating back to 2500 B.C., native Louisiana Indian pottery was first made around 1000 B.C. Some pottery was plain, and other pottery was decorated with careful artistic designs. Archaeologists have found large amounts of pottery at sites dated to this period.

The expansion of farming allowed more stable settlements for the Neo Indians. They were then able to build more permanent shelter.

POVERTY POINT

The Poverty Point site, built by the Neo Indians, is that culture's largest earthworks. This large complex of mounds, which has been recognized as a National Historic Landmark, was built between 2000 B.C. and 500 B.C. How people of that time created such a massive and elaborate structure puzzles all who see it. The area covers almost a square mile, about 400 acres. Viewing it by air is the only way to see the entire structure at once.

The huge design consists of six semicircular ridges, one inside the other, divided by four aisles. For this amazing creation, workers mounded 30 million loads of dirt. Scientists believe that each load weighed about 50 pounds and was carried to the site in baskets or animal hides.

The purpose of this tremendous human effort remains a mystery. A recent theory suggests the aisles may have been used for astronomical observations. Two of the aisles line up with the winter and summer solstice sunsets.

In its time, the Poverty Point site had the largest, most elaborate earthworks anywhere in the western hemisphere. This scale model gives visitors an idea of what the site looked like. The semicircular ridges can only be seen easily from an airplane.

The Poverty Point people undoubtedly gathered there for ceremonies and celebrations. Artisans (skilled crafts persons) and traders probably lived at Poverty Point throughout the year. Artifacts include trade goods from as far away as the Great Lakes region and the Appalachian Mountains.

Although this society is dated during the Neo Indian period, the Poverty Point Indians continued the traditions of the Meso Indians. They used spears with atlatls instead of bows and arrows; pottery had not yet replaced their carved sandstone and soapstone containers. The most commonly found objects — clay cooking balls — lined the cooking pits. These hand-formed balls were used like charcoal briquettes for roasting and baking. About two hundred balls lined each pit, and millions of balls have been found at the site. Some of the clay balls reveal the imprints of the people who shaped them, all those centuries ago.

Later, the Poverty Point Indians made pottery vessels and ornamental clay and stone figurines. They made beads from copper, clay, and exotic stones and crafted elaborate pendants in the shape of birds, insects, miniature tools, and geometric shapes.

Other artifacts included bolas, weapons weighted by teardrop-shaped stones called *plummets*. The plummets were made from magnetite and hematite, probably traded from Missouri and northern Arkansas. The stone was worth the trade, because the bola was a useful weapon. The weights helped the hunter wrap the bola around the feet of large waterfowl. The plummets were also probably used as weights for fishing nets.

The Poverty Point culture had disappeared by 600 B.C., and no evidence has been found to explain why. War and conflict usually leave signs as clues for later generations. Those who study Poverty Point must look for other reasons to explain its end. One theory suggests a change in the religious beliefs. Visit the Poverty Point site and form your own opinion.

The largest mound at Poverty Point is believed to have been in the shape of a flying bird, with a main ramp up the tail (above) and side ramps up each wing. The mound stands at the apex of the system of semicircular ridges (see photo opposite).

*Top: This burial mound is located at the Marksville State Commemorative Site. **Above:** Artifacts such as this ceramic pipe found at Marksville were often buried with the dead.*

During the early Neo Indian period, people built villages and occupied them on a seasonal basis, taking advantage of the available food supply. The development of the bow and arrow around 500 A.D. made hunting deer easier. The bow was made of a bent branch, such as hickory, and deer tendons were used to draw the arrow. The arrow shaft was made of local wood, and a stone point completed the arrow.

Mainstays of the Neo Indian menu were wild grapes, palmetto, fruits, pigweed, and amaranth. Amaranth was a seed-bearing plant that is now considered a weed. Fish, deer, and shellfish added more variety to their diet.

The early Neo Indians made more elaborate ornaments than people from earlier periods, and they traded for many items. They had copper ear spools and bracelets, beads, animal tooth pendants, pottery pipes, and figurines. These artifacts, along with other status symbols like marine and freshwater shells, were often buried with their dead in mounds.

LATE NEO INDIANS

The late Neo Indian period refers to the time from 800 A.D. until the Europeans arrived in the area. At this time, villages were larger and were located near waterways, which the Indians used for travel and as

a source of food. People built more permanent houses of *wattle and daub*, woven sticks covered with mud.

The late Neo Indians switched from gathering to **agriculture** (farming). By this time, they may have lived in one place year-round, so they could plant and harvest crops. Maize (corn), beans, squash, and pumpkins were their main crops. They grew those crops using a method called *intercropping*. This involved planting two or more crops with different harvest times in the same plot of land. The beans and pumpkins could grow and provide food in less time than it took the corn to mature.

During this time, the Indians built temples atop their mounds. These **temple mounds** were used for religious ceremonies. An open plaza between two or more mounds served as the ceremonial ground. At the Medora site in West Baton Rouge Parish, for example, there was a 400-foot plaza located between two mounds.

Top: These two pots are dated during the Early Neo period. *Above:* In the Late Neo period, pottery became more elaborately decorated. Designs were carved into the pot and colors used to highlight the design.

Do You Remember?

1. How do scientists believe that the first Indians arrived on the North American continent?
2. What improvement helped Meso Indians become better hunters?
3. During what period did the early Indians switch from gathering to farming?
4. What is maize?

HISTORIC INDIANS

The *historic* Indian period began when the Europeans came to North America. "The People," as the Native Americans called themselves, passed down their traditions and history through oral storytelling. This storytelling preserved the important truths for the next generation but did not include much information about daily life. As a result, most of the information about the first cultures of North America comes from archaeology, which cannot reveal the entire past.

When the Europeans arrived, they wrote letters and journals describing their encounters with the Native Americans. Unfortunately, the Europeans were not always the best observers of cultures that were far different from their own. The language and customs of The People were often misunderstood. Nevertheless, the Europeans' written descriptions give archaeologists more information as they study Louisiana's early inhabitants.

In 1539, Spanish explorer Hernando de Soto set out from Havana, Cuba, to explore the southern part of what is today the United States. He brought with him hundreds of mounted soldiers, his bloodhounds, and a huge herd of pigs. But this Spanish *conquistador* (conqueror) and others like him also brought along European diseases. The lack of **immunity** (natural resistance) to these diseases brought a sentence of death to many who never even saw the intruders.

When the French arrived in Louisiana in the early eighteenth century, they found far fewer people than earlier explorers had reported. The Native

Hernando de Soto became wealthy after serving in an expedition in Peru. He then began his own expedition, dreaming of riches to be discovered in what is now the southeastern United States.

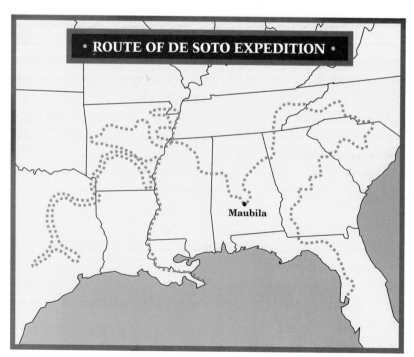

American population had been reduced by an estimated 80 percent, as village after village was hit by influenza, measles, smallpox, or cholera. Because of disease, some Indian groups had disappeared completely. The French were seeing the effects of the first European contact with Louisiana Indians, although this was only understood centuries later.

The early French explorers and trappers identified a number of tribes, recording names as they heard them. A **tribe** is a group of people who share a common ancestry, language, name, and way of living. The French sometimes made mistakes in identifying these tribes because the French did not understand the Indian alliances (tribal groupings). Today historians categorize the Indians of Louisiana according to six major language families: Atakapa, Caddoan, Chitimacha, Muskogean-Choctaw, Natchez, and Tunica-Koroa. All belong to the Eastern Woodlands culture of North America. Because of their location, the Caddo also shared some cultural traits with the Plains Indians.

Although tribes belonged to the same language group, they did not necessarily understand one another. To communicate

· LOUISIANA LANGUAGE FAMILIES ·

TUNICA-KOROA

CADDOAN

NATCHEZ

MUSKOGEAN-CHOCTAW

ATAKAPA

CHITIMACHA

with people who did not speak their language, Louisiana Indians used *Mobilian*. This trading language, based mainly on Choctaw, mixed gestures and words. Many of the Mobilian-Choctaw words became place names in Louisiana. For example, *Manchac* meant "rear entrance" and described the water route that was the back entrance to the Mississippi River.

Among the most significant tribes were the Atakapa, Caddo, Chitimacha, Choctaw, Houma, Natchez, and Tunica. Of these, the Natchez and the Atakapa no longer exist as tribes. After a confrontation, the Natchez were destroyed by the French. The Atakapa and the related Opelousas lived a primitive, seminomadic lifestyle in the Calcasieu Parish area. Early European observers and other tribes described them as cannibals. In fact, the name *Atakapa* means "eaters of flesh" in Choctaw. Their cannibalism was most likely a ritual or ceremony. To gain power, the Atakapa apparently ate parts of the bodies of their slain enemies. The Atakapa were later displaced when colonists moved into the area where they lived. First the French and then the Spanish maintained frontier forts in their region.

NATCHEZ

The primary village of the Natchez people, called Grand Village, was located near present-day Natchez, Mississippi, on the eastern bluffs of the Mississippi. On the west bank of the river, in northeastern Louisiana, lived the related Taensa and Avoyel tribes. Their flat-topped mounds and fortified villages were noted by the first Europeans. By 1700, they were more dispersed, with their villages scattered in the forests. However, mounds and temples continued to be part of their culture.

The Natchez had an unusual social structure. Their rigid class system consisted of common people (called *stinkards*), nobles, and chiefs. Everyone in the society, both men and women, wore tattoos indicating their status. Their ruler, known as the "Great Sun," was like a king and religious figure and held the power of life and death over his subjects. He rode in a litter and had a number of wives. When he died, at least some of his wives and other members of the tribe were killed and buried with him.

The Natchez liked to decorate their clothing with accessories such as belts of red-dyed opossum fur. The women wore the most elaborate clothing of any tribe. They used mulberry bark to make a thread for weaving, and the cloth they made was a homespun something like linen.

They strengthened their pottery with Spanish moss. This pottery was used to store and serve elaborate meals of deer, bison, bear, porcupine, and fowl. A variety of fruits and vegetables completed their diet. Much of their food came from skilled farming of the rich loess soil.

Ironically, it was this productive land that brought about the end of their way of life. Because the French wanted their farmland, relations between the French and Natchez were poor. In 1729, the Natchez attacked a French settlement at the site of present-day Natchez, Mississippi, killing about two hundred people. The French, with the help of the Choctaw, then drove the Natchez from the region. Some joined the Creek, Cherokee, and other Gulf tribes. Any descendants of the Natchez living today are mixed among those groups.

The Grand Village of the Natchez can be seen on the eastern bluffs of the Mississippi River near Natchez, Mississippi.

This illustration of a Tunica chief and his wife and child was painted in the 1730s by Alexander de Batz.

TUNICA-BILOXI

Both the Tunica and the Biloxi had lived in Mississippi. The Tunica lost their ancestral home when the Chickasaw drove them away. The Biloxi were pushed inland by the French and forced to leave their home near the Gulf Coast. By the late 1780s, both tribes had settled in Avoyelles Parish, in east-central Louisiana. The Spanish gave them a land grant, promising that they could keep their land.

The Tunica were great traders. After settling in central Louisiana, they continued this trading activity. They located their settlements near the junction of major waterways, taking advantage of an excellent trade route. They became major distributors of salt, a valuable trade commodity (good). They also traded arrow points, flint, and horses from New Mexico. As "money," the traders used shell beads, pearls, or quartz, and they kept trading records with bundles of sticks and knots of string.

The Tunica used their trade experience and good locations to gain power during the European colonial period. A French observer described the Great Chief of the Tunica: "He understands his trade very well. He has learned of us to hoard up money and he is reckoned to be very rich." In addition to trading, the Tunica hunted, farmed, and fished.

They were governed by both a war chief and a peace chief. The war chief was the military leader, and the peace chief was the tribal leader. Their **totem**, or tribal symbol, was the rattlesnake and represented the entire tribe.

In the 1980s, after a fifty-year effort, the Tunica-Biloxi tribe was recognized by the United States government. Federal recognition as a tribe is important for funding and for the legal right to govern themselves. The Tunica-Biloxi now have a reservation near Marksville in Avoyelles Parish with their own court and police system. When the business of the tribe is conducted, the elders may speak French, for no one today can speak the language of the Tunica. Storytellers still share the myths and tales of their ancestors, although they are told in English or French. Feeling this loss, the Tunica continue to rediscover and reclaim their heritage.

Do You Remember?
1. What signals the beginning of the historic Indian period?
2. Who was the Great Sun?

THE TUNICA TREASURE

In the 1970s in West Feliciana Parish, an untrained amateur discovered and excavated a very significant Tunica grave site filled with artifacts. Tribal custom was to bury the dead with their important possessions. Many of the artifacts uncovered were colonial European trade items. The treasure hunter claimed those priceless artifacts.

To the Tunica, the site was sacred because it contained ancestral graves. They considered the excavation to be desecration and grave-robbing, and they demanded the return of all the items taken. After years of legal battles, the Tunica regained the contents of the graves. Because of this court case, Congress passed the Native American Graves Protection and Repatriation Act, which was signed into law in 1990. The law states that objects buried directly with the dead belong to the descendants and must be returned to the tribes. Once their artifacts were returned, the Tunica built a museum and prepared a burial mound. The collection is now being restored.

The Tunica-Biloxi have established the first artifact conservation laboratory among Native Americans. Two members of the tribe have become full-time conservators, and others are learning as apprentices. Restored objects, including French trade goods and Native American pottery, are now on display at the museum.

The red and blue alligators outside the Tunica-Biloxi Museum in Marksville represent summer and winter in the Tunica creation story.

This Houma doll was made out of Spanish moss by Marie Dean of Dulac in the 1960s. Houma Indians greeted LaSalle's expedition when it reached the mouth of the Mississippi River in 1682.

HOUMA

The Houma Indians greeted the early French explorer Robert Cavelier de La Salle as he traveled down the Mississippi River in the late 1600s. Their primary village, a circle of about 140 cabins, was near the river at Angola in West Feliciana Parish. The Houma lost this location after a battle with the Tunica, and they moved further south. They first lived on Bayou St. John, moved to Ascension Parish in 1718, sold that land to the Acadians, and ended up in Terrebonne Parish.

Driven from their farmland, they had to give up their agricultural way of life. They learned to hunt, fish, and trap in the swamp and marsh. The crawfish was the totem of the Houma and served as a symbol of kinship and protection.

Another symbol of the Houma was the Istrouma (is TROO ma) or Isti Houma, the tall red pole on the banks of the Mississippi marking the boundary between the hunting grounds of the Houma and the Bayougoula. The French explorer Iberville called the marker *baton rouge*, French for "red stick." The name of Louisiana's capital city comes from this story.

The Houma today live mainly in Terrebonne and Lafourche parishes and number themselves at about 15,000. During the years they moved around Louisiana, they intermarried with the Bayougoula, Acolipissa, and Atakapa. This blurring of tribal lines has made it difficult for the Houma to verify their ancestry. Many who consider themselves Houma now speak French. They have lived among the Acadians for many years, with the two groups intermarrying and sharing their cultures.

The Houma are recognized as a tribe by the state of Louisiana. But the federal government has never granted this group tribal recognition. The Bureau of Indian Affairs claims they are not descendants of a distinct tribe, have not historically been a distinct community, and have not maintained political influence over their members. Today, the Houma continue to battle for federal recognition.

The Houma maintain a community center at Dulac. Lessons in weaving and woodcarving pass on the old ways. Palmetto baskets show a tradition that developed when local plants were used to make the containers needed. The use of herbalism by healers or *traituers* (Acadian French) was valued in both cultures and is still practiced by some members of the community.

At the Louisiana Folklife Festival, these Houma Indians demonstrate the traditional method of building a shelter using wooden poles and palmetto leaves.

CHITIMACHA

The name *Chitimacha* means "people altogether red." By 1650, over 4,000 Chitimacha lived in villages along Bayou Teche, Grand Lake, Butte LaRose, and the mouth of Bayou Plaquemine in South Louisiana. The Chitimacha were ruled by one male chief, who had charge over all the villages. The chief's position was an inherited one. Women could also hold political power and serve as healers, but they were not permitted to hold any powerful religious position. In the closed society of the Chitimacha, a child belonged to the clan of the mother, and the birth clan established the child's social class.

Important rituals were conducted in the dance house. These ceremonies of dancing and fasting sometimes lasted for six days. For a boy's rite of passage to manhood, he fasted (took no food or water) and sought a vision to help him direct his adult life.

Such was the way of life for the Chitimacha when the French arrived. They quickly became victims in the power struggle that followed. Fifteen French soldiers, helped by the Acolipissa and the Natchitoches tribes, captured twenty Chitimacha women and children, probably for slaves. When fighting broke out, the Chitimacha killed a French missionary. Bienville, the French governor, demanded that the Chitimacha turn over to him the killer of the priest. When they did, Bienville had him put to death. The Chitimacha later made peace with the French.

When the Acadians arrived, the lives of the Chitimacha changed again. In 1762, some of the Acadians settled near the Chitimacha. The two groups later intermarried, and French became their common language.

Although they were still living in their homeland at the time of the Louisiana Purchase, the Chitimacha were never offered a treaty by the United States. By 1905, they had lost much of their land. After a court struggle and help from Sarah McIlhenny, their neighbor from nearby Avery Island, the Chitimacha regained

John and Scarlett Darden are shown here making traditional Chitimacha baskets. Some Chitimacha baskets are so tightly woven, they can hold water.

174   *Louisiana: The History of an American State*

Nick Stouff of Charenton is a Chitimacha tribal historian and a former chief.

part of their ancestral homeland. By 1934, they had opened a school for their tribe.

In 1971, the tribe finally received federal recognition. Today, the Chitimacha reservation is almost three hundred acres in St. Mary Parish. As the twentieth century ended, Chief Ralph Darden said of his people, "To still walk this same land our ancestors walked. To again be able to care and provide for our people and those around us. To rekindle the pride in being Chitimacha. That is the greatest gift we can give our children."

CADDO

Caddo, or Kadochacho, was the name of a specific tribe, but the French applied it to a **confederation**, an entire group of related allies. Other tribes related to the Caddo tribe were the Natchitoches, Adai, Ouachita, and Hasinai. They lived in the land bordering the eastern woodlands and the western plains of North America. Border disputes between France and Spain and later between Spain and the United States centered in the land of the Caddo.

The Red River and its tributaries marked the traditional home of the Caddo. They had lived in Arkansas before moving into northwest Louisiana. On today's map, Caddo Lake and Caddo Parish are named for those first occupants of the land.

The Caddo shared this home with herds of bison, hunting them from horseback. The horses came from their neighbors on the western plains, who traded the horses for salt. The Caddo traded their surplus horses to their eastern neighbors, the Tunica.

Like those eastern neighbors, the Caddo were an agricultural people. Later, they added cattle, hogs, and poultry to their farms. In addition, fish from the many lakes, creeks, and rivers in their territory had long provided food.

After the Louisiana Purchase, the Caddo accepted American trade regulations. But the trade goods were inferior and often did not conform to the trade treaty. In 1815, the Caddo sold their land to the United States. They gave up one million acres of land for $80,000, part in cash and part in trade goods. The land included in the treaty extended from DeSoto Parish north to Texarkana. (A **treaty** is a formal agreement between two or more nations.) After the treaty, they joined other Caddo in Texas. The Caddo were forced to leave there when the Texans began driving out all Indians.

The present home of the Caddo people is a reservation in Oklahoma. An annual turkey dance continues a tradition that began in a time no one can remember. Some participants wear the special capes woven of seeds as they dance and sing the old songs.

This traditional Caddo village has been recreated at Indian City USA in Oklahoma. The headquarters of the Caddo tribe are in Binger, Oklahoma.

COUSHATTA

The Coushatta (Koasati) tribe belong to the Muskogean language group. They left their home on the Tennessee River after De Soto tried to force them to give him gold they did not have. Migrating south, they stayed until they felt the pressure of the British to the east. The Coushatta escaped the Indian slave traders by moving even further west.

Tribal traditions are passed down from one generation to the next. Here are two generations of Coushatta basket-makers, photographed at Elton. Lorena Langley (right) is shown holding a basket of pine straw animals. Her daughter Rose Medford (above) is making a small basket.

Coming from Georgia and Alabama, they settled in south-central Louisiana in the late eighteenth century. They became allies of the French and later the Spanish. After the Americans came to Louisiana, the Coushatta tried not to take sides in the conflicts between Spain and the United States. They moved around frequently along the border between Louisiana and Texas to avoid the clashes between the two countries.

The Coushatta lived in clans made of many families. A **clan** is a group of people who believe themselves related by blood. Respect for the clan of the mother gave women a special place in tribal life. Each family had its own animal totem.

The crafts of the tribe included weaving beautiful cloth, rope, and saddle blankets. The men made blowguns and bows and arrows for hunting. Like their neighbors, the Coushatta were also farmers.

By the nineteenth century, many Coushatta lived in Louisiana; by 1884, they had purchased their land near Bayou Blue in Allen Parish. The important federal recognition of their tribe came in 1973. Today, they have an active, organized tribal government and a vital and thriving community. Many tribal members are full-blooded, and all speak the Coushatta language. They follow their rich oral tradition to share the story of their past with the next generation. They still weave their intricate pine straw baskets.

These Choushatta animal dolls are made of pine straw and raffia, the leaf fibers of a type of palm tree.

CHOCTAW

When the Europeans came, the Choctaw were the second largest tribe in the southeastern United States, occupying an area that includes present-day Georgia, Alabama, and southern Mississippi and Louisiana. They were farmers living in permanent towns, and they also had extensive trade routes. Some roads in southeast Louisiana are still called old Choctaw roads.

The long-standing conflict between the French and the British spilled over to the New World and involved the Indian nations in the 1700s. The Europeans demanded that each tribe choose sides. The Choctaw chose the French. The Chickasaw, traditional enemies of the Choctaw, supported the British and hostilities between the two tribes increased. After the French and Indian War, the Choctaw formed two groups, one allied with the French and the other with the British. The conflict in the tribe led to an internal war.

A Choctaw militia fought the British in the American Revolution, and a unit of Choctaw warriors fought with Andrew Jackson at the Battle of New Orleans. But by the early 1830s, the Choctaw had ceded (given up) most of their land to the United States.

Most Choctaw descendants live on their reservations in Oklahoma or Mississippi. Several small groups of Choctaw continue to live in Louisiana. One group listed by the Intertribal Council of Louisiana is the Clifton Choctaw. The Louisiana Band is another, living mostly in the urban area of Baton Rouge.

The Jena Band of Choctaw is recognized by the federal government and has a tribal center in Jena, a town in Grant Parish. These Choctaw retain their language and many skills of the past. They make blowguns, fans of turkey feathers, and baskets of oak and pine straw. Skilled Choctaw crafters prepare deer hides using traditional methods.

Another group living in Louisiana today is the Ebarb-Choctaw-Apache tribe. Their tribal office is located at Zwolle in Sabine Parish. Here, near the Sabine River, Lipan Apache joined with a group of Louisiana Choctaw. The Apache had been brought to the region as Spanish slaves in the late seven-

Above: *This painting by Karl Bodmer depicts a Choctaw camp along the Mississippi River in the 1800s.* ***Left:*** *Bodmer painted "Tshanny, a Choctaw Man" near New Orleans during the period of the removal of the Choctaws to the west.*

teenth and early eighteenth centuries. Their culture today is a mixture of their native and Spanish heritage. The annual tamale festival features the community's food specialty and showcases their blended culture.

Do You Remember?

1. How did Baton Rouge get its name?
2. How did a Chitimacha boy prepare to become a man?
3. Which Indians hunted bison from horseback?

When the first Europeans came to Louisiana, the Native Americans who were living here had a rich culture.

CLOTHING

The Indians who lived in Louisiana wore simple clothing that suited the climate and that was made from available materials. Men wore breechcloths made from buckskin and held at the waist with a belt. The belts were made of fur, fiber, or buckskin and were often decorated. Buckskin leggings provided more covering, and men wore them when travelling or in severe weather.

The women wore variations of simple skirts. Natchez women were covered from the neck down with a garment of cloth made from mulberry bark. Choctaw women wove long skirts of buffalo wool or mulberry bark fiber. Women in other tribes wore simple skirts made of woven palmetto leaves, Spanish moss, other plant fibers, or buckskin. For warmth, Caddo women added buckskin or fur ponchos. Children were dressed very simply and sometimes did not wear any clothes during the summer. When they needed footwear, the Indians made moccasins from the skins of deer, bear, or bison.

Europeans most admired the Indians' feather cape, which was a woven net covered with turkey or duck feathers. Both men and women wore these elaborate and beautiful garments for special occasions.

Ornaments and body decoration were an essential part of their appearance, and tattooing was common to all groups. Sometimes the tattoos indicated important deeds or clan membership. Body painting had different purposes, and certain colors and designs had different meanings. Pierced ears were popular, and the Caddo pierced their noses in order to wear small silver ornaments. Their necklaces, bracelets, and rings were made of copper, silver, or gold.

WORK

The natural environment of Louisiana provided the Indians with the plants and animals to meet their needs. Those who lived near the coast often had no need for agriculture and survived on the huge supply of clams. Others planted crops in the rich soil to grow what they needed. The Indians also hunted, fished, and collected wild plants.

The men worked together to clear land, construct houses, and build boats. They partially burned cypress logs and scraped out the burned area with shells. These dugouts were good for bayou travel, and the French later named them **pirogues** (pe ROGS).

Women gathered together to weave baskets, make pottery, or craft other utensils. The double-walled baskets woven by Chitimacha

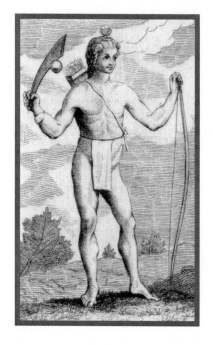

Above: *During the warm summer weather, Indian men wore little more than a breech-cloth.* **Opposite:** *The matchcoat in this 1730s painting by Alexander de Batz was made of bison skin and was a protection against the winter weather.*

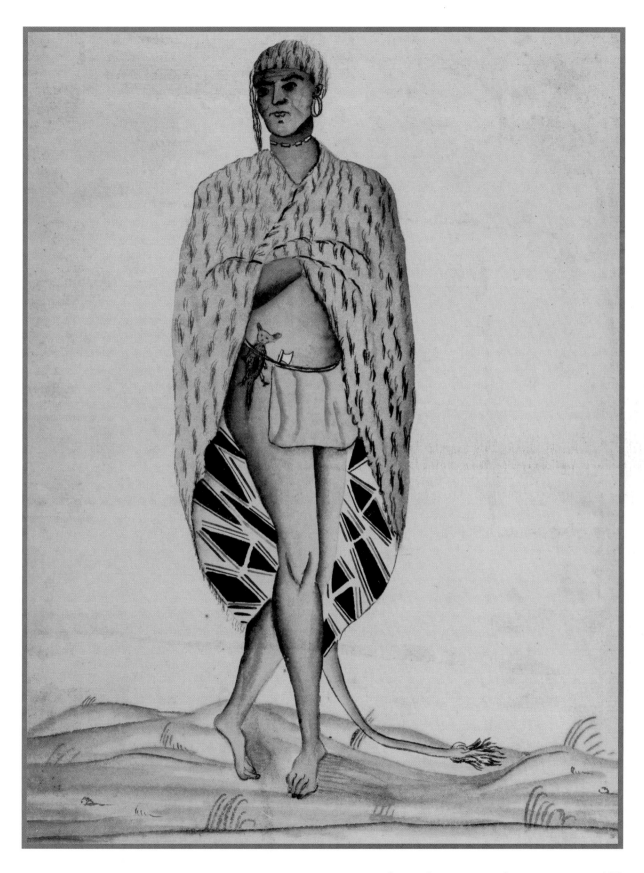

Chasse générale du Chevreuil.

women from river cane were so well designed that they could float.

Members of the tribe also spent their time preparing food and making essential clothing and tools. Any items they did not need were traded for additional supplies.

SHELTER

The Indians built their houses from available materials and adapted them to the climate. The Caddo built rectangular log houses, filling the cracks with clay mixed with deer hair to keep in the warmth. They also built a round summer house of woven grass. The Choctaw built a simple wood frame, plastered it with a clay and moss mixture, then thatched it with palmetto leaves. Most of the tribes used some variation of these three types.

The houses often had no window openings, and the small door faced east, the direction of the rising sun . The houses varied in size; in some tribes, they were quite large and accommodated several families.

FOOD

In the wild, the Indians found acorns, hickory nuts, mayhaw, blackberries, and many other plants, including 250 kinds of roots. One of these was a wild sweet potato, the forerunner of the yam grown in Louisiana today.

Above: Deer was an important animal to the Indians, providing both food and clothing. Opposite: The cabin of a chief (bottom) and a temple (top) depicted in this 1730s Alexander de Batz illustration are typical of the shelters built by the Native Americans in Louisiana.

This amazing list of foods was increased by farming. Long before the Europeans arrived, the people were successful farmers. At first, the Indians cultivated local plants such as the sunflower, amaranth, and tobacco. Trade with tribes in Mexico brought seeds for corn, beans, and squash, which soon replaced the earlier crops.

Corn became the mainstay of their meals. They ate boiled corn and a dish of corn mixed with beans and other vegetables or fruits. The dish with ground corn was called sagamite (sa GA me ta). Corn was dried, making it a portable food supply. Called "pinole" by the Spanish and "cold meal" by the British, this dried corn was the origin of the southern dish of grits. The dried corn was ground into meal and baked into bread. Another dried corn dish made by the Choctaw and Caddo included a meat filling, making a tamalelike dish.

TEMPLE des Sauvages, construit de Poteaux en terre, revêtû de [...] natte de Canne, er Couvert de même, [...] terminé par trois pi de Bois, de 3. pieds [...] de long, 18. pouces et 4. po d'aïpaisseur, [...] matachez et Scu grossierement les [...] 3. pyramides So natte garnie de [...] cañes pointû garentir, que [...] lon ne puisse monter auz [...] Figures qui rep -resente des [...] d'Indes part corps et [...] la queüe, la teste repr [...] esente celle de l'Aigle [...] ce que nous a parû de [...] plus aprochant

emme.   Sauvage   *Sau   vage*
                                                   ourson

terre

CABANE du Chef de poteaux en garnie de Bauge ou mortia de terre, Couverte aussy [...] de natte,
1ª Le temple a 22. piedic de [...] longueur et 14 pieds de large
il *se sert* de sepulture au [...] Chefs de la Nations .
Toutes les Caban [...] des Sauvages sont de pareille Construct [...] ion, etante toutes.
Rondes, celle cy [...] a 18. piedst de diametre.

Sauvage avec
son Calumet   *Jeunes Sauvags ou Banarets*
alo[...]   *Bra gueb.*

Levez et dessinez au Village des Colas-Pissas le quinze avril de la pr. année. Redigez a la nouvelle Orleans le vingt et deux Iuin 1732.

Dance générale.

To protect the supply of corn from hungry animals, the Indians built granaries high off the ground. This stored food helped the Indians make it through years when there were poor crops.

The Indians supplemented the vegetables and fruit with the meat of deer and bison. Bear provided not only meat but also oil. Bear oil was the best fat available and became a substitute for money in trade exchange.

RELIGION

The religion of the Indians was based on their concept of the world. Everything in the world had a place as part of a sacred whole. Preserving balance and harmony was the purpose of religious activities, which were supervised by priests, chiefs, and holy men.

The light of the sun represented a sacred power to several tribes. The Natchez believed that their main leader, the Great Sun, possessed special gifts from the sun. Fire was one symbol of the sun's power. Sacred fires and religious icons were often kept in special temples.

For most tribes, the annual celebrations included a new corn festival and a harvest festival. Some ceremonies continued for several days, with the participants getting little sleep or food. Dance and music were important in these religious festivities. Dances had specific meanings, and dancers often imitated animals to tell a story or teach a lesson. The musical instruments accompanying these songs and dances included drums and cane flutes.

Some Indian practices were not understood at all by the Europeans. The ritual of sacrifice seemed cruel and evil, especially to those who saw the Natchez women yield their babies to the death fire of a great chief. To the Natchez of the early eighteenth century, however, that act brought honor to the family and sent spirits to join the chief in the next world.

Above: The ceremonies of Louisiana Indians celebrated important events and gave thanks to their gods. Most ceremonies included dance.
Opposite: *In the 1730s, Alexander de Batz painted the Sacred Tree of the Natchez.*

This painting by Francois Barnard, "Choctaw Village near the Chefuncte," provides an opportunity for us to see history through the eyes of a person who actually lived it.

GOVERNMENT

A war chief and a peace chief usually led the tribe. The war chief was the military leader, the one who decided when to go into battle. The peace chief handled the domestic matters. Some tribes also had sub-chiefs. Some chiefs inherited their positions; in other tribes, they were selected, usually from among tribal elders. The Tunica-Biloxi and the Koasati still have a council of tribal elders to advise the chief.

The **calumet**, or peace pipe, was an important ceremonial possession of each chief. A calumet ceremony meant that war was averted. Because of its importance, each calumet was very carefully made and elaborately decorated. The pipe was usually made of clay or hollow cane and decorated with feathers and other significant items.

The reasons for going to war varied. The chiefs might feel menaced by a neighboring tribe. Sometimes the chiefs wanted to acquire captives, or the young men might want to improve their status by earning glory in battle. The Indians did not go to war without the required ritual and ceremony. They usually timed their wars for late spring or early fall when travel was easier and villages were safer without men.

The tactics of the Indians were completely different from the Europeans' experience. The Indians acted in secret, hoping to surprise their enemy. They depended on knives and war clubs in hand-to-hand combat. Captured women could marry into the tribe, and captured children were usually raised as members of the tribe.

The peace chief was responsible for the day-to-day activities within the tribe. He acted as judge when wrongdoings occurred. Criminal acts were not tolerated. Retaliation and retribution were demanded, and necessary to restore harmony. Punishment was severe and included beating, banishment, public humiliation, economic restitution, even death.

The interaction with the British, French, and Spanish changed the Indians' way of life forever. The colonial powers interfered with the internal affairs of the tribes and relocated many of them. They involved the tribes in their conflicts, enslaved them, and encouraged them to capture others as slaves. The early people of Louisiana changed from a hunting and agricultural society to one that depended on trade. But in that colonial trade economy, they were expected to serve as mercenaries (hired soldiers) to fight the battles of the Europeans.

THE VILLAGE

Community life was organized around a tribe or a clan, which was headed by a chief or chiefs. The kinship patterns were very important and, along with class ranking, directed much of a person's life.

Membership in clans was passed through the mother's side of the family. The Caddo and the Tunica ranked the clans, with some more powerful than others and chiefs chosen only from specific clans. The

Natchez had a caste system with several levels, and moving into a higher group was possible through marriage. A person could also lose rank by marriage. The Chitimacha followed a true caste system, in which people married only within their own rank.

Children were raised in these groups, often under the care of all the adults. In some tribes, the mother's brother handled discipline, and the father's role was more like that of a big brother. Discipline was mild, and the disapproval of the adults was usually enough to change unacceptable behavior.

Children's play often imitated adult work. In this way, they learned gender roles and the skills they would need as adults. But much of their childhood involved physical exercise, especially swimming and running, and they were not expected to do much work before age ten.

Games were an important part of village life. Much excitement centered around games like chunky and several kinds of ball games. Chunky was a one-on-one match in which a stone called the chunky was rolled between goals. One player rolled the chunky, while the other hurled a pole to hit it. Betting on the outcome was a key part of the activity. Other competitive matches included wrestling, racing, and archery.

Do You Remember?
1. What were the three basic types of Indian homes?
2. According to Native Americans, what was one sign of the sun's power?
3. Who were the leaders of a tribe?

SUMMARY

Native Americans lived in Louisiana thousands of years before any Europeans set foot here. Scientists have classified these prehistoric people into several periods — Paleo, Meso, and early and late Neo Indian groups — depending primarily on their hunting and settlement practices. By the time the Europeans arrived, Louisiana Native Americans had developed societies with distinct languages, social and political organizations, belief systems, and customs.

Historic Louisiana Native American groups include the Natchez, Choctaw, Tunica, Caddo, Houma, Chitimacha, and Atakapa. The dramatic encounter between the Europeans and Native Americans changed their history. From their mysterious past to their present-day contributions, Louisiana's Native Americans have left their mark on our state.

The Choctaw played ball games as a form of recreation as well as to help them improve their skills for hunting and war. George Catlin caught the spirit of these games in his painting "Choctaw Ball Game."

CHAPTER · REVIEW

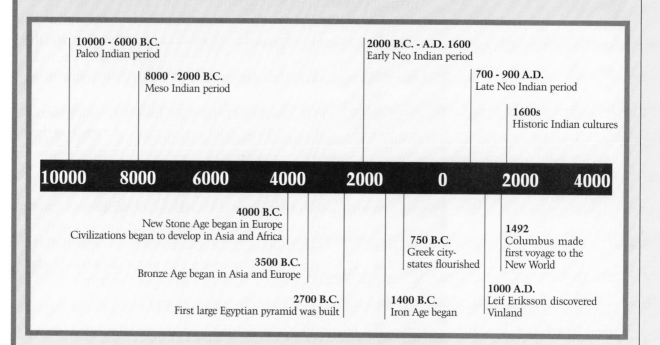

10000 - 6000 B.C.
Paleo Indian period

8000 - 2000 B.C.
Meso Indian period

2000 B.C. - A.D. 1600
Early Neo Indian period

700 - 900 A.D.
Late Neo Indian period

1600s
Historic Indian cultures

| 10000 | 8000 | 6000 | 4000 | 2000 | 0 | 2000 | 4000 |

4000 B.C.
New Stone Age began in Europe
Civilizations began to develop in Asia and Africa

3500 B.C.
Bronze Age began in Asia and Europe

2700 B.C.
First large Egyptian pyramid was built

1400 B.C.
Iron Age began

750 B.C.
Greek city-states flourished

1492
Columbus made first voyage to the New World

1000 A.D.
Leif Eriksson discovered Vinland

Reviewing People, Places, and Terms

Define, identify, or explain the importance of each of the following.

1. agriculture
2. ancestors
3. archaeologist
4. artifact
5. atlatl
6. calumet
7. clan
8. confederation
9. heritage
10. immunity
11. mastodon
12. midden
13. mound
14. nomad
15. temple mound
16. totem
17. treaty
18. tribe

Understanding the Facts

1. Why is there very little known for sure about the prehistoric peoples?
2. What are the four time periods archaeologists usually use to classify prehistoric peoples?
3. Why did prehistoric Indians stop hunting large animals like mastodons?
4. How did adding weight improve weapons for prehistoric Indians?
5. What was the biggest danger the Indians faced when the Europeans came?
6. How did tribes that did not speak the same language communicate with one another?
7. Where was the traditional home of the Caddo?
8. Which Louisiana tribe has managed to maintain its language?

Developing Critical Thinking

1. How did the prehistoric peoples interact with the environment? How did the environment affect where they lived? What they ate?

2. How can archaeologists tell much about a past culture by studying bits of old pottery, tools, or fragments of clothing? Why is an archaeologist's work important in understanding our culture and other cultures?
3. Why did De Soto bring a herd of pigs with him from Cuba?
4. List problems faced by Louisiana's Indian tribes today.

Using Your Skills
1. On a map of Louisiana, locate Bayou Blue, Jena, Marksville, Poverty Point, and Zwolle.
2. Locate a Web site on the Internet that will give you more information on Native Americans. Find five interesting items relating to Louisiana Indian groups to share with your classmates.

Special Projects
1. Research how archaeologists determine the age of artifacts. Prepare five questions that you could use to interview an archaeologist about this information.
2. Sagamite, the main staple of the Indian diet, consisted of boiled corn sometimes mixed with beans, other vegetables, or fruit. Starting with sagamite and ending with microwave popcorn, identify other uses of corn through American history. A timeline is one way you can show this progression.
3. The prehistoric peoples learned valuable lessons from those who lived before. For example, when one group learned how to store food, that technique was passed on to the next generation. Interview your parents or another adult. Find out what they consider to be the most important contributions made by *their* parents' generation.

Making Connections
1. How has the Native American Graves Protection and Repatriation Act changed the way we treat the artifacts of Native Americans?
2. Identify some of the knowledge and skills needed to be a conservator of artifacts.

Louisiana Lagniappe
- Some Indian hunters could catch wild geese with their bare hands.
- Sagamite was described often in French accounts of welcoming feasts.

• BUILDING SKILLS: UNDERSTANDING TIMELINES •

Keeping track of all the events you read about can be difficult. Timelines can help you remember events in the order they happened. Although a timeline can show events over a short period of time, most often it covers a period of years. Making a timeline is a useful way to organize the events that took place during a certain period of time. Sometimes it is not possible to include all events in a timeline; only the important events can be included. These important events then provide reference points for other events that occurred during the period covered by the timeline.

In your textbook, timelines appear in the Chapter Review section of many of the chapters, where they help you remember the events in the order they occurred during the chapter. They also help you place other events within the time frame of those on the timeline. You may want to expand these timelines and add other events to help you in your study of the chapter.

Try This! Make a timeline of your life or the life of one of your older relatives (mother, father, grandmother, grandfather, aunt, uncle). Start the timeline with the year you (or the other person) were born; end it with the present year. Show at least eight events in the order they occurred. You may also want to add other significant events to the timelines.

CHAPTER SIX

LOUISIANA'S FRENCH COLONIAL ERA: STRUGGLE AND SURVIVAL

We squared a tree and planted it in the ground, nailing to the side of the tree three copper fleurs-de-lis made from a cauldron. We made a cross, which we planted in the ground with this inscription on a lead plate: "Took possession of this land in the name of Louis XIV, King of France and of Navarre."
— From the journal of Minet, La Salle's engineer, on the 1684-1685 voyage to the Gulf of Mexico. Translation from *La Salle, the Mississippi and the Gulf*, Robert Weddle, editor.

SPICES FROM CHINA AND BEAVER PELTS from Canada triggered the contest to control North America. The powerful nations of Europe needed a shorter route to the spices and other exotic goods of the Far East. Seeking this route, the explorers found instead what they called the *New World*. When their ships delivered rich, new resources to the ports and palaces of England, Spain, and France, the race was on.

The rivalry expanded the struggle for military power and economic monopoly. At that time, the nations of Europe relied on an economic plan called mercantilism. As you learned in Chapter 3, under mercantilism a government expected its colonies to provide the raw materials the mother country needed for manufacturing *and* to serve as ready markets for the mother country's products.

This economic drive, plus their religious responsibilities, motivated the European rulers. Their struggle to control North America actually began on the Atlantic coast. The Spanish had established a colony at St. Augustine in 1565, the English one at Jamestown in 1607, and the French a colony at Quebec in 1608. The Mississippi River and the Gulf Coast became the stage for the eighteenth-century struggle.

Terms: Northwest Passage, expedition, colony, proprietorship, Superior Council, cash crop, speculator, land grant, Mississippi Bubble, slave, plantation, Code Noir, specie, casket girls

People: Louis Joliet; René Robert Cavelier, Sieur de La Salle; Henri de Tonti; Pierre Le Moyne, Sieur d'Iberville; Jean Baptiste Le Moyne, Sieur de Bienville; Antoine Crozat; Antoine de Lamothe, Sieur de Cadillac; Louis Juchereau de St. Denis; John Law; Etienne de Perier; Pierre Francois de Rigaud, Marquis de Vaudreuil; Louis Billouart, Chevalier de Kerlerec

Places: Louisiana, Ship Island, Fort Maurepas, English Turn, Fort de la Boulaye, Fort Louis, Natchitoches, New Orleans, German Coast, Fort Rosalie

Preceding pages: Fort St. Jean Baptiste, shown here as it was reconstructed, was built on the site of present-day Natchitoches. *Right:* Marquette and Joliet, traveling in canoes, explored the Mississippi River to the mouth of the Arkansas River.

EXPLORING THE MISSISSIPPI

The French established their first trading posts not on the Gulf Coast but in the cold Canadian north. They began trading with the local people for furs, including the beaver pelts that went to Europe to become fashionable hats. The hats became so popular that more and more furs were needed. This demand for Canadian furs provided the economic support that built New France (Canada).

Canadian traders wanted to expand their trading area by finding a river that would take them to China or to the Indies. They talked of the **Northwest Passage**, that mysterious water route through the North American continent. A great river described by the Iroquois might just lead them across North America to Asia. The western part of North America was unknown, so the traders thought this river might flow into the Gulf of California.

JOLIET AND MARQUETTE

In 1673, French fur trader Louis Joliet, Jesuit priest Father Marquette, and others set out to explore this river. They paddled and floated down the river in the birchbark canoes that their Indian allies had taught them to make. Indian food such as corn and dried buffalo meat nourished them on the trip.

These preparations and their determination took them as far down the Mississippi as the mouth of the Arkansas River. There, at the Quapaw Indian village, they learned that traveling further downriver could be dangerous. The powerful tribes living there could defend themselves with Spanish guns. Was there a Spanish fort somewhere to the south? Unwilling to risk an encounter with armed Indians or Spanish soldiers, the French exploring party returned north.

Robert Cavelier, Sieur de La Salle (above) came to Canada from France and established a fur trading post near Montreal. When La Salle learned of the exploration of Marquette and Joliet, he began his own adventure down the Mississippi River to the Gulf of Mexico in 1682. La Salle held a formal ceremony claiming the Mississippi Valley for France (left).

LA SALLE

René Robert Cavelier, Sieur de La Salle had long dreamed of finding a water route to China. La Salle's trading post in Canada was even called LaChine ("China") by other traders as they laughed at his obsession. But La Salle's goal and his hopes took him through years of delays and struggles until he was finally able to begin his journey.

His trip was made easier by his choice for his lieutenant, Henri de Tonti (TONE teh). An interesting and colorful character who was known for his bravery and courage, Tonti had lost a hand in a European battle. According to legend, he amputated the damaged arm himself. This story and his brave deeds earned him the respect of the Indians, who named him "Iron Hand." (Tonti wore a metal artificial hand.)

La Salle set out from Canada with Tonti, soldiers, priests, and Indians with their families. They entered the upper Mississippi River in

La Salle's dream of finding a water route to China ended in 1687 when his men mutinied and murdered him.

early February 1682. On April 9, they reached the mouth of the river. There, in a solemn and formal ceremony, La Salle claimed all the land drained by the Mississippi River for his king, Louis XIV. He honored the king by naming the land *Louisiana*, which means "Land of Louis." For the occasion, La Salle dressed in his ceremonial red coat trimmed with gold lace, which he had carefully packed for the journey.

Another purpose of the trip was to extend the official religion of France. A Catholic priest was part of the expedition, representing the church. (An **expedition** is a journey for a specific purpose, such as exploration.) The priest celebrated a mass with prayers and songs in Latin. Those words rang out from the natural levee somewhere in Plaquemines Parish. Today the location is marked with a monument topped with a large wooden cross. The monument represents the large log cross La Salle placed on the spot. A brass plaque inscribed in French tells the story of La Salle and the Mississippi River.

Eager to continue his important mission, La Salle returned to France to report his discovery to King Louis XIV. The king rewarded him with a small fleet of ships and three hundred colonists and directed him to establish a new colony. (A **colony** is a group of people who settle in a distant land but who are still under the control of their native land.)

La Salle's return trip, however, was not a successful one. After sailing into the Gulf of Mexico, La Salle missed the mouth of the Mississippi River and ended up at Matagorda Bay in Texas. The colonists were frightened and frustrated. Many had died at sea, and more died on the desolate beach. La Salle then set out to lead the remaining colonists overland to Canada. The journey was difficult and ended horribly when some of the men mutinied and murdered La Salle. La Salle's dreams had ended in a nightmare of failure.

Do You Remember?
1. What was the purpose of the French trading posts?
2. For whom was Louisiana named, and what does *Louisiana* mean?
3. What interest did Catholic priests have in exploration?

MEASURING LONGITUDE

The history of Louisiana might have been very different if the coastline had not been such a mysterious unknown to the French explorer La Salle. Today, La Salle might take advantage of the Global Positioning System, which uses a receiver to send a signal to a satellite. The receiver measures the amount of time the signal takes to reach the satellite and notes the satellite's position in orbit. With this information, the GIS (Geographical Information System) can determine and report latitude and longitude.

This 1700 French map of the New World shows the mouth of the Mississippi far to the west of its actual location. Inaccuracies like these likely contributed to La Salle ending up lost in Texas.

La Salle, unfortunately, had no way to accurately measure longitude, so he couldn't find the mouth of the Mississippi. He ended up lost in Texas. Like other explorers, La Salle was learning more about the earth as he traveled, trying to apply the knowledge of his time. Sailors and scientists had determined that the sun, moon, and stars could be used to determine latitude, but they were at a loss when it came to longitude. This problem was so important that, in 1714, British Queen Anne and Parliament offered a huge prize for the solution.

Scientists tried for many years, but it was a clockmaker named John Harrison who finally solved the problem. He developed a clock that could adjust itself for the movement of the ship and accurately measure time at sea. Harrison chose Greenwich, England, for the Prime Meridian, or the starting point. By comparing time at another location with the time at the Prime Meridian, he was able to accurately determine longitude. After forty years, Harrison's work was finally accepted; and he received his reward, several million dollars by today's standards. And now you should understand why the Prime Meridian was placed through England. After all, who solved the problem?

Iberville (above) was the son of a wealthy Canadian landowner. He became a war hero as a young man when he and other trappers drove the British from Hudson Bay. He was chosen by King Louis XIV (opposite) to carry out La Salle's dream of founding a French colony near the mouth of the Mississippi.

COLONIZING LOUISIANA

La Salle did not establish the first French colony on the Gulf Coast. But his claim in the name of France set off a chain of events that led to the first French colony.

When the other European powers heard of the French claim to the Mississippi, they reacted strongly. France's claims and plans for the Gulf Coast were a threat to Spain's New World. The Spanish government was determined to protect its colonies and built a fort on the Gulf of Mexico at Pensacola Bay. The English hoped to build a colony at the mouth of the Mississippi.

When Louis XIV heard of these plans, he knew he must establish a fort immediately. The Mississippi must be kept from England and guarded for France. To do this, the king needed a strong, experienced military leader familiar with North America. The wilderness experience of French Canadian officers made them suitable for this challenge. The king chose one of his Canadian commanders — Pierre Le Moyne, Sieur d'Iberville.

To accompany him on the expedition, Iberville chose his younger brother, Jean Baptiste Le Moyne, Sieur de Bienville. Although only eighteen, Bienville was an experienced and battle-scarred sailor. The two Le Moyne brothers would leave their names on the map and the history of Louisiana.

FORT MAUREPAS

The king charged Iberville with establishing a base from which to control the mouth of the Mississippi River. Iberville first had to explore the land near the river and choose a location for his headquarters. That site must also be a good location for a colony. Mercantilism required that the colony provide raw materials for manufacturers in France and serve as a market for French manufactured goods. Conditions in the colony itself were secondary. This attitude was one reason why the colony struggled from its beginnings.

Iberville's expedition stopped for supplies at the French colony of Saint-Domingue in the West Indies and then set sail for the Gulf of Mexico. Spanish soldiers had finished their fort at Pensacola Bay just months before the French arrived. When Iberville sailed into the Gulf, he found that the Spanish held the best harbor near the Mississippi River. Continuing westward, Iberville came upon a number of islands near the coast of present-day Mississippi. He named one Ship Island because it provided a good harbor for their ships. They built a few primitive huts for a temporary camp; then they set out to find the mouth of the

Henri de Tonti, the "Man with the Iron Hand," served as a lieutenant in La Salle's first expedition. On March 31, 1699, Tonti's unclaimed letter to La Salle told Bienville he had found the Mississippi River.

Mississippi. Iberville described the day of discovery in his journal: "March 3, Mardi Gras Day . . . I went up this river . . . two leagues and a half above the mouth it forks into three branches."

To make sure that this was the Mississippi, Iberville and Bienville questioned the local Indians. One chief they met told them of the "speaking bark" left by another Frenchman. Bienville offered a reward of an axe to recover that message. Soon, another chief brought him a letter Tonti had left for La Salle in 1685. La Salle never got that letter because he never made it back to the Mississippi. But more than thirteen years later on March 31, 1699, the unclaimed letter spoke an encouraging message to the French explorers. They had found the great Mississippi River.

The mouth of the river, however, was a poor location for Iberville's fort. The Gulf Coast offered a better harbor for ships and seemed to have better land for a colony. There were plenty of trees to build the fort. The completed fort, built near present-day Biloxi, was named Fort Maurepas (MOR eh PAH) to honor a French official.

AN UNEASY TIME

When the fort was finished, Iberville returned to France for more supplies, soldiers, and settlers. While he was gone, the little fort suffered from a food shortage and lack of supplies. The men were also afraid of an attack by the Chickasaw, who were allies of the British.

The British colonies along the Atlantic coast were a threat to French efforts to claim and control the Mississippi River Valley. While Iberville was in France, Bienville explored the river. On one trip, he encountered a twelve-gun British vessel coming up the river toward his much smaller boat. Pretending that he had many more ships with troops behind him, Bienville informed the British captain that he controlled the river. He hinted that he would attack if the British did not leave peacefully. The British captain believed Bienville's bluff, turned around, and sailed away. English Turn (Detour Anglais), south of New Orleans, is still marked on today's maps.

Bienville's action prevented the British from establishing a colony. A small group of French Huguenots (Protestants) were on board the British ship. They had hoped to claim the area for Great Britain and set up their own colony. Bienville, however, thwarted their plans and ensured that Louisiana would be a French colony.

The local Indians also presented a challenge to the French. In the beginning, the Indians shared their food and skills with the strangers. In his memoirs, a young ship's carpenter described one of those visits and the music and dancing the two cultures shared. A young soldier had brought along a special possession, his violin. With his music, the soldiers taught the Indians to "figure dance." In return, the Indians invited the soldiers to learn their dances. Later, when the soldiers were starving, they were invited to live with the Indians.

In spite of this acceptance, the French treated the Indians as a conquered people. They took Indians as slaves and started conflicts between tribes. Misinformation also created problems between the two cultures. Iberville had placed cabin boys with the Indians to learn their language and observe their culture. Several years later when Bienville was in charge, he was told that the Indians had killed one of these boys. He demanded that the person responsible for the boy's death be himself put to death. Later, however, the boy was found alive. The Indians responded to Bienville's unfair attack by killing several French traders and priests. But even more Indians died as Bienville quickly retaliated.

Fort Maurepas has been reconstructed in Ocean Springs, Mississippi.

BUILDING OTHER FORTS

The incident at English Turn convinced Iberville that a fort was needed on the Mississippi River. He chose a spot fifty-four miles above the mouth of the river. There, Fort de la Boulaye (usually called Fort Mississippi) was built in 1700. From this location, the fort could protect French claims to the river. Iberville placed his brother Bienville in charge of the fort.

Fort Maurepas, the French headquarters, also needed to be moved. Problems often developed with the first site chosen for a fort, and the forts were relocated several times during these early years. The first site

This painting of Fort Louis shows the fort as it might have appeared in the early 1700s.

for Fort Maurepas had flooded, and the sandy soil was useless for growing crops. The new fort, Fort Louis, was located where it would keep the English out of Mobile Bay. The fort later became the city of Mobile, Alabama. Henri de Tonti had returned to Louisiana to help with the new colony and for a time commanded Fort Louis. Tonti, however, died of yellow fever in 1704.

After setting up the new fort at Mobile, Iberville went back to France again. While he was there, the War of Spanish Succession broke out. The war had the full attention of the French government, and Iberville's request for colonists and supplies for Louisiana was ignored. The war created unrest and hard times in France and an even more dismal life in the colony. French supply ships sailed to places considered more important to the war effort. Abandoned, the colony was left without proper defense or assistance at a time when it was still very shaky.

Do You Remember?
1. Which countries tried to stop French efforts to colonize Louisiana?
2. Where was the first French fort established along the Gulf of Mexico?
3. How did Bienville keep the English away from the Mississippi River?

LOUISIANA AS A PROPRIETORSHIP

In 1701, young Bienville became the leader of the colony. The colony was so weak that Bienville had to obtain food from the French colony at Saint-Domingue and even from the Spanish at Pensacola. Iberville never did return to the colony. In 1702, he left Europe for Louisiana but died in Havana from yellow fever.

These two leaders of early Louisiana did not totally avoid controversy. After Iberville's death, an investigation was made of rumors that he had taken advantage of the war to make money for himself. Disgruntled officials or priests passed along to France various complaints against Bienville. However, Bienville's many supporters denied the complaints and blamed the problems on those who had complained.

The colonial officials quarreled throughout the French period. The structure of the colonial government contributed to many of those quarrels. The governor was usually a naval officer who was in charge of both the military and general administration. The *commissary commissioner*, or business manager, was in charge of the budget and certain parts of the judicial system. The responsibilities of the governor and the commissary commissioner made the power structure unclear and required the two officials to supervise each other.

Antoine Crozat, a French businessman who had loaned money to King Louis XIV, was the first proprietor of the Louisiana colony.

ANTOINE CROZAT

After the War of Spanish Succession ended, France once again turned its attention to Louisiana. The French king and his government were almost bankrupt because of the war, and the treasury could not really afford to maintain Louisiana. But France needed the colony as a buffer against the English. The well-established English colonies were pushing further and further inland to trade with the Indians.

France could keep the colony only if a new source of funding could be found. King Louis XIV decided to try the proprietory plan. A **proprietorship** gave an individual a charter (or contract) to operate the colony as a business. The proprietor was given almost total control and, in return, had to meet certain requirements. The proprietor had to send supplies and settlers to the colony regularly, and the colonial government had to follow French law.

In 1712, the French royal government gave the proprietorship of Louisiana to Antoine Crozat (KRO zah). This businessman had loaned money to the king from his vast fortune. To make more money, Crozat expected to find gold and silver mines in the colony. He had little interest in settlers and agriculture; his primary motive was profit.

After Crozat signed the contract for this new business venture, he selected a new governor for the colony. He chose an experienced colonial governor, Antoine de Lamothe, Sieur de Cadillac. Cadillac had set up a trading post that later became Detroit. Despite that success, Cadillac had difficulties as a leader and soon faced problems in his new appointment. His troubles began when he visited Indian villages along the river and refused to smoke the calumet when it was offered. (The calumet was the ceremonial pipe used by the tribal leaders.) Cadillac's refusal was more than an insult to his hosts; it was like a threat of war.

As governor, Cadillac had other difficulties. Some people complained of his abrasive personality. He also had to deal with the ongoing conflicts among government officials and the awkward organization that made those conflicts worse. But he deserves credit for his efforts to improve the colony. One of those improvements was in the organization of the colony. In 1712, he established the **Superior Council** to help govern the colony. The Council was in charge of judicial matters and was presided over by the commissary commissioner.

Some of Cadillac's ideas, such as taming buffalo to clip the wool, were completely impractical and must have amused the Indians. But he was the first official to suggest that cash crops, such as indigo and tobacco, be developed. **Cash crops** are those that are raised to make a profit. He also understood that colonists were essential, and he tried to convince Crozat to send more people to Louisiana.

Above: *The indigo plant produced a blue dye much valued in Europe. It was one of the colony's first cash crops.* **Opposite:** *Fort St. Jean Baptiste was reconstructed in Natchitoches using local materials and eighteenth-century technology. This photograph shows the interior of "Maison du Garde Magasin," the private quarters of the official appointed by the king to manage trade at the fort.*

NATCHITOCHES

Another of Cadillac's positive actions was selecting Louis Juchereau de St. Denis to establish a fort at Natchitoches. St. Denis was already familiar with this area, having earlier explored along the Red River. He had met the inhabitants, the Caddo Indians, and improved his knowledge of the Indian languages. These skills, his diplomacy, and his natural ability as a frontiersman built a career and a reputation for this Canadian-born, Paris-educated military officer.

Crozat and Cadillac needed to make a profit from the colony and wanted to build trade with the Spanish. Trade with outsiders was illegal in the Spanish colonies, but the French decided that the isolated presidios (forts) in Spanish Texas might be willing to overlook those laws.

St. Denis built Fort St. Jean Baptiste (present-day Natchitoches) on the banks of the Red River in 1714 to serve as his base of operations. Then he headed south to see if he could establish trade with the Spanish. At the Spanish fort in what is now Eagle Pass, Texas, he was detained but considered a guest. While he was there, he fell in love with and courted the granddaughter of the commandant.

Before the two could marry, however, the commandant sent St. Denis to Mexico City. The viceroy (the highest-ranking Spanish official) told St. Denis that trade between the Spanish colonies and French Louisiana would not be allowed. But rather than jailing him as a smuggler, the viceroy asked St. Denis to escort a Spanish priest and soldiers to Nacogdoches, Texas, to reopen an old mission and fort. The next time St. Denis returned to Texas, the new Spanish viceroy did not welcome him. He was jailed and then warned to stay out of Spanish territory.

But the Spanish colonists continued to trade with St. Denis, who now had a Spanish wife. The contraband (illegal) trade continued to be important to the border forts. French traders brought in pack trains with guns, ammunition, powder, knives, mirrors, and brandy to exchange for horses, cattle, animal hides, and silver. The Spanish wanted the French goods, especially medicine; the French wanted the Spanish silver.

Fort St. Jean Baptiste (top) is now a State Commemorative Area. Outdoor exhibits (above) and demonstrations (opposite, above) show visitors what life was like at the fort in the early 1700s. Eglise de St. Francois (opposite, below) is the reconstructed church at the fort.

NATCHITOCHES

A good place to see the early French history of Louisiana is in Natchitoches. The town was an important river landing. Just north of town, the towering red banks of the Red River are still called Grand Ecore, "big bluff" in French. A reconstruction of Fort St. Jean Baptiste hints of the French colonial life on the frontier.

Natchitoches is the oldest permanent settlement in the Louisiana Purchase. The historical district contains a number of houses built before 1850. The oldest house was built in the French colonial style in 1776, and others are almost as old. As the region became more settled and prosperous, plantation families added a second house in town. These elegant homes were their Nachitoches headquarters for church, business, and social events.

The biggest party in Natchitoches today — the Festival of Lights — is held in December, when thousands of visitors crowd the brick streets for a celebration of yesterday and today. The names of those brick streets honor the French who gave the town its yesterday. Today, it is neither hide canoes nor cypress pirogues but lighted party barges that cruise Cane River Lake . Reflections of thousands of Christmas lights sparkle in the calm water. Sharing the riverbanks with Santa Claus, angels, and Christmas trees is a large display decorated with a *fleur de lis*. The lights proclaim "Natchitoches, founded 1714."

Above: *Many of the early homes in Natchitoches have been restored, like the Lemee House, built in 1837.* **Right:** *The Ackel-Dranquet House, built in 1820, may have been the first brick house in Natchitoches.*

Above: *Many of the shops along Front Street have cast iron balconies, resembling those in the French Quarter of New Orleans.* **Left:** *The Tante-Huppé House, built in the 1820s, has been restored and is now a bed & breakfast.*

At the Fort St. Jean Baptiste State Commemorative Area, "interpreters" dress in colonial attire and answer questions from visitors.

CROZAT'S FAILURE

The colony, however, continued to struggle. When Louis XIV died in 1715, government support for the colony died too. The French settlers were for the most part not interested in agriculture. Trade with the Spanish was possible only through smuggling because the Spanish government would not ease its restrictions. Trade with the Indians was a failure because neither Crozat nor Cadillac encouraged it. British traders paid more for furs and sold European goods to the Indians cheaper.

As a businessman, Crozat failed to make a profit from the colony. He never sent the colonists supplies in the amounts required by his contract. He considered any money he spent on the colony as an expense, not as an investment that could lead to future profits. His biggest disappointment was that there were no gold or silver mines. The promised riches did not exist. With his business venture a major loss, Crozat surrendered the charter in 1717.

Do You Remember?

1. Why did the structure of the French colonial government cause problems in the colony?
2. Why did the French government try a proprietorship for the Louisiana colony?
3. Why did St. Denis go to Texas?

THE COMPANY OF THE WEST

The next proprietor of the colony was not an individual but a group of investors who pooled their money. The head of this group of investors — John Law — had organized the Bank of France and developed the paper money system for France. Law was considered to be a brilliant financier. But, he was also a gambler and a speculator. A **speculator** is one who buys items (such as land) hoping they will increase in value and, when sold, provide a profit.

In 1717, Law created the Company of the West, an investment company, to take over the proprietorship of the Louisiana colony. Law sold stock (shares of ownership) in the Company to individual investors. His goal was to make money for the investors as well as to increase income for the French government and improve the French economy. The Company of the West later expanded by buying other trading companies. In 1719, it became the Company of the Indies and was granted the right to coin all the French money and collect all taxes.

Law convinced people that the Louisiana colony would make a huge profit. The chance to share in this profit convinced more and more people to buy shares in the Company. The value of the Company began to rise. At one point, the price of a share increased from 500 to 18,000 livres (the French unit of money).

Meanwhile Law made plans to operate the colony. In 1718, Bienville was brought back as governor of the colony. Bienville had long wanted to build a town that would serve as a commercial center for the Mississippi Valley. Now, with the financial backing of the Company, he could begin his project. The site he had chosen was on a crescent (bend) of the Mississippi River and bordered by Lake Pontchartrain. In 1718, Bienville and the king's engineers designed and laid out the city of New Orleans. When he and his men arrived at the location, they had to chop

John Law killed a man in a duel in Scotland in 1694. He was arrested, jailed, and sentenced to death, but he escaped to Holland. In 1716, he bought a bank in France with money he acquired by gambling. A short time later, he obtained his lease on lands in America.

This illustration shows an early camp at New Biloxi that was home to some of John Law's early settlers.

their way through river cane as large as their legs while watching carefully for the alligators they heard roaring nearby.

However, this swampy wilderness could not become the new trading center without more people. All of the directors of the Company received large **land grants**, parcels of land given to the directors under the condition that they bring settlers to the colony. The plan seemed practical, but who would go to this faraway wilderness? The French peasants (poor, small farmers) did not want to go because life in Louisiana did not sound any better than their lives in France. The stories from Louisiana had been confusing during those early years. Frustrated fathers had threatened to send their misbehaving sons to the colony as punishment. Was it an untamed paradise or a cruel punishment?

A Search for Colonists

To change the image of Louisiana, Law launched one of the earliest real estate ad campaigns. When the French did not respond, he targeted an area of Europe where there had been a number of lengthy wars. The German farmers he hoped to attract read his glowing descriptions on handbills printed in their own language. Partly because of what they

read, and partly because their present situation offered no hope, they risked the change.

When these German farm families came to the colony, they settled on land above New Orleans. The French called this settlement *Cote Des Allemandes*, the German Coast. Those experienced and hard-working German farmers cleared the land and planted gardens. They are credited with saving the colony because they produced enough food to keep the people from starving. In fact, the people in the new settlement of New Orleans were so happy to see the food that, at one point, soldiers had to be dispatched to keep order.

Even more settlers were needed. Unfortunately, the next effort did not bring industrious farmers like the Germans. When no volunteers could be found, prisoners were sent to the colony instead of to jail. At first, the prisoners were nondangerous criminals such as debtors and smugglers. But these prisoners were still not enough. Before long, the new arrivals included more dangerous criminals, who were unwilling or unable to work.

More of a concern to the people in France was the search for vagrants (homeless persons) to ship to the colony. The Company paid a "finder's fee" for locating potential colonists; soon, citizens with jobs and families were being kidnapped to collect the finder's fee. Eventually, however, the king and the people halted these practices. But ending the exportation of the unwilling colonists did not end the problems.

Colonists complained that the Company never sent enough flour, fabric, wine, brandy, shirts, or shoes. When goods were available, they cost four times as much as they had in France. And when flour did arrive, it was usually bug-infested. The lack of flour was a major problem for the colony. Wheat would not grow in the warm climate, and the French did not consider corn a proper food. They especially hated corn bread, because wheat bread had long been the mainstay of the French diet. Occasionally, wheat was sent down the river from the Illinois country so the colonists could bake "proper" bread.

John Law's power and influence in France increased when he was appointed comptroller general, the official in charge of money for the French government. But when the Mississippi bubble burst in 1721, he had to flee Paris in disgrace.

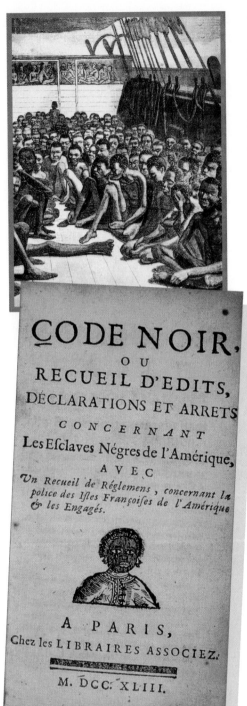

The Collapse of the Mississippi Bubble

As the colony struggled with these shortages and hardships, Law's publicity campaign was still promising that huge profits were just around the corner. People in France were still willing to invest in the hopes of making more money. The Company expanded, and the price of the stock rose — until the bubble burst. When the investors began to suspect that their investment was worthless, they withdrew their money. The Company collapsed because it did not have enough to pay back the investors. By 1721, the end had come to this huge risk, which was later called the **Mississippi Bubble**.

When the scheme collapsed, so did the world of John Law. Law's power and influence in France had increased when he was appointed comptroller general, the official in charge of money for the French government. But after the financial disaster in Louisiana, he had to flee Paris in disgrace.

The Company of the Indies, however, continued its responsibility for the colony because the king still did not want to bear the expenses of the colony. But to keep Louisiana alive, the French government could no longer ignore certain issues. The colony needed an adequate army, more dependable settlers, and a good export crop. This would require more money than the king wanted to spend, so the Company was given a new agreement. Bienville continued as governor, because he was considered the person most capable of dealing with the problems.

THE CODE NOIR

A **slave** is a person who is bound to a life of service to others and who is considered property. Shiploads of slaves were first brought to the colony in 1716. The numbers continued to increase, especially during the proprietorship of the Company. The slaves came from West Africa, where their cultures had long harvested rice and indigo. The Africans' ability to cultivate rice added another staple food to the diet of the colony. Their knowledge and experience also led to indigo and tobacco becoming Louisiana's first cash crops.

The large amounts of land available in the new colonies meant that vast areas could be planted once they were cleared. The **plantations** (large estates or farms) focused on one cash crop, growing as much of the crop as possible to make a profit. A tremendous amount of labor was needed to clear the land and produce the crops. At that time, slavery was an accepted way to obtain the large numbers of workers needed for the plantation agriculture system.

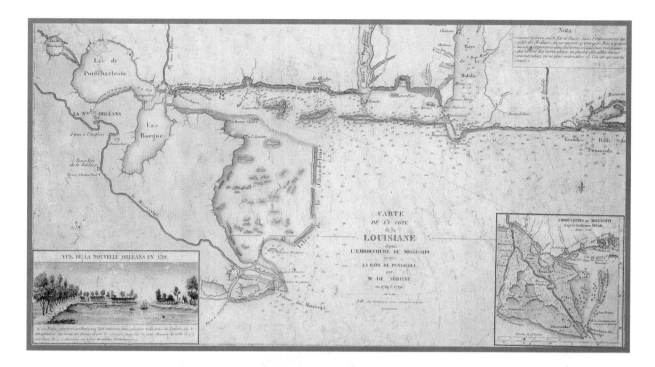

The slaves had also been essential in building New Orleans. Not only did they provide strong labor, but many were skilled at carpentry and metalwork. From the early years, the colony depended heavily on slavery for its success.

Nevertheless, the colony had to have a way to manage the increasing number of slaves. To do that, Bienville established the **Code Noir**, a set of laws governing the conduct of the slaves. Not only did these laws regulate slavery, but they also expelled Jews from the colony.

The laws, established in 1724, were patterned after laws governing slaves in other French colonies. Their purpose was to protect slaves as property. Rules were established for food, clothing, and health care. Slaves could not be forced to work on Sundays, and they were to be instructed in the Catholic faith.

The laws also established many restrictions on the slaves. They were not allowed to carry weapons unless they were hunting, and they could not assemble in crowds. The laws set out harsh penalties for runaway slaves.

A NEW GOVERNOR

During these years, Bienville continued to face criticism and complaints that seemed a constant part of the colonial government. Because he was governor, the settlers blamed him when things went wrong. The Company and the king blamed him because the colony was not profitable. Finally, he was ordered back to France to explain his decisions for the colony.

Above: The Louisiana coast and the area around New Orleans is depicted in this map by de Serigny, drawn around 1719-1720. **Opposite:** *Following the first shiploads of slaves brought to the colony in 1716, the numbers continued to increase (above). To manage this larger number of slaves, Bienville established the* Code Noir, *a set of laws governing the conduct of the slaves (below).*

The Company chose one of its own dependable, highly respected employees as the next governor — Etienne de Perier (PAH re a). Perier was sent to bring harmony to the colony. While he had no knowledge of or experience with the Louisiana colony, Perier was well respected in the French navy. His sense of fairness helped him deal with the problems, even without any colonial experience.

The recruitment of new settlers was one of Perier's priorities. To provide some economic stability for the colony, he was also expected to find more raw materials for export. He saw the forests of Louisiana as a source of resin, tar, and wood for barrels and ships' masts, all of which were needed in France. Perier also wanted to improve trade with the successful colonies of the West Indies and asked the French government to help.

However, an incident that took place while Perier was governor eventually led to the end of the proprietorship.

THE NATCHEZ UPRISING

In 1729, Captain Chépart (SHA pa) was the commander at Fort Rosalie. Bienville had built the fort in 1716 at the site of present-day Natchez on land belonging to the Natchez Indians. Early French visitors had described this tribe as the most civilized. The Natchez permitted the French fort in their homelands and were helpful to the colonists. A tobacco plantation had grown up around the fort. A crisis arose when Captain Chépart wanted the good land on which a Natchez sacred village stood. Chépart demanded that the Natchez move immediately.

Deciding that the French would never stop intruding on their land and lifestyle, the Natchez attacked Fort Rosalie without warning. Na-

This Alexandre de Batz drawing shows the Natchez Sun King being carried on a litter.

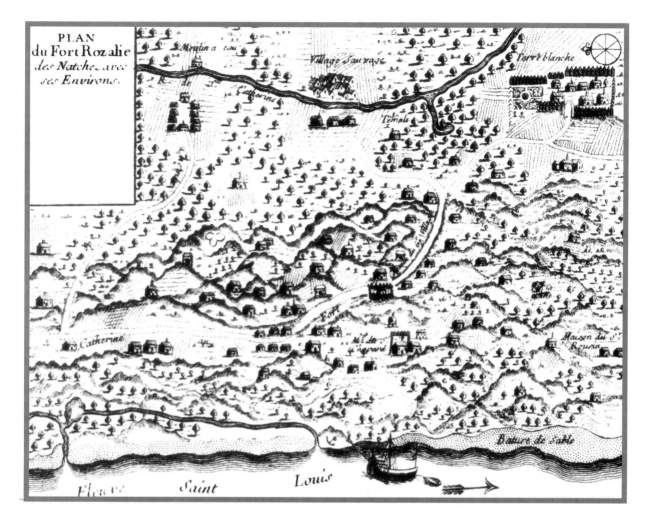

Bienville established Fort Rosalie in 1716 on a bluff above the Mississippi River on land that once belonged to the Natchez Indians. Note the Indian village (labeled "Village Sauvage") in the top center.

tive American historians call this event the Natchez uprising. Over 250 French colonists were killed. The French considered this a deceitful massacre, because it was so different from their idea of warfare.

Perier retaliated by destroying the Natchez as a tribe and scattering the few survivors. The French, however, held him responsible for the massacre because he had not intervened when Chépart first angered the Natchez. In addition, the French lost their most successful agricultural venture because few settlers wanted to stay in the area.

This loss and the poor morale were too much for the Company. The colony had never made any money for the Company, and the French government had never paid its share of administrative costs. By 1731, the Company handed the colony back to the king.

Do You Remember?

1. What was the purpose of the Company of the West?
2. How did the German settlers help save the colony?
3. Why did the Natchez Indians finally attack the French?

In 1732, Louisiana once more became a royal colony. France would hold on to the colony for another thirty troublesome years.

BIENVILLE BECOMES GOVERNOR ONCE MORE

When the king took control, Bienville was once again appointed governor of Louisiana. Many colonists were glad to see him return because of his experiences with the Indians. There was now great fear and resentment toward the Indians. Bienville's first task was to calm the settlers and restore his alliances with the Indians. He also faced other challenges.

Bienville recognized that the colony must be able to take care of itself. A thriving agriculture was important for success. But a shortage of livestock — farm animals such as horses, cows, pigs, chickens, and oxen — in the colony created hardships for everyone. The cows, pigs, and chickens provided much-needed food. The oxen and horses were needed for agricultural work, pulling the plows and carts. But what use was a team of oxen if the colonist had no plow? Even when good tools came from France, the prices were often too high for the people to buy them.

Another serious problem was the inadequate supply of money. There was little **specie** (gold or silver) in the colony. The colonists had not yet developed a stable cash crop, although some tobacco and indigo were being grown. The colonists continued to try to export forest products. But there were few ships available to transport goods, and those that were available charged high shipping rates. As a result, the colonists usually had to rely on barter and warehouse credit. That is, if the colonists could not get goods in return for their furs or crops, they were given credit to obtain the goods they needed when they became available.

Bienville struggled to ease the difficulties in the colony. He rationed the food supplies when necessary and pleaded with France for more supplies and soldiers.

WAR WITH THE CHICKASAW

The biggest problem Bienville faced, however, was the increased difficulty in keeping peace between the colonists and the Indians. Even before the Europeans came, relations between and among the tribes were not always peaceful. Some of the hostilities were long standing; others were more recent. Both the French and the British used these hostilities to pit one tribe against another for their own benefit. Each group struggled over the land and trade rights.

The Native Americans also recognized that their way of life was under attack. The presence of the European traders had changed the

Bienville (opposite) was the younger brother of Iberville. He was the founder of New Orleans. This statue of Bienville (above) stands in the the State Capitol in Baton Rouge.

existence of the Indians. The older chiefs lamented the increasing dependence on European trade goods. Tattooed Serpent, a chief of the Natchez, remarked, "Before the arrival of the French we lived like men who could be satisfied with what they have . . . now we are like slaves who are not allowed to do as they please."

The Choctaw generally preferred the French, although British trade goods were of much better quality and were delivered more dependably. The Choctaw chiefs were not above playing one colony against another for the benefit of their people. However, the French alliance with the Choctaw had been weakened by Governor Perier. He had insisted on the right to select chiefs, rewarding medals to many as he tried to gain allies. These "medal chiefs" were not always the tribal leaders and had no real power. By negotiating only with the medal chiefs, Governor Perier had disrupted the traditional tribal ways.

The Chickasaw occupied the important heart of the Mississippi Valley. They were trading partners and allies with the British and were enemies of the French and the Choctaw. The French became alarmed when the Chickasaw appeared to be making peace with their former enemies, the Choctaw. The French feared that the Choctaw might then also become trading partners and allies of the British. Such a situation would threaten France's claims and control of the Mississippi River and the Louisiana territory.

When Bienville returned as governor, he relied on his previous experiences with the Louisiana tribes. He demanded respect, using the Indians' own customs of tribal warfare. But this time, Bienville did so in the face of a shaky alliance with the Choctaw, the increasing power of the Chickasaw, and British interference.

After the Natchez uprising, some of the surviving Natchez had taken refuge among the Chickasaw. To show his power, Bienville demanded that the Chickasaw give up those Natchez to the French. The Chickasaw refused, and that refusal was intended as an insult. Bienville planned an attack.

Alexandre de Batz painted this Choctaw family in the 1730s. Notice the warriors have scalps hanging from their spears. The French paid the Choctaw for Chickasaw scalps.

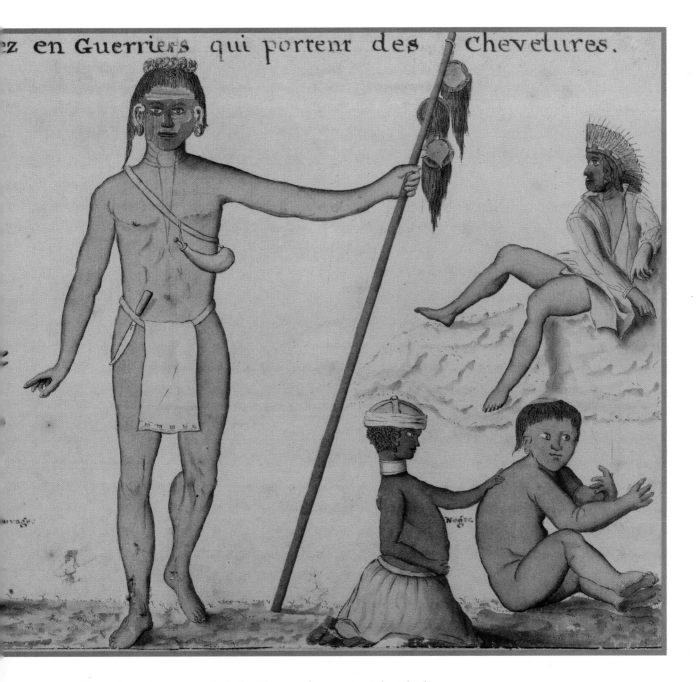

z en Guerriers qui portent des Chevelures.

First, a French commander led a Choctaw force against the Chickasaw. As the fighting increased, both the British and the French encouraged their Indian allies. The British supplied the Chickasaw with guns and ammunition; the French paid the Choctaw for Chickasaw scalps. At the same time, the British were promoting peace between the Choctaw and the Chickasaw. The Choctaw were tiring of the war, and the British were hoping to eventually gain control of trade with the Choctaw.

Meanwhile, Bienville received orders from France: He must defeat the Chickasaw or sign a peace treaty, and he must act quickly for the glory of

France. Bienville, however, had only about two hundred soldiers with which to fight the Chickasaw. With such a small army, he knew he could not march into Chickasaw territory and defeat them.

In 1736, he requested more troops from the commander of the Illinois country, Pierre d'Artaguette. D'Artaguette and his men arrived at the meeting place before Bienville. Instead of waiting for Bienville's forces, d'Artaguette attacked. The French forces were defeated, and d'Artaguette and some of his men were captured. When Bienville and his troops arrived a short time later, they too were defeated by the Chickasaw. The French had suffered a terrible blow, not only in the loss of life but also to their honor and to their standing with other Indian tribes. Bienville returned to the colony mourning the deaths of his friends.

France and Bienville tried to avenge their defeat. Several thousand troops, some from as far away as Canada, were sent to Chickasaw territory. There were more skirmishes (minor battles), and the war dragged on for over four years. Neither side achieved a true victory, although the Chickasaw eventually requested a peace treaty. Bienville described the results of his later meeting with the Chickasaw as "a peace of sorts."

Bienville viewed the Chickasaw War as a failure. Discouraged, he retired as governor in 1742. Bienville had lost the war, many friends, and his confidence.

Pierre Francois de Rigaud, Marquis de Vaudreuil, was appointed governor of the Louisiana colony at the age of thirty-nine.

A DIFFERENT KIND OF GOVERNOR

In 1742, the French government sent Pierre Francois de Rigaud, Marquis de Vaudreuil (VO drey) to Louisiana as the next governor. Louisiana offered Vaudreuil the opportunity to prove his ability as a leader. He hoped to become governor of Canada, as his father had been. His kindness and dignity calmed some of the internal conflicts among the many factions in the colony.

Cooperation among the colonists was important because Vaudreuil too had to contend with Indian conflicts. The new governor used his troops aggressively to halt Indian raids on settlements up and down the Mississippi River. After a major assault on the Chickasaw, Vaudreuil negotiated a final peace.

With the Indian threat reduced, the colony grew fairly prosperous and living conditions improved in New Orleans. As governor, Vaudreuil established formal ceremonies and parties that imitated the social life of the court at Versailles, the palace of the French king. His wife traveled the muddy streets of New Orleans in a four-horse carriage. He is even credited with having the first Louisiana Mardi Gras ball. As a compliment to his style, he was called "The Grand Marquis." The reception welcoming the next governor included fountains of wine and a fireworks show.

THE LAST ROYAL GOVERNOR

In 1752, Vaudreuil was appointed governor of Canada. Louis Billouart, Chevalier de Kerlerec (KAIR la rek) was appointed governor of the colony because of his strong military reputation. Those skills were needed to protect Louisiana from the British. When Kerlerec took office, the tensions between the French and the British were increasing and the stage for the French and Indian War was being set. The colony's defenses had to be strengthened.

Unfortunately, like other governors before him, Kerlerec became caught up in squabbles with the commissary commissioner. Kerlerec was a stern, blunt military man who found these arguments petty and annoying. The constant friction and the complaints sent to France interfered with Kerlarec's efforts on behalf of the colony and slowed its progress. The frustration of not having authority over the commissary commissioner must have also been difficult for this strong military commander. He quickly tired of his post and requested permission to leave. However, he remained as governor until 1762, when the colony was given to Spain.

Louis Billouart, Chevalier de Kerlerec, was the last royal French governor in Louisiana.

THE STRUGGLE TO SURVIVE

Did the French colony do as well as it could have under the whims and regulations of France? Did the hurricanes, mosquitoes, heat, and humidity overwhelm the colonists? Or, as so many historians have suggested, were the first colonists such a poor choice that they must be held responsible for the weaknesses of the colony?

Many of the early explorers and promoters were hardy French Canadians. The free-spirited woodsmen or *coureror-de-bois* ("woods runner" in French) came and went from the colony, preferring their

independent lifestyle to settling down in the colony. The early French colonists lacked the skills and drive needed to survive in the harsh environment. Many were more interested in looking for gold and silver than in making a home and life for themselves in the New World. It took the hardy German farmers to save the colony. And it was the labor of the African slaves that led to the economic growth of the colony.

The second Ursuline Convent, built in 1748-1753, is the only surviving building from the French Colonial period. Today it houses the archives of the Archdiocese of New Orleans.

Even the soldiers were considered the rejects of the army by their own leaders. On the other hand, their pay was low, and they often did not have enough food or clothing.

Women were scarce in the colony, and their absence contributed to the instability. At various times during the French colonial period, young women were sent to the colony. In 1712, Madame Cadillac chaperoned a group of girls sent to Louisiana to become brides of the settlers. After 1727, the Ursuline nuns cared for new arrivals at their convent in New Orleans until they were married. The best known of this group were the **casket girls** who came in 1728. The young women received that title because each girl brought her trousseau, or household goods, in a casket, or barrel-like chest. Some of the other women who came from France brought no trousseaus, just a bad reputation. These were women from the streets of Paris, who were shipped to the colony to get them out of France.

Choosing the right people for the colony was not the only challenge. The French colonial government suffered greatly from decisions made in France. These included trade restrictions and the lack of adequate funding and supplies. Every policy decision about Louisiana was made by those who had never seen the colony. No policy makers — Louis XIV, the royal advisors, Crozat, or John Law — ever ventured across the Atlantic to see the vast land they called Louisiana.

Do You Remember?
1. What mistake did Perier make with the Indians?
2. What actions by the Chickasaw led to Bienville's attack?
3. Who was the last royal governor?
4. Why did the casket girls come to Louisiana?

SUMMARY

In the late 1600s and 1700s, France struggled with Great Britain and Spain for control of North America. French explorations of the Mississippi River led to the discovery that it drained into the Gulf of Mexico. After French explorer La Salle claimed this territory for France, Louis XIV sent Iberville to protect his claim. The Spanish tried to stop the French with a fort at Pensacola Bay. The British also challenged the French with their nearby colonies.

The colony of Louisiana struggled through years of neglect. Lack of food and support from France created miserable conditions. The Indians accepted the colonists at first but soon resented them as intruders. When the colony became a financial burden to the king, he turned its management over to proprietors. The colony was never profitable, although conditions had improved by the end of the French period.

CHAPTER · REVIEW

1680	1690	1700	1710	1720	1730	1740	1750	1760

1673 Marquette and Joliet explored upper Mississippi

1682 La Salle claimed Louisiana for France

1699 Iberville established Fort Maurepas

1714 Natchitoches founded

1712 Crozat became a proprietor

1717 Company of the West became Louisiana proprietor

1718 New Orleans founded

1729 Natchez Uprising

1736 Chickasaw War

1762 France transferred Louisiana to Spain

1740 The population of the thirteen British colonies reached 1.5 million

1690 English East India Company founded the city of Calcutta, India

1736 John Wesley, founder of the Methodist church, arrived in Georgia

1682 Peter the Great became tzar of Russia

1732 Benjamin Franklin published *Poor Richard's Almanac*

1680 Rise of the Asante kingdom in West Africa

Reviewing People, Places, and Terms

Define, identify, or explain the importance of the following.

1. Jean Baptiste Le Moyne, Sieur de Bienville
2. cash crop
3. casket girls
4. Code Noir
5. colony
6. expedition
7. Pierre Le Moyne, Sieur d'Iberville
8. René Robert Cavelier, Sieur de La Salle
9. land grant
10. John Law
11. Mississippi Bubble
12. Northwest Passage
13. plantation
14. proprietorship
15. slave
16. specie
17. speculator
18. Superior Council

Understanding the Facts

1. Why were the French exploring North American waterways?
2. Why was La Salle never able to establish a colony in Louisiana?
3. Why was Louisiana deprived of supplies and leadership from France?
4. Why were colonists so important to the settlement of Louisiana?
5. How did John Law convince people to buy shares in the Company of the West?
6. Why did neither proprietorship work?
7. How did the death of Louis XIV affect the colony?
8. Why was life so hard for the French soldiers sent to Louisiana?

Developing Critical Thinking

1. How did mercantilism set off the struggle to control North America?
2. What was the significance of English Turn?

1. Locate these places, established in the French colonial period, on a Louisiana map: Baton Rouge, les Allemands (German Coast), Natchitoches, New Orleans, Pointe Coupee, Poste de Attakapas (St. Martinville), Poste de Opelousas (Opelousas), Poste de Rapides (Pineville).
2. Using a present-day Louisiana map, make a list of the French place names you find.

Special Projects

1. Much of what we know about French Louisiana comes from the journals of people who lived at that time. Think of a recent event that might give someone in the future insight into the lives of students today. Write a journal entry describing this event.

2. Archaeologists excavating early French Louisiana settlements have found artifacts that tell the stories of the past. Gather ten "artifacts" that an archaeologist two hundred years in the future might use to tell *your* story. Share these items and their significance with the class.

Making Connections

1. How could knowing longitude have helped La Salle?
2. How did Harrison's skills as a clockmaker help solve the problem of longitude?

Louisiana Lagniape

• Berries from the myrtle wax shrub were boiled to make wax. Colonists hoped to get rich exporting this candle wax to Europe.

• BUILDING SKILLS: FINDING THE MAIN IDEA •

When you read about a topic, don't try to remember every detail. Identifying the main idea of a paragraph will help you organize information and remember more of what you read.

The main idea of a whole paragraph is often stated in the first sentence of the paragraph. The other sentences in the paragraph provide supporting details.

The main idea of the following paragraph is stated in the first sentence. The other sentences in the paragraph provide the supporting details.

The king charged Iberville with establishing a base from which to control the mouth of the Mississippi River. Iberville first had to explore the land near the river and choose a location for his headquarters. That site must also be a good location for a colony. Mercantilism required that the colony provide raw materials for manufacturers in France and serve as a market for French manufactured goods. Conditions in the colony itself were secondary. This attitude was one reason why the colony struggled from its beginnings.

What are some of the details provided by the other sentences? You are correct if you said that the fort had to be near the river, that the site had to be a good location for a colony, that the colony was expected to provide raw materials to France and buy its finished goods, and that the king did not really care about the conditions in the colony.

Do you think it is necessary to remember all the details in the paragraph? If not, which ones do you think are most important? It is not necessary to remember all details, but try to pick out the major fact from a paragraph.

Read the second paragraph under the head "Colonizing Louisiana" on page 200 and answer the following questions.

1. What is the main idea of the paragraph?
2. Which sentence in the paragraph states the main idea?
3. Which sentences in the paragraph provide supporting details?
4. For what reason did the Spanish build a fort at Pensacola Bay?

CHAPTER SEVEN

LOUISIANA'S SPANISH COLONIAL ERA: STABILITY AND SUCCESS

My position is most extraordinary. I command for the King of France and at the same time I govern the colony as if it belonged to the King of Spain.
— Charles Philippe Aubrey,
Acting Governor of Louisiana, 1765-1766

THE STRUGGLE FOR NORTH AMERICA ESCALATED. From 1689 to 1763, France, Spain, and Great Britain fought a series of wars in Europe and in North America. The names of the wars changed, and the official reasons for them changed too. Sometimes a war started when a king died and a struggle resulted over who would hold the power. One war was called the "War of Jenkins' Ear" because the Spanish cut off the ear of a smuggling British sea captain.

The key war in this long list was called the Seven Years' War in Europe and the French and Indian War in America. The British colonists called it the French and Indian War because they fought against the French and their Indian allies. The British victory in the war sent France home to Europe. The French colony planted on the Mississippi sixty-three years earlier now belonged to Spain.

Destrehan Plantation is the oldest surviving Creole-style plantation home in the Mississippi Valley. The main part of the house was built from 1787 to 1790 by Charles, a free man of color.

CHAPTER · PREVIEW

Terms: French and Indian War, rebellion, treason, Cabildo, imports, surveyor, neutral, ally, militia, siege, right of deposit

People: Jean-Jacques-Balise d'Abbadie; Antonio de Ulloa; Charles Philippe Aubry; Alejandro O'Reilly; Luis de Unzaga y Amezaga; Bernardo de Gálvez; Esteban Rodriguez Miro; Francois-Louis Hector, Baron de Carondelet et Noyelles; Etienne de Boré

Places: Florida Parishes, Nova Scotia, Monroe

George Washington, a colonel in the Virginia militia, was defeated in a skirmish with a French scouting party near present-day Pittsburgh. That clash ignited a war in both Europe and America.

THE FRENCH AND INDIAN WAR

By the 1750s, the French had pushed into the Ohio River Valley, intending to control the fur trade of the area. The British were eyeing the same territory. The British government wanted the fur trade, and its colonists wanted the land. A young George Washington led a troop of Virginians to investigate the French activity near present-day Pittsburgh. He warned the French to get out, but they refused.

When the British tried to force their claims to the area in 1754, the French retaliated. Thus began the **French and Indian War**. The heaviest fighting between Great Britain and France took place in Canada, which had long been the center of their struggle. In 1758, the French lost Fort Louisburg, which protected the approach to the St. Lawrence River. The loss of this stronghold opened the way to the heart of New France. Quebec fell to the British on September 18, 1759; the French surrendered Montreal almost exactly one year later. The British continued to seize French territory, but fighting shifted to other areas.

Spain entered the war in 1762 to help the French. The kings of France and Spain had signed an earlier agreement, the Family Compact of 1757, pledging to support each other. These royal relatives were cousins, both of the Bourbon dynasty.

RESULTS OF THE FRENCH AND INDIAN WAR

The fighting ended in North America in 1760, but a settlement was not signed until 1763. In the Treaty of Paris, the three European nations divided up North America as a war prize. Spain traded Florida to Great Britain in return for Cuba, which the British had captured during the war. Spain needed its port of Havana back because the silver-laden Spanish ships from Mexico always stopped there before heading home.

Spanish Florida became British. What was once British East Florida is today the state of Florida. British West Florida is now part of Louisiana, Mississippi, and Alabama. Louisiana residents still call this section of our state "the Florida Parishes."

France lost all of its land in North America, which pleased the British. Great Britain received Canada and the French territory that lay east of the Mississippi River. The French colony of Louisiana became a Spanish possession. The British diplomats were also pleased with this transfer and hoped that operating this expensive colony would further weaken Spain.

Spain and France, however, had already transferred Louisiana — in 1762, during the war. They had negotiated a secret treaty, the Treaty of Fountainebleu. France had needed a loan and military assistance from Spain. In payment, France gave up Louisiana west of the Mississippi

British General Edward Braddock was sent to America in 1754. His continental style of fighting made him and his army easy targets for the French and the Indians. Braddock was mortally wounded in a battle near present-day Pittsburgh. His death and the defeat of his army was a terrible blow to the British.

and the "Isle of Orleans." The arrangement was hidden from Great Britain, because it might have affected the war and its results. If the British knew Louisiana already belonged to Spain, they might have demanded the colony in the war settlement. They did try to bargain for New Orleans, but failed. The capital of the French colony became the capital of Spanish Louisiana.

SPAIN ACCEPTS LOUISIANA

The Spanish government anticipated the big expense of its new colony. The military expense alone would be tremendous; maintaining a soldier in Louisiana cost five times as much as in Spain. Nevertheless, Spain saw advantages in owning the colony.

Louisiana would serve as a buffer — keeping the British away from the Spanish silver mines in northern Mexico. Spain's control of the Mississippi River offered even more protection for Mexico. With the river, Spain also had better control of the Gulf of Mexico.

The strategic location of the colony made it worth the cost to the Spanish. They also took the colony because they expected France to pay for Spain's heavy losses. Since the Spanish had entered the war on France's side, they expected compensation.

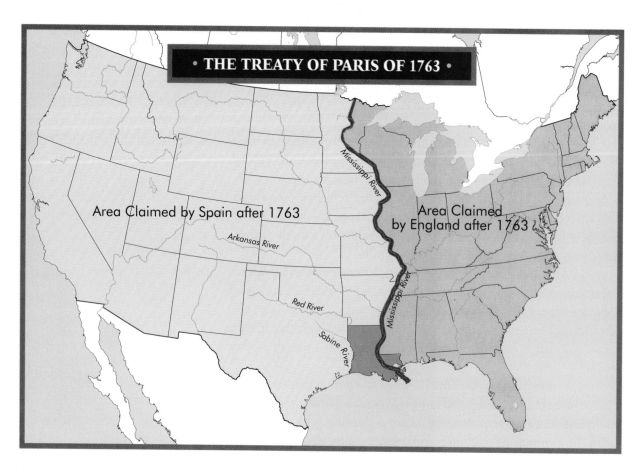

THE TREATY OF PARIS OF 1763

Area Claimed by Spain after 1763

Area Claimed by England after 1763

Mississippi River

Arkansas River

Red River

Sabine River

THE ACADIANS

The French and Indian War also brought new colonists to Louisiana. The Acadians were exiles from French Acadia, which had become the British Nova Scotia in 1713.

The Acadians were peasants who had come from France to Canada in 1632. In Acadia, they were frugal and hard-working trappers and farmers. The land, their families, and their Catholic faith defined their lives. Even though Canada changed hands several times, the Acadians continued to farm and live their simple lives. They ignored the clashes in Europe that spilled over into North America, until the violent conflict pushed its way into their villages. All around them, the French and English settlers struggled for control of land and forts.

In 1755, early in the French and Indian War, Major Charles Lawrence, a British officer, declared that these farmers were enemies because they refused to take an oath of allegiance to the Protestant British king. Lawrence evicted them from their land, decreed that they must "learn to become good British subjects," and sent them to the British colonies on the Atlantic Coast. After the tragic events of this journey and the years following, some of the Acadians began to make their way to Louisiana beginning in 1764. There, at least, they expected to hear their own language.

The British doubted the loyalty of the French colonists in Acadia (present-day Nova Scotia). In 1755, during the French and Indian War, the British evicted the Acadians from their land. Many eventually found their way to southern Louisiana.

The king of France had arranged for the Acadians to go to Louisiana but had not provided any other assistance to help them get settled. The confusion in the colonial government increased their problems. But the French colonial officials were sympathetic to the newly arrived Acadians. They gave the new settlers supplies from the government warehouses and sent them to live in the Attakapa region. The prairies there offered a place to raise livestock, as they had done in their homeland. Other Acadian settlements developed in the colony. Today Louisiana is home to the descendants of these hardy people.

Do You Remember?
1. Who fought in the French and Indian War?
2. How did the Florida Parishes get their name?
3. Where were the Acadians before they moved to Louisiana?

Handling the transfer of Louisiana for the French was the responsibility of the French Director General, Jean-Jacques-Blaise d'Abbadie (da ba de). When he arrived in 1763, he inspected the colony. In his report to France, he described the government as understaffed, demoralized, and corrupt and the warehouse and the treasury as nearly empty. The French government was almost bankrupt and could send the colony little other than complaints about its expense. These conditions continued for another two years.

Louisiana was left to manage on its own. The problems continued; the colony's finances were in disorder and supplies were short. Because France did not send supplies, the officials of the colony had to ask the British at Pensacola to sell them flour. In addition, the poor conditions made keeping order more difficult. More troops were needed, but France sent no aid. Neither did it reveal word of the colony's transfer to Spain, and the colonists had no idea of the changes ahead.

Finally, on September 30, 1764, d'Abbadie officially announced the agreement to transfer Louisiana to Spain. The news had already begun to leak out, and the colonists were very bitter about this betrayal by their country. After they received official word of the tranfer, the colonists held a meeting. Delegates from the colony headed to France to ask the French government to stop the transfer. Leading the group was a wealthy merchant, Jean Milhet. He spent almost two years in Paris, pleading the colony's cause. He was joined in this effort by Bienville, who was now eighty-six and retired to France. The king, however, did not want to hear from the representatives of his former colony, and all the other officials refused to help French Louisiana. The people in the colony struggled along, hoping that a change in government would not come.

King Carlos III of Spain was the cousin of French King Louis XV and came to his aid during the French and Indian War. To keep Louisiana out of the hands of the British, Louis XV gave the colony to Spain in 1762.

THE FIRST SPANISH GOVERNOR

The Spanish government sent Antonio de Ulloa (ool YO a) to Louisiana as its governor. Ulloa was a high-ranking and competent naval officer with colonial administrative experience. However, he was not a forceful leader but a reserved intellectual. It was his quiet manner and low-key style that made him ineffective in Louisiana.

Ulloa arrived on March 5, 1766, with only seventy-five soldiers and one ship. The New Orleans weather that day hinted at his unpleasant stay in the colony. A heavy downpour made his entrance less than dignified, and the small number of soldiers disembarking added to the poor impression.

Arriving with such a small force was not Ulloa's intention. He had asked for seven hundred troops, but this request was not filled. Instead, he was told that the French soldiers in the colony would join his military forces. But the few French troops considered themselves French, not Spanish, subjects. The soldiers and the other colonists hesitated to transfer their loyalty to Spain.

Almost as soon as he arrived, Ulloa made unpopular changes. Following orders from the Spanish King Carlos III, he announced that the colony must now follow Spanish trade laws. Those regulations meant that the colony could trade only with Spanish ports. Spain did not believe in helping other nations develop their trade by using their markets.

To the colonists, the Spanish trade laws spelled ruin. While they were under French control, the colonists had traded with the French ports in the Caribbean. Equally important, they maintained a busy but illegal trade with the nearby British colonies. The successful merchants resented the loss of this business.

When he arrived, Ulloa did not take full control of the government. Captain Charles Philippe Aubry (o BRY) had become the acting French governor when d'Abbadie died suddenly in 1765. So as not to disturb the colonists even more, Ulloa worked through Aubry. Ulloa did not include the French Superior Council in government decisions, but neither did he abolish it. He conferred with French officials on some decisions, but orders were issued to the colonists under Aubry's name. This strange dual government confused the people and encouraged them to think the transfer might be temporary. In fact, members of the Superior Council became the organizers of the dissent against the Spanish.

The Spanish governor's social behavior also led to complaints. The French governors had held ceremonies and provided formal entertainment in New Orleans. The social life in the city had been led by the governors, and the French colonists expected this lifestyle to continue. However, just six months after he arrived, Ulloa left New Orleans for the Balize, a fort at the mouth of the Mississippi River. The colonists in New Orleans assumed he did not want their company. Unaware that he had offended anyone, Ulloa had gone to the Balize to await and greet his South American bride. As a sheltered young Spanish woman who spoke no French, she preferred a small marriage ceremony at the fort. This private wedding was considered an insult in New Orleans, where

Antonio de Ulloa was the first Spanish governor of Louisiana. A noted scholar, Ulloa tried to impose Spanish trade rules on the colony. That eventually led to a rebellion in 1768.

In 1768, the citizens of Lousiana appealed to King Louis XV of France (above) to take back control of the colony. He refused.

the wedding was expected to be a big social event. Even when Ulloa and his wife returned to New Orleans, they did not participate in the town's social activities.

As a result, the colonists gave Ulloa little credit for his positive actions. To improve the colonists' safety, Ulloa toured and inspected the forts. He communicated with the nearby British governor in West Florida to establish diplomatic ties. Ulloa also took steps to ensure the goodwill of the Indians. He gave them more gifts than the French had given them, even more than the amount the Spanish government had allotted.

THE REBELLION

The people had other fears. Would the Spanish culture be forced upon them? Would Spanish become the official language? When they cheered "Long live the king," must they now say *Viva el Rey* instead of *Vive le Roi*? These fears, the strict enforcement of the Spanish trade laws, and Ulloa's other actions added to the growing disrespect.

By October 28, 1768, an armed mob had gathered in New Orleans. The merchants of New Orleans and the members of the Superior Council were its chief organizers. The leaders, however, made sure that all the colonists were represented in order to present a unified front. The Germans came because they wanted to be paid for the produce purchased from their farms. The Acadians wanted payment for the paper currency they had brought from Canada. They also came because Ulloa had forced some of them to settle near Natchez, instead of allowing them to join relatives near St. Gabriel.

As the crowd grew larger and more unruly, Aubry suggested that Ulloa and his family seek refuge on the only Spanish warship at the dock. Aubry and Ulloa could do little to stop the **rebellion** (open resistance to authority). The entire military force available to them totaled about one hundred men. There were only ten Spanish soldiers in New Orleans because the others had been sent to guard the frontier forts. Without enough soldiers to resist the rebellion, Ulloa was forced to leave the colony.

After Ulloa left Louisiana, the people tried to justify their actions to the French king. They wrote a lengthy explanation in "The Memorial of the Planters and Merchants of Louisiana." In it, they argued that Ulloa had never taken proper possession of the colony because he had not formally presented his credentials to the Superior Council. They also complained about Ulloa's leadership style and his trade policies. The people appealed to the king to return Louisiana to the French family.

Their pleas fell on deaf ears. King Louis XV did not want to offend his ally, King Carlos III of Spain. In addition, the colony had always been an expensive burden. Why would Louis want it now?

After this rejection, the leaders of the rebellion knew they would need the protection of a European country. Spain would certainly retaliate against them. So they contacted the British governor at Pensacola to ask for the protection of the British. But King George III was already hearing rumblings from his own colonies and did not want more troubles.

Turned down by King Louis XV, the leaders of the rebellion turned for help to British King George III (above). But the king was facing serious resistance in his own colonies and did not want to become involved in a squabble with Spain.

Do You Remember?

1. Who was the first leader Spain sent to Louisiana?
2. What positive actions did Ulloa take for Louisiana?
3. Why did Ulloa flee the colony instead of putting down the rebellion?

THE ARRIVAL OF O'REILLY

When Ulloa reached Havana, he reported the rebellion to the king of Spain. To the Spanish, the colonists' actions were **treason** (the crime of trying to overthrow the government of one's own state or country), and the rebellious colony must be regained and controlled. A strong and forceful military leader—Alejandro (Alexander) O'Reilly—was selected for this assignment. O'Reilly had been born in Ireland but had come to Spain when he was young. He became a hired soldier, then a hero. He had once saved the king from a mob, proving his bravery and gaining the king's favor.

Three thousand soldiers and twenty-four ships provided the strength O'Reilly needed to carry out the king's orders. (The total population of New Orleans at that time was less than four thousand.) This mighty fleet arrived in August 1769. O'Reilly first stopped at the Balize, to prepare for his formal entry into the city. When word of his presence reached New Orleans, the ringleaders of the rebellion wasted no time. Rushing to the Balize, they told O'Reilly their version of the events. Their major spokesman was the attorney general of the Superior Council; another ringleader of the rebels was the French commissioner who was officially ordered to carry out the transfer of the colony from France to Spain.

In 1769, King Carlos III named Alejandro O'Reilly (above) governor of Louisiana and gave him orders to put down the rebellion. He arrived in Louisiana in August 1769, ten months after Governor Ulloa had left the colony.

O'Reilly politely heard their complaints against Ulloa and their assurances that they had defied Ulloa, not Spain. They interpreted his courteous reception as an acceptance of their defense. They left the fort and returned to New Orleans, apparently thinking they were safe.

O'Reilly headed for New Orleans, to make his next move. His carefully planned arrival displayed the strength and power of Spain. His troops paraded in the Place de Armes (present-day Jackson Square) while cannons fired. Red and gold Spanish flags flew from every post, announcing the Spanish presence. The Spanish officials hosted a formal ceremony in the church, where all important occasions occurred. The people were reminded of the connection between their religion and the king's authority with the Latin words of the Mass. Speeches by O'Reilly and other officials emphasized Spain's control.

To continue his message, O'Reilly reviewed his troops on the parade grounds. This military procedure showed the skill and number of the Spanish soldiers. Backed by his huge army, O'Reilly asserted the power of Spain. Louisiana was now a Spanish colony and must conduct itself properly.

O'Reilly's next step was to get a full report from Aubry. This cooperation with the Spanish led to Aubry's being labeled as a traitor to his people. His death at sea on his way back to France was seen as a just punishment by his enemies in the colony.

O'Reilly wasted no time. Within three days, he had invited thirteen of the leading rebels to his home. Arriving at what they thought was a social visit, they were arrested and imprisoned. O'Reilly's action greatly offended the French, who viewed it as a violation of hospitality. The other people in the city were terrified, fearing what his next action might be. To ease their fears, the Spanish general announced that no one else would be charged with treason.

In the next phase of the investigation, O'Reilly followed Spanish law and procedure exactly. A trial for treason was conducted according to the Spanish justice system; the trial lasted two months. The prisoners and witnesses were questioned secretly. A judge decided and delivered the verdicts (juries were not used in Spanish courts). Six of the defendants were sentenced to death; one died before the executions were held. The usual method of execution was hanging. But because O'Reilly could find no one willing to act as hangman, the prisoners faced a Spanish firing squad. The others were sentenced to prison and had to forfeit their property. The ringleaders had been punished, and the revolt ended.

O'Reilly then issued a proclamation pardoning all others who might have been involved. At an assembly, all of the colonists were asked to take an oath of allegiance to Spain. Spanish officers went to rural inhabitants to offer them a pardon also. Anyone not willing to take the oath had to leave the colony.

The treason trial and the verdicts that resulted in the death sentences did not endear O'Reilly to the colonists. In fact, the French called him "Bloody O'Reilly" for years afterward, and New Orleans schoolchildren even memorized a poem about the evils of O'Reilly. However, at the time, the Spanish king was concerned that the unrest in the British colonies might spread, and he wanted all Spanish colonies to know that rebellion would not be tolerated. O'Reilly was sent to Louisiana as the agent of the king, with written orders to take control of the colony. Treason was punishable by death throughout the world, and lesser crimes such as theft often brought the death penalty also. O'Reilly's actions were thus in accordance with the laws of his country.

ESTABLISHING A SPANISH GOVERNMENT

O'Reilly was also charged with removing French power and French law from this now-Spanish colony. He restructured the government and the military organization of the colony according to the Spanish colonial policies.

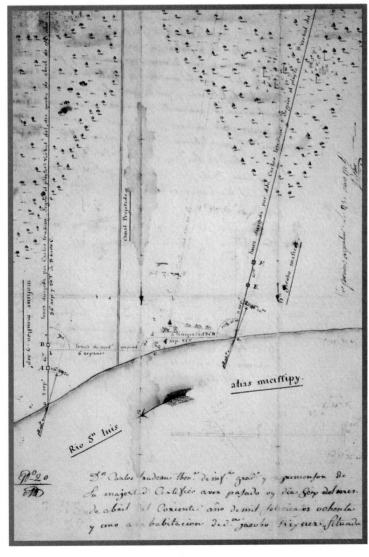

One of O'Reilly's accomplishments was to put in place a system to measure and mark off boundary lines for property. This official survey of a Spanish land grant along the Mississippi River was prepared in 1787.

O'Reilly modified the Spanish colonial law (the Law of the Indies) for Louisiana and replaced the French Superior Council with the Spanish **Cabildo**. The Cabildo functioned as a town council and as a court of law. Its duties included making legal decisions, setting policy for the colony, and advising the governor. The Cabildo had ten members, all voting delegates. But any vote they took could be vetoed by the governor, who presided over the meetings.

The members of the first Cabildo were selected by O'Reilly. Later, in the accepted Spanish custom, the positions were bought. As time went on, the duties of the governmental body broadened, and it took on more responsibilities. The New Orleans building constructed for its meetings was also called the Cabildo.

BRINGING ORDER AND ORGANIZATION

Smuggling violated Spanish trade laws, and O'Reilly intended to stop the British smugglers. British traders in the Manchac settlement had customers across the bayou in Louisiana. After France stopped sending goods, these smugglers were the colonists' only source of needed supplies. To provide a legal trade source for the colonists, O'Reilly offered import tax breaks to Cuban merchants so they would send goods. (**Imports** are goods brought into a country to sell.)

Continuing the reorganization, O'Reilly visited the interior districts of Louisiana. He created subdistricts at St. Louis and Natchitoches and appointed a lieutenant governor for each. Anthanase de Mezieres, the son-in-law to St. Denis and the French commander at Natchitoches, was promoted to the position at Natchitoches.

Spain still had a fort at Los Adaes, near Natchitoches. This fort had always been poorly maintained and generally ignored because it was hundreds of miles from the nearest Spanish settlement in Texas. After Natchitoches became a Spanish fort, Los Adaes was finally abandoned in 1773.

After examining the frontier forts, O'Reilly turned to other problems. Because the prices merchants charged for food were too high, O'Reilly set the prices that they could charge. He made changes in the Code Noir and abolished Indian slavery. He improved Indian relations by continuing to give them gifts. To provide more information for the records required by the Spanish government, O'Reilly ordered a very detailed census. An official **surveyor** was appointed to measure and mark off boundary lines to establish land ownership. No complete surveys had been done by the French.

Hovey Cowles (left, as a leather-armoured Spanish soldier) and Gus Martinez (right, as an ensign) are "interpreters" at Los Adaes SCA. Los Adaes was a Spanish fort built in 1721 to protect Texas from the French.

Spanish-born Colonel Francisco Bouligny came to Louisiana from Havana, Cuba in 1769, as an aide-de-camp to Governor O'Reilly. In 1779, he founded the town of New Iberia.

Now Louisiana was a true Spanish colony. O'Reilly had ended the rebellion and brought order and organization to the colony. In October 1770, Alejandro O'Reilly set sail for Spain. Before he left, he turned the colony over to its new governor.

LOUISIANA UNDER UNZAGA

Luis de Unzaga y Amezaga had been sent with O'Reilly to become the civilian governor once the colony was under control. To continue to maintain order, Unzaga needed to have good relations with the French. One of his earliest decisions helped win them over because it improved their economy and their lifestyles.

As governor, Unzaga continued to face the problem of illegal trade with the British. The restrictions established by the first two Spanish leaders had only increased the smuggling. But Unzaga decided to quietly overlook those regulations. He realized that doing so was the only way to keep the economy alive. And so, in 1772, Unzaga allowed British colonial merchants to set up shop in New Orleans. This trade and the sound Spanish coin money improved the colonial economy.

Religious problems also troubled Unzaga. The close relationship between the royal Spanish government and the Catholic church brought government officials into disputes about religious life. For example, the French priests wanted to stay in the colony, and the people wanted to keep those French-speaking priests. So the Capuchins (KAP u chin) were allowed to stay in the colony for ten years. The Spanish priests were unhappy with this decision because they wanted the permissive French priests removed.

Unzaga handled all of these problems with his mild manner and efficient organizational style. His willingness to appoint many French to official positions reduced the hostility toward Spanish authority. He ensured his acceptance when he married one of the daughters of a wealthy French merchant. His was among the first of many marriages between Spanish officers and the daughters of the French colonists.

Goodwill in the colony was essential to Unzaga because of the growing hostilities in the British colonies. This neighbor across the Mississippi might explode at any time and spill over into Louisiana. Unzaga did what he could to strengthen his forts by repairing them and bringing in more soldiers. He also sought the loyalty of Indian tribes by continuing to sell them firearms. These warriors would be needed as allies if war broke out with Great Britain.

THE ISLEÑOS

The possibility of war made loyal colonists in Louisiana essential. King Carlos III, however, still doubted the loyalty of his new French colonists. The Spanish government, therefore, looked for a group of loyal Spanish subjects. The group selected to fill this need came from the Spanish Canary Islands, which lay off the northwest coast of Africa. These Canary Islanders called themselves *Isleños*, the Spanish word for "islanders."

The Isleños came to Louisiana beginning in 1777. Their journey across the Atlantic was subject to the same tragedies that befell most voyages: disease, hurricanes, lost ships, delays. Many of the Isleños who left the Canaries never reached New Orleans, but those who did settled throughout the colony. The Isleños had also been brought to Louisiana to join the military. But a soldier's low pay was not enough to support a family in the colony, and the Isleños families were directed to become farmers instead. The Spanish government gave them land, houses, cattle, poultry, farm implements, and food to tide them over.

Tommy Benge and Blaine Benge, dressed in the typical fiesta dress of Gran Canaria, receive flowers from Dorothy Benge during the 1998 Isleño Festival. The Benges are descendants of the Molero family, who came to Louisiana from the island of Tenerife, in the Canary Islands.

Do You Remember?
1. How did Alejandro O'Reilly show Spain's military strength?
2. What Spanish governing body replaced the French Superior Council in Louisiana?
3. Who were the Isleños?

NEW IBERIA

New Iberia or *Neuva Iberia* means "new Spain." In 1779, a Spanish official named Colonel Francisco Bouligny founded this town on Bayou Teche. Today, he is honored with a bronze statue in Bouligny Plaza in the city.

Colonists from Malaga, Spain, were brought to the new settlement to grow flax. But when they discovered flax would not grow in Louisiana, they raised cattle and grew corn. Soon these early Spanish settlers merged with the French culture. Spanish names in Iberia Parish today include Segura, Sanchaz, and Miguez. But these descendants of the Malagans are more likely to speak Cajun French than Spanish.

New Iberia's most famous house stands on a Spanish land grant on Bayou Teche. This house, known as Shadows-on-the-Teche, is a wonderful example of the Louisiana of yesterday. William Weeks gained title to the land in 1792; his son built the imposing mansion in 1831. William Weeks Hall (great-grandson of the original owner) restored the white-pillared plantation house to its former grandeur. Today, the National Trust for Historic Preservation guards this American architectural treasure. The Old Spanish Trail (today's Highway 90) passes in front of the house.

Sugar built this house, the port, and the town of New Iberia. When sugar cane became a profitable crop, the land around New Iberia produced tons of this white gold. Steamboats traveling Bayou Teche brought greater prosperity.

The "Queen City on the Teche" celebrates this heritage during its Sugar Festival. Iberia Parish also salutes the Tabasco factory at Avery Island and the Konriko Rice Mill in New Iberia. Is there any wonder that people in New Iberia take pride in their famous foods?

Today, New Iberia has shopping centers and petroleum supply businesses. From its Spanish beginnings in the eighteenth century, the city is now the twelfth largest in Louisiana.

Above: *Sunlight filtering through the trees inspired the name for the Shadows-on-the-Teche plantation house, built in 1831.*
Left: *The spicy Tabasco sauce has been produced on Avery Island since 1868.*

THE SPANISH ROLE IN THE AMERICAN REVOLUTION

Unzaga was the Spanish governor of Louisiana during the period of growing tensions between Great Britain and its American colonies. In 1776, those colonies began their revolution. Spain was glad to see its old enemy Great Britain in trouble. The Spanish secretly supported the American side, and the American Continental Army received supplies from New Orleans. But as Spain was pushed closer to war, a governor with a strong military background was needed in Louisiana.

In 1777, Spain named Bernardo de Gálvez (gal VAZ) as the next colonial governor of Louisiana. Gálvez was increasingly forced to focus on the American Revolution; other officials handled colonial business. But as long as Spain was officially **neutral** (not taking sides), everything Gálvez did to aid the Americans had to be done in secret. The Spanish governor of Louisiana prepared for war and waited for word from his commander in Cuba.

From New Orleans, American agent Oliver Pollock directed the secret Spanish assistance to the Continental Congress. An experienced trader throughout the West Indies, Pollock had helped the Spanish in Louisiana set up trade with other Spanish ports. Because of this good relationship with the Spanish, he was allowed to collect guns, gunpowder, medicine, and cloth for the Americans. Most of these munitions and supplies went to help George Rogers Clark win the western front.

SPAIN ENTERS THE WAR

In 1779, Spain entered the war, but as an ally of France. An **ally** is a person or country that cooperates with others on some projects. France had signed an alliance with the United States in 1778. But the Spanish considered the Americans unacceptable allies because they would not agree to contain themselves between the Atlantic Ocean and the Allegheny Mountains. Also, the Spanish king was reluctant to openly support a rebellion against another monarchy.

Gálvez received orders to expel the British from the Mississippi River, Mobile, and Pensacola. He went on the offensive. He wanted to weaken the British before they could seize New Orleans, which American ships used as a base. Taking New Orleans would also give Great Britain access to the Mississippi River and the British forts along the upper river. The British would then have an advantage in their efforts to put down the rebellion.

To stop the British, Gálvez organized a force of Spanish soldiers and local **militia** (citizen-soldiers). Men between the ages of sixteen and sixty-five were required to serve in the militia. Thus, the Louisiana militia included wealthy merchants and planters from New Orleans, the

*Opposite: Bernardo de Gálvez was governor of Louisiana during the American Revolution. When Spain entered the war in 1779, Gálvez attacked and defeated British forces along the lower Mississippi River and the Gulf of Mexico. **Above:** During the American Revolution, American George Rogers Clark benefitted from the support of the Spanish of Louisiana.*

Isleños, the Acadians, the Germans, rural farmers, and free men of color. Slaves and the Choctaw served as scouts at the front of the line.

Gálvez left New Orleans on August 27, 1779, with almost 1,500 men. The oppressive summer heat, mosquitoes, and the thick canebrake made traveling miserable. More than half of the men got sick along the way. After marching over a hundred miles, they reached Fort Bute at Manchac. On September 7, 1779, Gálvez and his army captured the British fort. From there, Gálvez took his men upriver. The next British fort, New Richmond, was located at the site of present-day Baton Rouge. Gálvez seized the fort on September 21, and the British commander also surrendered Fort Panmure at Natchez. The British had lost all their forts along the Mississippi in British West Florida. Gálvez had captured 28 British officers and 550 troops; he had lost one man and had two wounded.

Gálvez next launched a naval attack to take the British forts on the Gulf of Mexico. His main target was Pensacola, the capital of West Florida. Before the war, the British commander had been visited by a Spanish officer, who said he came to discuss runaway slaves. He actually had been sent by Gálvez to spy on that fort and the fort at Mobile.

Before he could take Pensacola, however, Gálvez first had to capture Mobile. In early 1780, he set out to begin this military mission with thirteen ships. However, a hurricane stopped him, the second time that a hurricane had slowed his progress. Before he had set out on his land march to capture the British river forts, a hurricane had hit and destroyed his supplies.

After reorganizing his ships, supplies, and troops, Gálvez captured Mobile after a four-day battle. He was now ready to attack Pensacola and went to Cuba himself to assemble the forces and supplies he needed.

For his victories during the American Revolution, the king of Spain honored Bernardo de Gálvez by giving him a title of nobility. Gálvez's coat of arms included a battleship and the phrase Yo solo *("I alone").*

In October 1780, Gálvez left Cuba with a huge fleet of sixty-four ships. Unbelievably, a third hurricane struck. After that storm, Gálvez regrouped and headed for the fort at Pensacola. On March 9, 1781, the Spanish began a **siege** of the British fort, surrounding the fort and preventing any supplies from reaching it. On May 8, a Spanish shell blew a hole in the fort. Gálvez took advantage of the situation and stepped up the attack. On May 10, the British general surrendered, giving up British access to the Gulf of Mexico. Losing these forts and the Gulf of Mexico kept the British from launching any more attacks in the area.

For his victory and his bravery, the king of Spain honored Bernardo de Gálvez with a royal title. He also was allowed to add a battleship and the motto *Yo Solo* ("I alone") to his coat of arms. His success is still celebrated today when the descendants of the Louisiana militia meet to honor the Spanish hero of the American Revolution. The United States honored his contributions with a statue in the nation's capital.

THE TREATY OF PARIS OF 1783

When the war ended, Spain was rewarded with much of the territory it had sought. Florida became Spanish again. King Carlos III now held both banks of the Mississippi. This marked the height of Spain's power in the Americas.

To protect these possessions, the Spanish government improved the *Camino Real* ("Road of the King"). This road connected Natchitoches, New Orleans, and St. Louis with San Antonio. San Antonio, the capital of Spanish Texas, had become a major horse market. The route from Texas to Louisiana was used by *vaqueros* (cowboys) to drive over 9,000 head of longhorn cattle to New Orleans. This beef fed the Spanish soldiers during the American Revolution. Today, Highway 90 in Louisiana follows the route of part of this old Spanish trail.

LOUISIANA UNDER MIRO

Gálvez was promoted to another assignment in colonial Spain after his success in the war, and another governor was sent to Louisiana. Esteban Rodriguez Miro had to deal with the problems caused by the war.

One of those problems was the relationship with the Native Americans. Since the days of the French, the Indians had come to rely on trade with the whites. After losing the British traders, the Indians wanted to trade with the Americans in Georgia and the Carolinas. Fearing that the Indians might become allies of the Americans and pose a threat to Spanish Louisiana, Miro worked hard to continue trade with the Indians.

Esteban Rodriguez Miro was governor of Louisiana from 1785 to 1791. Louisiana prospered under his leadership, and many Americans began to move into the area. The city of Monroe began as Fort Miro, named for this Spanish official.

Settlers began to encroach on Spanish territory. After the war, the Americans swarmed over the Allegheny Mountains, heading west. Spain feared that if this region filled with the land-hungry, aggressive Americans, the United States would become a stronger threat to Spain's North American holdings. It tried to stop the American expansion by encouraging Indian opposition and by limiting traffic on the Mississippi River.

Spain did encourage immigration to Spanish Louisiana and set aside funds for that purpose in the colonial budget. But Miro had to use those funds to feed his soldiers. The Spanish, like the French, often did not

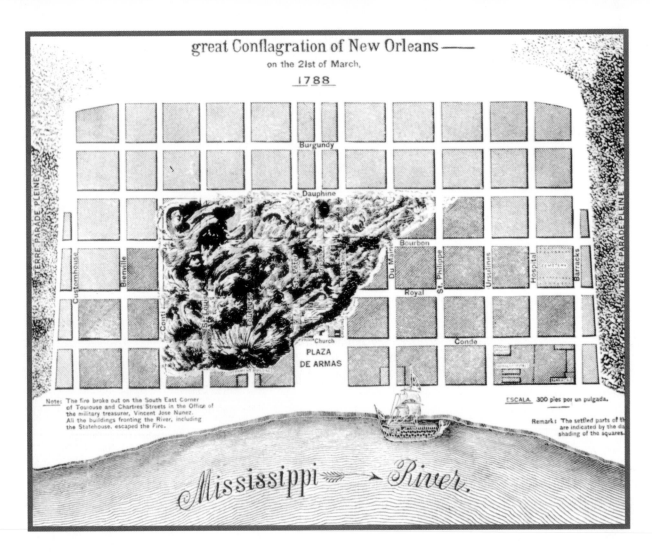

great Conflagration of New Orleans ——
on the 21st of March,
1788

Note: The fire broke out on the South East Corner of Toulouse and Chartres Streets in the Office of the military treasurer, Vincent Jose Nunez. All the buildings fronting the River, including the Statehouse, escaped the Fire.

ESCALA. 300 pies por un pulgada.

Remark: The settled parts of the are indicated by the da shading of the squares.

More than eight hundred buildings were destroyed in the Great New Orleans Fire of 1788. This map shows the extent of the fire. Another devastating fire struck in 1794.

send enough money to provide for all of the colony's needs. Like many other Louisiana colonial governors, Miro had to set his financial priorities. But even without government help, many people moved to Louisiana. The Spanish allowed the Americans to come to Louisiana, expecting them to be loyal to the colony. If the Americans took an oath of allegiance to Spain, they were given a land grant. Protestants had to agree not to worship openly, but they were not required to convert to Catholicism. This was a change in policy; previously, Spain had required all colonists to become Catholics.

When Miro realized that many Americans were settling in the colony, he tried to place them in organized communities like Natchez. By adding the newcomers to established areas, he hoped to keep them loyal. He also recognized the danger of their presence. Abiding by the new immigration regulations, he sent for Irish priests. He hoped the English-speaking clergy would encourage the Americans to voluntarily become proper Catholics as well as good Spanish subjects.

In 1788, Miro faced a major disaster. A fire burned much of New Orleans, destroying 856 homes and leaving 1,000 people homeless. The fire damage went beyond the immediate loss of homes and property, however. The effect on life in the city was devastating, and the loss of stored food threatened a famine. The colonial government was disrupted by the fire. The simple building where the Cabildo met was burned, as were the prison and the police station. Obviously, the prison and the police station had to be replaced first; a new building for the Cabildo was not finished until 1799. New Orleans suffered another fire in 1794. Again many buildings burned, including the recently completed firehouse.

Miro's handling of these problems and the willingness of Spain to loosen trade laws improved life in the colony. The population increased, and new settlements were established. The city of Monroe began as Fort Miro, named to honor this Spanish governor. The fort was established in 1790 in North Louisiana to protect the Spanish territory.

Francois-Louis Hector, Baron de Carondelet et Noyelles, became governor of Louisiana in 1791. Governor Carondelet loosened Spanish trade laws to improve the colony's economy, established the first newspaper in Louisiana, installed the first street lights in New Orleans, and signed treaties with the Indian tribes.

Do You Remember?

1. Why was Spanish aid to the Americans in 1777-1779 kept secret?
2. How did the king of Spain honor Gálvez for his part in the American Revolution?
3. Who was the governor of Louisiana after the American Revolution?

SPANISH LOUISIANA GROWS

The next Spanish governor was a highly energetic leader — Francois-Louis Hector, Baron de Carondelet et Noyelles. Constant action marked his years as governor. Spanish trade laws had been loosened during Governor Miro's term, but Carondelet exceeded the new policy by allowing free trade with the United States. He also permitted foreign trade ships to enter the port of New Orleans. The "official" records listed these ships as Spanish. Carondelet had to walk a tightrope because he could not openly violate the Spanish trade policies. But only with this outside trade could the colony's economy survive.

COLONIAL NEW ORLEANS

Visitors to New Orleans marvel at the Old World charm of the Vieux Carré ("old square" in French) or French Quarter. The Creole architecture found in this historic section reflects the cultural changes of the French colonial, Spanish colonial, and American eras. The early French and Spanish colonial buildings were lost in the fires of 1788 and 1794.

After the second fire, the wealthiest Spanish colonial official, Don Andre Almonester y Roxas loaned the city the money to rebuild the Cabildo. The front of this structure is similar to the government house in Oaxaca, Mexico, built around 1780. Don Andre also provided the funds to rebuild St. Louis Church.

The new houses and businesses built in the city after the fires reflected both French and Spanish influence. The roofs were required by law to be tile, an effort to prevent another major fire. Some of the houses had a flat roof, which was used as a patio, in the Spanish style. The houses faced inward to a courtyard for privacy. These courtyards, or patios as they were also called, served as outdoor living areas. Exterior stairways led to the second-floor rooms. The rooms opened into each other since the Creole-style house did not have hallways.

The main decoration on the facade of the buildings in Creole New Orleans was the now famous iron balconies. At first, this ornamental work was hammered or forged by hand. Later, cast iron made in molds was used.

Left: St. Louis Cathedral is one of the oldest and most photographed churches in the country. The Presbytère, next to the cathedral, was begun in 1793 and now serves as a museum.

The exterior of these buildings was usually painted stucco. The French and Spanish did not like exposed brick and used an overlay of stucco to cover it. One of the practical reasons for covering the brick was to protect the house from damage by the high humidity of the region. Historic preservation projects in New Orleans today still struggle with the effects of the moisture-laden air of the city built on the swamp.

"Lafitte's Blacksmith Shop," built around 1788, is a typical Creole-style cottage. There are no interior hallways, and the exterior wall is bricks between posts, covered by stucco.

After the execution of King Louis XVI (above) during the French Revolution, many members of the French nobility made their way to Louisiana.

THE FRENCH REVOLUTION

The outside world brought more than trade to Louisiana. From across the Atlantic came reports of the French Revolution in 1789. The spread of "the Age of Enlightenment" brought changes. Any government that insisted on absolute control over its citizens was threatened. When those new ideas and terrible living conditions kindled the French Revolution, the Spanish government watched nervously. After French King Louis XVI was beheaded, Spain's King Carlos IV could no longer ignore the threat. In 1793, Spain declared war on France.

Even before Spain entered the war, Louisiana's sympathy for the French Revolution concerned Governor Carondelet. Talk of the revolution captured the interest of the people. The French blood in many of the colonists produced a loyalty for the citizens of France. In addition, the ideas of freedom and individual rights appealed to these people who had lived far from a king for several generations. In the streets of New Orleans, people sang the anthem of the French Revolution, "Le Marseillaise." In Natchitoches, revolutionary clubs supported the French cause.

The colonists' increasing involvement brought action from Carondelet. He sought support among the Indian tribes just in case he faced any actual rebellion. He improved the safety of New Orleans by establishing a police force and adding street lights. He carefully monitored the activities of the people as they moved about the colony; any mobs expressing sympathy for the French Revolution could thus be stopped more easily.

In France, the situation became less controlled and more violent, and "the Reign of Terror" began. Those French who were loyal to the king were in constant danger of joining the long lines at the guillotine. Fearing execution, they escaped from France when they could. The French-speaking colony of Louisiana with its royal government offered refuge to some of the French nobility. Records show that they came to New Orleans, St. Martinville, and New Iberia in 1793 and 1794.

The words of freedom and the rights of man spreading around the world were also heard by the slaves in colonial Louisiana. By 1795, a group of slaves in Pointe Coupee planned an uprising, encouraged by their belief that the attitude about slavery was changing. Their plan, however, was reported and the uprising stopped.

BOUNDARY DISPUTES

Carondelet constantly heard rumors that Americans along the Mississippi planned to come and take New Orleans. These angry western farmers threatened to seize the port they needed in order to get their products to market. Some of the plots went beyond that goal and included overthrowing the Spanish and taking the West.

After the American Revolution, travel on the Mississippi had been a major issue between the Spanish and the American farmers who lived in the West. Without access to the river, the farmers could not get their crops down river to a port. Their complaints to the new Congress and their threats to take action brought about a treaty in 1795. According to Pinckney's Treaty, the Americans gained free navigation of the river. Once they reached New Orleans, they could "deposit" or store their goods in warehouses before loading them onto ocean-going ships. This agreement was called the **right of deposit**. The arrangement was not completely satisfactory, because the right of deposit was granted for only three years.

The treaty also set the boundary between the United States and the Spanish territory. The agreement set the southern boundary of the United States at the thirty-first parallel.

THE FINAL SPANISH YEARS

As Louisiana grew, both in population and in importance, progress and change increased the demand for information. *Le Moniteur de la Louisiane*, the first newspaper in the colony, began publication in 1794. It was printed in French, indicating that, although the Spanish held the colony, the people still spoke their native language.

Sugar cane brought further progress to the colony. Many people contributed to this agricultural effort, but Etienne de Boré was the first really successful sugar producer. In 1795, he improved an experimental process and manufactured a good quality sugar. Other experienced sugar planters moved into Louisiana from Saint-Domingue (Haiti) after

Sugar cane became the leading cash crop in Louisiana after Etienne de Boré (above) succeeded in producing a crop that yielded about 100,000 pounds of sugar in 1795.

the slave rebellion there. This infusion of knowledge and skilled workers made sugar cane the leading cash crop.

That slave rebellion in Haiti frightened the planters in Louisiana, and they no longer wanted slaves from the West Indies. Because of this fear of rebellion, Carondelet stopped the importation of slaves for a time.

Louisiana continued to cost Spain more than it returned. In fact, the expenses were ten times the profits Spain gained. At the end of the 1700s, more secret negotiations about the colony would soon change the direction of life in Louisiana again. The colony would be traded again by the European powers who controlled its destiny.

After being returned to France for a brief period, the Louisiana people were headed for the biggest change in their tumultuous history. These French-speaking Spanish citizens would soon be American. Once again, the colonists knew nothing of the looming changes.

Above: A family of slaves, c. 1798. The slave rebellions in Saint-Domingue forced Governor Carondelet to ban the importation of West Indian slaves for a time. *Right:* Free blacks from Saint-Domingue. Skilled workers from the sugar plantations of Saint-Domingue immigrated to Louisiana and helped establish the sugar industry.

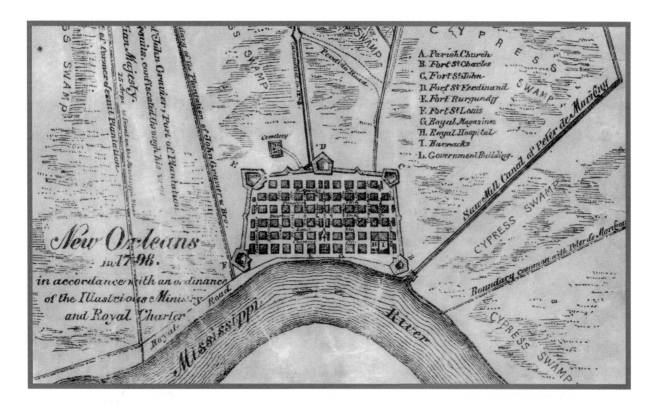

Labels on map:
- A. Parish Church
- B. Fort St. Charles
- C. Fort St. John
- D. Fort St. Ferdinand
- E. Fort Burgundy
- F. Fort St. Louis
- G. Royal Magazines
- H. Royal Hospital
- I. Barracks
- L. Government Building

Do You Remember?

1. Where did French nobility seek refuge during the French Revolution?
2. What is the right of deposit?
3. Did Louisiana make a profit for Spain?

SUMMARY

The control of the Louisiana territory and the Mississippi River brought conflict among the major European powers. After years of struggle and great expense, France decided it could no longer afford to keep Louisiana. And so, in 1762, France traded Louisiana to Spain in return for much-needed money and military assistance. Spain looked upon Louisiana as a buffer for Mexico and as a means to control the Gulf of Mexico.

Although Spain anticipated some of the great expense of maintaining Louisiana, it was rarely able to send the soldiers and supplies the struggling colony needed. And at first, the French-speaking citizens of Louisiana resisted Spanish control.

Spain allied itself with the American forces during the American Revolution. In return for its help, Spain regained Florida. It also gained new neighbors, the Americans, who soon began to move into the Louisiana territory. Unable to stop their expansion, Spain reluctantly accepted these new settlers and established trade agreements. In the end, Spain, like France, was unable to maintain the high cost of Louisiana.

This map detail shows New Orleans in 1798. The city was a strategic port for both Spain and the young United States. Events set in motion when Spain refused to renew the right of deposit would soon lead to a monumental change for the city.

CHAPTER · REVIEW

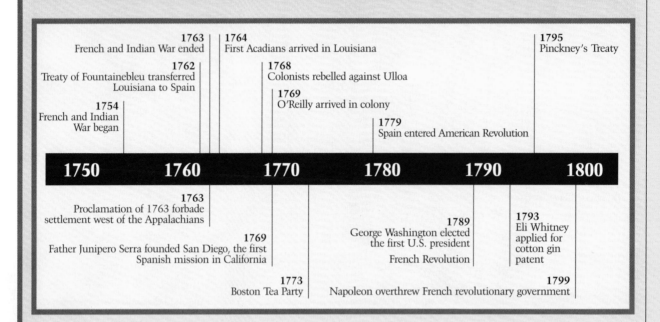

1763 French and Indian War ended

1764 First Acadians arrived in Louisiana

1795 Pinckney's Treaty

1762 Treaty of Fountainebleu transferred Louisiana to Spain

1768 Colonists rebelled against Ulloa

1754 French and Indian War began

1769 O'Reilly arrived in colony

1779 Spain entered American Revolution

1750 1760 1770 1780 1790 1800

1763 Proclamation of 1763 forbade settlement west of the Appalachians

1769 Father Junipero Serra founded San Diego, the first Spanish mission in California

1789 George Washington elected the first U.S. president

French Revolution

1793 Eli Whitney applied for cotton gin patent

1773 Boston Tea Party

Napoleon overthrew French revolutionary government **1799**

Reviewing People, Places, and Terms

Define, identify, or explain the importance of the following.

1. ally
2. Cabildo
3. French and Indian War
4. imports
5. militia
6. neutral
7. Alejandro O'Reilly
8. rebellion
9. right of deposit
10. siege
11. surveyor
12. treason
13. Antonio de Ulloa

Understanding the Facts

1. What lands did France lose in the French and Indian War?
2. Why were the Spanish willing to take on the heavy cost of owning Louisiana?

3. How did Ulloa anger the French colonists?
4. What was "The Memorial of the Planters and Merchants of Louisiana"?
5. What did O'Reilly do to earn the nickname "Bloody O'Reilly"?
6. Who was the first Spanish civilian governor of Louisiana?
7. How did Gálvez help the Americans win the American Revolution?
8. What did Spain receive in the Treaty of Paris of 1783?
9. How did Miro handle the Americans who wanted to settle in Spanish Louisiana after the American Revolution?
10. What became Louisiana's major cash crop in the late 1700s?

Developing Critical Thinking

1. What did the Louisiana colonists lose and gain as a result of the rebellion against the Spanish?
2. How did the French Revolution affect the citizens of Louisiana?

Using Your Skills

1. Locate the thirty-first parallel on a map of the United States. Name all the present-day states that touch this parallel. Which states use this parallel as a boundary?

2. On a map of Louisiana, locate the following towns. These are most of the settlements that existed at the end of the Spanish colonial era: Baton Rouge, Donaldsonville, Madisonville, Marksville, Monroe, Natchitoches, New Iberia, New Orleans, Opelousas, Pointe Coupee (New Roads), Rapides (Pineville), St. Francisville, Springfield, Vermillionville (Lafayette), and Vidalia.

Special Projects

1. Using reference sources, investigate one of the towns listed in Using Your Skills #2. Find some information about this town that could be added to the "Louisiana Lagniappe." Present your information to the class in an interesting format.

2. Using reference sources, find the name of a school in the town you researched. Write a letter to a student in that school, telling that student what you have learned about his or her town. Ask the student to reply telling you more about the town.

Making Connections

1. People often adapt their buildings to the local climate and geography, but sometimes they continue to use building practices from their former regions. Do you think a flat-roofed building was a good choice for New Orleans? Why or why not?

2. Do Louisiana architects today still adapt their designs to suit the climate and geography? Give some examples.

3. What role has technology played in the architectural styles found in Louisiana today?

Louisiana Lagniappe

- Ulloa learned to speak French when he was invited to join a group of scientists on a South American expedition led by the French Royal Academy of Science. The group completed a scientific study to measure the length of the equator.

- New Orleans merchant Oliver Pollock created the dollar sign, "$," by modifying a Mexican symbol.

• BUILDING SKILLS: FINDING INFORMATION •

As you continue your study of the history of Louisiana, your teacher may assign topics for you to research. In addition to the card catalogue of your school media center, there are numerous reference books available. Here are the types of information you are likely to find in some of them.

- **Almanac:** Facts about a variety of events and dates, often in date order
- **Atlas:** Maps and place information
- **Dictionary:** Meanings, spellings, pronunciations, and origins of words
- **Encyclopedia:** Important details about people, places, and things, usually arranged alphabetically by subject or topic

Read the following descriptions and determine in which reference source you would find the information. Some information can be found in more than one reference source or in reference sources that are not listed here.

1. Distance between New Iberia and Natchitoches
2. The date Louisiana became a state
3. The average annual rainfall in Louisiana
4. The capital of Louisiana
5. An explanation of how Cane River Lake was formed
6. The location of Driskill Mountain
7. The parishes of Louisiana
8. Louisiana's state song
9. A biography of Bernardo de Gálvez
10. Major crops grown in Louisiana

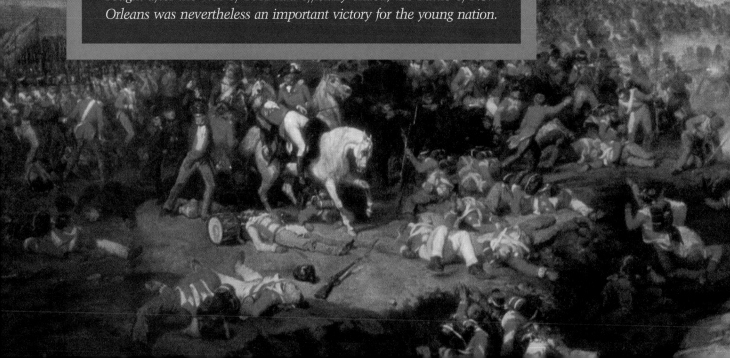

CHAPTER EIGHT

LOUISIANA'S EARLY AMERICAN ERA: PURCHASE AND PIONEERS

Let the land rejoice, for you have bought Louisiana for a song.
— General Horatio Gates to President Thomas Jefferson, July 18, 1803

ONE OF THE GREATEST REAL ESTATE DEALS IN history added a "new, immense, unbounded world" to the United States. The Louisiana Purchase transformed the colony of Louisiana and its new country. The bargain buy included Louisiana and all or parts of twelve more states. Almost 900,000 square miles were added to the United States. It was Napoleon Bonaparte's ambition that doubled the size of the United States.

Fought after the War of 1812 had officially ended, the Battle of New Orleans was nevertheless an important victory for the young nation.

Napoleon Bonaparte, shown here on horseback crossing the Alps, seized power in France after the French Revolution. His plans to re-establish France's New World empire were thwarted when he could not regain control of Haiti.

NAPOLEON'S FRENCH LOUISIANA

After the French Revolution, Napoleon seized power in France and set out to conquer the world. Restoring the French empire in the New World was one part of his grand plan, and Louisiana would provide the base for his military operations in North America.

First, Napoleon persuaded the Spanish to give up Louisiana. However, the Treaty of San Ildefonso (signed in 1800) between France and Spain was kept secret, and the formal transfer of Louisiana did not take place for over two years.

Next, Napoleon sent troops to regain control of Saint-Domingue. He hoped to use the island as the center of his North American campaign. From this wealthy and well-placed location in the West Indies, he could guard the Mississippi Valley, an important food and trade center.

But the French had lost control of Saint-Domingue. Toussaint L'Ouverture, a former slave, led a revolution against French control in 1801 and now controlled the island. L'Ouverture renamed Saint-Domingue after one of its original names — Haiti. In 1802, Napoleon sent 20,000 French troops to Haiti. The French dictator expected his army to regain the island. But yellow fever changed Napoleon's future and the history of Louisiana. An epidemic of the disease killed most of the French soldiers in Haiti.

Referring to Louisiana, Napoleon said, "I have scarcely received it before I risk losing it." Without Haiti, he could not protect Louisiana. In addition, he could not risk sending more troops to take Haiti because he was at war with Great Britain and that war required all of his available troops. The war also required huge sums of money. Napoleon knew that the United States wanted New Orleans. The Americans west of the Ohio River needed access to a port and had been frustrated with foreign control of the Mississippi River. To Napoleon, selling Louisiana was now an attractive option.

Toussaint L'Ouverture, leader of the slave revolution in Saint-Domingue, gave the island its present name, Haiti.

THE LOUISIANA PURCHASE

In 1802, the Spanish suspended the right of deposit at New Orleans. That meant Americans could no longer store their goods in New Orleans while waiting to load them onto ships. This Spanish interruption of western American trade created a storm of protest. In Washington, the Federalists (the political party whose members favored a strong federal government) talked of war.

The western farmers demanded action. The governor of Kentucky wrote to President Thomas Jefferson, "The citizens of this state are very alarmed and agitated, as this action of the Spanish government will, if not altered, at one blow, cut up the present and future prosperity and interests by the roots." Jefferson had been in Congress in 1783 and 1784 when Spain threatened to end the right of deposit. He knew very well the value of the Mississippi River.

American unrest increased when the United States learned Napoleon owned New Orleans. President Jefferson understood the threat. Napoleon's hand on New Orleans could become a choke-hold. And because France was a much stronger nation than Spain, the United States might be forced to rely on its old enemy, the British. Thomas Jefferson wrote that "the day France takes possession of New Orleans, . . . we

*Top: French Minister of Finance Barbe-Marbois negotiated the sale of Louisiana. **Above:** Robert Livingston served as U.S. minister to France from 1801 to 1804. **Right:** This map shows New Orleans and the surrounding area in 1803, the date of the Louisiana Purchase.*

PLAN DE LA ET DES ENVIRONS LAUSSAT ET COMMISSAIRE DE PAR VINACHE CHEF DE BAT:. DU GÉNIE

N⁰. ORLÉANS DEDIÉ AU CITOYEN PRÉFET COLONIAL LA RÉPUBLIQUE F.⁴ᴵᴿᴱ SOUS-DIRECTEUR

must marry ourselves to the British fleet and nation." Jefferson the **diplomat** (one who is skilled in dealing with others) intended to avoid war.

Robert Livingston served as the United States minister to France. He and French Minister Barbe-Marbois met unofficially to discuss the situation. President Jefferson sent an additional diplomat to assist Livingston. Jefferson's choice — the farmer and statesman James Mon-

THOMAS JEFFERSON'S LETTER TO JAMES MONROE

Thomas Jefferson realized that skilled diplomacy was needed if the United States ever hoped to get New Orleans from Napoleon. He sent James Monroe as a special diplomat to work with the American Minister to France, Robert Livingston. The following is an excerpt from Jefferson's letter to Monroe, explaining this assignment.

The agitation of the public mind on occasion of the late suspension of our right of deposit at New Orleans is extreme. In the Western country it is natural and grounded on honest motives. In the seaports it proceeds from a desire for war, which increases the mercantile lottery; in the Federalists, generally, and especially those of Congress, the object is to force us into war if possible in order to derange our finances, or if this cannot be done, to attach the Western country to them, as their best friends, and thus get again into power. Remonstrances, memorials, etc., are now circulating through the whole of the Western country. . . .

It was essential, then, to send a minister extraordinary to be joined with the ordinary one, . . . well impressed with all our views and therefore qualified to meet and modify to these every form of proposition which could come from the other party. . . . You [James Monroe] possessed the unlimited confidence of the administration and of the Western people and generally of the Republicans everywhere, and were you to refuse to go, no other man can be found who does this. The measure has already silenced the Federalists here. Congress will no longer be agitated by them, and the country will become calm fast as the information extends over it. All eyes, all hopes, are now fixed on you. . . . For on the event of this mission depend the future destinies of this republic.

In 1803, President Thomas Jefferson (top) sent James Monroe (above) to Paris to try to purchase West Florida and the city of New Orleans.

roe — pleased the westerners. To them, Livingston was an eastern aristocrat who did not understand their needs. Livingston and Monroe had instructions to purchase New Orleans and as much more of the Gulf Coast as they could for $2 million.

The diplomats negotiated for weeks, awaiting Napoleon's decision. Suddenly, in April 1803, Napoleon offered to sell the entire Louisiana

This late nineteenth-century illustration shows French finance minister Barbe-Marbois negotiating the Louisiana Purchase with James Monroe and Robert Livingston.

territory, not just New Orleans. The Americans were shocked but soon worked out the details of the **Louisiana Purchase**. According to the terms of the treaty, the United States agreed to buy hundreds of millions of acres for less than 5 cents an acre. When asked to identify the boundaries, French Foreign Minister Talleyrand said, "I can give you no directions. You have made a noble bargain for yourselves and I suppose you will make the most of it."

Livingston and Monroe had exceeded their instructions. The Americans had been sent to buy New Orleans. When Napoleon threw in the rest of the territory at the last minute, they acted decisively. They could not write to Washington and wait months for a reply. By that time, Napoleon might have withdrawn his offer.

Their diplomatic success stunned Washington, and Congress faced a challenging decision. The U.S. Constitution did not include a procedure for adding new territory to the United States. But the Constitution did give the president treaty-making power, and so the Purchase was submitted to Congress as part of a treaty. Congress had to decide whether to accept and ratify the treaty that had already been signed in France.

Congress convened early for this important vote. Opponents of the treaty feared that the port of New Orleans would have special commercial privileges, and the merchants of the eastern United States resented competition from another port. Some Americans were against admitting "foreign" people to the United States. Others argued that the treaty was not binding — how could France sell the territory to the United States without the consent of the people of Louisiana? Another group complained about the high price. Finally, however, the United States Senate voted 24 to 7 to ratify the treaty. The young United States had to borrow some of the money from banks in London and Amsterdam to buy the land, but the Purchase was completed.

Above: Earlier U.S. negotiations with French Foreign Minister Charles Maurice de Talleyrand-Périgord were unsuccessful. When it appeared that war would soon break out between England and France, Napoleon told Talleyrand to sell Louisiana.
Left: Under a portrait of Louis XIV, who established and gave his name to the Louisiana colony, Napoleon is seen signing the Louisiana Purchase treaty.

SPAIN TO FRANCE TO THE UNITED STATES

Spain watched the negotiations and protested the sale of Louisiana. Napoleon had violated his treaty with Spain; the Treaty of San Ildefonso stated that France would return Louisiana to Spain if France chose not to keep it. Napoleon's sale of Louisiana to the United States also threatened the Spanish presence in the Gulf of Mexico. But Spain had no power to stop the sale. If it did not agree to the sale, it would be forced into war with the United States and France. The Spanish government finally gave the order to transfer Louisiana to France.

When the people of New Orleans heard about this change, reactions were mixed. Some were excited to be French citizens again. Others preferred the Spanish management of the colony.

The French government designated a representative to accept the colony from Spain. On a rainy New Orleans day, at the Cabildo, a formal ceremony marked the changeover. In the typical formal European style, the Spanish official presented the keys to the fort on a silver tray. The French representative accepted this symbol of Spanish authority on November 30, 1803.

Just twenty days later, the colony watched as yet another flag was raised in the parade ground. The "Stars and Stripes" announced the United States's claim to Louisiana. The American secretary read the treaty in a loud voice. After this announcement, the French official spoke to the people. He released them from their fidelity to France. All who stayed in Louisiana would be Americans. Cannons fired and troops paraded, symbolizing a new chapter in Louisiana's story. Louisiana must now learn to be American. And the American government must deal with this unknown and little understood region.

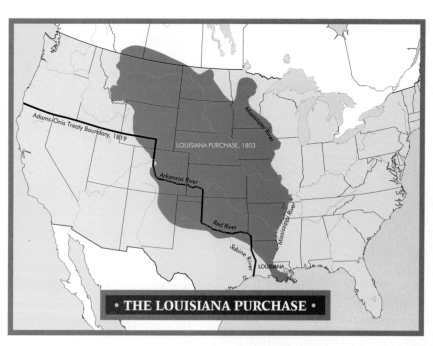

Above: *This map shows the vast area acquired by the United States in the Louisiana Purchase.*
Opposite: *In a formal ceremony on December 20, 1803, the American flag was raised for the first time in the Place de Armes, now Jackson Square.*

Do You Remember?

1. Why did Napoleon want Louisiana?
2. Who was the president of the United States in 1803?
3. Why did the United States want New Orleans?
4. How much did the United States pay for Louisiana?

THE TERRITORIAL PERIOD

The Louisiana Purchase more than doubled the size of the United States. All of this new territory had to be explored, organized, and made part of the government. After Congress approved the Purchase, it planned the government for this vast new area. Because of the size, Congress created two territories in March 1804. The Territory of Orleans contained most of the present state of Louisiana. The remaining land became the District of Louisiana within the Indiana Territory.

General James Wilkinson became the governor of the District of Louisiana, which had its **capital** (seat of government) at St. Louis. William C. C. Claiborne was appointed territorial governor of the Territory of Orleans. Although he was young (just one year older than the United States) and spoke only English, Claiborne was experienced. He had earlier served as the governor of the Mississippi Territory.

Governor Claiborne faced tremendous challenges in his new assignment. One of the first problems he had to deal with was the Spanish officials, who had not yet left Louisiana. The Spanish governor said he was taking a hunting trip on the frontier. Actually, he was exploring the border between Louisiana and Texas and trying to stir up opposition to the Americans. Finally, in 1806, the president instructed Claiborne to send the troublesome Spanish out of the territory. But even after the Spanish had gone, their system of land claims and titles caused problems. Land grants had often been given without clearly established boundaries, and the documentation of ownership of the land was often confusing and contradictory.

Opposite: President Jefferson appointed William C. C. Claiborne the first governor of the Territory of Orleans. Above: General James Wilkinson was one of the officials who accepted Louisiana from the French. He was the first governor of the District of Louisiana.

THE PEOPLE OF LOUISIANA

It was up to Governor Claiborne to convince the people of Louisiana to become American. Claiborne called the French Creoles the "ancient Louisianians." The early definition for Creoles referred to all persons born in the Louisiana colony. In fact, the term orginated from a Portuguese word meaning "of the colony." These French-speaking Creoles were not eager to change. Their strong Catholic roots led them to resist the ways of the English-speaking Protestants who now possessed their land.

The revolution in Haiti had driven French planters to Louisiana. They brought their slaves, expecting to continue their plantation lifestyle. They associated with the French of Louisiana rather than with the Americans.

Free people of color had also fled Haiti. In French colonies, *gens de couleur libre* was the legal identification for those of mixed race. Former

This 1806 view of New Orleans is from the Marigny plantation. An American eagle in the sky holds a ribbon that reads "Under my wings, everything prospers."

slaves who purchased their freedom were also identified with this term. In New Orleans, they joined a large established community of free people of color. Many families were wealthy, educated, and cultured. They honored their Catholic and French heritage, had their own schools, and attended the theater regularly. Many free people of color were skilled workers in New Orleans — carpenters, masons, cigar makers, shoemakers, clerks, mechanics, coopers, barbers, blacksmiths, and butchers.

Some of the people in the Territory of Orleans wanted immediate statehood. President Jefferson, however, had informed Congress that the people of Louisiana were "as incapable of self-government as children." Their colonial experience had not prepared them for this kind of government. Louisiana had been founded and maintained as a colony

Pitot House in New Orleans was the home of James Pitot, a refugee from the Saint-Domingue slave rebellions. In 1803, he became the first elected mayor of New Orleans. The house reflects a Caribbean influence common in Louisiana houses.

of royal governments. A royal government meant total authority, not involvement by the citizens. The king controlled the government, and paid officials took care of government matters. Louisianians considered jury duty and voting an imposition, rather than a right. Jefferson wanted to give them time to learn about democratic government. In addition, some members of Congress wanted more Americans to move into the territory before they would approve statehood for Louisiana.

Many of the first Americans who came to Louisiana were the "Kaintucks." These westerners with their different language and strange culture came down the Mississippi River on their flatboats. Because of their behavior, the Louisianians assumed all Americans were rough, violent, and rowdy.

The Hypolite Bordelon House in Marksville (top) is an example of Creole architecture in the late 1700s and early 1800s. The walls (above, left) are bousillage, a mixture of mud and deer hair or Spanish moss. The dining room in the house (right) was one of the two main rooms. The netting in the bedroom, the other main room (opposite page) protected the sleeping occupants from mosquitoes.

BORDER DISPUTES

The huge tract of land that was the Louisiana Purchase was largely unknown. President Jefferson sent out expeditions to survey and map the territory. The most famous was the Lewis and Clark expedition.

The undefined boundaries of the Louisiana Purchase strained the relationship between the United States and Spain. In 1806, Zebulon Pike set out to explore the southern border of the Louisiana Purchase and to determine the source of the Red River, which the Spanish regarded as the western border of the Purchase. To settle disputes with Spain, this river had to be accurately mapped.

The area along the Sabine River had belonged to the Spanish colonies of Texas and Louisiana. Now, that border too provoked an ongoing argument. Some of the Americans claimed that the Sabine River was the western border between the United States and Spanish Texas. In addition, there were rumors that the Spanish planned a push into American territory, while westerners crowded toward the Spanish territory.

Finally, in 1806, the two governments established a neutral buffer zone between Louisiana and Texas. As part of the agreement, no troops from either government entered the neutral ground. This so-called Sabine Strip became a no man's land, a lawless hideout for bandits. Outlaw gangs made their headquarters here, robbing the traders who traveled from Mexico to Louisiana.

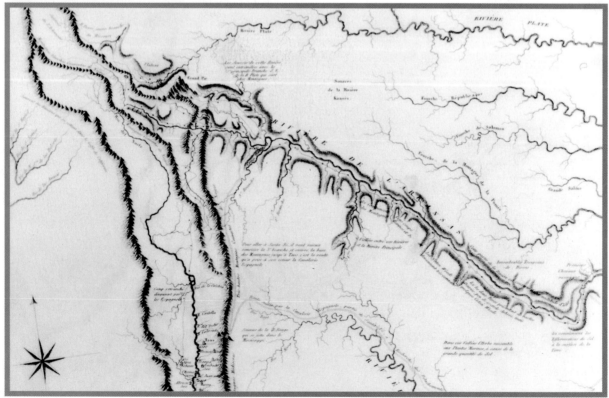

THE BURR CONSPIRACY

Intrigue and plotting swirled through the western United States before and immediately after the Louisiana Purchase. One of those conspiracies involved Aaron Burr, a former vice president of the United States. Burr had fallen from power after he killed Alexander Hamilton in a duel.

Burr saw the competition to control New Orleans as his chance to regain power. He expected Spain to declare war to regain the port, and so he began working behind the scenes with the Spanish. Later, he was accused of planning his own empire with land he hoped to seize from the southern United States and Mexico.

Burr's conspiracy was stopped by General Wilkinson, governor of the District of Louisiana. In 1805, Wilkinson reported Burr's plans to bring an armed flotilla (fleet of boats) down the river toward New Orleans. Burr then hoped to start a rebellion among the French settlers. Wilkinson's letter to President Jefferson led to Burr's arrest for treason. Although Wilkinson was the chief witness against him, Burr was acquitted.

Wilkinson's role in this intrigue was unclear. Burr once wrote to Wilkinson, "The gods invite us to glory and fortune. It remains to be seen whether we deserve the boon." But Wilkinson apparently turned against Burr when he saw the plan was doomed. General Wilkinson was a double agent, working with the Spanish while he served the United States. He had negotiated the agreement that established the Sabine Strip. Some historians now suggest that he arranged this compromise because he was working for both sides.

THE WEST FLORIDA REVOLT

West Florida was not included in the Louisiana Purchase; it remained Spanish. West Florida included the part of the state on the east side of the Mississippi River today called "the Florida Parishes." These parishes include East Baton Rouge, East Feliciana, Livingston, St. Helena, St. Tammany, Tangipahoa, Washington, and West Feliciana. New Orleans was the only place east of the Mississippi River that was included in the Louisiana Purchase.

However, from the time of the Louisiana Purchase until the Adams-Onis Treaty of 1819, Spain and the United States disputed the ownership of the West Florida area. The area had not been clearly specified when the land was transferred from Spain to France, nor had Napoleon specifically mentioned it in the Purchase.

Many Anglos lived in Spanish West Florida. They were disappointed when West Florida was not included in the Louisiana Purchase and talked of rebelling against the Spanish. Fort San Carlos, the fort on the east side of the river at Baton Rouge was the closest Spanish authority. As early as 1804, just a year after the Louisiana Purchase, the east-side settlers tried to seize the fort. They failed, but it did not end their plotting to gain control

Above: Aaron Burr, Thomas Jefferson's vice president, was involved in a conspiracy against the United States. He was tried for treason but acquitted.
Opposite page, above: In 1806, General Wilkinson sent Zebulon Pike, explorer and soldier, to find the headwaters of the Red and Arkansas rivers. During that trip, he discovered the mountain named for him, Pikes Peak.
Opposite page, below: This map detail shows the results of Zebulon Pike's exploration of the Red River.

JACKSON

The Feliciana Parish courthouse in Jackson was built in 1816. When the parish was divided into East and West Feliciana in 1824, Jackson lost some of its importance.

Louisiana's Florida Parishes include the Felicianas, East and West. This historic region reflects the changes that took place in Louisiana during its early years. The early French settlements in this region were located close to present-day Natchez. The land south of Natchez did not see many settlers until the British took control of the region in 1763.

After that time, people from the British colonies migrated to this rich land. These Anglos brought their own heritage to the Felicianas. The early architecture mirrored their Carolina homes, rather than the French Creole West Indies. Historic towns in East and West Feliciana, such as St. Francisville and Clinton, preserve the history of those days. Only hints, however, remain of the large settlement, Bayou Sara, that existed during the steamboat days.

Jackson, another Feliciana town, developed under several names. At first, the settlement was called Bear Corners by hunters and traders. When it became an official town, it was called Buncombe. Colonel John Horton had donated the land and named the town after his home in North Carolina. After the Battle of New Orleans, the citizens decided to honor Andrew Jackson and changed the name of their town once again.

After Louisiana became a state, Jackson became the parish seat of Feliciana Parish. The first courthouse in Jackson was built in 1816. In 1824, the parish was divided into East Feliciana and West Feliciana. Clinton became the parish seat of East Feliciana, and Jackson lost some of its importance.

But in 1826, the College of Louisiana was chartered in Jackson by the state legislature. At first, it occupied the old Jackson courthouse, but later a new school with two dormitories was built. When enrollment declined, state support stopped and the college closed in 1845.

During the same period, the Methodist church was operating a struggling college in Mississippi. In 1846, the two schools merged at the Jackson campus and became Centenary College of Louisiana. Centenary College remained in Jackson until 1908, when it was relocated to Shreveport. The West Wing still stands at the site of the old school. It has been listed on the National Register of Historic Places.

Centenary College in Jackson is on the National Register of Historic Place. The West Wing (left) was built as a dormitory in 1837. This professor's house (top, above), an original faculty building, dates from the 1890s.

of the land east of the Mississippi. In 1810, they were ready to try again. By then, Americans were in the majority in Spanish West Florida.

Unrest in Spain gave them the reason they needed to rebel against the Spanish government. Napoleon had invaded Spain in 1808 and put his brother Joseph on the Spanish throne. Supporters of the Spanish royal family resented Napoleon's action and stood behind the former Spanish king, Fernando VII. Several Spanish colonies used the change of government as an excuse to revolt. The Anglos in Spanish West Florida used opposition to the new Spanish government to justify their plan.

Fort San Carlos was still in Spanish hands. Seventy men, led by Philemon Thomas, followed an unguarded cow path into the fort. They easily captured the fort, killing two Spanish soldiers during the fighting. The West Florida revolution had succeeded.

For a brief period, West Florida was an independent nation. In December 1810, however, the United States annexed the area. (To **annex** is to add territory to an already existing governmental unit, such as a city, state, or nation.) When Louisiana became a state in 1812, the Florida Parishes were not included. But in its first official act, the new state legislature annexed West Florida and made it a part of the state of Louisiana.

Philemon Thomas led a militia group to capture the Spanish fort at Baton Rouge, Fort San Carlos.

THE GREAT SLAVE REVOLT OF 1811

After 1808, slaves could not be legally imported into the United States. This did not, however, stop the trading of slaves among the states. In addition, smugglers continued to bring slaves into Louisiana from other countries.

After the Louisiana Purchase, the economy of Louisiana improved. As the plantations grew, more workers were required. Slaves were needed to work the valuable Louisiana crops — sugar cane and cotton. By 1812, the slave population in Louisiana was about 35,000.

As the number of slaves increased, the unrest among them spread. In 1811, a major slave uprising took place near the present-day town of Norco in St. Charles Parish. The leaders of the revolt organized the escaping slaves into companies complete with officers. They had no weapons except those that they had fashioned from farm tools.

Numbering several hundred, the slaves marched along the river toward New Orleans. Regular troops of the United States Army joined with the Orleans militia to stop them. Some slaves were killed in the fighting; others were executed later. Their heads were displayed on poles to remind other slaves of the punishment they could expect for revolting.

Do You Remember?

1. Name the two territories carved from the Louisiana Purchase.
2. What was the Sabine Strip?
3. What were the Florida Parishes?

STATEHOOD

More and more settlers moved into Louisiana. Some began pressing for statehood as soon as they arrived. But the process established by Congress required that a territory have at least 60,000 residents before it could become a state. By 1809 the territory had reached the population required, and the territorial legislature sent a request for statehood to Congress. Governor Claiborne, however, did not support this petition because he did not think the Creoles were ready for citizenship. He wanted more Americans to move into Louisiana before the territory became a state. Congress took no action on the 1809 petition. In 1811, however, Congress did vote to admit Louisiana as the eighteenth state. The statehood bill was signed by President James Madison on February 16, 1811. The official date for statehood was set for April 30, 1812.

LOUISIANA'S FIRST CONSTITUTION

Before it became a state, Louisiana had to write a constitution. The constitution of Kentucky, written in 1799, was used as a model. As a citizen of Kentucky, Governor Claiborne had helped write that constitution. Louisiana's constitution provided that the legislature would select the governor from the two leading candidates in the popular election. The governor, who was limited to one 4-year term, had extensive power to appoint other officials. Judges, who were also appointed by the governor, served for life. Only white male property owners could vote or hold office.

Julien Poydras of Pointe Coupee served as president of the 1811 constitutional convention.

Julien Poydras of Pointe Coupee was the president of the constitutional convention. In a speech following the signing of the constitution, he described his new American government as "the most perfect the human mind has hitherto framed." The Creoles were ready to be Americans.

New Orleans continued as the capital of Louisiana. The first election for governor lasted three days, as required by the constitution. William C. C. Claiborne was elected as the new state's first governor, surprised that he was asked to lead the "ancient Louisianians."

EARLY PROBLEMS

Statehood did not end the conflicts between the Creoles and the newly arrived Americans. Language and cultural barriers increased the distrust. Matters were made worse when a Philadelphia newspaper printed Governor Claiborne's private comments about the inferiority of the Creoles.

Claiborne also had to settle the problem of the Caddo Indians. The tribe tried to continue its agricultural lifestyle in Louisiana after statehood, but increasing numbers of white settlers encroached on Caddo land. Governor Claiborne negotiated a treaty to buy the Caddo land near the Red River. The tribe then moved west to Texas.

Smuggling was a serious problem during Claiborne's administration. Established during the French colonial period as a necessity, this illegal trade was still tolerated. The largest band of smugglers operated from a base along the Gulf Coast at Barataria. These **privateers** preyed on Spanish and British ships, with the full backing of countries that were at war with Spain or Great Britain. Most of the privateers sailed under the flag of Cartagena (now Colombia), which was then a Spanish province. Jean Lafitte led the Baratarians.

Claiborne tried to stop Lafitte's operations and his illegal smuggling of slaves. Finally, he offered a $500 reward for Lafitte's capture. The bold Lafitte posted notices around New Orleans and raised Claiborne's $500 reward to a $5,000 reward for the governor! The story of Claiborne and Lafitte took an interesting turn when the War of 1812 reached New Orleans.

Above: Jean Lafitte, shown here gambling with several pirates, was the leader of the privateers and smugglers known as the Baratarians. Opposite: General Andrew Jackson arrived in New Orleans in December 1814 to defend the city against an attack by the British.

LOUISIANA AND THE WAR OF 1812

The War of 1812 is sometimes called the "second war for independence." The United States was young but looking for the respect of other nations, including Great Britain. The British, however, did not treat the United States as an equal. Thirty years after the American Revolution, the British continued to occupy American territory along the Great Lakes. British agents encouraged the Indian tribes in their struggles with the Americans. Trade issues also created conflict.

But the British angered the Americans most by the **impressment** of American sailors. That is, the British stopped American ships on the high seas and seized able-bodied seamen, claiming they were British deserters. These sailors were then forced to serve in the British navy. (France, with whom Great Britain was at war at the time, also stopped American ships. But Americans directed most of their anger at Great Britain since it had a larger navy and was a stronger nation.) The United States declared war on Great Britain on June 18, 1812.

PROTECTING NEW ORLEANS

During the early years of the War of 1812, the British were also fighting France in Europe. Nevertheless, they were able to turn back American attacks on British Canada and Florida. The few American victories

involved battles at sea. In 1814, the British defeated Napoleon and could then direct their full strength to the war with the United States.

Governor Claiborne prepared for an attack on New Orleans. If the British succeeded in taking New Orleans, they would gain access to the entire Mississippi Valley. The United States tried to strengthen the forts near the mouth of the Mississippi River and protect this vital port.

Claiborne expected the state militia to defend the city. In a letter to the captain of the militia in Pointe Coupee, Claiborne ordered him to assemble his troops for exercise twice a week and to "be in readiness for actual service at a moment's notice." But he wondered whether these French-speaking Louisianians would consider themselves American and fight the British.

In the fall of 1814, British warships entered the Gulf of Mexico and **blockaded** New Orleans. That is, the British positioned their ships to isolate the city and prevent any ships from entering or leaving the port. The United States sent Major General Andrew Jackson to defend the city after his success in defeating the Creek Indians in the Mississippi Territory. In the Creek War, Jackson had earned the nickname "Old Hickory" because his men claimed he was as tough as a hickory tree.

Jackson gathered his forces and prepared the defenses for the city. His troops included the regular United States Army, Kentucky sharpshooters who had served with him in the Creek War, the local militia, and the Choctaw. Like Claiborne, Jackson doubted the loyalty of the French in New Orleans. But after a huge public meeting, they swore their support. A U.S. Army major described Jackson's ability to motivate his New Orleans troops by noting "he electrified all hearts." A French Louisianian described their feelings, "Nationalities no longer count. We are all Americans."

Even Jean Lafitte and his Baratarians offered to fight with the Americans after refusing a British request for their help. In return, Lafitte got some of his men released from jail and some of his property returned. He and his men joined Jackson to fight the British.

British naval forces defeated the Americans at the Battle of Lake Borgne in December 1814. It was the first of the battles leading up to the Battle of New Orleans.

THE BATTLE OF NEW ORLEANS

The Battle of New Orleans was actually the last in a series of battles that began in December 1814. The British fleet approached the city through Lake Borgne, where the first battle occurred. The British warships were too large to enter Lake Borgne, but their small sloops were able to outmaneuver and defeat the six American gunboats. Although

the British won the first battle on Lake Borgne, their progress toward New Orleans was slowed.

The British army landed some of its troops across the lake and started for New Orleans. Jackson surprised the British with a night attack, which again slowed their approach. British General Edward Pakenham led two more attacks, but Jackson's troops held their ground.

The two armies met on January 8, 1815, "on the plains of Chalmette," just south of the city. On that foggy morning, the battle lasted less than an hour. Jackson and his five thousand assorted troops soundly defeated eight thousand professional British soldiers. More than two thousand British soldiers were killed, while only eight of Jackson's men died in battle that day.

Ironically, the two generals did not know that the war was already over. On December 24, 1814, a treaty ending the war had been signed. But news of the Treaty of Ghent (in Belgium) did not arrive in the United States until weeks later. The battle could have been avoided.

But the victory was not meaningless. The British had been forcefully shown that the Americans were willing to take on the world's mightiest nation and fight it to a draw. If the Americans had been defeated, the British might have stopped the peace process. If the British had won, they might have given Louisiana back to their Spanish allies.

Fourth of July celebrations in New Orleans had new meaning. The Battle of New Orleans brought all of Louisiana's citizens together to fight for the American cause. After the battle, New Orleans honored Jackson and the United States in a patriotic ceremony. The hero of the Battle of New Orleans is still honored today. A statue of Andrew Jackson guards the city from the center of the Place de Armes, now called Jackson Square. The statue, cast from a cannon used in the battle, was completed in 1856. Jackson himself laid the cornerstone in 1840.

Above: *In this painting of the Battle of New Orleans, Andrew Jackson can be seen on the right, mounted on a white horse.* ***Left:*** *British General Pakenham was killed in the battle.*

SETTLING BOUNDARY DISPUTES

The War of 1812 had settled somewhat the conflict between the United States and Great Britain. But the issue of the boundary between Louisiana and Spanish Texas was still unsettled. The Spanish claimed all of the land as far east as the former Spanish fort of Los Adaes. They considered the Arroyo Hondo ("dry gulch") in Natchitoches Parish their boundary indicator. The United States believed that the Sabine River — or even the Rio Grande River — should be the boundary.

The issue was not settled until February 1819, when the Adams-Onis Treaty set the boundary at the Sabine River. Spain also ceded (gave) East Florida to the United States. The United States gave up its claims to Texas, at least for the time being.

A U.S. military post, Fort Jesup, was built in 1822 at the boundary line between the United States and Spanish Texas. Later, this outpost served as the headquarters for the Western division of the U.S. Army, which covered the territory from Florida to Lake Superior. Fort Jesup has been reconstructed at its site in DeSoto Parish. The nearby town of Many (MAN e) was named for the commander of the fort, Colonel John Many. The main street of Many follows the old San Antonio Trace (now Highway 6), a Spanish trail that ran from Natchitoches to San Antonio, Texas.

Do You Remember?
1. Who was elected the first governor of the state of Louisiana?
2. Who commanded the American forces at the Battle of New Orleans?

Fort Jesup in Many has been designated as a National Historic Landmark. The soldiers' mess (opposite, above) is the only original building remaining. The mess hall has been furnished (below) as it would have been in the 1840s. The reconstructed officers' quarters (left) houses a museum. Costumed interpreter Cornial Cox (opposite, below) portrays the camp baker and private cook for Colonel Many.

Steamboats were important for transporting people and goods, and they contributed to the importance of New Orleans as a port. This drawing was created by Captain Basil Hall using a camera lucida, a precurser of the camera which used a lens to project an image onto a piece of paper, where it could be traced.

THE EARLY YEARS OF STATEHOOD

The period after the War of 1812 was a time of growth and progress for Louisiana. New Orleans developed into the largest city in the South and one of the largest cities in the United States. Its growth was due to its importance as a port.

STEAMBOATS

New Orleans had seen birchbark canoes, cypress pirogues, French and Spanish sailing ships, Kentucky flatboats, and keelboats travel the waters of the Mississippi River. But on January 10, 1812, a history-changing vessel landed at the docks. Nicholas Roosevelt had come from Pittsburgh with his steamboat, the *New Orleans*. The trip down the river had taken 259 hours.

With its speed and ease, the steamboat changed Louisiana. A flatboat was basically a raft that was guided with an oar and moved by pushing poles into the river bottom. Built for about $35, it was good for only one trip down river. Traders who came down the river on a flatboat had to find another way to get back. Keelboats could be steered and could make the return trip upriver — but the trip took three months of back-breaking poling.

Built to carry both cargo and passengers, the steamboat used steam power to travel up and down the rivers. Roosevelt's steamboat cost a thousand times more than a flatboat. But the value of his investment was soon clear. The steamboat earned a $20,000 profit for Roosevelt before it sank.

Soon, dozens of steamboats lined the river landings. By 1821, the port of New Orleans registered more than seventy-five steamboats. All the goods of the new country's economy filled the boats. Piles of pelts, stacks of lumber, barrels of corn whiskey, bales of cotton, and hogsheads (barrels) of sugar covered the docks at New Orleans.

Steamboats became the most popular mode of transportation. At their peak, the floating palaces usually associated with the era offered their passengers luxuriously furnished cabins, banquet rooms, ladies' sitting rooms, gambling parlors, and promenade decks. The smaller steamboats were not nearly as elegant; often, they were crowded and dirty.

All steamboats, grand or simple, carried risk. Obstacles in the river, such as a sunken log, could damage and sink the boat. The changeable river channels made navigation very difficult. Sometimes steamboats ran aground when the water level of the river was low. The most feared disaster involved overheated steam boilers that exploded.

Famous Americans like Mark Twain signed their names on the pages of Louisiana's steamboat days. One tall, lanky boy from Indiana jumped

Some steamboats were rough and uncomfortable, while others were luxurious and had elaborate woodwork and decorations. This 1861 painting of the salon of the Princess *by Marie Adrien Persac is the earliest known interior view of a Mississippi River steamboat.*

to shore from his flatboat. He decided to return home the easier way, going upriver on a new steamboat. The fascinating port of New Orleans amazed the eighteen-year-old Abraham Lincoln.

CLEARING THE RED RIVER RAFT

Steamboats navigated a number of the rivers of Louisiana. But boats on the Red River could only get as far as Natchitoches. A huge tangle of logs and brush had jammed the river and made travel further upriver impossible. The debris had become so thick that cottonwood trees actually grew in the logjam! The logjam, or "the Great Raft" as it was called, clogged the river northward for about two hundred miles. The Great Raft blocked not only the river but progress itself.

Captain Henry Miller Shreve agreed to help clear the river. First, he designed a snagboat to pull the logs from the river. Then, in 1833, he began work with a crew of over one hundred men and three boats. He worked for years trying to open the river. Funding for the project came from the federal government. Often, the project ran out of money and the river became blocked again. It was not until 1873 that the Red River was totally opened.

The map of northwest Louisiana is a tribute to Shreve's efforts. The city of Shreveport was named to honor him. It was at this site that a trading post was established after Shreve cleared the Red River. That trading post developed into the city that bears his name.

Captain Henry Miller Shreve worked for years to clear the 160-mile-long "raft" on the Red River. The snagboat on the right is removing the snagged logs.

LOUISIANA'S PIONEERS

When Louisiana became an American territory, people came down the Mississippi from the "western country," Tennessee and Kentucky. They also crossed overland from the Mississippi Territory and from Georgia. First, they settled in the Florida Parishes and in South Louisiana. The prairie areas around Opelousas and the old Attakapa region of St. Martinville attracted American cattle farmers.

Later, the newcomers began to move into North Louisiana. The area around the old Spanish fort on the Ouachita River was one of the first areas of settlement. Abraham Morehouse brought pioneers from Kentucky into this region as early as 1804. People also crossed the river at Natchez to live near Vidalia. This settlement was named for Jose Vidal, an early Spanish official.

The clearing of the Red River opened up North Louisiana to the pioneers. Many traveled overland in wagons pulled by oxen. Often, the travellers were groups of family and friends. Some came with minimum supplies and few assets. Others moved from once-prosperous cotton plantations whose soil had worn out. Those newcomers brought their slaves and expected to create other plantations.

This Washington Parish log cabin, built around 1810, has been relocated to the LSU Rural Life Museum. The log cabin was actually lived in until 1960.

This dogtrot cabin is an exhibit at the LSU Rural Life Museum in Baton Rouge. A typical dogtrot cabin has front and rear porches and a central open hallway.

One Louisiana family has passed down the story of the pioneer ancestor who arrived in North Louisiana in the late 1830s. As a boy, he had come up the Red River with his family and vividly recalled gripping the steamboat's rail as the captain ordered more wood for the boiler. The captain just could not resist a race up the river on the way to Shreveport. Major James Dyer, another pioneer and a veteran of the War of 1812, settled in North Louisiana in 1822. He had come from Missouri. When Claiborne Parish was established, he became its first representative to the state legislature.

The northwest corner of Louisiana became the state's Texas connection. Mexico began a war of independence from Spain in 1810, finally winning its independence in 1821. Mexico still held Texas, but in the 1820s Americans began moving into the region. Many of these pioneers traveled the trails of North Louisiana "going to Texas." These Americans did not leave their democracy behind when they crossed the Sabine River. Soon, talk of "freeing" Texas was heard at the inns and taverns along the route. The plots were whispered about in Texas and in Washington.

Finally, in 1836, the Americans in Texas declared their independence. The heroes of the Texas revolution died at the battle of the Alamo. The people of North Louisiana had seen these Texans travel through their land. After the Alamo, Louisiana supporters joined the Texans in their fight for freedom. The streets of the town square of Shreveport, laid out the same year that Texas won its independence, were named to honor the Texans. Texas Street is still the name of the street in front of the Caddo Parish courthouse.

1. What was the name of the first steamboat to dock in New Orleans?
2. For whom was the town of Shreveport named?

SUMMARY

The sale of the Louisiana territory to the United States ushered in a new era. The Louisiana Purchase brought new leadership, new ideas of democracy, and new English-speaking settlers to the area. It also caused new problems. Boundary disputes strained relations with Spain. Conspiracies and revolts added to the unease in the territory.

But with statehood granted in 1812, Louisiana's identity in the United States was firmly established. In the War of 1812, the United States fought its "second war of independence." At the Battle of New Orleans, the country — and all of the state's citizens — demonstrated its determination to protect the important port of New Orleans. A new invention, the steamboat, brought tremendous growth to New Orleans and increased trade along Louisiana waterways.

The talk of "freeing" Texas led to the Battle of the Alamo (below), where many of the heroes of the Texas Revolution died.

CHAPTER · REVIEW

1800	1811	1812
Treaty of San Ildefonso	Slave revolt	Louisiana became a state

1801
Jefferson became president

1810
West Florida revolt

1812
Louisiana became a state
War of 1812 began
First steamboat arrived in New Orleans

1803
Louisiana Purchase

1815
Battle of New Orleans

1800   **1810**   **1820**

1806
Noah Webster published his first dictionary

1815
Battle of Waterloo, final defeat of Napoleon

1799
Napoleon seized power in France

1803
Matthew Flinders sailed around Australia and named it

1812
First tin cans made in England for preserving food

1822
Liberia founded as home for freed U.S. slaves

Reviewing People, Places, and Terms

Define, identify, or explain the importance of the following.

1. annex
2. blockade
3. capital
4. diplomat
5. impressment
6. Andrew Jackson
7. Jean Lafitte
8. Louisiana Purchase
9. privateers
10. Territory of Orleans

Understanding the Facts

1. Why did Napoleon sell Louisiana to the United States?
2. What was the Spanish reaction to Napoleon's sale of Louisiana?
3. Who was appointed territorial governor of the Territory of Orleans?
4. What was the Burr conspiracy?
5. What were the results of the rebellion by the Anglos in West Florida?
6. The importation of slaves into the United States was forbidden after 1808. Did this end the slave trade? Why or why not?
7. When did Louisiana become a state?
8. Why was the Battle of New Orleans significant?
9. What border dispute did the Adams-Onis Treaty settle?

Developing Critical Thinking

1. Zadok Cramer, a nineteenth-century writer, referred to New Orleans as "the grand mart of business . . . the Alexandria of the Americas." What do you suppose he meant in making this comparison?
2. William C. C. Claiborne was elected the first governor of the state of Louisiana. The traditional voting period lasted for three days. Why do you think so much time was allowed for voting? What problems might have resulted from such a lengthy election time?

1. President Jefferson paid $15 million for the territory in the Louisiana Purchase. The area totaled about 828,000 square miles. How much was that per square mile?
2. The population of Louisiana increased from 75,000 in 1810 to 150,000 in 1820. What was the amount and the percentage of increase?

Special Projects

1. The chapter mentioned that the Louisiana Purchase included Louisiana and all or parts of twelve other states. Make a list of those states.
2. Andrew Jackson's victories during the War of 1812 made him a national hero. Some even began to mention his name for president. Research Jackson's life to determine what characteristics he displayed as a general that would make him an effective president.
3. The 1904 World's Fair in St. Louis celebrated the Louisiana Purchase and introduced new technology. List three technological innovations of 1904 that were not available in 1804 and that will no longer be needed in 2004.

Making Connections

1. Thomas Jefferson recognized that different groups of Americans pushed for the right of deposit in New Orleans for different reasons. How did he describe the motivation of the Federalist party in this situation?
2. What did Jefferson mean when he said, "All eyes, all hopes, are now fixed on you"?

Louisiana Lagniappe

- British General Pakenham was killed at the Battle of New Orleans. His body was shipped home to England in a hogshead (barrel) of rum. He was buried on his English estate.
- Some pioneer Louisiana hunters claimed they could lasso the wild turkeys that were so plentiful in the forests.

• BUILDING SKILLS: UNDERSTANDING CAUSE AND EFFECT •

Historical events happen because something makes them happen. What happens is the *effect*. The person, condition, or event that makes the effect happen is the *cause*. The connection between what happens and what makes it happen is known as the *cause-effect relationship*.

Not all cause-effect relationships are clear-cut. And sometimes an event may have more than one effect, and an effect may have more than one cause. At other times, an effect may not appear for a long time. The following guidelines will help you identify cause-effect relationships in written material.

1. Statements often contain "clue words" that alert you to cause and effect. Watch for words or phrases such as *because, led to, brought about, produced, as a result of, so that, thus, since, outcome, as a consequence, resulted in, gave rise to,* and *therefore*. For example: *Because* of their behavior, the Louisianians assumed all Americans were rough, violent, and rowdy.
2. There may not be any clue words. In their place, may be the word *and* or a comma. For example: Often, the project ran out of money *and* the river became blocked again.
3. It usually takes more than one sentence or paragraph to describe a cause-effect relationship. If you're not sure whether a description illustrates a cause-effect relationship, ask yourself if economics, geography, religion, or technology is involved in the event or condition being studied. These are major forces in history.

Try This! Make a chart with a Cause heading and an Effect heading. Find three examples of cause-effect relationships in this chapter. Place each cause and its effect under the correct heading.

CHAPTER NINE

ANTEBELLUM LOUISIANA: RICHES AND REPRESSION

We are now within sight of Baton Rouge. It is a fine looking town with a stately Capitol, towering with bastions, towers and battlements far above the other buildings. At a distance, its white appearance and bulk in the shining reflection . . . give it the look of an iceberg. . . .
— Unknown traveler, Baton Rouge *Daily Advocate*, July 13, 1855

WHITE COTTON AND WHITE COLUMNS are the expected symbols of Louisiana's **antebellum** era (the period before the Civil War). However, a careful look reveals a more intricate tapestry. This era is woven from the culture of Louisiana's different people, their politics, and economy.

The people of the new state of Louisiana had united against their enemy, the British. Louisiana's Creoles fought beside the Americans to win the Battle of New Orleans. But their common tie soon unraveled.

The Americans envisioned a typical American territory after the Louisiana Purchase. The French language of those going to Catholic Mass seemed foreign to them. After all, citizens of the United States spoke English and were mostly Protestants. The Americans' attitude offended the French Creoles, and the ancient Louisianians resented the criticism of their way of life. They had lived in Louisiana for generations and did not consider their lifestyle inferior or in need of change.

This cultural conflict became the focus of the political, economic, and social life of Louisiana. Neither group could understand the other. Language was not the only barrier; there were other differences that ran much deeper. During the early years of the antebellum period, the political struggles centered on those clashes.

Terms: antebellum, writ of habeas corpus, discrimination, immigrant, famine, faction, compromise, suffrage, tariff, depression, exports, factor, canal, internal improvements, tutor

People: James Dakin, Norbert Rillieux

Places: Donaldsonville, Baton Rouge

Preceding pages: Antebellum New Orleans was a bustling port and came to be called the "Queen City of the South."
Right: It was the Creoles of antebellum New Orleans who promoted opera and theater in the city. Charles Colson painted this "Portrait of a Creole Woman."

THE PEOPLE

After the Louisiana Purchase, ambitious Americans headed to Louisiana to build their fortunes and reputations. Many were from successful families in the original thirteen colonies. One young Rhode Islander said, "This is the most promising country for a young man to . . . get a living."

LOUISIANA CREOLES

The Creole descendants of the early French and Spanish colonists treasured their traditions in the face of American change. They spoke French and continued their long-established lifestyle. Louisiana had been their home long before the Anglo-Americans arrived.

More French Creoles came to Louisiana after the revolution in Haiti, seeking shelter among people who shared their heritage. By 1810, al-

most 10,000 of these Creoles had come to New Orleans. Their arrival doubled the population of the city and strengthened the Creole culture.

FREE PEOPLE OF COLOR

The Creoles who came from Haiti included many free people of color, or *gens de couleur libre*. In the early 1800s, they had a sizable population in New Orleans. They joined the free people of color who had already established their own society in New Orleans.

Many were well educated and considered middle class. Their society included Paris-educated professionals who established their own newspaper and published a literary magazine. Some were skilled artisans, and others operated profitable stores. One successful merchant was Madame Marie-Justine Ciraire Couvent, who had been brought from Africa as a slave. She died a wealthy free woman in 1837 and through her will established a school for the children of her community.

The legal rights of free people of color fell between the rights of whites and those of slaves. They were entitled to the presumption of innocence, a trial by jury, and the writ of habeas corpus. A **writ of habeas corpus** is a court document that ensures a person cannot be held unlawfully. However, free people of color were not allowed to serve on a jury, which meant that any jury they appeared before was all white. They were also subject to specific laws that said they could not insult whites. As restrictions tightened during the later antebellum period, free people of color faced increasing legal and social discrimination. **Discrimination** refers to any actions that deny people their rights because of prejudice. For example, free people of color had to carry papers proving their freedom.

Free people of color in antebellum Louisiana were often well educated and included artisans, artists, businesspeople, and professionals.

FOREIGN FRENCH

Political unrest in France had pushed more French people to Louisiana during and after the French Revolution. Both royalists (those who supported King Louis XVI) and the soldiers of Napoleon fled the unrest. Again, Louisiana offered a French-speaking home. The state's native

French people labeled these newcomers the "foreign French." The take-charge attitude of these outsiders offended the Creoles, but their political skills were valued. During the antebellum period, the so-called foreign French influenced the politics of Louisiana.

IMMIGRANTS

Other **immigrants** (those who move into a new country in order to settle there) added to the tapestry of cultures in Louisiana. A series of potato **famines** (extreme and prolonged shortages of food) in Ireland led to the arrival of the largest group of immigrants. Multitudes of starving Irish fled to the United States. Ships filled with cotton sailed from New Orleans to Liverpool. On the return voyage, those same ships transported the Irish to New Orleans. The ships were crowded and the conditions miserable. In some cases, only half of those who set sail survived the trip. Those who did survive took the jobs in New Orleans that no one else wanted. Irish workers became the cheapest labor, used instead of slaves for the most dangerous work. Planters hired the Irish to clear land and dig ditches. If the Irish workers died, the planters lost nothing. According to one observer, the bones of the Irish workers are "lying up and down the Mississippi River."

Problems in other parts of Europe brought more immigrants to New Orleans. German intellectuals fled their homeland after a failed revolution there in 1848. About half of these Germans were Catholic, and their relaxed Sunday behavior offended the Protestant Americans. The Germans gathered at beer gardens on Sunday afternoons.

By 1850, almost half of the people in New Orleans had been born in another country. These new residents changed the political and economic outlook for Louisiana. An already complicated culture became even more confusing.

AMERICAN PIONEERS

American pioneer families began moving into Louisiana in larger numbers. Many of them settled in North Louisiana, and others built communities in the Florida Parishes. These immigrants from the other southern states had English, Scottish, and Irish roots. Many of these pioneers lived a frontier life, while others established cotton plantations and large farms like those they had left in Virginia or the Carolinas.

John Davidson of Poydras Plantation was a Scottish immigrant. John moved to the South in the 1830s, eventually establishing a successful slate-importing business in New Orleans. This 1858 portrait by William Rumpler is of the two Davidson daughters, Elizabeth (center) and Henrietta (right) with their nurse Annette and Newfoundland dog.

ACADIANS

The Acadians did not become absorbed into the larger culture at this time. They continued to live their simple lifestyles along the bayous. There they farmed and fished, continued to speak French, and practiced French folkways that had developed through the years.

The prairie Acadians owned cattle ranches. These *vacheries*, as they were called, existed long before the "Wild West" became famous. A good cowboy and his horse knew how to bring a herd of cattle out of the marsh.

Above: This cabin, now located at the LSU Rural Life Museum, is typical of those built by the Acadians. Right: At Vermilionville, near Lafayette, costumed artisans and crafts people recreate life in Acadian and Creole South Louisiana. This man is demonstrating the skills of an Acadian blacksmith.

NATIVE AMERICANS

By 1850, many of the first inhabitants of Louisiana had disappeared. In 1835, the Caddo sold their land and moved to Indian Territory (present-day Oklahoma). The groups that were left lived in quiet isolation in the forests and along the smaller waterways. Some of them farmed near the Acadians and the hill farmers.

SLAVES

Slaves created a lifestyle for themselves within the slave community. Aside from the work they did, slave life centered around the slave quarters. Only recently have archaeologists begun to excavate slave quarters to study their culture.

At Ashland-Belle Helene Plantation in Ascension Parish, for example, the slave quarters consisted of double rows of two-room cabins. Slaves gathered around the cabins to enjoy games, food, and conversation. Slaves' free time was limited to Sundays, although some plantation owners also gave the slaves Saturday afternoons off.

Sometimes music and dancing were allowed at the end of the work week. Dancing and singing allowed slaves to blend their African cultural traditions and their present experiences. Work songs helped the laborers

Few Native Americans remained in antebellum Louisiana. This 1847 painting by Alfred Boisseau, however, depicts a Choctaw family near Bayou St. John.

English artist John Antrobus painted "A Plantation Burial" from life in 1860, on a northern Louisiana plantation. Sympathetic portrayals of slaves were a rarity in the antebellum South.

push on, and spirituals comforted the weary. Musical instruments were homemade and usually included a fiddle or banjo, which was an African instrument. Drums, another important African instrument, were not permitted on plantations. Owners feared their slaves would use these drums to communicate with the outside world or signal a slave revolt.

The slave diet was very basic. Rations (food supplies) usually included salt pork or bacon, corn or cornmeal, and molasses. Owners provided just enough rations to keep the slaves healthy for working. On some plantations, slaves were allowed to have their own gardens where they might grow sweet potatoes, collard greens, turnips, cabbage, and black-eyed peas. A favorite crop was okra, which was an African vegetable. Sometimes slaves also raised chickens and hogs. Fishing and trapping small animals such as rabbits added more food to their diet.

Food preparation was another element of community life. The older slaves were often responsible for food preparation. On large plantations, food might be prepared in a cookhouse, but slaves usually prepared their own food in the slave quarters.

Do You Remember?
1. What is a writ of habeas corpus?
2. Who were the foreign French?

SLAVE MUSIC

Music was an integral part of ceremonies and festivals in West African society. The music brought cheer to celebrations and to everyday life. Through slavery, African musical traditions reached the New World.

"Musicianers" played a key role in the slave community as teachers, entertainers, and preservers of African folk culture. Slave musicians played every instrument, and string instruments were prized the most. In the slave community, the fiddle was even more popular than the banjo, which was an African instrument. To be nicknamed "fiddler" was a high honor.

Slave holders feared African drums and prohibited their use. They believed that drums might be used to signal a slave revolt, as, in fact, they were during the 1739 Stono Rebellion in South Carolina. To preserve the complex rhythms of West Africa, slaves resorted to "jubba patting," which was hand clapping, body slapping, and foot tapping.

Slaves had many restraints on their freedom of expression and few outlets for their creativity or feelings. Slave songs provided both. The songs were also an "allowed" form of protest. "The songs of the slave," Frederick Douglass wrote, "represent the sorrows of his heart." Often, the songs conveyed images of broken families, the burden of work, and cruel treatment. But just as often they were filled with joy, deliverance, and the hope for a brighter future — even if that future lay in the next world.

African musical traditions were kept alive in the slave community. The fiddler was held in high esteem and many times his music was accompanied by the hand clapping, body slapping, and foot tapping known as "Jubba patting."

POLITICS

When Louisiana became part of the United States, the government in Washington appointed officials to govern the territory. The Americans assumed most of the leadership positions formerly held by the French. When Louisiana became a state, these Americans were elected to state offices. A Creole leader once complained that Virginia would have to run out of sons before Louisiana could elect one of its own.

National party issues were not important in the developing state; every election focused on the Americans versus the Creoles. During the antebellum period, other political factions formed throughout the state. (A **faction** is a small group with common goals within a larger group.) For example, people outside New Orleans resented that city's influence on state politics. Cotton planters and sugar planters did not agree on the ways the government should help the economy.

The settlers in North Louisiana believed the government was neglecting their area of the state. The population in the northern part of the state increased dramatically between 1830 and 1840. More people should have meant more representatives, because legislative districts are based on population. But the boundaries for the districts were not reapportioned (redrawn) even though the population had increased. The people in North Louisiana were not fairly represented.

A CLASH OF CULTURES

Each faction struggled to gain political power. But the underlying conflict in the state was always between the Americans and the Creoles. From the time that the first governor was elected until just before the Civil War, these two factions selected the candidates for governor. Historians have concluded that the two sides had informally agreed to alternate between American and Creole governors.

The list started with the American William C. C. Claiborne. The second elected governor, Jacques Villere, was a Creole who worked out compromises between the two groups. In a **compromise**, each group gives way a little in its demands in order to settle a disagreement. The next governor, Thomas Bolling Robertson, was an aggressive American who increased the conflicts. The two groups became caught in a power struggle, and the plan to alternate between American and Creole governors was abandoned.

The legislature reflected the same factional differences. Legislators spoke in either French or English, with translations immediately following. In one account, a legislator stood silently as he was being insulted by a colleague. When he heard the foreign words translated into his own language; he answered with rude comments.

Top: Jacques Villere was a Creole who was elected as the second governor of Louisiana. **Above:** *Anglo-American Thomas Bolling Robertson was the third governor of the state.* **Opposite:** *In 1849, the capital was moved to Baton Rouge. James Dakin designed the Capitol building to look like a castle. It is now referred to as the Old State Capitol.*

The American legislators objected to meeting in New Orleans, the center of Creole power. In 1823, they tried to move the capital to the West Florida region, the Anglo-American stronghold. The Creoles blocked that move, and this argument almost ignited a riot. Fear of bloodshed forced the leaders on both sides to calm down.

The hostilities and tension between the two groups eased during the Marquis de Lafayette's visit to New Orleans in 1825. His French heritage and his heroic role in the American Revolution brought both Creoles and Americans out to cheer him. Huge crowds of people paraded and celebrated his arrival. City officials even remodeled the Cabildo for his temporary residence.

CREATING A NEW CAPITAL

Governor Henry Johnson took advantage of this temporary peace and goodwill. He led the legislature to compromise about the capital, and Donaldsonville was selected as the new location. The capital was removed from New Orleans, which pleased the Americans. But Donaldsonville was still within the Creole sugar bowl along the Mississippi River.

Unfortunately, the compromise did not work out. The legislature met in Donaldsonville in 1830 for only one term, complaining that the town was just too small. By the next term, they had returned to New Orleans with its hotels, restaurants, and entertainments.

In 1849, the Americans succeeded in moving the capital to Baton Rouge. The cornerstone for the State Capitol in Baton Rouge was laid on November 3, 1847. The imposing building cost $100,000 and took two years to build. A new technique — using cast iron instead of masonry supports — made the building stronger and less costly. Cast iron was also used for the window frames, sills, battlement caps, cornices, and columns.

Other state capitols built in the same era copied the U.S. Capitol in Washington, D.C. Architect James Dakin designed the Louisiana Capitol to look more like a castle than a government building. Dakin's radical design shocked some and pleased others. Mark Twain ridiculed the building, calling it a "sham castle." Others were impressed by the huge white building that overlooked the Mississippi River. This monument to the past still stands today.

POLITICAL PARTIES

Andrew Jackson's presidential campaigns created Louisiana's first, strong interest in national political parties. The people remembered the hero of the Battle of New Orleans and helped elect him president in 1828. The ideas of Jacksonian democracy appealed to many. Jackson distrusted the wealthy upper class and its dominance of the political system. The candidate of the "common man," Jackson believed that

One attraction of the Old State Capitol's interior is a large iron spiral stairway crowned by this beautiful stained glass dome. The building was one of the first in the South to be constructed of brick on a cast iron frame.

all people had the right to participate in their government. Those who supported Jackson called themselves the Democratic-Republicans, which was later shortened to Democrats.

A government of the people demanded broader voting rights. Before the Jackson era, most states required that voters be property owners or taxpayers. But by 1828, many states had extended **suffrage** (the right to vote) to all white males over twenty-one years of age. The American

Henry Clay of Kentucky was one of the leaders of the Whig party. His stand on protective tariffs attracted many Louisianians, particularly the sugar planters, to the Whig party.

newcomers in North Louisiana welcomed these ideas and joined the Democratic party.

Not everyone agreed with Jackson, his policies, or his methods. The Whig party was formed in the 1830s to oppose Jackson, and many Creoles became Whigs. Henry Clay of Kentucky was one of the leaders of the Whigs. Among other issues, he supported protective tariffs. **Tariffs** are taxes on imports designed to keep out foreign competition.

This issue soon attracted Louisianians to the Whig party. The sugar planters in Louisiana needed protection against the lower prices of sugar from the West Indies. In fact, the sugar planter faction organized the Whig party in Louisiana in 1834, and the leaders of the Whig party in Louisiana came from this wealthy and powerful group. Alexander Porter was an early Louisiana Whig leader. He had left Ireland for political reasons and emigrated to the United States. Later, he became a prosperous sugar planter on Bayou Lafourche. Henry Clay visited Porter's Oak Lawn Plantation to discuss Whig plans for the state. However, increasing national conflicts over slavery killed the Whig party. The many factions within the party could no longer compromise on that issue.

Increasing tensions in a growing country led to the formation of a new party about this time. Officially called the American party, the party was opposed to immigrants and Catholics. Members soon became known as the "Know Nothings" because they always answered "I know nothing" when asked about their organization. The party blamed recent immigrants for problems in the United States such as unemployment and wage cuts and proposed that immigrants wait twenty-one years before they could become citizens. They also wanted elected offices to be limited to native-born Americans. The Know Nothings accused the Catholic Church of having too much influence, especially over newly arrived immigrants.

In Louisiana, the American party focused more on the immigrants in New Orleans than on the Catholic Church. Louisiana's strong Catholic heritage would have made an American party challenge against Catholics unwise. The Know Nothings blamed the immigrants for the increasing violence among workers in the growing port of New Orleans. The party gained control of the New Orleans city government in 1854 and maintained that control until the Civil War. The Democratic newspaper accused them of using "the gun and the Bowie knife" to achieve that control. Several riots did, in fact, occur, and in one riot two Irish policemen were killed.

Strong opinions about politics did not always lead to violence. Political campaigning added to the social life and entertainment of the antebellum period. Crowds gathered to hear politicians' long-winded speeches. One campaigner spoke for six hours. He gave his two-hour speech first in English, then in French, and finally in Spanish.

Barbecues attracted audiences for the lengthy speeches. One Whig barbecue held to celebrate a political victory was reportedly attended by six thousand people. The huge crowd was entertained by several bands. A celebration by Andrew Jackson's New Orleans supporters included the barbecue of a bear.

REWRITING THE LOUISIANA CONSTITUTION

The growth of Jacksonian democracy eventually led to a new constitution for Louisiana. The first state constitution, written in 1812, limited voting rights and representation. In addition, a depression struck the nation in 1837 (called the Panic of 1837). A **depression** is a severe, continued downturn in the economy where sales and prices drop, manufacturing decreases, businesses close, banks fail, and people lose their jobs. The state's leaders wanted to include economic and banking controls in the new state constitution.

The resulting Constitution of 1845 was more democratic. Owning property was no longer a requirement for voting or holding office. However, the right to vote was still limited to white males over twenty-one years of age. The biggest battle over this constitution repeated the same arguments heard in Philadelphia when the U.S. Constitution was written. What was a fair way to decide representation?

Each faction had its own interests in mind. The New Orleans delegates wanted to count the number of voters to determine the number of legislators. The planters opposed that plan fearing they would lose their power because they would be outnumbered by the city voters. The planters wanted to count the total population, including slaves. In a compromise, the two groups shared the power. Representation in the house of representatives was based on the number of registered voters; in the senate, it was based on the total population.

The Constitution of 1845 never pleased many people. Some felt it was still too undemocratic. Others complained that the banking regulations were too strict and stifled economic growth. Because of these concerns, another constitution was written a few years later—in 1852.

Again, the major argument centered on representation. This time, the planters won and representation in both houses of the legislature was based on the total population. The 1852 constitution loosened banking regulations to promote a growing economy. It allowed the state to help fund companies. This action led to state financing for canals, roads, and, most importantly, railroads.

Judge Alexander Porter was an early leader of the Whig party in the state. Henry Clay visited Porter's Oak Lawn Plantation to discuss Whig plans for the state.

Do You Remember?
1. What were the two major political factions that existed in Louisiana during the antebellum period?
2. Why was the Louisiana constitution rewritten in 1845?

DONALDSONVILLE

Buildings record history. And so does a vacant lot in Donaldsonville. Even though the capitol built in Donaldsonville is gone, you can still find its story.

"The founder of the village of Donaldson has been summoned by The Angel of Death," announced the *New Orleans Courier* in November 1813. William Donaldson died before he could see the state capital moved to his town. As early as 1812, Donaldson had offered to donate eighteen lots in his new town for a capitol building fronting Opelousas and Claiborne streets. The legislature did not accept his offer, but it did agree to incorporate the town on March 18, 1813. Over the years, the community has had several names — Lafourche, Donaldson, and finally Donaldsonville. In 1830, when Donaldsonville became the capital, the town boasted 492 residents (261 whites, 76 free people of color, and 155 slaves).

The state legislature set aside $30,000 for a building in which it could meet. The furniture arrived by steamboat from New Orleans before the building was finished. In January 1830, the legislature arrived in Donaldsonville, but the building was still not finished. Until the building was ready, the senate met in a tavern and the house of representatives used the parish courtroom.

*Top: This late nineteenth-century doctor's office on the courthouse square is now a tourism office. **Above:** Listed on the National Register of Historic Places, the Lehman Store is now a museum.*

Legislators complained about the capitol building and the town, and they soon headed back to New Orleans. In 1848, the capitol building was torn down and the bricks used to reinforce the banks of Bayou Lafourche. A historical marker labels the spot where the Donaldsonville capitol once stood.

Another significant building in Donaldsonville is the Church of the Ascension. The parish, in fact, was named for this church. The Acadians built the first church in 1770; the present church is the fourth and was completed in 1896.

The nearby three-story brick convent of the Sisters of Charity of St. Joseph was finished in 1850. In 1854, it also became an orphanage for children whose parents died in the yellow fever epidemic of 1853. During the Civil War, the convent was hit by Union gunboats as they bombarded the town.

Lehman's Store is another noteworthy building. The founder of this business, Jacob Lehman, began as a peddler. In 1876, he hired an architect to design and build this imposing structure. The building, listed on the National Register of Historic Places, covers a whole block on Mississippi Street. The store was a true general store, selling hardware, feed and seed, clothing, groceries, and almost anything available at the time.

Even the cemetery in Donaldsonville has architectural significance. An imposing above-ground tomb was designed in 1845 for the Landry family. James Dakin created this Egyptian-style tomb after he designed the Capitol in Baton Rouge.

Top: Donaldsonville's parish, Ascension, was named for the Church of the Ascension.
Above: James Dakin, architect of the Old State Capitol, designed this tomb for the Landry family.
Left: The Ascension Parish courthouse was built in 1889 by James Freret.

THE LOUISIANA ECONOMY

Louisiana's economy grew in spite of the political unrest. The plantation system had already been well established by the Creoles. The American newcomers bought existing plantations or created new ones along the Mississippi River. These plantations created some of the wealthiest people in America.

The profitable plantation economy relied on the port city of New Orleans. The only larger United States port was New York, and only three world ports had a larger export volume. (**Exports** are goods sent or sold to another country.) New Orleans was the state's commercial urban center.

This 1858 painting of the port and city of New Orleans was done by Marie Adrien Persac.

BANKING

New Orleans also developed as the banking center for Louisiana. The growing economy required investment capital (money that could be put into or loaned to businesses to help them grow). People needed loans to buy land. Those who operated businesses or plantations needed to borrow money to pay expenses. The planters wanted ready access to the money they needed to operate and expand.

The factor system developed partly from the planters' need for quick financial and business assistance. A **factor** is a commercial agent. The factor represented the planter in the sale of a crop and by doing so earned a percentage of the profit. During the year, the factor might advance money to the planter for various expenses. Some factors also represented

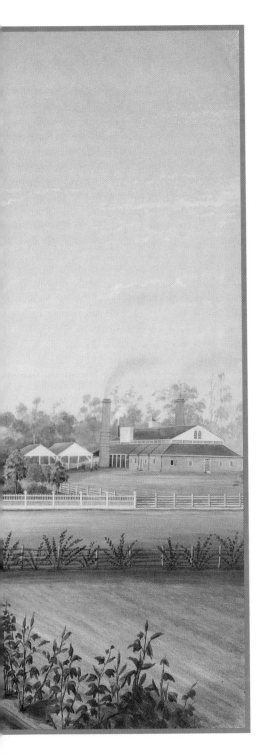

the planter by buying needed goods and sending them to the plantation. If the planter needed a large loan, the factor often agreed to repay the loan if the planter could not. The plantation economy made many factors as wealthy as the planters.

The early banks in Louisiana were sounder than those in much of the United States, but they could not avoid the national banking crisis of 1837. Many who had borrowed money to pay for land could not repay their loans. Louisiana dealt with these banking problems through new banking laws and provisions in the constitutions of 1845 and 1852. By 1860, Louisiana banks ranked among the best. Those banks supported the commercial interests and the plantation system.

THE PLANTATION SYSTEM

Cotton became a profitable southern crop when Eli Whitney designed an efficient cotton gin in 1793. The gin (short for *engine*) removed the cotton seeds from the cotton fibers, a task that was incredibly time consuming when done by hand. The cotton gin soon became a fixture on the Louisiana landscape and led to an increased use of slaves.

Above: *St. John Plantation was a sugar plantation in St. Martin Parish.* **Right:** *At 12,000 acres, Houmas House was the state's largest sugar plantation.*

Rosedown Plantation (above) in St. Francisville is an Anglo-style plantation. The main house contains much original furniture (top left). The 28 acres of gardens (left center) are historically important. The kitchen has its own vegetable garden (below left).

Laura Plantation in Vacherie (top left) is a Creole-style plantation with slave cabins (below right). Rooms like the dining room (above) and bedroom (center right) are less ornate but brightly decorated.

Factories in the North and in Great Britain turned the South's cotton into cloth. Industrial progress — steam engines, automatic spinning machines, and power looms — made it easier and cheaper to produce cloth, which increased the demand for cotton. While not quite spinning gold from straw, growing cotton created great riches.

Louisiana wanted a share of this wealth. Both large plantations and small farms could produce cotton. A farmer could grow a few acres of cotton, sometimes with just the help of his family. As profits increased, the farmer bought more land and planted more cotton. Long grown in Louisiana, cotton soon became a major cash crop.

The boom in agriculture was not limited to cotton. Sugar plantations were even more profitable than cotton plantations, but they required a larger capital investment of workers and equipment. The South Louisiana climate was perfect for growing sugar cane. Sugar was the main plantation crop in the West Indies. Immigrants from that region brought their sugar-producing skills to Louisiana. An invention by Norbert Rillieux, a free man of color from New Orleans, revolutionized sugar production, just as the cotton gin increased cotton production. Rillieux invented a vacuum pan evaporator for refining sugar. Rillieux's invention resulted in finer, whiter sugar with a huge reduction in costs and labor. The device made the crop even more profitable.

One of the richest sugar planters was John Burnside of Houmas House in Ascension Parish. He owned 22,500 acres of land and 1,000 slaves. His huge plantation made him very wealthy and enabled him to live the lifestyle usually associated with the plantations. For example, guests were offered portable bathtubs filled with water and blocks of ice to provide relief from the muggy Louisiana heat. At the time, ice was an expensive luxury that had to be brought from northern lakes. Steamboats carried the ice, packed in sawdust, to Burnside's landing on the Mississippi River.

Some slaves were skilled workers such as carpenters. Others worked inside the home, such as this maid (opposite). The hardest jobs were those of the field hands. Women often worked the fields (above).

SLAVE LABOR

Behind this view of luxury was another scene. Slavery supported this lifestyle and economic structure. Not only did slaves provide the labor in this economy but it was their status as property that made slave owners wealthy. It was slave labor that produced the plantation crops. But slaves also did basic manual labor, worked in the plantation houses, and performed skilled tasks. Skilled workers such as blacksmiths and

coopers (barrel makers) were valuable assets. These skilled slaves were
often hired out; field hands too might be hired out to bring in crops.

Plantation owners hired *overseers* to supervise work on the plantations. Some slaves were selected to be *drivers* and were held responsible for the work of other slaves. Slaves worked long hours from "can
to can't," meaning from daylight ("can see") to dark ("can't see"). A bell
or horn started their work day before dawn. Every hour of a slave's day
was structured to produce as much work as possible and to keep the

slaves subdued. They were allowed to leave the plantation only with permission and a written pass.

Punishment was used to keep order and control in this rigid system. Slaves were disciplined when they stole, ran away, or did not work. Documents from the time show that the punishment varied from fairly mild to extremely cruel. Whipping was the most common form of punishment. But even under the best conditions, the slave system was paternalistic. The plantation owners controlled all aspects of their slaves' lives and felt responsible for them.

A journalist from the North reported finding at Richard Taylor's Fashion Plantation in Ascension Parish the best conditions he had ever seen for slaves. But he also learned from the carriage driver that the good treatment did not lessen the slaves' desire for freedom.

FARMERS

Slave-holding plantations dominated Louisiana's antebellum economy. They are often presented as representing the entire history of antebellum Louisiana. But more than 71 percent of the white population did not own slaves. These people included merchants, skilled craftsmen, professionals, laborers, and small farmers.

While the planters' goal was profit, the small farmers were mainly concerned with feeding their families. Generally, the small farmers owned just enough land to raise crops for their own use. Sometimes the farmers had excess crops that they could sell for cash. The farmers and their families provided the labor.

Above: These preserved slave cabins from a Louisiana plantation are exhibits at the LSU Rural Life Museum. ***Above left:*** Slaves were considered property and were bought and sold at auctions, as seen in this engraving of the Rotunda in New Orleans.

Antebellum Louisiana: Riches and Repression   **329**

Steamboat travel was the main method of transport along the Mississippi until the coming of the railroads in the late 1870s.

Farmers also raised cattle and hogs. The animals were branded or had their ears notched for identification and were allowed to roam the nearby woods. The corn crop helped feed these animals as well as the farm families. In fact, the basic farm diet was often described as "hog and hominy" (*hominy* was a dish made from corn).

The small farms were basically self-sufficient. But peddlers traveled to isolated farms, bringing goods the farm could not provide. Coffee and sugar were two of the prized items purchased from these traveling salespeople.

Do You Remember?

1. What was the only port larger than New Orleans in the antebellum United States?
2. How did the cotton gin increase cotton production?
3. What was the difference between drivers and overseers?

TRANSPORTATION

Imagine a ten-mile trip taking six days. This was not uncommon on the roads of antebellum Louisiana. Wagons pulled by teams of oxen often had to struggle through deep, muddy ruts on the wilderness roads. Rural residents urged the state government to improve roads because they needed the access to markets. But rainfall and the type of soil in Louisiana made road-building difficult. In 1827, the first road-improvement bill funded the road from Covington through Washington Parish to Mississippi.

Water travel was always easier than trying to build a Louisiana road. The coming of the steamboat in the early nineteenth century made water travel faster, and canals provided shorter water routes to markets.

WATER TRAVEL

The steamboat developed as the primary means of transportation in Louisiana. Not only did the steamboats travel the state's rivers, but they also transported freight through **canals**, manmade waterways that connected Louisiana's rivers and bayous.

The first canals were dug by private *investors* (people who risked their own money on a project) who charged users a fee. Later, banks and the government funded canals in New Orleans and outside the city. In 1831, a special bank was organized to build the New Basin Canal in New Orleans.

Water-filled Louisiana required another major improvement. An extensive levee system was needed to protect the plantation economy. From the time of the French era, the government had required individuals to build and maintain their own levees. Now, the demand for government-funded levees became a major political issue.

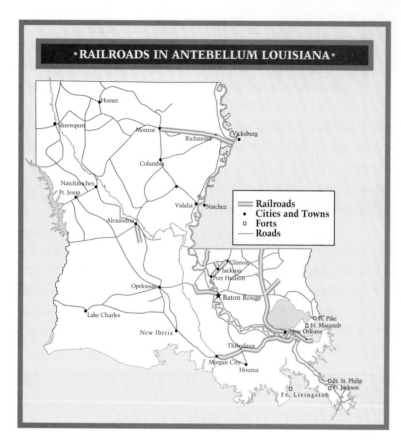

In 1832, the state created the Board of Public Works, which gave special attention to waterways, including levees. In 1856, the board developed a system of levee districts to maintain the levee by sections. These districts made some efforts, but not as much as was needed. Then the Civil War halted further efforts for flood control.

RAILROADS

The political and economic focus on **internal improvements** (roads, bridges, canals, and other transportation needs) increased with the coming of the railroad. The Pontchartrain Railroad was the first railroad west of the Alleghenies. Begun in 1831, the six-mile-long track ran between New Orleans and Lake Pontchartrain.

Passengers on the earliest railroads in Louisiana paid a 25-cent fare for an exciting but not always pleasant ride. The train often slipped off the unstable tracks. Getting the train going again required the passengers' help. Other obstacles were common. One traveler described in graphic detail the cow that was run over by the train.

Building and improving the railroads cost huge sums of money, but New Orleans needed those railroads to compete with the North. As the demand for the railroads increased, the state and the city of New Orleans helped finance the railroad building. By the 1850s, three major railroad lines had been funded in this way. One line linked New Orleans with Nashville, bringing goods to the port from the North. Another line ran westward from New Orleans to Texas. The third line connected Shreveport and Vicksburg.

The Panic of 1837 slowed the growth of the railroads in Louisiana. When the Civil War started, railroad building in Louisiana stopped completely. But by that time, Louisiana had 334 miles of track, built at a cost of $12 million.

DAILY LIFE

During the antebellum period, Louisiana was changing from a colonial and frontier world. Small towns and villages had grown, adding some of the basics of urban life. In rural Louisiana, however, some people still lived closer to the frontier lifestyle, self-sufficient and independent.

New Orleans had already become the fourth largest city in the United States and one of the premier ports in the world. As the city expanded, the Americans and the Creoles built separate communities in different sections of the city. The Americans built their own neighborhood with a grand display of architectural styles. Known today as the Garden District, this section exhibits that antebellum splendor. The Creole community was the Vieux Carre, or French Quarter.

By 1836, the disputes between the districts split the city government. New Orleans was divided into three separate municipalities, each with

In the antebellum period, the Creoles lived in the Vieux Carre, or French Quarter. The Spanish-style architecture there created quiet courtyards such as this one at the Raymond Gallard Cottage.

its own government. In this way, each group could provide for its own neighborhood. The separate districts merged into one city government again in 1852.

COMMUNICATION

The lack of roads and the resulting isolation made communication and the spread of information difficult. Delivery of mail was quite a challenge. Some mail was carried by stagecoaches traveling between the larger towns. But often the mail carrier rode a horse. If the horse had to ford a river or bayou, the mail arrived wet. Once a mail rider reported that the mail was lost because his horse was swept away and drowned. He hoped that when the flood waters went down, he could find the horse with the mailbag still attached. Then the mail would go through.

When they could get mail, people throughout Louisiana eagerly looked forward to the arrival of newspapers. New Orleans printed different newspapers in English, French, Spanish, and German. The *New Orleans Picayune* was founded in 1837. The price of the paper was 6¼ cents, which was the value of a coin called a picayune. Small-town newspapers also existed in places like Franklin and St. Francisville. The papers published news and influenced public opinion. Some newspapers slanted their views toward certain political groups, and some were funded by political party leaders.

Newspapers and letters mailed from New York took two weeks to reach New Orleans. But, the speed of communication changed dramatically in July 1848 when the telegraph reached New Orleans. Businesses telegraphed many messages a day, at about 5 cents a word. In its excitement, the New Orleans *Daily Crescent* reported that "Distance and time are annihilated."

Bringing this "lightning system" to Louisiana presented obstacles. "Cypress sawn square" poles had to be used to prevent rot in Louisiana's rainy weather. Storms, floods, and fallen trees could quickly down telegraph lines and stop service. Fallen lines created additional hazards. One traveler complained when his horse and buggy became entangled in fallen wires. Despite the problems, Samuel Morse's dot-and-dash code improved communication and brought progress.

EDUCATION

The first schools in colonial Louisiana were taught by nuns and priests. As the Protestant churches grew, they added schools of their own. Some children were taught at home, and the wealthy planters often hired **tutors** (private teachers). One such tutor was John James Audubon, who came to Oakley in the Felicianas to teach dancing and drawing.

Opposite, above: This engraving depicts a typical street in one of the French neighborhoods of New Orleans. ***Opposite, below:*** In the American Garden District of New Orleans, you will see villas and neo-classical mansions such as this, many surrounded by ornamental iron fences. **Below:** Many of the early schools in Louisiana were Catholic, reflecting the heritage of the early settlers. This is the Academy of the Sacred Heart in Grand Coteau, built in 1821.

Above: This one-room plantation schoolhouse is on exhibit at the LSU Rural Life Museum.
Opposite: John James Audubon, famed naturalist and artist (below right), was hired to teach drawing to Eliza, daughter of Mr. and Mrs. James Pirrie, at Oakley Plantation (below left) in St. Francisville, home of the Pirries. This Audubon lithograph (above) depicts a pair of black-crowned night herons, a common bird on the bayous of Louisiana.

The state's first attempts at public education offered students scholarships to private schools. But the small number of openings and the perception of charity resulted in few children going to the schools. The Constitution of 1845 was the first to establish free public schools in the state and fixed the school age between six and sixteen. However, the state's new public school system struggled with funding and public support. Many children were still taught in private schools or at home. And many more children who lived outside the cities and towns received little education.

An early one-room schoolhouse in Claiborne Parish was typical. School "took in" at 8:00 a.m. and "turned out" at 5:00 p.m. There was a lunch break from 12:00 to 1:30 and two short recesses. The school term was usually six months or less. The textbooks were Webster's "Blue-Backed Speller" and Smiley's arithmetic. The teacher kept a good supply of switches on hand with which to discipline students. Naughty boys experienced hardwood switches, while girls were punished only with softwood.

Cholera, yellow fever, and other diseases struck often during the antebellum period. This painting depicts the Duchamp family in mourning for Mr. Duchamp who died in 1832, the year of the great cholera epidemic.

DISEASE AND HEALTH

Medical progress in this era did not include conquering the most dangerous enemies. Cholera and yellow fever frequently attacked the population. The worst cholera epidemics occurred in the 1830s. A cholera epidemic of 1832 killed 6,000 people throughout Louisiana, including almost 20 percent of the population of Baton Rouge. Conditions in New Orleans were so awful that hundreds of people were buried together in the same trench or grave.

Old cemeteries still tell the story of the worst yellow fever epidemic. The headstones of entire families are dated 1853. In that year, yellow fever killed 9,000 people in New Orleans alone. Thibodaux lost 224 people, 15 percent of the town. Even working through the night, the grave diggers could not keep up. Cannons boomed every twenty minutes in New Orleans in an attempt to clean the air of the disease. Smaller towns burned buckets of sulphur to try to protect themselves.

Even though cholera and yellow fever were known as killers, more people suffered from digestive diseases. Diarrhea was a common and serious ailment. The usual treatment was a harsh laxative, which only made it worse and caused dehydration.

These epidemic diseases touched everyone in Louisiana. One cholera epidemic killed the speaker of the house of representatives during a session of the legislature. Early in the century, Governor Claiborne lost two wives to yellow fever. Poor sanitation and limited medical knowledge made nineteenth-century Louisiana an unhealthy place.

RELIGION

France and Spain had allowed only the Catholic Church in colonial Louisiana. Built in 1794 facing Jackson Square, the St. Louis Cathedral symbolizes the Catholic Church in Louisiana. Some of the early churches still offer Sunday mass to Louisiana's large Catholic population.

When Louisiana became part of the United States, Protestants moved into the territory. By 1805, the Protestants in New Orleans were ready to build a church. The group, which represented several denominations, voted to establish an Episcopal Church.

The Protestant revival that swept America in the 1800s sent ministers on horseback into Louisiana. These *circuit riders* came to preach and to establish churches. An early Methodist minister built a simple log church with his own hands.

Even more Protestants arrived when North Louisiana was opened to settlement. There, camp meetings served as religious and social gatherings. A makeshift church, called a *brush arbor*, was built, and people camped for days at these revival meetings.

The first synagogue was built by the Jewish community in New Orleans in 1828. One wealthy member, Judah Touro, is remembered in New Orleans for the contributions he made to the

While Louisiana was a French and Spanish colony, only the Catholic Church was permitted in the territory. St. Louis Cathedral, completed in 1794, is actually the third Catholic Church on this site. The spires were not added until the church was rebuilt in 1847.

city. He donated money for a hospital, libraries, and parks. Other members of the Jewish community included German immigrants who came to the city in the 1840s.

ENTERTAINMENT

As a city, New Orleans offered a fascinating variety of entertainment for visitors and residents. More than two thousand people could attend performances at the French Opera House. Theaters were very popular, and traveling troupes visited the small towns to perform.

Dancing was popular in the ballrooms of the plantations, in the cabins of the Acadians, and in Congo Square in New Orleans, where the slaves were allowed to dance on Sunday. Plantation dances included an elaborate midnight supper with flowers at every place setting. When the guests left at dawn, they were given strong coffee and hot gumbo. The people in North Louisiana danced to fiddle music, part of their Celtic heritage. As the Protestant religions grew stricter, dancing was forbidden by many churches. However, some forms of dancing survived when they were labeled party games.

Louisiana also loved horse racing. The largest and most elegant track was the Metairie Race Track. In 1854, some 20,000 people, including former President Millard Fillmore, watched a horse race between Lexington and LeCompte. LeCompte, the Louisiana horse, was honored by having a town in Rapides Parish named for him.

Do You Remember?
1. What is a picayune?
2. What were the two deadliest diseases in antebellum Louisiana?
3. What forms of entertainment did the people of antebellum Louisiania enjoy?

SUMMARY

Antebellum Louisiana, in its early years of statehood, faced many challenges. The blending of the people, their politics, and the economy brought both change and complications. The clash of cultures between the Creoles of New Orleans and the English-speaking Americans affected both politics and the economy.

Some grew rich as their cotton or sugar plantations flourished. Inventions such as the vacuum pan evaporator and the cotton gin brought great wealth to Louisiana. Others worked hard to build businesses in growing cities. Farmers struggled to provide for their basic needs. And some experienced the oppression of slavery. New Orleans developed into one of the major ports of the world. By the time of the Civil War, Louisiana had a well-established economy.

The constitutions of 1845 and 1852 emphasized the growing need for reform. For the first time, public education in Louisiana was addressed. The capital moved to Baton Rouge.

Opposite, above: The church held a very important position in a community. Grace Episcopal Church in St. Francisville, established in 1827, is the second oldest Episcopal congregation in Louisiana. **Opposite, below:** *Judah Touro of New Orleans is remembered for the many contributions he made to the city.* **Above:** *Most slaves were given Sundays off. Some were able to enjoy dancing in Congo Square in New Orleans.*

CHAPTER · REVIEW

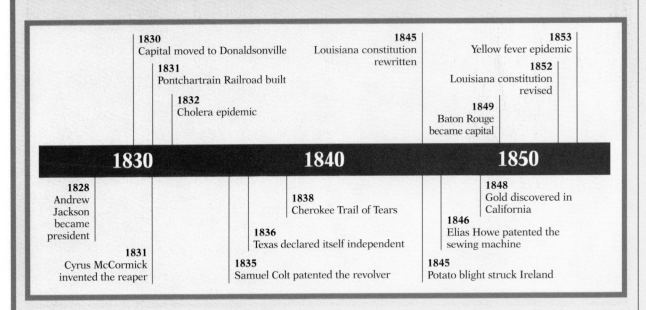

1830
Capital moved to Donaldsonville

1831
Pontchartrain Railroad built

1832
Cholera epidemic

1845
Louisiana constitution rewritten

1853
Yellow fever epidemic

1852
Louisiana constitution revised

1849
Baton Rouge became capital

1830   **1840**   **1850**

1828
Andrew Jackson became president

1831
Cyrus McCormick invented the reaper

1838
Cherokee Trail of Tears

1836
Texas declared itself independent

1835
Samuel Colt patented the revolver

1848
Gold discovered in California

1846
Elias Howe patented the sewing machine

1845
Potato blight struck Ireland

Reviewing People, Places, and Terms

Define, identify, or explain the importance of the following.

1. antebellum
2. Baton Rouge
3. canal
4. compromise
5. depression
6. discrimination
7. exports
8. faction
9. factor
10. famine
11. immigrant
12. internal improvements
13. suffrage
14. tariff
15. tutor
16. writ of habeas corpus

Understanding the Facts

1. What brought the Irish to Louisiana?
2. What were vacheries?

3. Why did the people in North Louisiana believe the state was neglecting them?
4. Why did the Americans want to move the capital from New Orleans?
5. Name the three political parties that formed in the early 1800s.
6. Which of Louisiana's constitutions extended suffrage to all white males over the age of twenty-one?
7. How was the number of legislators for each district determined in the Constitution of 1852?
8. What was the factor's role in the state's plantation economy?
9. Why did road building become so difficult in Louisiana?

Developing Critical Thinking

1. Why did the American and the Creole cultures clash?
2. Why were free people of color denied the same rights as other free people?
3. "Irish need not apply" signs were sometimes seen in New Orleans. How does this discrimi-

nation against Irish workers explain the growth of the American party?

4. Discuss the interrelationship of cotton (or sugar) production, slavery, and the economic and social development of Louisiana.

Using Your Skills

1. A yellow fever epidemic in Thibodaux killed 224 people, which was 15 percent of the town's population. What was the total population before the epidemic?

2. The Vicksburg, Shreveport, and Texas Railroad was planned to run from the Mississippi state line to the Texas state line. How many miles would this have involved? When the Civil War started, the line extended only from Vicksburg to Monroe. How many miles were finished? How many miles were left to build?

Special Projects

1. The planter and the slave have quite different views of a typical work day on a Louisiana plantation. Write a one-paragraph description from the planter's point of view. Write another paragraph from the slave's point of view.

2. Buildings are one of the things that help us learn about the past. Select a building in your parish that can help tell the history of Louisiana. Take a photograph, draw a sketch, or make a model of this building. Using your visual aid as a prop, tell the story of this building to your classmates.

Making Connections

1. How did "slave music" make life more bearable for the slaves?

2. It was mentioned that slave songs were an "allowed" form of protest. Can you think of other ways in which music has been used as a form of protest?

Louisiana Lagniappe

• New Orleans hosted its first formal Mardi Gras parade in 1838.
• A hogshead, a large wooden barrel, held a thousand pounds of sugar or seventy gallons of molasses.
• Passengers jokingly complained about the Pontchartrain Railroad by calling it the "Smoky Mary."
• *Gumbo* is the African word for okra.
• The capitol building in Donaldsonville was 100 feet long and 15 feet wide.

• BUILDING SKILLS: READING FOR DETAILS •

Reading for details often requires different techniques than reading for an overview or to see the big picture. To read for details, follow these guidelines.

1. Slow down in your reading. Look for key words, concentrating on a few words at a time.

2. Look for phrases that explain. Often the important terms are defined either right before or right after a key word.

3. Look for verbal clues. The first sentence usually gives an idea of what the paragraph is about. Details and examples follow this topic sentence. Look for words such as *for example, such as*, and *that is.*

4. Look for visual "tricks" in the text and in the design of the page. Numbers, dashes, and other graphic devices such as bold or italic print are sometimes used to make major points or details.

Reread the section on Politics, which begins on page 310. Answer the following questions based on the details in this section.

1. What political factions developed in antebellum Louisiana?

2. What two languages separated antebellum political factions?

3. Why did the legislature move the capital from Donaldsonville back to New Orleans?

4. Why did sugar planters support tariffs?

CHAPTER TEN

LOUISIANA'S CIVIL WAR ERA: CRISIS AND CONFLICT

What may be the fate of this horrible contest, no man can tell, and none pretend to foresee. . . .
— Judah Benjamin, *The Daily Delta*, January 16, 1861

THE CIVIL WAR CAME AFTER YEARS OF STRUGGLE over the issues of slavery and **states' rights** (the principle that the rights and responsibilities of the states should take precedence over the rights and responsibilities of the federal government). Lousiana's political leaders had hoped that the Missouri Compromise and the Compromise of 1850 would protect slavery and preserve the Union. But the state's planters saw the increasing pressure from abolitionists as an economic threat. Louisiana, like the other southern states, could not see the desolation that lay ahead when it entered a war expected to last only a few weeks.

Confederate General P. G. T. Beauregard was born in 1818 near New Orleans. He commanded the artillery that fired the first shots of the Civil War at Fort Sumter, South Carolina. This statue of Beauregard is located near the New Orleans Museum of Art.

HEADING FOR WAR

In 1819, the Territory of Missouri applied for statehood as a slave state. An amendment was added to the statehood bill requiring Missouri to abolish slavery. When the bill was rejected, Congress worked out a compromise in 1820 that maintained the balance between the number of slave states and free states. Missouri entered the Union as a slave state, and the new state of Maine was a free state. A line drawn westward from Missouri's southern border marked the division between slave and free states. This decision was known as the **Missouri Compromise**.

The problem of slavery, however, was not settled. The annexation of the lands taken from Mexico after the war of 1846 led to another debate over which states would be slave states and which would be free. Congress settled that debate by passing the **Compromise of 1850**. California was admitted as a free state and part of Texas was given to New Mexico. Slavery in some of the western territories was to be determined by a vote of those living there. Congress also passed a stronger fugitive slave law. Many hoped that the compromise had permanently settled the dispute over slavery.

The American Anti-Slavery Society had been formed in 1833 and called for an immediate end to slavery. The Society worked to convince people that slavery was evil and that slave owners were sinners. These **abolitionists** (people who wanted to free the slaves) launched bitter attacks on slavery and slave owners. The antislavery novel *Uncle Tom's Cabin*, written by Harriet Beecher Stowe, was published in 1852. Some people believe that the author based her story on a Louisiana Red River plantation. The book increased abolitionist efforts and brought more pressure to end slavery.

The Missouri Compromise provided for a balance between free and slave states. A line drawn westward from Missouri's southern border marked the division of free and slave states.

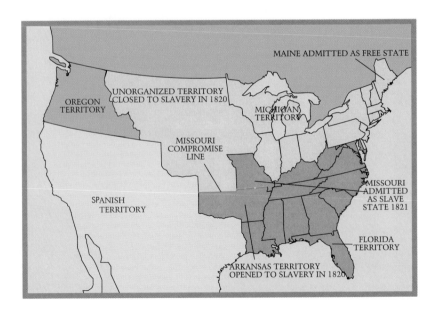

Tensions increased even more when Congress passed the Kansas-Nebraska Act in 1854. The bill allowed those territories, both of which were north of the Missouri Compromise line, to decide for themselves whether to permit slavery. Fighting between the proslavery and antislavery factions broke out in Kansas. John Brown was one of the leaders of the antislavery militia forces there. The Kansas-Nebraska Act also led to the formation of a new political party in 1854. Members of the antislavery movement united to form the Republican party.

The pressure of the slavery issue split the Democratic party convention wide open and led to a presidential election in 1860 with four candidates. Northern delegates to the Democratic convention supported Stephen A. Douglas of Illinois, but the southern Democrats disagreed with his position on slavery. The extremists among the southern Democrats, labeled "fire-eaters" because of their passionate speeches, led a walkout at the convention. They then held their own convention and named

Henry Clay of Kentucky argued in favor of the Compromise of 1850 in the U.S. Senate.

John C. Breckinridge of Kentucky as their candidate. Another faction of southerners, which included many former Whigs, hoped to preserve the Union. They formed the Constitutional Union party and nominated John C. Bell of Tennessee. The Republicans nominated Abraham Lincoln of Illinois, who was a moderate compromise candidate.

The election of 1860 was like a dress rehearsal for the coming conflict. Abraham Lincoln said, "You think slavery is right and ought to be extended. We think it is wrong and ought to be restricted. . . . It is certainly the only difference between us." Southerners heard this as the words of an abolitionist. Lincoln had actually said that he would not interfere with slavery where it already existed.

The split among the Democrats handed the Republicans the victory. To southerners, a Republican was the enemy and a threat to their way of life. The Republican party did not exist in Louisiana, so Lincoln's name was not even on the ballot. The new president of the United States had not received one vote in the state.

Lincoln's election aroused immediate reaction. One New Orleans newspaper said the Republican party opposed the "dignity, interest and well-being of Louisiana." Another predicted, "You might as well try to breathe life into a mummy of ancient Egypt as to expect the Union to be preserved."

Talk of **secession** (the withdrawal of a state from the Union) filled the South. The cry for secession spread as quickly as a yellow fever epidemic, and the results were just as deadly. But in 1860 Louisianians could not see what lay ahead. They heard speeches loaded with words like *honor*, *self-respect*, and *principle*. They heard Lincoln labeled a "black Republican Abolitionist" who would end their way of life. In St. Charles Parish, a man was ordered to leave because he cheered Lincoln and expressed opinions that were different from those of his neighbors. A Boston piano manufacturer in Shreveport was advised to leave town. He had identified himself as a supporter of Lincoln.

·THE ELECTION OF 1860·

TERRITORIES

■ Abraham Lincoln (Republican)
■ John Breckinridge (Democrat, Southern)
■ John Bell (Constitutional Union)
■ Stephen Douglas (Democrat, Northern)

*Top: Abraham Lincoln's election as president in 1860 drew the nation closer to war. **Above:** The 1860 election split the country along sectional lines. Compare this map with the map of the Confederate States of America on the opposite page.*

Do You Remember?

1. What were the provisions of the Missouri Compromise?
2. Who were the fire-eaters?

SECESSION

Was secession a right or was it treason? Southerners insisted that each state had the constitutional right to withdraw from the Union. In the North, some said "Let them go." But others insisted that secession was an act of treason. The Union formed by the U.S. Constitution could not be dissolved. When he was inaugurated, President Lincoln had sworn to "preserve, protect, and defend the Union."

The election of a Republican president brought a swift reaction in Louisiana. South Carolina had seceded on December 20, 1860. Louisiana's legislature and its governor called for a special convention to vote on secession in January 1861. The delegates to that convention held various positions. Some wanted the state to secede immediately. Others wanted to wait to see what the other southern states did. A few announced their total opposition to secession.

Louisiana would lose much by leaving the United States. Although it was a southern plantation state, Louisiana was different in important ways. New Orleans depended on the commerce from the North, and the sugar planters needed the protective tariff the federal government enforced. The other southern states opposed tariffs because the tariffs did not help their economies.

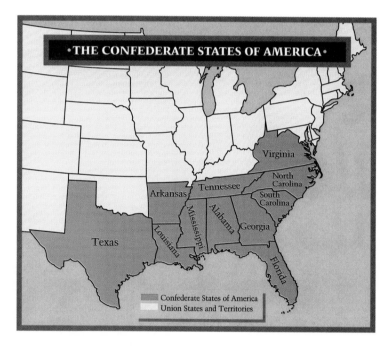

Powerful propaganda influenced public opinion. A well-known New Orleans minister preached a sermon supporting slavery and favoring secession. His message was reprinted on handbills and distributed around the state. Some voices warned of the risk secession would bring, but gradually they realized they had no chance to be heard. Some of these people later joined the Confederacy, but others supported the Union throughout the war.

Few secessionists believed that leaving the Union would bring war. Those who did were not heeded. Richard Taylor, son of Zachary Taylor, warned that war would follow secession. The *New Orleans Picayune* warned that the only way the Union could be severed would be with a sword and a "baptism of blood."

Even before the Secession Convention met, Governor Thomas Moore took action against the Union. The state militia seized Fort Jackson and Fort St. Phillip, the two forts below New Orleans on the Mississippi River. Then the governor demanded the surrender of the arsenal at Baton

Rouge. (The *arsenal* stored weapons and supplies for the federal troops stationed in Baton Rouge.) Governor Moore justified his action to the legislature by saying he was protecting Louisiana citizens "to prevent a collision between the federal troops and the people of the state."

Louisiana seceded from the Union on January 26, 1861. When the Secession Convention met in Baton Rouge, it voted 113 to 17 to adopt the Ordinance of Secession. Judge James G. Taliaferro (TOL eh ver) of Catahoula Parish was the most outspoken opponent. He warned that secession threatened the interests and the destiny of Louisiana. He predicted war, ruin, and decline. His opinion, however, was not included in the official record of the proceedings.

Most citizens celebrated secession. Pine torches lighted a night parade in New Orleans. The governor called for homes and businesses to put lights in their windows to show their support. People cheered in the streets as fireworks exploded and cannons fired. That sound of cannon fire would soon create a very different emotion in a city under attack.

*Top: Judah P. Benjamin served in the cabinet of Confederate President Jefferson Davis. **Above:** John Slidell worked to gain recognition for the Confederacy. **Right:** The legislature debated secession then called for a special convention. **Opposite, above:** After secession, the state seized the U.S. Mint in New Orleans.*

Louisiana's senators and representatives withdrew from Congress in February 1861. Soon afterward, the state seized all of the remaining federal property. More than $600,000 in federal funds was taken from the U.S. Mint in New Orleans. Louisiana had clearly acted against the United States government.

Louisiana called itself a country for less than two months. On March 21, 1861, the Republic of Louisiana joined the **Confederate States of America**, the name of the government formed by the southern states that had seceded. The newly formed Confederate government gained the political skills of Louisiana's former United States senators. Judah P. Benjamin, called "the brains of the Confederacy," served in Confederate President Jefferson Davis's cabinet. John Slidell spent most of the war trying to persuade European nations to support the Confederacy. Louisiana also contributed four key generals to the Confederate Army — Braxton Bragg, Leonidas Polk, Richard Taylor, and P. G. T. Beauregard.

PREPARING FOR WAR

History records April 12, 1861, as the date the Civil War began. The place was Fort Sumter, South Carolina. Confederate General P. G. T. Beauregard ordered the Union commander to surrender the fort.

MUSTERING TROOPS

One of the first tasks of the Confederacy was to build an army. Louisiana responded immediately with 5,000 volunteers. Around the state, they organized themselves into companies. They chose names like Louisiana Swamp Rangers, Crescent City Guards, Vienna Rifles, Irish Brigade, Carondelet Invincibles, Franklin Sharpshooters, and Caddo Greys. These names and their colorful uniforms seemed suitable for the short and glorious war southerners expected. They would "teach the Yankee a lesson and . . . settle matters inside 60 days."

The spirited soldiers drilled to "save the South." Camp Walker, located at the Metairie Racetrack, became the first training site. The last horse race was run there on April 9, 1861. Soon afterward the grounds were covered with marching soldiers preparing for a very different contest. The camp, although close to New Orleans, was soon abandoned. Surrounded by swamp and with no healthy water, the camp was a poor location for an army.

An area to the north of Lake Pontchartrain attracted the Confederate commanders to a site with hills, tall pines, and good water. Camp Moore became the main training location for Louisiana's soldiers. But the experience proved less than glorious. Providing adequate food and supplies was a constant problem. Diseases spread quickly through the troops. Epidemics such as measles killed many soldiers before they ever left the camp.

Once war became the ugly reality of blood and death, fewer men wanted to enlist. When the first soldiers left home, they expected to return quickly. Instead, the war dragged on and families suffered. To encourage enlistment, the Confederate government paid a bounty and some local governments paid additional bounties. The **bounty** was a one-time reward for enlisting.

Finally, the Confederacy had to make service mandatory. A draft or **conscription** required all men of a certain age to enlist in the army. The law, however, included a substitution clause, which allowed a man to pay someone else to take his place. Newspapers carried the names of men who were willing to serve as substitutes. The Confederate draft also exempted (excused) anyone owning twenty or more slaves. Combined with the right to pay a substitute, this made the law seem aimed at the poor man. Soldiers on both sides called the Civil War "a rich man's war and a poor man's fight."

Above: New recruits were drilled at training sites, first at the Metairie Racetrack and later at Camp Moore. **Opposite:** *Louisiana native P. G. T. Beauregard was a key Confederate general.*

GATHERING SUPPLIES

In 1861, Louisiana was ready for war only in attitude. But motivation alone was not enough. The focus shifted frantically to equipment and supplies.

In the early days of the war, equipment and supplies were furnished by parish governments, wealthy individuals, or the soldiers themselves. Although Louisiana imported most finished goods, some manufacturing did exist. A New Orleans factory switched from making clothing for plantations to making uniforms. Converted factories made weapons from scrap iron collected by the citizens.

Ranches in southwest Louisiana and Texas supplied the cattle for a slaughterhouse south of Alexandria. The beef was preserved by salting it. This method, however, left the meat tough and very salty. The soldiers had to boil the meat for hours to make it edible. They learned to ignore the bugs floating on the water.

The salt for preserving the beef came from several salt deposits around the state. Brine (a mixture of salt and water) was pumped out of the ground and boiled down in kettles to get the salt. Discovering the extensive salt deposits at Avery Island gave the Confederates a valuable resource.

The women of Louisiana also helped "The Cause." Ladies' sewing circles made uniforms and cartridge bags. Their new sewing machines became part of assembly lines. But too soon the ladies stopped designing battle flags to make bandages. Monogrammed linen pillow cases became sandbags at Port Hudson, and treasured carpets became blankets for freezing soldiers.

Do You Remember?
1. How did Louisiana history change on January 26, 1861?
2. Where did the Civil War begin?
3. Where was the main training camp for Louisiana's Confederate soldiers?

THE WAR IN LOUISIANA

The first eager volunteers from Louisiana fought with General Robert E. Lee's army in Virginia. One famous company was known as the Louisiana Tigers. They gained a reputation as being wild and uncontrollable off the field but heroic fighters once the battle began.

However, the bodies shipped home from Shiloh silently predicted what lay ahead. This reality brought fear and anxiety. There were few troops left in Louisiana for protection. The state was almost defenseless against an attack.

This 1861 map entitled "Panorama of the Seat of War" gives a bird's eye view of the Gulf Coast of Louisiana, Mississippi, and Alabama.

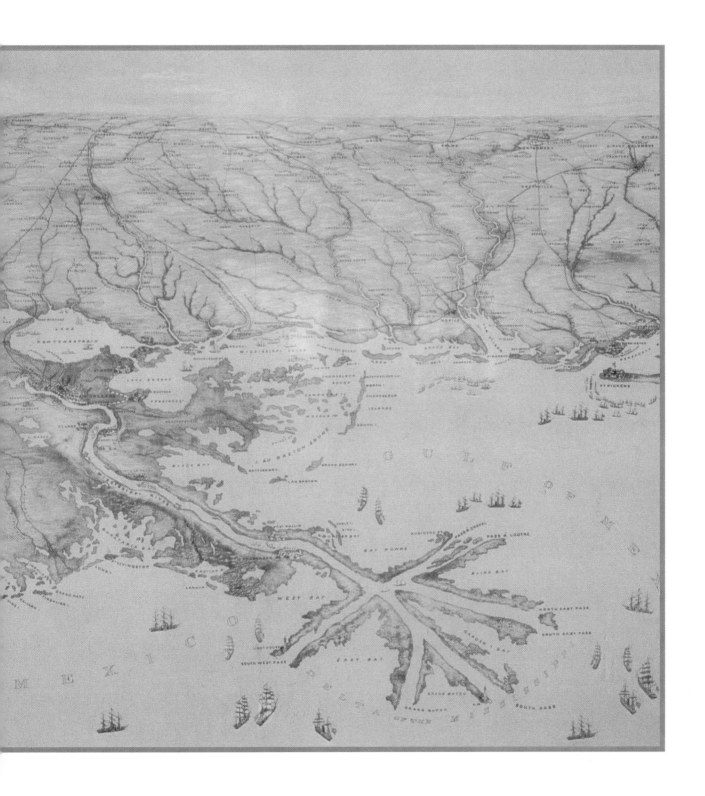

THE FALL OF NEW ORLEANS

The most vulnerable and valuable spot was New Orleans. The port was a key location for the state and for the Confederacy. The Union Navy had already blocked the mouth of the Mississippi. If the Union could seize New Orleans, the Confederacy would be crippled. General Beauregard had warned the Confederate government not to leave New Orleans unguarded. But Confederate President Jefferson Davis thought the Union would attack from upriver. The Confederate Navy was not sent to protect New Orleans.

South of the city, the Confederates held the river with Fort Jackson and Fort St. Phillip. They added to the defense by blocking the river with chains. All of the vessels tied up in New Orleans were ordered to contribute their mooring chains. Along with the chains across the river were cypress rafts carrying pine knots and cotton ready for burning.

The Union threat came when the U.S. Navy sent forty-seven ships under the command of Admiral David Farragut up the river. He ordered

David Porter, the commander of the Union gunboats, to open fire on the two forts on April 18, 1862. The constant shelling was heard fifty miles away. One soldier described the noise as being like an earthquake. But the forts held.

On the night of April 23, Farragut decided to take his ships past the forts. The exploding shells lit the night to the brightness of day. The Confederates at the forts saw excitement and fear on the faces around them. When the Union ships broke the Confederate chain, no barriers were left between the Union fleet and New Orleans.

The river was high with spring floods, and the ships easily sailed up the river. Union gunboats faced directly into Jackson Square. The church bells warned that the city had fallen. The children and teachers in their schoolrooms counted the twelve bells and left their books, crying "The Yankees are here." Panic filled New Orleans.

Once the people knew the city was lost, they refused to allow the Union Army to seize their goods. The wharf blazed with 29,000 bales of burning cotton. The huge fire also consumed warehouses filled with rice, corn, sugar, and tobacco. An amazed onlooker reported that molasses flowed in the gutters. The wealth of the city was destroyed.

On May 1, 1862, Union General Benjamin Butler took command of the city. Once again, the city saw a conquering army parade in Jackson Square as Butler and his troops entered New Orleans. The residents lived through the war in an occupied city, isolated from the rest of Louisiana.

Above: "Farragut's Fleet Passing the Forts below New Orleans" was painted by Mauritz F. H. de Haas. **Right:** In this engraving, the Confederate ship Governor Moore *is firing through its bow at the Union ship* Varuna. **Opposite, below:** *Admiral David Farragut led forty-seven Union ships up the Mississippi River, capturing New Orleans.*

BATON ROUGE FALLS

Admiral Farragut then headed up the Mississippi to take the state capital. Union gunboats fired on the unprotected city, which surrendered on May 7, 1862. The Union Army moved in to hold the location.

The Confederates under General John Breckinridge tried to retake Baton Rouge on August 5. They attacked by land from the east, but the Union gunboats stopped their drive at the river. The Confederate iron-clad *Arkansas* was to have taken part in the attack. But it did not reach Baton Rouge in time to join the battle. As the ship rushed south from Vicksburg, its engine overheated. The *Arkansas* was burned to keep it out of Union hands.

The Union Army left Baton Rouge on August 21, when the Confederates threatened to recapture New Orleans. But federal troops returned to Baton Rouge before the year's end. In December 1862, the State Capitol burned, and many official state records were lost. The fire was apparently caused by careless troops. The Union commander did try to prevent the building from burning.

THE LAFOURCHE AND TECHE CAMPAIGNS

In the fall of 1862, General Butler turned his attention to the rich Bayou Lafourche. This plantation region helped support the Confederate Army. Butler wanted to seize the riches and supplies of the region for the Union Army instead. He ordered that any goods belonging to "disloyals" along the bayou be confiscated (seized). This included the valuable hogsheads of sugar ready for shipping.

As the Union and Confederate armies moved through southeast Louisiana, much action took place along Bayou Lafourche and Bayou Teche. The residents of this region faced either battles or an occupying Union Army during most of the war.

Above: *The burning of the capitol at Baton Rouge.* ***Above, left:*** *The* Arkansas *was burned to keep it from Union hands.*

MAURICE

FRANK H. SCHELL

Union General Winfield Scott advised President Lincoln to take the Mississippi River. Early in the war, the Union's strategy was to block all of the Confederate ports and seize the Mississippi. Taking control of the river would split the Confederacy in two, leaving Arkansas, Texas, and Louisiana stranded. This strategy was called the "Anaconda Plan" because it would squeeze the Confederacy to death, just as the huge anaconda snake does to its prey.

If the Union plan worked, the Confederacy would not be able to send supplies to its troops on the eastern front. However, Vicksburg and Port Hudson stood in the way of the Union plan. Both stood high above the river on bluffs, which gave the Confederates an advantage.

For six weeks, the Union Army laid siege to Vicksburg, Mississippi, finally capturing it on July 4, 1863. The defeat of the Confederate army at the Battle of Gettysburg on the same day was the turning point in the war.

VICKSBURG

Union General Ulysses S. Grant began preparing to take Vicksburg in late 1862. The land to the north and east was swampy, and there were few roads. Because of the Confederate guns high on the bluffs, Grant needed to find another approach. Above Vicksburg on the Louisiana side of the river, he hoped to dig canals as a shortcut. Once the canals were complete, he could carry his troops past Vicksburg's guns and attack from the south. But despite the hard work of the troops and many former slaves, the canals collapsed.

Grant had to march his army along the swampy Louisiana riverbanks. Ferries took the men across the river south of Vicksburg. The Union troops then laid siege to the Mississippi city.

PORT HUDSON

At Port Hudson, 150 miles south of Vicksburg, the Confederates had stopped Union forces from moving supplies upriver to Grant's army. The fort controlled a large bend in the river. From its high bluffs, the Confederates fired on Union ships heading north from New Orleans. An assault by the Union Navy failed to silence the Confederate guns.

The next Union attack came by land. On May 23, 1863, General Nathaniel Banks surrounded the 4½ miles of Confederate fortifications at Port Hudson, trapping the Confederate Army within the earthworks

(embankments) and trenches. For forty-eight days (the longest siege of the Civil War), the 30,000-member Union Army assaulted the 6,800 Confederate troops.

In the hot Louisiana summer, soldiers collapsed from the heat and sickened from the bad water. The tiniest enemies — mosquitoes and lice — tormented both armies. The worst were the snapping beetles, which crawled into the ears of sleeping soldiers. Bounded on all sides by Union troops, the barefoot and ragged Confederate troops ran out of food. Their hunger forced them to eat the horses, the mules, and finally the rats.

Despite these hardships, the Confederates held out until they learned that Vicksburg had fallen on July 4. A Union officer claimed he informed the Confederates by wrapping the surrender notice around a stick and throwing it into their trenches. An official dispatch from General Grant informed General Franklin Gardner, the Confederate commander, that Vicksburg had fallen. General Gardner then surrendered to General Banks. The long siege at Port Hudson ended on July 9. Later, Lincoln praised the Union victory by announcing, "The father of waters again flows unvexed to the sea."

Union troops under General Augur cross Bayou Montecino on their way to Port Hudson, the last Confederate stronghold on the Mississippi River.

ADMIRAL FARRAGUT'S Attack upon & Passage of the
Rebel Batteries at PORT HUDSON, March 14. 1863.

Hartford, Capt Palmer, bearing the Admiral's Flag.
Albatross, Lt Com'r Hart.

Richmond, Com'r Alden.
Genessee, Com'r McComb.

PORT HUDSON

The town of Port Hudson is gone, but today the Civil War site is a State Commemorative Area and a National Historic Landmark. The wooded, well-kept park has over six miles of hiking trails. You can climb the earthworks and hide in the trenches prepared by the Confederate soldiers. You will hear birds, the wind in the trees, and children laughing and roughhousing.

You will not hear the boom of cannons and shouted warnings like "Rats, to your holes" as you and your fellow Confederates scramble into the trenches. You will not hear the ping of rifle fire as you look frantically for a hidden sniper. You will not see a moss-covered Confederate hiding in a cypress tree. You will not hear an order to advance and join the charge of your fellow soldiers in the Corps de Afrique. You are more than a century too late. The sounds and the sights of the summer of 1863 are gone. You can only imagine the experience.

To hear the horror of war, imagine the boys who laughed and roughhoused here in 1863. Some of them were as young as thirteen years old, and many were not yet twenty. The young soldiers waited for battle by sharing the games they played at home. Marbles and leapfrog filled time in the summer heat. The Union troops even played their new game of baseball. They played their games one day and died from sniper bullets the next. They now fill the cemetery next to the battle site.

Above: *This painting depicts the U.S. Navy's assault on Port Hudson, Louisiana.* **Left:** *Civil War enthusiasts portray Confederate infantry at a re-enactment of the battle of Port Hudson.*

THE RED RIVER CAMPAIGN

The final Union campaign in Louisiana headed toward Shreveport and Texas. (A **campaign** is a military plan with a specific goal.) By 1864, Shreveport was the Confederate capital of Louisiana and the headquarters for the Confederate command west of the Mississippi. The Confederates shipped cotton from Shreveport through Texas to Mexico. Eager European buyers bought all the cotton the southerners could supply. Often, the cotton was exchanged for essential supplies.

The Union planned to seize Shreveport and confiscate the cotton from the Red River Valley. To prepare for this assault, federal troops moved north along Bayou Teche. They intended to destroy the Confederate troops and capture the Confederate fortress at Butte La Rose. That would have given them control of the Atchafalaya River and an approach to the Red River. Along the way, the Union Army seized horses and anything else they found useful. After they had passed, the people along the bayou had little left.

From there, the federal army headed to Alexandria. The Union Navy's gunboats moved up the Red River to join them. On March 16, 1864, Union forces took Alexandria. General Banks then led his troops upriver to Natchitoches. He turned away from the river and headed toward Shreveport, choosing the shorter and more traveled route. When Banks moved his army away from the river, he lost the protection of Admiral Porter's gunboats. Confederate General Richard Taylor used this to his advantage. The outnumbered Confederates, led by General Taylor, waited for Banks in the wooded hills forty miles south of Shreveport.

At the Battle of Mansfield, Union forces were led by General Nathaniel Banks (above), Union leader at Port Hudson. Confederate forces were led by General Richard Taylor (opposite), the son of President Zachary Taylor. The Confederate victory stopped the Union from advancing into Texas.

The fierce Battle of Mansfield was fought on April 8, 1864. The Confederate cavalry and infantry charged the Union forces, following Taylor's orders to draw first blood. Their respected General Alfred Mouton was killed as he led his men in battle. Later, General Taylor commented, "The charge made by Mouton and his men across the open was magnificent." More than 1,500 Union soldiers were killed, wounded, or captured during the attack.

Amid the confusion, General Banks called for a night retreat. The next afternoon, at Pleasant Hill, twenty-two miles further south, Taylor

again struck the Union Army. This battle had no clear winner, but Banks continued retreating.

By the time the Union troops returned to Alexandria, the level of the Red River had fallen. Their gunboats were now trapped above the rapids. But Union Army engineer Joseph Bailey developed an amazing plan. Union troops built a *wing dam* to force the water to back up and deepen along a narrow channel. To the surprise of all, **Bailey's dam** worked. The water level rose, and the boats floated past the rapids. The Union Navy was finally able to leave Alexandria after two weeks of hard work on the makeshift structure.

As Union troops left the city, a fire was set. At least twenty-two blocks of the city, including the courthouse and the Episcopal and Methodist churches were burned. It is unclear who started the fire. Some residents blamed Union soldiers, while others blamed outlaws. General Banks did not order his troops to burn the town, but records do show that Admiral Porter considered the action "a fitting termination of the Red River expedition." One resident reported that some Union officers tried to help save homes while other soldiers looted and robbed.

General Banks took his army back to New Orleans. He claimed victory in the Battle of Mansfield, but his fellow officers did not agree. Admiral Porter reported to General Sherman that "the army was shamefully beaten by the rebels."

Do You Remember?

1. How did the Confederates try to stop Union ships from reaching New Orleans?
2. What happened to the Louisiana State Capitol in December 1862?
3. What land features made Port Hudson a good defensive location for the Confederacy?
4. What happened to the Union gunboats when the level of the Red River went down?

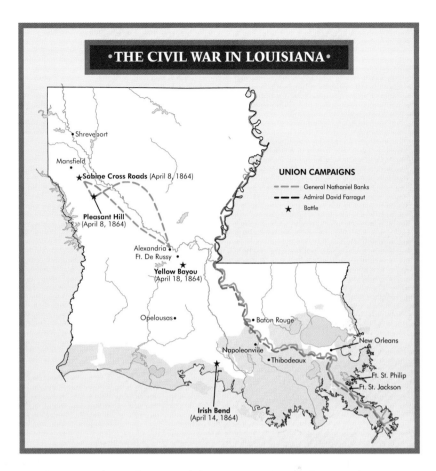

·THE CIVIL WAR IN LOUISIANA·

UNION CAMPAIGNS
--- General Nathaniel Banks
--- Admiral David Farragut
★ Battle

Shreveport
Mansfield
★ Sabine Cross Roads (April 8, 1864)
★ Pleasant Hill (April 8, 1864)
Alexandria
Ft. De Russy
★ Yellow Bayou (April 18, 1864)
Opelousas
Baton Rouge
Napoleonville
Thibodeaux
New Orleans
Ft. St. Philip
Ft. St. Jackson
★ Irish Bend (April 14, 1864)

Opposite, above: A re-enactment of the Battle of Mansfield. These men are portraying Union cavalry. *Opposite, below left:* Monument to Prince de Polignac ("Lafayette of the South"). After the death of General Mouton at Mansfield, French-born General Polignac led the Confederate troops to victory. *Opposite, below right:* This fence in the woods at Mansfield marks the position of the Union line.

PHOTOGRAPHY IN THE CIVIL WAR

The Civil War was the first major national event to be photographed. In 1839, a Frenchman named Daguerre developed a process to take a picture using a copper plate coated with silver. Samuel F. B. Morse (inventor of the telegraph) happened to be in Paris then and learned the process. Back in New York, Morse opened a studio, and the photography craze soon swept America.

When the Civil War came, some 3,154 Americans listed their occupation as photographer. At least 1,500 of them took war photographs, and practically all of these worked with Union forces. The Union block-

ade made it difficult for southern photographers to get the chemicals needed to coat plates and develop them.

Photographers usually reached the battlefields after the fighting was over. And because exposure times were long, photographers took pictures of still scenes: dead people and animals, splintered trees, destroyed buildings, and the debris of war. The most popular pictures were those of individual soldiers. Illustrated newspapers bought photographs from which they made wood engravings. Important photographers included Mathew Brady, Edward and Henry Anthony, Alexander Gardner, George Bernard, Timothy O'Sullivan, and Henry P. Moore.

Artists argued about whether photographs were art. Some people regarded them as depictions of reality. Others argued that the photographers posed their subjects, determined the light, and thus took pictures that had the elements of art. Art or not, the nation is fortunate to have an extensive pictorial record of the Civil War.

Mathew Brady (opposite page, above) took this photograph (opposite page, below) at the Battle of Chancellorville on May 3, 1863. The photograph above shows the destruction of Confederate railroad tracks in Georgia during Sherman's "March to the Sea" in 1864.

CIVILIAN LIFE

Whatever southerners' reasons were for entering the war, defending their homes became the reason for continuing. The Union policy of total war destroyed parts of Louisiana. Known as the "scorched earth policy," the intent was to leave nothing for the Confederates to use to make war. Making life miserable for the civilians in order to end the war sooner was also part of the Union goal.

Some troops were ordered to pillage (to take goods by force), but others vandalized even against orders. Federal troops were sent to destroy a railroad bridge at Pontchatoula. Instead, they destroyed the town. The uncontrolled vandalism fueled the civilians' hatred. Mailbags were slit open, and the mail was scattered in the streets. Private homes were ransacked and treasured possessions were lost.

At Baton Rouge, a Union officer filed a complaint about a Massachusetts company who considered pillaging their right. But another officer said he deliberately left "nothing but blackened chimneys as monuments to the folly and villainy of the owners." Baton Rouge was saved from burning only when another officer reminded General Butler about the orphanage there.

Above: Union troops pillaged the countryside while they were in the state. Troops, like these shown near Baton Rouge, left little for the civilian population.
Opposite: *Union General Benjamin Butler commanded the land forces that captured New Orleans and from May to December 1862 was military governor of the city. His actions provoked charges of corruption and earned him the nickname of "Beast Butler."*

Another threat to the citizens came from the Jayhawkers. Confederates labeled these men draft dodgers, but they called themselves irregular guerrillas. A **guerrilla** is a member of a small military group that harasses the enemy. Some Jayhawkers helped the Union Army, and some just hid out. But others robbed their neighbors. The Catahoula and the Pearl River swamps harbored gangs of these men. These were often the poor whites who felt that this was not their war.

Not all guerrillas were Union sympathizers. Later in the war, the citizens in the Florida Parishes asked for protection from the Union soldiers. Confederate officers gave their approval for guerrilla activity. These irregulars were often hard to control. They took no prisoners and sometimes bushwhacked their enemies by hiding in the bushes and shooting them in the back.

It wasn't only the Union Army that brought misery to the people. Confederate troops also foraged (searched) for food, horses, and cattle. The shortages caused by the war forced them to take their supplies from the people. "Hungry Confederate troops took what the Yankees had left," said one farm woman.

The Federal naval blockade of New Orleans was a death threat for the city. This painting by William Challoner shows the Confederate sidewheeler Webb *attempting to run the blockade.*

SHORTAGES AND SACRIFICES

Once the war began, people at home suffered. The federal blockade of New Orleans at the beginning of the war quickly created shortages. For a city based on trade, the blockade was a death threat. Speculators drove up the prices of basic goods. Counterfeiters made Confederate money even more inflated and worthless.

Shortages affected every area of life. People were hungry for news of the war, but newspapers struggled to survive during the war years. A shortage of paper forced the Shreveport newspaper, *The Weekly News*, to become the *Semi-Weekly News*. The editor was finally forced to print his newspaper on the back of wallpaper rolls! Coffee was another item for which people had to improvise and substitute. Acorns, parched cornmeal, and okra seeds were all tried.

These substitutes and "make do" items were soon labeled "Confederate." For example, a Confederate bridle was a rope halter, and a Confederate bonnet was a simple hat woven of palmetto. Confederate flour was poor quality cornmeal.

The items that were available were often so inflated in price that few could buy them. The price of a dozen eggs reached $5, as did a pound of butter. An apple cost 50 cents — if one could be found. Often there was no flour, sugar, or meat available at any price. High prices, almost worthless Confederate money, and a shortage of money choked the economy.

As the war dragged on, people reverted to the skills of the past. They made what they needed from scratch. The oldest women in the communities remembered how to weave cloth on the old looms and the plant dyes used to color the handwoven cloth. Confederate Governor Allen encouraged this home manufacturing.

FREEING THE SLAVES

Life for the slaves during the war years was filled with hope, fear, confusion, and disappointment. When the Union Army arrived, slaves came to them seeking freedom. At first they were told to return to the plantations. Later, General Butler followed his contraband policy. That is, he gave his soldiers the right to take any Confederate-owned property, including slaves. This was his interpretation of the **Confiscation Act**. This act, passed by the U.S. Congress in July 1862, said that the property of rebels could be taken by the government.

Thousands of slaves flocked to the Union camps. As the Union Army moved through the Teche region, a vast line of slaves followed. Union soldiers wrote about lines of slaves that were longer than the columns of marching troops. Young and old, sick or strong, the slaves looked for freedom. Sometimes with a few meager possessions in a bundle and sometimes with nothing, they looked for freedom.

Providing for these people became the responsibility of federal authorities. The first solution was to set up camps for the slaves. Like all refugee camps, they were crowded and filled with disease. Some of the former owners of the slaves even complained about the poor care the slaves received in these camps.

The huge numbers of slaves presented management problems for Butler. Some of the slaves were put to work as laborers in New Orleans. Then they were assigned to work with the military. They built forts on the Red River and dug Grant's canals at Vicksburg. During the war, some slaves who were under Union protection were sent back to work the confiscated plantations for the federal government. The slaves were paid a low wage for this work.

On January 1, 1863, Abraham Lincoln acted boldly to increase pressure on the Confederacy. With his **Emancipation Proclamation**, he announced that slavery was the issue of the war. He stated that all slaves "within any state . . . under rebellion against the United States" were now free. What Lincoln's proclamation did was remove all possibility that Great Britain would enter the war on the side of the Confederates. The British people and the British press supported this move against slavery.

As the war continued, both the former slaves and the free men of color were allowed to join the Union Army. At the beginning of the war, Louisiana's Native Guards (the militia composed of free men of color) helped the Confederacy protect New Orleans. The grandfathers of these

Some former slaves worked for the Union Army. These helped dig General Grant's canals at Vicksburg, Mississippi.

The Louisiana Native Guard, composed of free men of color, served first the Confederacy and later the Union.

men had formed the Native Guards to defend the city at the Battle of New Orleans in 1815. But in 1862, after New Orleans fell to Union forces, the free people of color aligned themselves with the Union Army. They approached General Butler and volunteered to fight with his army.

Like many other Union officers, Butler feared black troops. He appreciated the education of the free men of color but hesitated to arm any former slaves. However, the need for more troops and the need to provide for the many former slaves after the Emancipation Proclamation led the Union Army to allow black troops. The Louisiana Native Guard organized three regiments for the "Corps de Afrique," and the members of the Native Guard served as the officers. Although they met prejudice from Union officers and soldiers, these Louisiana regiments made history at Port Hudson, their first combat action.

Do You Remember?
1. Why did General Butler decide not to burn Baton Rouge?
2. What was Confederate flour?
3. What was the Corps de Afrique?

LIFE IN OCCUPIED NEW ORLEANS

During most of the war years, New Orleans was an occupied city, isolated from the rest of the state. After April 1862, the city was under the control of the United States Army. General Benjamin Butler and his troops were responsible for maintaining order and running the city.

General Butler was determined to have control of the city. In his words, "New Orleans is a conquered city. And, by the law of nations, lies subject to the will of the conqueror." Butler clearly informed the citizens of New Orleans that he would tolerate no disrespect for the United States. He ordered that William Mumford be hanged for pulling down the American flag. This was the first of many acts that enraged the citizens.

Butler was furious at the attitude displayed toward his troops. He retaliated when he heard reports of the rude comments made to his soldiers by Confederate women, whom he privately called "she-rebels." Saying that no lady would make such remarks, Butler issued Order No. 28. The order said that any woman who insulted any officer of the United States would be treated like a "woman of the town plying her avocation."

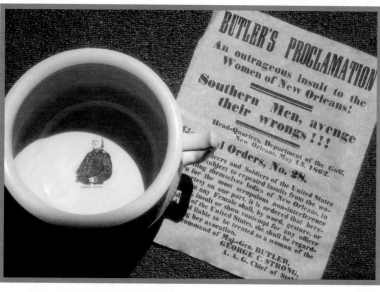

Butler's action was criticized around the world. One northern newspaper even joined in the name calling, labeling him "Beast Butler." The British Parliament and the London *Times* also condemned his order. Generations have repeated the story of the ladies' revenge against Butler. They placed his picture at the bottom of their chamberpots!

In other actions, General Butler knew that a prosperous New Orleans would help the Union war effort. He re-opened the port to international trade. The citizens of New Orleans benefitted when goods became available and the economy improved.

He ordered his soldiers to respect private property and not to enter homes or businesses without authority. However, when the U.S. Congress passed the Confiscation Act, Butler interpreted it strictly. By September 1862, anyone who had not signed an oath of allegiance to the United States could lose his or her property. Many accused Butler of using this law for his own benefit. The confiscated property was sold at auction, with General Butler's brother in charge. The secretary of the U.S. Treasury even warned Butler to "avoid the appearance of evil."

Top: General Butler imprisoned "she-rebel" Eugenia Levy Phillips on Ship Island for several months for "laughing and mocking at the remains of a Federal officer." Above: A poster protesting General Butler's Order No. 28, next to a "Butler chamber pot."

Above: Colonel George F. Shepley served as military governor of occupied Louisiana.
Right: This caricature of "Beast Butler" reflects the outrage generated by Butler's Order 28.

While some felt Butler's actions were unjust and harsh, others believed he did what he had to do to control the city. Many of his programs helped the city and its people. He kept the city clean and its citizens fed. The poor were paid to clean the city, and this "broom battalion" kept the city so clean that disease was greatly reduced. There were no outbreaks of cholera or yellow fever during the occupied years.

Butler was diligent but controversial. The foreign diplomats complained to Washington, D.C., about him because his actions frequently affected them. For example, when he took weapons from the Confederates, he also seized the weapons of the foreign nationals. At the end of 1862, Butler was replaced by General Nathaniel Banks.

General Banks was more moderate in his treatment of the city. One of the first things he did was re-open the Episcopal churches, earning the gratitude and approval of the city. Butler had closed the churches because the pastors prayed for Jefferson Davis instead of President Lincoln.

GOVERNING THE STATE

During the war, Louisiana actually had two state governments. The Confederate government controlled all of the state outside the Union lines. That government had to relocate several times to avoid capture by the Union Army. After New Orleans was captured, President Lincoln worked to restore a loyal government to the state.

STATE GOVERNMENT IN OCCUPIED LOUISIANA

According to Lincoln's plan, once 10 percent of the voters signed a loyalty oath, an election could be held. People loyal to the Union soon formed political associations and began preparing for elections.

Lincoln directed General Banks to hold an election in occupied Louisiana as soon as possible. He wanted to show that the state, and the other seceded states, could easily return to the Union. In the elections that were held, only those who had signed loyalty oaths were allowed to vote.

In February 1864, Michael J. Hahn was elected the governor of Louisiana for the occupied region. He replaced Colonel George F. Shepley, who had been the military governor. The elected government worked with the military commanders in occupied Louisiana. During the war, this was the state government recognized by the United States.

STATE GOVERNMENT IN CONFEDERATE LOUISIANA

The state government that functioned while Louisiana was part of the Confederacy faced tremendous obstacles. The capital was moved several times — from Baton Rouge to Opelousas to Shreveport — to avoid the federal troops.

The most urgent problem for Confederate Louisiana was funding for the war. This need for money made life in Louisiana even more difficult. First, the Confederacy sold bonds to raise money. When this voluntary approach to raising money no longer worked, an income tax was established. Still later, a tax-in-kind required that 10 percent of every crop be given to the Confederate government.

Providing for the needs of the people in the state while supporting the war effort was almost impossible. The governor who was elected to head Confederate Louisiana in 1863 won the gratitude of the people at that time and the respect of historians today. Henry Watkins Allen was an injured Confederate officer who took charge of the state when the fall of the Confederacy already seemed likely. His creative and practical programs kept Louisiana from starving and lessened the suffering. His leadership was amazing under the circumstances.

In his inauguration speech, Allen called for relief (financial aid) for soldiers' dependents and pensions for wounded soldiers. He wanted to control the manufacture and importation of liquor, because he believed

Michael J. Hahn of New Orleans was the first elected governor of occupied Louisiana.

the corn was better used to feed people and livestock than to make whiskey. He set up a factory to make medicine at the old Mount Lebanon College in Webster Parish. He kept the trade routes to Mexico open and imported the medicine that could not be made.

Cotton "cards" were made and distributed so that cotton could be carded (cleaned and combed), spun, and woven. This move ensured that

*Above: General Robert E. Lee surrendered the Confederate forces to General U.S. Grant, ending the Civil War. **Right:** This plaster cast was used to make the statue of Governor Henry Watkins Allen, that stands in the State Capitol.*

there would be a supply of cloth to replace what could no longer be imported.

By this time, Louisiana was almost entirely cut off from the rest of the Confederacy. Allen told the Confederate government that he needed to take care of the people of Louisiana and could no longer refuse to sell the cotton to Europe. He financed his state aid by buying cotton and sending it through Texas to the blockade runners at Galveston. State stores provided what the people needed. Those who could not pay were given what they needed.

THE WAR ENDS

On April 9, 1865, General Robert E. Lee surrendered his Confederate Army to Union General Ulysses S. Grant in Virginia. The Confederate trans-Mississippi forces surrendered in June. The war took its toll on Louisiana. More than six hundred Civil War battle, engagement, and skirmish sites mark the map of Louisiana.

Governor Allen led the troubled state through the last days of the war. He told Louisianians to "submit to the inevitable" and "begin life anew." These words foreshadow the years to come.

Do You Remember?
1. What Louisiana city served as the state capital at the end of the Civil War?
2. Who was the governor of Confederate Louisiana? Of occupied Louisiana?
3. When did the Civil War end?

SUMMARY

By 1860, politics in Louisiana had focused on national issues rather than on local conflicts. Lincoln's election to the presidency pushed Louisiana and other southern states to secede from the Union. Residents of Louisiana could not predict the economic and social changes that were to come.

Louisiana prepared for the coming war by seizing federal property, training troops, and gathering supplies. The Union Navy blockaded the port of New Orleans, making it difficult to get supplies. The city fell into Union hands early in the war.

As the war progressed, battles at Baton Rouge, Port Hudson, and Vicksburg gave the Union its Mississippi River goal. The Union Army marched up the Red River to take Shreveport but was turned back by Confederate forces. By 1864, however, Louisiana and the other southern states admitted defeat.

General Ulysses S. Grant, commander of the Union forces, accepted Lee's surrender at Appomattox Court House on April 9, 1865.

CHAPTER · REVIEW

1861	1862	1863	1864	1865
(Jan.) Louisiana seceded	*(May)* Union Army took New Orleans	*(Jan.)* Confederate government moved to Shreveport	*(Apr.)* Battles of Mansfield and Pleasant Hill	*(Apr.)* Lee surrendered to Grant
(Mar.) Louisiana joined the Confederacy	*(May)* Capital moved to Opelousas	*(Jul.)* Confederates surrendered Vicksburg and Port Hudson		*(Jun.)* Confederates surrendered at Shreveport
(Apr.) Civil War began				
(May) Union forces blockaded New Orleans				

1860	**1861**	**1862**	**1863**	**1864**	**1865**

1861	1864
First transcontinental telegraph message sent	Red Cross formed in Switzerland

1860
Lincoln elected president

1862
Homestead Act passed by Congress
Transcontinental railroad authorized

1863
President Lincoln declared Thanksgiving a national holiday

Reviewing People, Places, and Terms

Define, identify, or explain the importance of the following.

1. abolitionist
2. Henry Watkins Allen
3. Bailey's dam
4. bounty
5. Benjamin Butler
6. Camp Moore
7. campaign
8. Compromise of 1850
9. Confederate States of America
10. Confiscation Act
11. conscription
12. Emancipation Proclamation
13. David Farragut
14. guerrilla
15. Abraham Lincoln
16. Missouri Compromise
17. Thomas Moore
18. Port Hudson
19. secession
20. states' rights

Understanding the Facts

1. Which political party was formed to oppose the spread of slavery?
2. Who were the candidates for president of the United States in 1860? What were their political parties?
3. What property did Louisiana seize from the United States government? Why did it do this?
4. Why did many consider the Civil War "a rich man's war and a poor man's fight"?
5. Why was salt important to both the Confederate and United States troops?
6. What was the Union's Anaconda Plan?
7. Where did the longest siege of the war take place? How long did it last?
8. What was the goal of the Red River campaign?
9. How did the Union naval blockade affect New Orleans?

Developing Critical Thinking

1. Why was it important for the South that the number of slave states and free states be kept even?

2. What issues besides Lincoln's election in 1860 led the southern states to secede?

3. Do you think states should have the right to secede from the Union? Why or why not?

4. Why do you think Louisiana joined the Confederate States of America instead of remaining an independent country?

Using Your Skills

1. On a map of Louisiana, mark the cities that served as the state capital during the Civil War. Determine the distance of each move.

2. Select one Confederate officer and one Union officer of the Civil War. Make a chart showing how their lives before the war were alike and how they were different. What does your completed chart reveal about the people involved in the Civil War?

Special Projects

1. Civil War ironclads changed naval battles. For example, the Confederate ironclad *Arkansas* did not reach Baton Rouge in time to save the city. Research a Civil War ironclad. Describe your choice in writing or art.

2. How close did the Civil War come to your community? There are over six hundred sites in Louisiana where fighting took place during the Civil War. Find one of those sites near your home. Write a description of the site today and compare it with its 1860s appearance.

Making Connections

1. From a library or other reference source, find a photograph taken during the Civil War that you find particularly moving.

2. Have photographic images affected people's impressions of or reactions to wars or fighting in recent times? Explain.

Louisiana Lagniappe

• The Secession Convention took only three days to make the decision to secede.

• The half-brother of Mary Todd Lincoln was killed in a battle at Greenwell Springs, Louisiana, fighting for the Confederacy.

• The constitution written for Louisiana during the Confederacy period was published in both French and English.

• After the Union Army occupied Baton Rouge, many huge trees were cut down because they blocked the view of the river.

• BUILDING SKILLS: DISTINGUISHING FACT FROM OPINION •

A *fact* can be proven by examining it against other information or by your own observations or research. For example, "Eighteen-year-old U.S. citizens have the right to vote" is a statement of fact. This can be proven by reading the Twenty-sixth Amendment to the U.S. Constitution.

An *opinion* is something a person thinks, believes, or feels is true. For example, "A person should not be allowed to vote until she or he is twenty-one years old" is a statement of opinion. This may be the way someone feels. It may also be shared by others, but it is a personal opinion.

Examine the following statements, then decide which statements are fact and which are opinion.

1. General Butler was responsible for maintaining order in New Orleans.

2. General Butler's hanging of William Mumford was controversial.

3. The women of New Orleans deserved Order No. 28.

4. General Butler should no longer be called "Beast Butler."

5. General Butler made the city of New Orleans a cleaner place to live.

6. General Butler was more strict with the city than his successor, General Banks.

CHAPTER ELEVEN

LOUISIANA'S RECONSTRUCTION ERA: RIOTS AND REBUILDING

Broken eggs cannot be mended, but Louisiana has nothing to do now but to take her place in the Union as it was, barring the already broken eggs.
— Abraham Lincoln to New York banker August Belmont, July 1862

BRICK CHIMNEYS STANDING ABOVE BURNED LAND signaled the Confederate defeat. One southern writer described those chimneys in Georgia as "Sherman's sentinels guarding the ruins he had made." The South in 1865 reflected its status as a war zone. Like every war zone throughout history, more than the landscape was damaged.

After most wars, the defeated people come together in their misery and in their hope for the same future. This was not true in the South after the Civil War. One class felt crushed and conquered, while another group felt liberated and uplifted. Whatever the feelings, the war affected Louisiana like an earthquake. No one could avoid the aftershocks.

This memorial in Monroe is a reminder of the great human losses suffered by Louisiana during the Civil War.

Many Louisianians returned from the war with serious injuries. This card is from an organization soliciting funds to care for disabled veterans.

Civilians living in the regions hit by the war lost almost everything. Both the Union and the Confederate armies foraged for food and supplies among the civilians. After the armies left, outlaws often stole anything that remained. The economy was stalled. There was no money to buy anything, but there was also nothing to buy.

The clashing armies left a barren land. Union General Banks followed General Sherman's "scorched earth policy" in central Louisiana. Banks burned plantations and towns as his army marched through the state. Houses, cotton gins, sugar mills, and barns were charred ruins. Fences had been burned to warm the troops. The number of cattle, horses, mules, hogs, and other animals had dropped drastically. It took twenty-five years for the livestock count in Louisiana to reach prewar levels.

Towns with their stores and supplies had also been destroyed. When courthouses had been burned, the parish's legal records were permanently lost. Railroads, bridges, roads, and levees were damaged and needed maintenance. Damage was even visible in the regions the armies had not crossed. Weeds grew in the fields, and the slaves had left the plantations.

Many soldiers came home from the war with empty sleeves or on crutches. For some families, no one came home. A woman in West Feliciana Parish watched her husband and six sons march off to war. She faced the aftermath of the war alone.

The end of the war brought confusion for the newly freed slaves. The promise of a new and better life was not quickly fulfilled. Chaos and poverty deprived the former slaves of a real place in the economic and social system. According to one twentieth-century historian, "They had

received their freedom but not the right to exercise it in the 'American tradition.' "

The **freedmen** (former slaves) wanted a better future, while the planters wanted to restore the past. A journalist noted, "It is admitted that . . . the freedman has . . . ceased to be the property of a master; it is not admitted that he has the right to become his own master."

LOUISIANA RETURNS TO THE UNION

War—and its aftermath — brings a special set of problems. This pattern, observed throughout history, appeared after the Civil War in the United States: Economic recovery became more important than anything else. Some people took advantage of the economic changes to get rich. Controversy and corruption troubled the federal government. The northern states experienced an economic boom, while the war-torn South struggled to survive.

And, as in every war, the death of so many promising young men affected the South's recovery. The loss of those potential leaders affected Louisiana, the South, and the nation.

ABRAHAM LINCOLN'S RECONSTRUCTION

President Lincoln recognized that restoring the nation after the war was crucial. He announced his plan before the war had ended, in his Reconstruction Proclamation. (**Reconstruction** refers to the steps taken to restore the southern states to the Union and to rebuild the South.) He wanted to restore the Union rather than to punish the South.

In Lincoln's view, secession was unconstitutional. He considered the Confederate states still part of the Union. He believed that men who were willing to swear their loyalty should be allowed to elect state and local governments. Lincoln put his plan into effect in occupied Louisiana during the war. In the election held in occupied Louisiana (the fourteen parishes in southeast Louisiana), Michael J. Hahn became the governor. He was elected by those voters who had signed an oath of allegiance to the United States.

To continue the process of restoring a loyal state government, delegates were also elected in 1864 to write a new state constitution.

President Abraham Lincoln was assassinated by John Wilkes Booth in April 1865. Had he lived, the conditions of Reconstruction imposed on the South might not have been so harsh.

Vice President Andrew Johnson became president upon the assassination of Abraham Lincoln. He favored a Reconstruction plan much like Lincoln's but was forced by the radical Congress to adopt stricter measures.

Louisiana's 1864 constitution abolished slavery, but it did not grant the freedmen the right to vote.

This right became an issue during the war. A delegation of the free men of color in New Orleans traveled to Washington to ask President Lincoln for their right to vote. Lincoln was impressed by their arguments and considered their request. He suggested to General Banks that blacks who owned property or who had fought for the Union be allowed to vote.

The assassination of Abraham Lincoln changed the direction of Reconstruction. John Wilkes Booth changed history in a way he did not intend. A Union Army commander's wife believed Louisiana would not have suffered so greatly if "Lincoln could have been spared to bring his justice and gentle humanity" to the conquered South.

ANDREW JOHNSON'S RECONSTRUCTION

When Vice President Andrew Johnson assumed the presidency after Lincoln's death, he faced difficulties almost immediately. He clashed with Congress as he tried to continue Lincoln's Reconstruction plan. Johnson began to readmit the southern states to the Union after voters in a state ratified the Thirteenth Amendment to the U. S. Constitution. The Thirteenth Amendment abolished slavery.

President Johnson also pardoned many former Confederate officers, which meant they could get their land back. The land had been seized under the terms of the Confiscation Act. Some of the radical Republicans in Congress had intended to distribute that confiscated land among the freedmen — the beginning of the rumored promise of "forty acres and a mule." (A **radical** is one who holds extremist views or wants drastic changes.) The radical Republicans disagreed with President Johnson on Reconstruction; they believed that the South should be punished for the war.

Congress and President Lincoln had also disagreed about Reconstruction, but Lincoln had had enough power to keep his more lenient plan. Without the political support in Congress, however, Johnson could not carry through his Reconstruction plans. President Johnson found it impossible to negotiate compromises. One of his critics observed that Andrew Johnson's biggest enemy was Andrew Johnson. During this power struggle, President Johnson was impeached and came within one vote of being removed from office.

Do You Remember?

1. What happened to the economy of the northern states after the war?
2. Who became president after Abraham Lincoln was assassinated?
3. What did the Thirteenth Amendment to the United States Constitution do?

LOUISIANA GOVERNMENT

While the presidential plan for Reconstruction was in effect, state government in Louisiana began to return to its prewar style. The presidential Reconstruction plan allowed former Confederates to vote once they had signed a loyalty oath. With their support, the state's antebellum leaders returned to power when the war was over.

In the first statewide election following the war, many former Confederates were elected to the legislature. They made their political views clear when they hired their doorkeeper. They chose a Confederate veteran who had lost both arms in the war. Every day when he assumed his post, he wore his Confederate uniform. The radical Republicans were greatly offended by this show of support for the defeated Confederacy. At this point, however, they could do little about it; the returning Confederates had more power. But Louisiana's Republican party (made up mostly of free people of color, former slaves, and northerners) gained strength during Reconstruction.

The governor at this time was James Madison Wells. He had been elected lieutenant governor of occupied Louisiana in 1864. When Michael Hahn was elected as the state's U.S. senator, Wells became the governor. Wells was elected as governor on his own in 1865. Wells was a Unionist and former slaveholder from Rapides Parish. (A **Unionist** is a person who had supported the Union during the entire war period.) Nevertheless, Wells quickly learned to cooperate with the Confederate legislature.

James M. Wells was elected lieutenant governor of occupied Louisiana in 1864. When Governor Hahn resigned to become a U.S. senator, Wells became governor.

THE FREEDMEN

Much of the political struggle during these years involved the former slaves either directly or indirectly. General Banks had asked the plantation slaves what they hoped the Union victory would bring them. Their first response was that their families not be separated. For their children, they wanted an education. For themselves, they wanted to know they would not be flogged, that they would not have to work on plantations where they had been abused, and that they would be paid reasonable wages.

With their new freedom, some former slaves moved to the towns. Some of them returned to the plantations, but others found work as laborers and craftsmen. During the Reconstruction years, the increased number of freedmen living in towns caused conflict.

One of the first actions of the restored legislature was to pass laws to control the former slaves. The free movement of the former slaves offended and frightened the whites. The laws, called the **Black Code**, restricted the freedmen's actions, movement, and conduct; the Code even included sections about rudeness to white people.

The other purpose of this legislation was to control the work force. regulation of the freedmen's labor had begun during the war. The plantations needed labor. Union Commanders Butler and Banks both developed strict controls. The former slaves were encouraged to work on the plantations, which were sometimes leased to Union supporters.

The laws passed by the legislature required freedmen to sign one-year labor **contracts** (formal, written agreements). If they did not sign a work contract, they could be forced to do public work under the vagrancy laws. (A *vagrant* is a person with no home or job who idly wanders from place to place.) If the freedmen were arrested for vagrancy and could not pay their fine, someone else could pay the fine and demand that the freedmen sign a work contract in order to pay off the fine.

In 1865, the federal government established the **Freedmen's Bureau.** Its original purpose was to provide aid — food, clothing, and basic medical care—to former slaves and other needy southerners. The Bureau also established some schools. The adult slaves who had been forbidden to learn to read and write could now become literate. The Freedmen's Act of 1866 expanded the authority and responsibility of the Bureau. An agent and a small group of soldiers were sent to each of the districts in the state. It became the agent's job to negotiate work contracts between the freedmen and the planters.

As the freedmen began exercising their new rights, more local restrictions came. Some towns added laws regulating the movement of freedmen. In Opelousas, for example, a freedman could not be on the streets after 10 p.m. and could live there only as the servant of a white resident.

Most of the other southern states also enacted Black Codes. Northerners disapproved of the increasing limits placed on the freedom of the former slaves. They believed that the South still wanted slavery. To

stop the enactment of more restrictive laws, Congress passed the Fourteenth Amendment to the U.S. Constitution. This amendment was intended to ensure the rights of the freed slaves. It granted citizenship to the freedmen, guaranteed them due process of law, and gave them the right to vote. (*Due process* refers to the judicial procedures set up to protect the rights of individuals.) The southern states were expected to ratify this amendment; states that refused to do so would have their representation in Congress reduced.

Louisiana and almost all of the other southern states refused to ratify the amendment. Most white southerners did not believe that the former slaves were ready for citizenship. Even more tension developed between those who wanted to restrict the freedmen and those who wanted to give them their full civil rights.

By 1866, Louisiana's Republican party had increased the pressure on the state legislature to give the freedmen their full citizenship rights, including suffrage. Governor Wells agreed with their plan to reopen the 1864 constitutional convention. They were to meet at the Mechanics Institute Building in New Orleans to discuss suffrage and other issues.

The city's mayor, John T. Monroe, was concerned about the safety of the citizens. He threatened to arrest anyone attending the meeting and sent police. The Republicans responded with a call for support and strength.

Armed whites attacked a group of blacks going into the building. Soon a riot broke out, and police fired into the crowd. In the fighting, three whites and more than thirty blacks were killed; more than one hundred blacks were injured. The riot put an end to the constitutional convention.

Before the riot, *The Picayune* had described the white treatment of the freedmen as "kindly good will . . . rarely exhibited in any country by a superior to an inferior race." These words reflect the attitude of superiority held by whites of the time. Unfortunately, that kindly goodwill was not demonstrated at the Mechanics Institute meeting. The violence brought strong reaction from northern newspapers and Congress. A Congressional committee investigated the New Orleans riot, and Congress began to believe that the South would have to be forced to give the freedmen their rights.

MILITARY RECONSTRUCTION

Congress then established a Joint Committee on Reconstruction to examine the situation in the South. The committee reported that "the feeling toward the emancipated slaves, especially among the ignorant and uneducated, is one of vindictive and malicious hatred." After the report was issued, Congress passed a new Reconstruction Act in 1867. The legislation placed the southern states under strict military control,

*Opposite, above: New Orleans Mayor John T. Monroe asked the city's people not to support the 1866 meeting of the Constitutional Convention. **Opposite, below:** Fighting broke out at the Mechanics Institute, site of the Constitutional Convention, and quickly turned into a riot. **Above:** General Phillip Sheridan was appointed military commander of District 5, in which Louisiana was placed.*

complete with military courts. Five military districts were established, each commanded by a general of the United States Army. This control would be removed only after the state had ratified the Fourteenth Amendment and written a new constitution that included universal male suffrage (the ability of all men to vote).

Louisiana, along with Texas, was part of District 5. General Phillip Sheridan was the military commander of the district. He removed Governor Wells from office because Wells was uncooperative and would not give blacks the right to vote. Sheridan called Wells "an impediment to reconstruction" and said he had no honest friends. Wells had been called a Jayhawker by his Confederate neighbors, but his opposition to rights for the freedmen lost him his position as governor. Wells had tried to get along with both groups but did not get along with either.

Under military Reconstruction, stricter loyalty oaths were required. The former Confederates had controlled the state for two years, but now most of those people could no longer hold public office. The loyalty oath required under the presidential Reconstruction plan focused on the future. Those taking that oath had to swear that "I will be loyal to the United States." The new loyalty oath examined voters' past behavior. The voter had to be able to swear "I have been loyal."

To the radicals in Congress, this was appropriate punishment for the war and the restrictions placed on the freedmen after the war. To southerners, this was an attempt to put power in the hands of Republicans. Louisiana spent ten troubled years under military control.

Do You Remember?
1. Who were the Unionists?
2. What rights did the Fourteenth Amendment protect?
3. What was the purpose of the meeting at the Mechanics Institute in New Orleans?

In 1868, Henry Clay Warmoth was elected governor. Born in Illinois, Warmoth was known by some as "Louisiana's Carpetbagger Governor."

THE STRUGGLE FOR CONTROL
OF STATE GOVERNMENT

The former Confederates could no longer participate in the political process. They were forced to sit by as the radical Republicans took control of state government. The Civil War had ended, but Louisiana was still not at peace.

THE RADICAL REPUBLICANS TAKE CONTROL

In 1868, Louisiana wrote the new constitution required by the 1867 Reconstruction Act. This constitution protected the freedmen's civil rights and extended suffrage to all black males over the age of twenty-one. Former Confederates who wished to vote had to sign a loyalty oath.

This was also the first Louisiana constitution to have a bill of rights. Only those who had taken the new loyalty oath and sworn that they had never aided the Confederacy could vote to ratify this constitution. That loyalty oath prevented many white Democrats from voting.

The 1868 governor's race was won by a newcomer to Louisiana. Henry Clay Warmoth had been a Union officer in New Orleans during the Civil War military occupation. He returned after the war to open a law practice. Charm and skill brought him to the head of the line of ambitious politicians trying to run Louisiana.

Warmoth had enough influence at the 1868 constitutional convention to ensure that the constitutional age requirement allowed him to run for governor; he was twenty-six when he was elected. Warmoth supposedly said "corruption is the fashion" and described himself as being as "honest as any other politician." He may not have taken money from the state, but he did make a personal fortune while he was in office. When he was inaugurated, he talked about the "growing spirit of harmony and good will." His days as governor, however, did not fulfill this promise.

Elected in 1868 as lieutenant governor was Oscar J. Dunn, the first black to be elected to a statewide office. He gained the respect of his party, the Republicans, and many conservative observers. Dunn was part of an influential group of African-American political activists. Also part of the group were Dr. Louis Roudanez and his brother, Jean Roudanez. They published a bilingual newspaper called *The Tribune*, which became a voice for African-American rights.

At the same time that the Louisiana Republican party was taking control of the state government, it

Oscar J. Dunn was elected lieutenant governor of Louisiana in 1868. He was the first black to be elected to statewide office.

was struggling with factionalism. The party had been established by the Unionists, but there were conflicts within the group. Some conservative Unionists had hoped to maintain slavery. They soon lost control of the party to the northerners who moved in after the war. Throughout the South, these people were called **carpetbaggers**. A *carpetbag* was a satchel or suitcase made of carpeting. The term meant that these were people who packed up their few belongings and headed south to make their fortune. To the white southerners, they were interfering outsiders. Henry Clay Warmoth, in fact, became known as Louisiana's carpetbagger governor. Southerners gave the local white Unionists who joined the Republicans a different name. They called them **scalawags**, as an insult. The scalawags often joined the Republican party for personal gain.

The results of elections during Reconstruction were often suspect. In 1872, William P. Kellogg was declared the governor by the federal government.

THE REDEEMERS

As part of the military Reconstruction plan, General Sheridan set up a system to register black voters. In 1868, almost 50 percent of the house of representatives and 25 percent of the senate were African Americans.

The former Confederates — generally members of the Democratic party — opposed the state government elected in 1868. The Democrats were angry at being subjected to a government based on the votes of former slaves and resented not being allowed to vote. They vowed to regain the power they had had before the war. They preferred to call themselves Conservatives or "Redeemers." They wanted to "redeem" or reclaim the state from the hands of the Republicans, carpetbaggers, and scalawags.

After the state election in March 1868, violence increased. A masked group called the **Knights of the White Camellia** used threats and physical violence to keep the freedmen from voting or to force them to vote for Democrats. Some voters were controlled by telling them they would be fired if they voted for Republican candidates. Merchants let voters know they had to vote "right" in order to buy at their stores. By the time the 1868 presidential election took place in November, the threats had worked. The Republicans had lost the majority of votes they held in the election for governor.

Governor Warmoth reacted to this by appointing the Returning Board. (Election results are referred to as *returns*.) The board checked election results to make sure they were fair. The Returning Board had the authority to throw out the votes from any polling place where it determined fraud had taken place. (**Fraud** is deliberate deception for unfair or unlawful gain.)

By the 1872 governor's election, the friction was not only between the Democrats and the Republicans. The Republicans were also fighting among themselves. The Republican party had two factions — one that supported President Ulysses S. Grant and one that opposed him. In Louisiana, the party had to hold two conventions because of its factional fighting. The leader of the Grant faction called out federal marshals with Gatling guns to control and protect his meeting. The Republicans ended up choosing William P. Kellogg as the gubernatorial candidate.

To try to hold onto his power, Governor Warmoth and his faction of Republicans allied themselves with the Democrats. They supported the Democratic candidate, John McEnery. After the election, both men claimed victory. Even the Returning Board was split and could not agree on a winner. Both the Republican Kellogg and the Democrat McEnery took the oath of office. The federal government, under President Grant's direction, declared Kellogg the governor.

During this power struggle, the legislature impeached Governor Warmoth on charges of corruption. Lieutenant Governor Dunn had died suddenly in 1871, and State Senator P. B. S. Pinchback, also an African American, was chosen to replace Dunn. Pinchback became the acting governor in December 1872 when Warmoth was removed from office during the impeachment proceedings. This made Pinchback the first African American to serve as the governor of any state. He served for one month.

Do You Remember?
1. What was a carpetbagger?
2. Who was Louisiana's carpetbagger governor?
3. Who was the first African American to serve as governor of Louisiana?

In December 1872, P. B. S. Pinchback became the first African American to serve as the governor of any state.

The End of Reconstruction

Early in this period, Governor Warmoth recorded in his diary that another Republican said "he [Warmoth] intended to beat the rebels and keep them from power [even] if in doing so he destroyed the state government and produced anarchy for twenty years." This promise was almost fulfilled. **Anarchy** is an absence of government or a state of lawlessness. Louisiana came very close to anarchy during the last years of Reconstruction.

MOUNTING VIOLENCE

Because of voter intimidation in the South, Congress passed the Enforcement Act in 1870 making it a crime to interfere with the rights of a citizen. But federal laws did not stop the violence and political fighting in Louisiana. The state spiraled out of control.

One bitter clash took place in Colfax. Grant Parish was one of the new parishes formed by the Republican government during Reconstruction. The parish was named for President Grant, and the parish seat was named for his vice president, Schuyler Colfax. The new town of Colfax was established at the site of a former plantation. In fact, the plantation's old stable was used as the parish courthouse.

After a contested election in 1872, a conflict developed over whether the Republican candidate (a black) or the Democratic candidate (a white) had the legal right to take office as sheriff. The events of April 13, 1873 — Easter Sunday — became known as the Colfax Riot. Both sides armed themselves, and a battle was fought for control of the courthouse. More

Violence sometimes erupted when both parties claimed victory in an election. The so-called Colfax Riot in Grant Parish was one example. Over twenty-five people were killed in the fighting.

than twenty-five blacks died in the fighting. Some accounts set the number much higher and include a number of unarmed black farmers who had come to the courthouse for refuge from the whites.

THE UNIFICATION MOVEMENT

There was one attempt to seek a peaceful solution to the strife. Some businessmen realized that the political chaos was keeping the state from economic recovery. They decided that only compromise could save the state. Meetings of the so-called Unification Movement took place in New Orleans in 1873. The group included two former Confederate generals and two of the most influential free men of color in the city.

The group planned to push for suffrage for freedmen and to develop some arrangement between whites and blacks for sharing political offices. However, it was soon obvious that no one could bring so many conflicting opinions and political agendas together. The radical Republicans opposed the idea because they would lose power. The Redeemer-Democrats did not even want to consider allowing the freedmen to vote. The freedmen themselves did not trust the group's intentions. So this effort, set in motion mainly to save the economy, failed. And the economy continued to suffer because of the political unrest.

THE WHITE LEAGUE

Whites began to organize to reclaim control of the state government. One newspaper, *The Caucasian*, was established in Rapides Parish to "unite the white people." Reporting on a mass meeting, it described one speaker "carried away by the power of his arguments and the heat of passion . . . [who] advocated the murder of the Republican candidates and offered to lead the mob."

In 1874, a group known as the **White League** was established. Its stated purpose was "the protection of our own race against the increasing encroachment of the Negro" and the removal from office of those who "lord it over us." Working whites wanted to ensure no black would be hired for any job a white would do. The White League intended to restore political power to the prewar white Democrats, and it did not hesitate to use violence to achieve that end. The term it used for the intimidation was "bulldozing."

Bulldozing was enough to drive some Republicans out of office in some parishes; in others, violence erupted. Red River Parish saw some of the ugly violence of the time. Red River Parish was one of the new parishes set up during Reconstruction. A carpetbagger, Marshall Twitchell, came to the area as an official with the Freedmen's Bureau. He soon married the daughter of a local family and established himself in the area. He then brought many of his relatives from Vermont to join him. Soon Twitchell and his family were politically powerful and

Members of the White League did not hesitate to use violence. Here, White Leaguers are manning a streetcar barricade in New Orleans.

The Battle of Liberty Place took place in New Orleans when the Metropolitan Police tried to keep a shipment of arms from the White League. The White League seized the New Orleans City Hall and forced Governor Kellogg to flee. Federal troops finally restored order.

prosperous. He arranged for Red River Parish to be created from several existing parishes.

As in other parishes where radical Republicans controlled the government, conflict flared. After hearing rumors of an uprising by the freedmen, a huge mob of White Leaguers gathered in Coushatta in Red River Parish. Accused of encouraging an insurrection, the white Republican officeholders were shot.

Violence also struck New Orleans. The Metropolitan Police had been created by Republican Governor Warmoth. Under the leadership of former Confederate General James Longstreet, they served as the military arm of the radical Republicans and were used to maintain order. The Redeemer-Democrats claimed that the Metropolitan Police were also used to intimidate them to keep the Republicans in power.

By September 1874, Louisiana was almost at the point of civil war. The White League had ordered a large shipment of weapons. General Longstreet moved to seize those weapons. A full-scale battle broke out between 4,000 Metropolitan Police and 8,000 members of the White League. This "Battle of Liberty Place" gave the White League the opportunity to seize the New Orleans City Hall and the State House. President Grant had to send federal troops and six warships to restore order.

THE 1876 ELECTIONS

The 1876 gubernatorial election was as controversial as the one before it had been. The violence and voter intimidation that marked the campaign made the results questionable. The Republicans claimed that their candidate, Stephen B. Packard, had won. The Democrats said the fair winner was their candidate, Francis T. Nicholls.

Once again the Republicans appealed to Washington for help. But this time the answer was different. President Grant did not want to send troops again to ensure that the Republican governor held the state. He sent a letter saying that national public opinion no longer favored using federal military force to keep an unpopular state government in power.

The Republicans' real concern was keeping the presidency in their party. The recent presidential election had the politicians in a turmoil. Rutherford B. Hayes of Ohio was the Republican candidate, and Samuel J. Tilden of New York was the Democratic candidate. Neither candidate had a majority of the votes, and the returns in three southern states (Florida, Louisiana, and South Carolina) were disputed.

Finally, a compromise was reached. The Republicans in Washington agreed to end military Reconstruction and remove federal troops from Louisiana and the rest of the South. In return, the state's electoral votes and those of the other two states were awarded to the Republican candidate, Rutherford B. Hayes. The compromise meant that the Republicans would no longer help keep the Louisiana Republicans in power. In 1877, President Hayes withdrew the last federal troops from the South; Reconstruction was over. The Redeemer-Democrats soon took control of state government in Louisiana.

In the 1876 election, Republican presidential candidate Rutherford B. Hayes promised to withdraw federal troops from the South in return for the electoral votes of Louisiana and two other states.

REBUILDING THE ECONOMY

During the Reconstruction period in Louisiana, politics overshadowed economic planning. The Congressional Reconstruction plan focused on punishment and political control. There was no master plan — or even consideration — for rebuilding the South's economy.

To most people, the political struggle was important only in the ways it affected their daily lives. Most Louisianians wanted peace around them and prosperity for their families. Restoring the plantation economy seemed logical. But rebuilding the plantation system required money, and banks were reluctant to make loans to the planters because they no longer had slaves for collateral. (*Collateral* is something of value pledged as security for a loan.) Many planters lost their land because they could not make the mortgage payments or could not pay their taxes.

A currency shortage also made the state's financial recovery difficult. Confederate money was worthless. One planter paid his

Blacks continued to provide most of the labor in the cotton fields, but now they worked as sharecroppers. Conditions, however, were close to slavery.

employees with written notes, "Good in thirty days to any merchant in Alexandria that furnishes Willis Washington a half barrel of flour."

Finding workers for the plantations was a constant struggle. Rather quickly, *brokers* began operating almost like slave traders, charging a fee for finding workers. Sometimes they cheated the workers, and sometimes they cheated the planters. Some of the workers were freedmen from other states. Workers were paid more in Louisiana because the land produced more cotton than in the eastern states.

One way to keep workers was with a contract. Labor contracts were started by the Union commanders during the war. Under the contracts, workers were paid wages, but they had to stay on a plantation for a year. Often, a part of their wages was held until after the crop was sold. This contract method worked well on the sugar plantations but not on the cotton plantations.

On a cotton plantation, there were several months when workers were not busy. In addition, planters did not have the cash just after the war to pay wages, and crops failed because of floods and insects. For these reasons, **sharecropping** developed. The planter provided the land, the tools, and a cabin. The workers labored all year in return for a share of the profit when the crop was sold. Typically, both the workers and the planter bought the year's supplies on **credit**. That is, they bought what they needed and agreed to pay for the items over a period of time. The store owner usually agreed to take part of the crop in payment at the end of the year. This form of credit was called the *crop lien system*. Sharecropping became a way of life for most freedmen, and later for many poor whites. Merchants who sold on credit charged high prices, and the workers' share of the profit was rarely enough to pay off the store owner. As a result, the sharecroppers were always in debt.

Natural disasters increased the struggle for economic survival. In 1866-1867, major floods hit Louisiana. Because the levees were not maintained during the war, the flooding was widespread. Even when there was enough of a crop to sell, it was difficult to get it to market. The railroads had been heavily damaged during the war. Only the line from Algiers (near New Orleans) to Brashear City (now Morgan City) was in good shape.

After the war, the small towns slowly began to recover. This is a view of New Iberia in 1866.

After 1867, agriculture and the rest of the economy began to improve slowly. Some sawmills were set up to handle the huge old cypress trees being cut in the swamps. Spanish moss was baled for sale. And professional hunters brought ducks and other game to market in the cities and towns.

The towns began to report some rebuilding. Shreveport and Marksville added several new buildings. Small factories in the towns built wagons, buggies, carts, and railroad cars. The system for buying cotton shifted from the factors in New Orleans to towns near the plantations. These towns had cotton buyers, gins, a big general store, a drugstore, a doctor, a school, a saloon, and several churches. Often, the general store doubled as the post office.

But the state's economic recovery halted in 1873 when a national depression stopped the country's growth. Louisiana stayed poor well into the twentieth century.

Do You Remember?
1. What was the Enforcement Act?
2. Why did some freedmen move to Louisiana at this time?
3. What is sharecropping?
4. Why was it difficult to get crops to market?

EDGAR DEGAS, THE IMPRESSIONIST

The famous French impressionist Edgar Degas has Louisiana connections. Degas was the son of a wealthy Paris banker and an American mother whose family were Creoles from New Orleans. He visited the city in 1872 and painted at least seventeen of his works of art while living in New Orleans. The most famous of these paintings shows his uncle at work in the Cotton Exchange. That 1873 painting, "The Cotton Exchange at New Orleans," was purchased by a Paris museum, the only Degas painting acquired by a museum during his lifetime. It was also the first impressionist work selected by any museum.

The impressionists were part of an art movement of the late 1800s that featured contemporary subjects and informal scenes. Their paintings used a variety of brush strokes and emphasized texture and light. Many of the impressionist paintings were done outdoors, a new idea at the time. Among the impressionists, Degas is the recognized master of drawing the human figure in motion. Ballet dancers and racehorses were among his favorite subjects. As he began losing his eyesight in his later years, he created bronze sculptures, usually of dancers or horses.

Above: *Edgar Degas' painting "The Cotton Exchange at New Orleans."* ***Left:*** *This portrait is of Edgar's American mother, Mme Auguste de Gas (left), and her sister, Duchess de Rochefort.*

During his stay in New Orleans, Degas painted portraits of many of his relatives. He lived with his mother's relatives, the Musson family. He felt an attachment to his family and to the city and said, "Louisiana must be respected by all her children, of which I am almost one." The Musson home is now open as the Degas House, a museum showing the life of Degas and the city at that time.

DAILY LIFE

Politics and the economy were not the only things in Louisiana that needed rebuilding after the war. People — black and white — had to rebuild their social lives.

ENTERTAINMENT

The return of the circus helped the children forget the war years. They were entertained and distracted by trained animals, acrobats, and clowns. Shreveport was excited by a visit from the famous General Tom Thumb, a tiny man who stood only 40 inches tall. A traveling group shocked the town of Shreveport with the can-can dance. Critics denounced the performance as being a place "a gentleman should be ashamed to be seen." The circuses and other entertainers traveled on the riverboats that soon filled the waterways.

The riverboats themselves provided part of the excitement of the times. Scheduled races attracted onlookers to town landings. In the most famous race, the *Natchez* and the *Robert E. Lee* steamed up the river from New Orleans to St. Louis in 1870. Because he was a friend of the owner, Governor Warmoth was a passenger on the *Robert E. Lee*. In his memoirs, he told how he watched the loading of more wood during the race. Another steamboat came alongside and the wood was transferred without either boat slowing down. The *Robert E. Lee* won the race in three days, eighteen hours, and fourteen minutes.

People also created their own entertainment. Amateur theater groups were formed in Alexandria and other towns. Parties and dances continued, although they were not as elaborate as in antebellum days. Charades was a popular party game. Making and pulling taffy candy was a special treat for young people.

Above: This 1872 painting is entitled the "Volunteer Fireman's Parade." Volunteer fire departments often served as social clubs. **Left:** *Steamboat races were a popular form of entertainment. Perhaps the most famous was the race between the* Natchez *and the* Robert E. Lee. *In the actual race, the boats were never this close together.*

After the war, baseball became popular. Baseball teams were formed as this new sport began to earn its nickname as "America's favorite pastime." The New Orleans Southerns traveled as far away as Brooklyn, New York, to play. The Baton Rouge team was called the Red Sticks, and Shreveport had two teams — the Quicksteps and the Country Boys.

New Orleans continued to be the only true city in the state, providing both entertainment and excitement. Visitors reported on the shocking behavior they saw and often described it as an immoral city. Gambling flourished. A new entertainment, the concert saloon, became popular. But along with the saloons and dance halls, New Orleans was also home to operas and the theater.

LSU RURAL LIFE MUSEUM

Rural life in Louisiana before and after the Civil War is easier to imagine when you stand on the grounds of the LSU Rural Life Museum. The buildings were all moved to the 450-acre site in the center of Baton Rouge to create this history museum. The different types of buildings are examples of *folk architecture*; that is, the people built them without architectural plans. You can see a one-room schoolhouse waiting for its pupils, a grist mill waiting for a wagonload of corn, and a country church waiting for Sunday worshipers.

You can also see a country store waiting for some barefoot children in overalls to come for penny candy. The store once served as a commissary on a plantation farmed by sharecroppers. As you step inside, you will soon realize that goods were limited, and many were very different from what you buy today. Horse collars hang on the wall alongside rub boards for scrubbing clothes. Instead of ready-made clothes, the store sold bolts of gingham fabric and sewing notions. Sugar, rice, and flour were kept in large wooden barrels and measured out by the pound. The prices of items were very different too. That gingham cost 20 cents a yard, and sugar cost $1 for eleven pounds.

The country store at the Rural Life Museum was also a social center, where people came to get mail, supplies, or a little gossip. The store had a wooden post office window with mailboxes. A pot-bellied stove heated the store and the men who sat around telling tales. When the weather was warmer, the porch benches held the visitors.

The LSU Rural Life Museum in Baton Rouge has over twenty buildings that depict life in nineteenth-century Louisiana. The buildings show how people lived (top) and where they shopped (above and opposite).

At the corner of the porch, a hitching post waited for a boy to tie his horse or mule. Then he could fill his can with the kerosene needed for the lamps at home. The storekeeper recorded the purchase in the account book under the family's name.

There are other country stores around the state to remind us of this time. The Webb store was moved from Caspiana, in south Caddo Parish, to the campus of LSU Shreveport. The Alma Plantation store on Highway 415 in Pointe Coupee Parish still sells to workers on the nearby sugar plantation. The Kleinpeter store in East Baton Rouge Parish has been converted to a feed store.

General Tom Thumb (whose real name was Charles Sherwood Stratton) and his wife Lavinia toured all over the United States, including Shreveport.

One new organization had an important community purpose. Volunteer fire departments were organized in several towns. The fire departments also served as social clubs, and the members of clubs like the Ascension Hook and Ladder Company met regularly. Local parades often included decorated firewagons. Special young ladies were honored when the fire engines were named for them.

EDUCATION

During the war years, education received little attention except in New Orleans. There, the military commanders established schools and brought teachers from the North to teach the freedmen how to read and write. The Freedmen's Bureau operated these schools after the war.

The Reconstruction government directed that the public schools be open to all students, but only a few schools in New Orleans functioned that way. Wealthy whites continued to send their children to private schools. But many children, both black and white, received little or no education. In some parishes, the public schools were controlled by an African-American school board. White parents refused to send their children to these schools. In parishes where whites controlled the schools, the African-American children were not allowed to attend. The corruption and confusion of these years affected education and the state's future.

Many northern churches helped provide for the needs of the freedmen after the war. Their most lasting contribution, however, was their involvement in education. The first colleges for African Americans in Louisiana were started by these missionary groups and became important institutions in the African-American culture. These included the University of New Orleans, Leland College, and Straight University. The University of New Orleans and Straight University later merged to become Dillard University.

AFRICAN-AMERICAN CHURCHES

An important cultural development after the war was the growth of the African-American churches. In antebellum times, slaves usually attended the white churches. The slaves were expected to sit in a special section and worship in the style of their masters. Now African Americans wanted their own churches.

Records of the Beulah Baptist Church of Chenyville in Rapides Parish show that the members met in July 1865 to discuss the attitude of their "colored members." The church voted to tell these members to report and repent of their behavior. Instead, the former slaves petitioned to begin their own church.

Some churches for African Americans had already been established. The African Methodist Episcopal Church was started in New Orleans in the antebellum era. Before the war, many of the free people of color were

Catholic. Their association with the Catholic Church was a result of their French heritage. Some of the slaves had also been Catholic. Now, however, most of the blacks chose to join another church. Some of the former slaves wanted to form Methodist churches, but most of the churches established were Baptist.

The church organizations were a source of strength for the African-American community. It was in these churches that the former slaves found the most freedom from interference in their lives. Here they developed their leaders and their sense of community.

The first colleges for African Americans in Louisiana, like Leland College (above), were started by missionary groups.

Do You Remember?

1. What new sport became popular after the Civil War?
2. What agency operated schools for the former slaves after the war?

SUMMARY

Soldiers returning home after the Civil War found a Louisiana physically neglected and politically troubled. Presidential Reconstruction, the first plan to restore the South, failed after President Lincoln's death.

The struggle for control of state government between the radical Republicans and the former Confederate Democrats fed the political unrest in Louisiana. Laws passed by the Confederate-Democrat legislature to control the newly freed slaves brought strong reactions from Congress. States were required to ratify the Fourteenth Amendment or face reduced representation in Congress. Louisiana and most of the other southern states refused.

As a result, Congress carried out its plan of military Reconstruction. Former Confederates who refused to take the "iron clad" oath of allegiance to the United States lost their political power. General Sheridan took command of Louisiana in 1867, and the state suffered from the civil unrest for the next ten years.

The political turmoil slowed the healing processes needed after the war. The Louisiana economy suffered from neglect, and many people struggled to secure even the basic needs. Louisiana citizens slowly began to rebuild their lives.

CHAPTER · REVIEW

	1866 Mechanics Institute riot 1865 James Madison Wells elected governor 1864 New state constitution written	1867 Congress established military Reconstruction 1868 Louisiana's Reconstruction constitution adopted Henry Clay Warmoth elected governor	1873 Colfax Riot 1874 White League formed Coushatta massacre Battle of Liberty Place	1877 Reconstruction ended
1865		**1870**	**1875**	
	1865 Abraham Lincoln assassinated Freedmen's Bureau established 1867 United States bought Alaska from Russia	1871 Most of Chicago destroyed in Great Fire 1869 First transcontinental railroad completed	1876 Alexander Graham Bell invented the telephone	

Reviewing People, Places, and Terms

Define, identify, or explain the importance of the following.

1. anarchy
2. Black Code
3. carpetbagger
4. contract
5. credit
6. Oscar J. Dunn
7. fraud
8. freedmen
9. Freedmen's Bureau
10. Knights of the White Camellia
11. radical
12. Reconstruction
13. scalawag
14. sharecropping
15. Unionist
16. White League

Understanding the Facts

1. What was President Lincoln's Reconstruction plan?
2. Why did the legislature pass the laws known as the Black Code?
3. What is due process and why is it important?
4. What was Louisiana required to do in order to remove military Reconstruction?
5. Why did the white Democrats call themselves the "redeemers"?
6. What was the Returning Board?
7. Why was the Unification Movement started?
8. How did the 1876 presidential election bring about the end of Reconstruction?
9. What is the crop lien system?

Developing Critical Thinking

1. Why do you think the radical Republicans wanted to punish the South?
2. The Louisiana Constitution of 1868 denied the right to vote to former Confederates. What arguments might delegates have used for and against this action?
3. Identify some of the reasons that made Louisiana's economic recovery after the Civil War so difficult.

1. It probably took weeks for a Confederate soldier to return home to Louisiana from Appomattox, Virginia. Using a modern highway map, calculate the distance from Appomattox to your home town. Suppose you made this trip and covered three hundred miles each day. How many days would it take for you to reach home?

2. During Reconstruction, new parishes were created from parts of existing parishes. On a present map of Louisiana, identify the following Reconstruction Era parishes: Acadia, Cameron, East Carroll, Grant, Iberia, Lincoln, Red River, Richland, Tangipahoa, Vernon, Webster, and West Carroll.

Special Projects

1. During Reconstruction, African Americans gained a political voice in Louisiana for the first time. P. B. S. Pinchback, Oscar J. Dunn, C. C. Antoine, and James H. Ingraham were key leaders. Locate and list several sources that tell you more about them. Write a biographical sketch of one of these men.

2. Newspapers during Reconstruction influenced people's opinions about issues. Today's newspapers use editorials and editorial cartoons in the same way. Find a recent example. Identify the issue, and summarize the opinion given. Write one paragraph evaluating the editorial or the editorial cartoon. Did it influence your opinion of the issue?

Making Connections

1. Degas painted "The Cotton Exchange at New Orleans" because this was where his uncle worked. List two or three possible subjects an artist might paint that would show the economy of our time, the way this painting does for the 1870s.

2. Using the Internet or library resources, find a book or Internet site that shows Degas paintings. Select a painting you like, describe it, and tell why you like it.

Louisiana Lagniappe

• George Armstrong Custer spent time in Louisiana as a military officer before he went west to meet his fate at the Battle of Little Big Horn.

• The president of the 1868 constitutional convention was James Taliaferro, who had argued so strongly against secession at the 1860 convention.

• Michael J. Hahn established Hahnville in St. Charles Parish.

• By 1872, New Orleans had an ice company making its own ice.

• BUILDING SKILLS: EXAMINING ALL SIDES OF AN ISSUE •

There are few issues on which everyone agrees. And people usually have a wide variety of reasons for feeling the way they do about an issue or for making the choices that they do. Often, when making decisions, it is important to examine *all* reasons or alternatives in order to make the best decision possible.

When Confederate soldiers returned to Louisiana after the Civil War, they faced three choices: Support the federal government, support former Confederate leaders, or remain neutral. Supporting the federal government would give them the power and freedom of their former lives. Remaining loyal to the Confederacy meant keeping friends but losing privileges.

Put yourself in the place of a Confederate soldier returning from the war, and analyze the reasons for and against each of the three choices given in the previous paragraph. On a sheet of paper, make three columns with these headings: Union, Confederacy, Neutral. Under each heading, make a "for" and an "against" list. In other words, list the reasons why that choice should be supported and the reasons why it could be a mistake to make that choice.

CHAPTER TWELVE

LOUISIANA'S TRANSITION ERA: POPULISM AND POWER

I remember these: horse-drawn carriages, button shoes, corsets and feathered hats for women, maypoles in the school yards in spring time, quiet orderly school rooms, five-cent soda pop and snack foods, mule-drawn wagons and plows, quilting bees, spelling bees, magic lanterns, and silent movies . . . steam locomotives, Civil War veterans reunions, Victorian attitudes . . . long flannel underwear, Model-T Fords, frequent and sudden fatal diseases, depressing funerals held in family parlors . . . religious revivals under big tents. Some of these things were splendid, others struck terror, especially in the hearts of the young.

      — From *When the Century Was Young,* by Dee Brown,
           a writer who spent his early years in the Bienville Parish
           sawmill town of Alberta, at the turn of the century

THE DEPARTURE OF THE FEDERAL TROOPS signaled drastic changes in Louisiana. After 1877, the president and Congress no longer interfered in Louisiana's government. Political control shifted from the radical Republicans to the Redeemer-Democrats.

The Democratic party soon directed Louisiana's political life. Without support from Washington, the Republican party could not maintain power in Louisiana. Without the strength of the Republicans, the political voice of the African Americans was gradually silenced.

This painting of turn-of-the-century New Orleans by Philip Poincy shows a mixture of the old and the new with modern conveniences like electric streetlights, telephone poles and streetcar tracks.

THE LOUISIANA LOTTERY

In 1868, the state had granted a 25-year charter (permission to operate) to the **Louisiana Lottery Company**. The Louisiana Lottery was a private company; that is, it made money for the company's owners, not for the state. In fact, the only benefit the state received was a small payment of about $40,000 a year for the charity hospitals. This was less than 1 percent of the income the lottery made. It usually brought in more than $20,000,000 a year and kept at least half of that as profit. During that same period, the average worker made $2 a day.

The lottery drawings were probably not rigged. Cheating seemed unnecessary because the company was making so much money. To appeal to the public, two old Confederate generals supervised the drawings. Advertisements announced that honest "orphan boys" drew the winners.

During Reconstruction, the lottery company gained a great deal of political power. It held political influence over the radical Republicans and later the Democrats by contributing large sums of money to elected officials. Opponents called the money "bribes" rather than campaign contributions.

The lottery controlled the Reconstruction government so completely that a top lottery official became the state treasurer. E. A Burke was penniless when he arrived in New Orleans after the war and took a $1-a-day job. He claimed to be a former Confederate Army major, but his critics said he had actually been a Yankee spy. Burke is sometimes called the ultimate carpetbagger.

At the same time Burke served as state treasurer, he expanded his influence on the state as the managing editor of the *New Orleans Times*, a newspaper owned by the lottery. This paper later merged with another, thereby increasing its political strength.

THE BOURBON DEMOCRATS

The Redeemer-Democrats who were now the political leaders of Louisiana saw themselves as southern gentlemen. Others, less complimentary, called them **Bourbons**. This term referred to the kings of France, whose royal family name was Bourbon. Louis XIV, the most powerful Bourbon king, said, "I am the state." This attitude was shared by those Louisianians labeled Bourbons. They believed their background, education, and success meant they should lead the government. These Louisiana Bourbons wanted to continue their way of life and did not accept the need for change. The Louisiana Bourbons continued their prewar beliefs in states' rights and in their superiority to the former slaves. They were accused of looking to the past yet not learning from it.

Some of the Bourbons also saw themselves as responsible for others who needed help. This attitude of taking care of the less fortunate is an example of **noblesse oblige**, which is a French phrase meaning "a noble obligation." In other words, a person who has wealth and position should help those who do not.

Other Bourbons, however, wanted to keep their wealth for themselves and were not concerned about the needy. Those Bourbons could be labeled **reactionary**; they strongly opposed progress. They usually described the best government as the least government. The reactionary Bourbons resented paying taxes for government programs. They succeeded in reducing the money spent on public schools and on social programs to improve the quality of life for fellow citizens.

THE DEMOCRATS IN POWER

The Louisiana Bourbons did not create a new political party but built their power within the Democratic party. As a result, the Democratic party became the party of whites in the South.

Whites gained and held onto their political power by manipulating the votes of the blacks. Whites controlled those votes with economic or physical threats. An employer told his workers how to vote. If they did not vote that way, they could and did lose their jobs. Anyone who tried to be an independent voter was threatened with physical harm. If necessary, the actual votes were simply ignored to give the Democrats the victory. The Returning Board was no longer around to ensure that elections were valid; it had been eliminated when the Republicans lost power.

The first Democratic governor after Reconstruction was Francis T. Nicholls, who was elected in 1877. This former Confederate officer was a classic example of the noblesse oblige approach to politics. Even an African-American newspaper said he tried to be just and impartial, but other politicians thought he was too generous toward blacks.

Nicholls had high ideals and was not afraid to take a stand. He criticized some of the wealthy Bourbons in his party for not paying their

The Louisiana Lottery Company was a private, for-profit organization. This is an engraving of its headquarters in New Orleans.

Francis T. Nicholls was elected governor in 1877. When the state constitution was revised, the governor's term was reduced to one year. This was a result of Nicholls's challenge of the Louisiana Lottery Company.

property taxes. Then, Nicholls challenged the Louisiana Lottery, but he was no match for the powerful lottery. There were more lottery supporters than opponents in the legislature. Burke and other powerful lottery officials engineered a call for a convention to revise the state constitution.

THE CONSTITUTION OF 1879

In the new 1879 constitution, the lottery charter was renewed. Lottery supporters also used the new constitution to reduce the governor's term by one year. Nicholls was thus punished for fighting the lottery.

The writers of the constitution of 1879 intended to change the radical Republican direction of the state government and return to home rule in Louisiana. But they feared federal reaction and so did not take suffrage away from the African Americans. They were also afraid that doing so might drive their workers out of the state. But some of the rights that had been put into place by the constitution of 1868 were removed. For example, the equal rights amendment was not included in the 1879 constitution. To separate black and white students, Southern University was established as a black college.

Other constitutional changes were made to please those in power. The property tax was lowered, and more restrictions were placed on borrowing money for state improvements. The powers of the governor were increased while those of the legislature were decreased. Separate public school systems were established for both races, but they were not well funded.

THE END OF THE LOTTERY

In 1888, Francis T. Nicholls returned as the governor. He still strongly opposed the lottery and its hold on the state. More and more people agreed with Governor Nicholls's opposition to the lottery.

In 1889, a scandal involving the lottery broke. E. A. Burke was accused of stealing more than a million dollars of state funds while he was the state treasurer. He fled to Central America, and the money was never recovered. Burke had already established business ties in Honduras and operated a mail-order lottery from there.

The Louisiana Lottery, however, was still powerful. It expected Louisiana to extend the company's charter. In fact, in 1890, it offered to give the state $1.25 million a year if the legislature extended its charter. The legislature voted to put the lottery extension before the voters in the 1892 election. Governor Nicholls refused to sign the bill saying, "At no time and under no circumstances will I permit one of my hands to aid in degrading what the other was lost in seeking to uphold . . . the honor of my native state." (Nicholls had lost one hand and one foot in a Civil War battle.)

The 1892 campaign for governor centered on lottery supporters and opponents. In the election, the voters chose Murphy J. Foster as governor. Foster had campaigned against the lottery as a "polluting monster" and promised to remove this corruption. The voters also rejected the amendment to renew the lottery's charter. The Louisiana Lottery Company finally ceased its operations in the state in 1893.

Do You Remember?
1. How was the state's portion of the lottery money spent?
2. What was the political party of the Louisiana Bourbons?
3. Who was the first Democratic governor elected after Reconstruction?

Murphy J. Foster ran as an anti-Lottery candidate. His election as governor ensured the death of the Louisiana Lottery.

THE POPULISTS

After the Civil War, many new political ideas spread across the United States. America's farmers were at the forefront of one of the new political movements.

The farmer's place in the economy had changed. The independent, self-sufficient farms were disappearing. In Louisiana, cotton became the farmers' main crop, and farmers' economic futures depended on the crop lien system. As a result, farmers got caught in a credit cycle. They relied on next year's crop to pay this year's expenses. But the farmers could not predict what profit they would earn. Many factors, some beyond the farmers' control, affected their income.

It was natural for farmers to get together and talk about their mutual problems. In 1867, an organization called the National Grange was founded to help farmers. This group was never very strong in Louisiana, but other farm organizations soon developed. One group that gained members in Louisiana was the Farmers' Alliances, which started in Texas in 1876. This movement was followed some years later by the **Farmers' Union**, set up in 1888.

The Lincoln Parish Farmers' Club was organized when a group of farmers discussed their problems after church one day. Their leader said they proposed to "protect the farmers of our country from these thieving pirates of modern civilization." Farmers' Union chapters or branches organized in several parishes. In Caddo Parish alone, there were six chapters of the Farmers' Union.

The Farmers' Union urged members to work together to keep costs down. For example, a merchant might agree to keep the costs reasonable in return for the business of Farmers' Union members. One store owner in central Louisiana charged 20 percent interest on credit accounts, which was considered a good rate at that time. Farmers in Sikes in Winn Parish operated their own cooperative store, while the Farmers' Union in Grant Parish expanded its efforts to include a private school.

THE POPULIST PARTY

These organizations of American farmers led to the birth of a new political party in 1891 — the Peoples' party, whose members were called **Populists**. The party's platform (a statement of the principles and policies the party supports) stated, "We believe that the powers of government should be expanded . . . to the end that oppression, injustice, and poverty shall eventually cease in the land." The

This "Gift of the Grangers" poster depicts the contributions farmers made to the nation's welfare. The Grange, however, was never very strong in Louisiana.

Populists believed that middlemen and manufacturers were taking too much of the farmers' profit. They wanted the government to make changes to help the small farmers. They promoted government ownership of the railroads so that transporting goods to market would not be so expensive. The Populists also wanted changes in money and banking.

FUSION

When Louisiana farmers and other voters left the national Democratic party to become Populists, political strength in the state shifted. The sugar planters no longer supported the national Democratic party because President Cleveland did not support a protective tariff. In Louisiana, they voted for the Republican candidates. In 1896, the Republican planters decided to oppose the Democratic candidate for governor. John Pharr, a wealthy sugar planter himself, was their choice. Pharr sought and received the support of the Populists.

The Republicans and the Populists saw an opportunity to join forces. This political strategy was called the **fusion movement**. The fusionists — the Republicans and the Populists — hoped to end Democratic control in the state. The sugar planters could provide Republican votes with their plantation workers. They could also influence these African-American voters to vote for the fusion candidate.

The Democrats expected to re-elect Murphy J. Foster. The campaign that followed was bitter. Threats and violence inflamed the voters, and accusations of fraud marred the Democratic victory.

THE CONSTITUTION OF 1898

The 1896 election and the fusion movement threatened Democratic control. The Bourbon Democrats reacted to this threat by writing a new constitution. One delegate described the constitutional convention as being like a family meeting of the Democrats. They intended to use the new constitution to maintain their control of the state, without bringing down federal disapproval.

The new constitution was much like the previous one. The major addition was the requirement that voters own property, be literate (able to read and write), and pay a poll tax. These restrictions virtually **disfranchised** (took the right to vote away from) the freedmen. The Democrats, however, did not want to lose any white voters because of the restrictions. A special section of the constitution protected this group. Called the **grandfather clause**, it stated, "No male person who was on January 1, 1867, or at any date prior thereto entitled to vote . . . shall be denied the right to register and vote in this state by reason of his failing to possess the educational or property qualification prescribed by this constitution." In other words, white males would not have to pass a literacy test or own property. However, because the freedmen did not receive the right to vote until 1868, the grandfather clause did not apply to them. The restrictions were very effective. In 1896, there were over 130,000 African Americans registered to vote. But by 1900, that number had shrunk to about 5,300. In 1904, there were only 1,300 registered black voters.

President Grover Cleveland was not popular with Louisiana planters because of his opposition to a protective tariff.

Do You Remember?

1. What political party attracted Louisiana farmers?
2. Who were the fusionists?
3. How did the constitution of 1898 affect African Americans?

SEGREGATION, DISCRIMINATION, AND CONFLICTS

As Louisiana approached a new century, major social and economic struggles continued. Those who preferred the traditional way of life clashed with those who wanted a better future. Their clashes were often violent.

Already disfranchised by the Bourbon Democrats, Louisiana blacks at the turn of the nineteenth century found their personal freedom resticted by the passage of Jim Crow laws.

SEGREGATION

The Bourbon Democrats were not content with disfranchising the blacks. Near the end of the nineteenth century, they also passed new laws that restricted blacks' personal freedom. These laws imposed **segregation**, public and social separation of the two races. The laws were known as **Jim Crow laws**, the name of a black character in a stage show. Jim Crow laws were found in every southern state, as well as many other parts of the United States. They resulted in separate restrooms, water fountains, railroad cars, waiting rooms, dining areas, and schools. Facilities for blacks were separate but rarely equal to those for whites. This segregation remained the law and the way of life in Louisiana until the civil rights movement of the 1960s.

The educated Creole African Americans of New Orleans did not accept this loss of their rights without a legal battle. They formed the Comitè des Citoyens, an early civil rights organization. In the early 1890s, one of its members, Homer Plessy, challenged the Louisiana law requiring blacks to ride in a separate car on trains. Because he was so light-skinned, he had to tell the conductor he was a black man. He was then arrested for riding in the white car.

Plessy sued to have the Louisiana law overturned, arguing that it violated the Thirteenth and Fourteenth amendments. The case was appealed through the court system and reviewed by the U.S. Supreme Court. In 1896, the high court upheld the Louisiana law. This court decision, referred to as *Plessy v. Ferguson*, legally established the **separate-but-equal concept**. The majority of the judges ruled that states could legally require separate facilities as long as they were equal. From 1896 until 1954, when it was successfully challenged, segregation was legal in the United States.

VIOLENCE

The attitude that fostered Jim Crow laws also generated violence. Every election brought out brutality against voters. Candidates themselves resorted to violence to settle their differences. Some followed the formal code of duels, but others reacted immediately. Two candidates had a shoot-out on Main Street in Farmerville in Union Parish. Milder conflict led to insults and name-calling; one candidate, for example, called his opponent a buzzard and a parasite.

The violence spread beyond campaigns and elections. Communities believed they had the right to carry out their own justice. The definition of "justice" depended on who had the power. Lynching (mob murder, usually by hanging) was not uncommon. Large mobs sometimes gathered for these vigilante actions. (A *vigilante* is a member of a self-appointed group that presumes to interpret, rule on, and carry out sentences on matters of law or morals.) Plans for some lynchings were even reported in newspapers in advance. The worst violence was directed at black men, but the violence also involved blacks against whites and blacks against blacks.

Immigrants were the object of violence from both blacks and whites. In the late nineteenth century, many immigrants left the poverty of Sicily and came to the United States. Some of them settled in Louisiana, with the largest number in New Orleans. In 1890, the city's police chief was murdered, supposedly by a secret Italian organization called the Mafia. Nineteen Italians were arrested, tried, but not convicted. Nevertheless, a mob took them from the jail and killed them. This episode created a major international incident. Some of the men who were killed were Italian citizens. Newspapers around the United States criticized the mob mentality of New Orleans. In 1907 in Jackson Parish, a clash occurred between a group of blacks and some European immigrants over lumber mill jobs.

This 1891 Harper's Weekly *cover illustrates the mob's murder of six of the Italians in the New Orleans incident.*

Above: Leased convicts were used to build the New Orleans Pacific Railroad in Natchitoches Parish. ***Opposite, above:*** *Laurel Valley Plantation Village outside Thibodaux is the largest surviving sugar plantation in the United States. This was the plantation store.* ***Opposite, below:*** *Sugar workers at Laurel Valley Plantation lived in these houses. The sugar workers tried unsuccessfully to improve their living and working conditions by forming a labor union.*

CONVICT LEASE SYSTEM

Another aspect of Louisiana life that also involved violence was the **convict lease system**. After the Civil War, several states, including Louisiana, devised a new scheme for cheap labor. To earn money, a state leased convicts from the state penitentiary for work outside the prison.

In Louisiana, one man received a contract requiring that he pay the state a certain amount of money for the prisoners. He then leased (rented) the men to other people. The convicts were soon doing all of the dirtiest, most dangerous work in the state — building levees, roads, and railroads.

Their working and living conditions were brutal. A man who was sentenced to life in prison was usually dead within seven years. A Clinton newspaper commented, "The men on the [public] works are brutally treated and everybody knows it." The writer concluded with his opinion that their suffering was a thousand times worse than the law intended as punishment for their crimes.

THE PROBLEMS OF LABORERS

As Reconstruction ended, the former slaves faced an even harder life. Rumors spread throughout the South about the opportunities available in Kansas. There, it was said, a black man could start his own farm. By

1879, thousands of black farm workers in Louisiana were willing to gamble on this new life. They were called *Exodusters*, because they took part in the exodus to Kansas.

The possible loss of their labor force greatly disturbed the planters. Workers were threatened and even physically stopped at the steamboat landings. The freedmen who reached Kansas were disappointed in the climate and in the treatment they received. To regain their workers, some planters paid their return fare.

Blacks were not the only ones hoping to improve their lot. All workers were concerned about better working conditions after the Civil War. By the 1870s, the Knights of Labor, an early labor union, organized in the United States. A **labor union** is an organization of workers formed to improve wages, benefits, and working conditions for the workers. In Louisiana, black sugar plantation workers joined this union.

At about the same time, sugar planters formed the Louisiana Sugar Planters' Association. They wanted to control their laborers and improve their sugar production. After a poor crop in 1886, the planters' organization proposed lowering wages for the next season.

The workers, who had wanted a wage increase, threatened to strike. A **strike**, a labor union's main weapon, occurs when workers refuse to work. One slogan of the sugar cane workers was "A dollar a day or fight." When sugar cane is ready to be cut, there is only a short time to gather in the harvest. The threatened strike meant the crop might be lost.

Above: The Watkins Syndicate and other land companies brought experienced wheat farmers from Iowa to apply their skills to rice cultivation. With new scientific agricultural methods and new machinery, they established profitable farms, like this one in Crowley, *Opposite, below:* With exhibits from all over the world, the 1884 Cotton Centennial Exposition in New Orleans represented Louisiana's attempt to become part of the "New South."

Many workers left the plantations and came into Thibodaux, where the Knights of Labor had rented houses for the strikers. To control the workers, the authorities declared martial law. During the riot that followed, shooting broke out and more than thirty workers were killed. Many others were wounded. The strike was broken, and the powerless strikers were forced to return to harvest the sugar cane.

Unions did not succeed in improving working conditions for timber workers either, but they did create conflict. The Southern Lumber Operators' Association was formed in 1906 to combat the union's efforts. The Brotherhood of Timber Workers was organized in Louisiana in 1910. Two years later in Alexandria, it merged with the Industrial Workers of the World (IWW), whose members were known as "wobblies." The founder described this organization as the "Continental Congress of the working class." The IWW was closely associated with the Socialist party and did not shy away from violence.

Two violent labor conflicts took place in 1911 and 1912 in the lumber towns of Graybow and Merryville in Beauregard Parish. Workers were arrested and charged with conspiracy, but they were acquitted.

Do You Remember?

1. What were southern segregation laws called?
2. What group of immigrants faced violence in New Orleans in the late nineteenth century?

AGRICULTURAL AND INDUSTRIAL PROGRESS

Louisiana had a mild climate, abundant water resources, low-cost fuel, a large labor supply, and rivers for transportation. The new century brought new industry to the state. New discoveries and developments made the resources of the state more valuable.

AGRICULTURE

After the railroad was built, southwest Louisiana became the rice center of the state. Land companies such as the Watkins Syndicate owned huge amounts of land in the prairies. They hired the head of Iowa's Agricultural College to bring farmers to Louisiana. These experienced wheat farmers applied their skills to growing rice. With new scientific agricultural methods and new machinery, they established profitable farms.

This agricultural progress and plans for more economic growth led to the 1884 Cotton Centennial in New Orleans. Exhibits from all over the world filled the area that is now Audubon Park. This exposition represented Louisiana's attempt to become part of the "New South." Even the Bourbons who did not want social change approved of economic growth. One Centennial speaker noted, "We must develop our great resources. We must multiply sweat in steam, and multiply muscle in machinery."

LUMBER

The huge forests around the state attracted outside investors, and the railroads that were built in the state in the late 1800s ensured easy transportation for the lumber. The lumber industry grew rapidly, peaking between 1880 and 1920. The lumber companies harvested yellow pine from many areas of the state and cypress from the swamps of South Louisiana. The cypress lumbermen, in fact, were usually called "swampers." Massive trees provided billions of board feet of lumber. Some pine logs measured seven feet in diameter, and many cypress logs were even larger.

One of the first major sawmills was Pharr and Williams's Sawmill at Patterson in St. Mary Parish. The lumber industry also developed around Bogalusa in Washington Parish. There, the Great Southern Lumber Company established one of the largest lumber mills in the world.

These early lumber mills produced railroad ties and telephone poles. Coopers purchased wooden staves (narrow strips) to make barrels. Shingles, lumber, and cypress for fine-finishing work left the mills for construction sites around the United States. The *Southern Lumberman* said Louisiana cypress "makes up easily, finishes beautifully, and lasts without end."

Wages for lumber workers varied from $2.50 to $10.00 a week. They were often paid in *scrip*, paper certificates used in place of money and usually only good at the commissary store run by the company. The work was hard and dangerous. It was common for old loggers to be missing fingers, if not arms or feet. Falling trees or the slip of an ax could end the life of the lumberman.

When Louisiana's big lumber boom began, more than 75 percent of the state was covered in forest. By the 1920s, however, much of those forests had been reduced to cut-over land with only stumps left standing. Sawmill towns became ghost towns as workers moved on.

Above: The state's pine forests yielded thousands of huge trees such as the one being cut here. *Right:* Log trains transported cut timber to the lumber mills around the state.

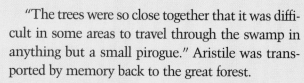

"TREES"

In the following story, Aristile "Vieux Pop" Guilbeau, a Cajun fisherman born in the Atchafalaya Basin, tells his grandson, Alexson "Ti Frere" Shellgrave, about the swamp before the lumber companies harvested the huge cypress trees.

Ti Frere often wandered in the Basin during the low water stage of fall. It was a favorite activity for the growing boy. "Why are the stumps so big and the living trees so small?" he asked Vieux Pop, who was cooking a big chicken and sausage gumbo over a low fire at the woodstove.

"In the late 1800s and early 1900s the lumber companies came in and bought the land cheap. To make money on their investment they hired logging crews to cut the trees, for the valuable cypress lumber."

"But, Vieux Pop, why did they cut all the big trees? Why can't I see what the forest looked like? Was it beautiful? Do you remember?"

"Yes, it was beautiful! The trees were magnificent." Vieux Pop began to gesture with his hands; "Most of them were bigger in diameter than the outhouse in our backyard, eighty or ninety feet tall before the first branches, huge columns, straight, round, solid. Standing in a forest of big trees, even at midday, you might have guessed, if you didn't know better, that the light was that of early morning or late afternoon because the huge trunks and leafy branches blocked out so much of it. There was a canopy a hundred feet up that looked like the ceiling of a great cathedral.

"The trees were so close together that it was difficult in some areas to travel through the swamp in anything but a small pirogue." Aristile was transported by memory back to the great forest.

"But why did they cut down all the trees?" Ti Frere insisted.

"Well, it was a business, you know. The companies that had bought the swampland wanted to make money by selling the lumber. Those people didn't live here, and they didn't care about the future," Vieux Pop explained. "Old cypress was a very valuable wood. You could build anything with it—boats, houses, barns, furniture, barges, water tanks, fence posts, anything. It was easy to work and durable." And then he continued, in Cajun English: "Well, you know, Ti Frere, not'ing lasses fuh evah, not even somet'ing big an' strong like dose ol' tree."

Vieux Pop gets a sad look on his face that I can never quite understand. He is looking right through me, as if I'm not even there anymore. What is he seeing? The big trees maybe? Some memory from his youth? I try to bring him back: "I'll be able to see the big trees one day, won't I, Vieux Pop, if I live to be as old as you?"

"No, no! Not hif you live to be twice as old like me. Every lass one of dose big tree was older den 500 year. Some was older den 2,000 year. No, nevah again. Hit's too late." Then he sometimes walks outside to chop firewood, or clean his nets, or repair something; and I know that the talk is ended. Sometimes I know, too, that he is close to tears. I wonder why he gets like that.

"Why didn't you stop them, Vieux Pop? Why didn't you just make them stop? he repeated. It was Ti Frere's belief that his grandfather could do anything he wanted — could solve any problem, right any wrong.

"There were times when fishing and moss-picking didn't supply enough money for those who lived on the bayou — times when fish would not get into the nets. At other times, there were plenty fish, but the buyers paid so little for them it was pointless to catch the fish and take them to market, because the fishermen were working hard only to lose money. I remember days when you couldn't have found twenty-five cents in this house. Plenty days were like that. Then the land company men came to the fishermen and said, 'We own these swamps covered with cypress trees. We will pay you well, if you work for us. Cut these trees, float the logs out to the mills that we're building along the edges of the swamp.'

"So the people of the swamp said, 'All right, we love the trees, but there are so many of them. It won't really make any difference.' Everywhere you looked there were huge old cypress trees, so they told themselves and each other, 'O.K., we will do this thing for a certain time. We'll cut the trees, make some money, buy some better clothes to replace our rags, a new shotgun to provide food for the table. We'll buy nets and crawfish traps and boat engines and fuel so that we might have a better chance to make a living fishing.' But once they had started cutting the trees, there was no end to it. They couldn't seem to find a way to stop. They earned enough to buy not only the things they needed, but even to save some money. They were not wise, Ti Frere. They didn't know or didn't want to know that north of them in the swamp and south of them and in every direction there were logging crews like theirs cutting the trees. So they cut and cut, and they let themselves forget that the great trees were many hundreds of years old and that the beauty and tranquility and peace they provided, as well as safe homes for wildlife, would all be gone — forever.

"Without realizing the meaning of what they were doing, they themselves changed the great cypress forest into cutover swampland. We, of all people, *they*, I mean, should have known better. They had come to live here because of the big trees and the abundant wildlife that the forest supported. Then they allowed, and even helped the landowners, including the state of Louisiana, to nearly destroy their chosen homeland. They were not wise; they did not think ahead. They placed the need for having jobs and making money above the value of the big woods. For the landowners it was a business; for my friends it was a job; for you it is a loss that can never be corrected, *never*.

"The swamp is beautiful now, you know it is, and you know that I've said to you more than once, 'I wish you could have seen the swamp the way it was when I was a boy.' Yes, it is still a thing of great beauty, and I know that you will someday say to your own children and grandchildren those same words; 'I wish you could have seen the swamp the way it was when I was a boy,' for this place continues to change, to fill up with sand and silt that come into the Basin from the Mississippi River. And it has become more and more a victim of people who don't understand, people who litter and who destroy things, people who lessen the quality of a place by their presence alone.

"One standing tree like those I've told you about could provide homes for hundreds of creatures: squirrels, raccoons, wood ducks, hawks, herons, owls, song birds, tree frogs, lizards, woodpeckers. Imagine a tree 180 feet tall, six feet in diameter — what a creation this is! When they cut the trees, they didn't think about the effect it would have on the wild creatures living in them, nor on ourselves who lived below them."

Vieux Pop sends me out for wood, but I know what he's doing. He's getting rid of me so I can't see him crying, but I saw already. I saw one big ol' tear rolling down his face, takin' a crooked path through his beard stubble and fallin' right in the gumbo. I even heard it; that's how quiet it was just before I stepped through the doorway. If one of my buddies at school had seen that, it'd be all over for me. Shame, shame, Ti Frere's grandfather is a crybaby. So much for his reputation as the toughest man on the bayous, and so much for my reputation as anything.

Source: Greg Guirard, *The Land of Dead Giants* (St. Martinville, La.: Greg Guirard, 1991), pp. 42-45.

OIL AND GAS

As the lumber industry declined, an even bigger economic boom occurred. In 1902, the first successful oil well in the state was drilled in Jennings in Acadia Parish. Louisiana had another resource to sell to the world.

The state's second major oil field was found in Caddo Parish. It was there in Caddo Lake that the very first offshore oil well was drilled in 1911.

New boom towns, like Oil City in Caddo Parish, developed as the oil industry grew. These towns, filled with oil workers, gained the reputation of being rough and wild. The Oil City hotel was a tent, but it had a reputation for good meals. The general store also served as a post office, billiard parlor, and an auditorium. The railroad and telegraph offices were operated from freight cars.

Money was made by both those with oil on their land and those who supplied the oil industry. One storekeeper in Mooringsport received $30,000 a month from land that he had purchased for 70 cents an acre. His neighbors made money selling supplies to the oil companies.

Above: A replica of the small wooden oil rig used to drill Louisiana's first oil well is on display at the Louisiana Oil and Gas Park in Jennings. *Right:* Here, Southern Well #3 is gushing oil near Crowley.

By 1910, Standard Oil Corporation had completed a pipeline to Baton Rouge. That 8-inch pipeline carried northwest Louisiana crude oil to the company's new refinery. By 1911, the Baton Rouge refinery was producing more than 7,000 barrels of oil a day.

Drillers often found natural gas while they were looking for oil. At first, it was burned off as a nuisance, but around the turn of the century drillers discovered its value. Oil producers began transporting the natural gas through pipelines. Cities began using the natural gas as fuel and for lighting. One of the largest natural gas fields was discovered near the city of Monroe in 1916.

SULPHUR AND SALT

Another important mineral had been mined in Louisiana even before oil drilling began. The first sulphur deposits were discovered in 1869 in Calcasieu Parish, but commercial mining did not begin until 1895.

In 1891, Dr. Herman Frasch developed a method of mining sulphur using superheated water to melt the sulphur underground. The liquid sulphur was then pumped to the surface. Using this technique, Frasch and his Union Sulphur Company made huge profits.

By 1914, Calcasieu Parish was providing 75 percent of the nation's sulphur. The town of Sulphur grew up around the Calcasieu Parish mine. This Calcasieu Parish sulphur field, however, was exhausted by 1920.

Salt had been discovered and used before the Civil War. But commercial salt mining at Avery Island in Iberia Parish did not begin until 1879. By the early twentieth century, Louisiana produced much of the salt used in the United States.

Although salt had been discovered in Louisiana and used before the Civil War, it did not become profitable until the late 1800s.

NEW TRANSPORTATION

Louisiana's agricultural and industrial progress would not have been possible without transportation improvements. The state's dirt roads turned into mud during the rainy season and were almost impassable. People had tried several techniques to improve the roads. First, they put logs on the roads, making a road they called *corduroy*.

In 1875, Judge John W. Watkins of Minden came up with a better plan. He had a covered road built from Bossier Parish to Webster Parish through the swamp. The finished road was less than ten miles long and was called the Shed Road. The "shed," built of heart pine planks, was eighteen feet wide and high enough for a wagon with three bales of cotton to pass under. Each mile of Shed Road cost about $8,500 to build. Watkins made a $20,000 profit by charging a toll of $1.50 for a wagon with four oxen and $1.00 for a wagon pulled by four mules. The road was very profitable — until the railroad came through.

*Above: This young boy is enjoying an old locomotive during the Railroad Days Festival in DeQuincy. **Opposite, above:** Engineer James Eads developed a plan to deepen the mouth of the Mississippi River by using a system of jetties. **Opposite, below:** The jetties at the mouth of the Mississippi were constructed of woven willows, stone, and heavy timbers.*

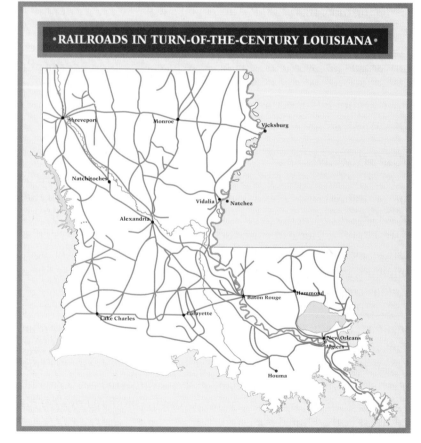

• RAILROADS IN TURN-OF-THE-CENTURY LOUISIANA •

RAILROADS

Most railroad construction in Louisiana took place between 1880 and 1910. The Kansas City Southern Railroad was built in the 1890s, opening up western Louisiana. It was a railroad company owned by Jay Gould that finally built the line from New Orleans across Louisiana to Marshall, Texas. The company received a land grant of more than a million acres of land as an incentive to lay track on that land. Later, the railroad company established towns on that land and sold lots.

Other developers brought additional railroad lines into Louisiana. By 1910, some five thousand miles of track crossed Louisiana.

JETTIES

The coming of the railroads did not mean that water transportation was no longer important. The Mississippi River was still a valuable transportation route. But the shallow mouth of the river made it difficult for large ships to navigate the passes. An engineer in Iberville's day concluded that narrowing the channel near the passes would help. The swifter current would then scour the river bed and clear away the mud. Efforts had been made to dredge (deepen) the river before the Civil War, but the Mississippi continued to deposit sediment.

In 1873, engineer James Eads presented his plan to deepen the river's mouth. He proposed building a system of jetties that would extend into the river and increase its flow. With the support of Congress, Eads built what were essentially retaining walls of woven willows weighted with stone and held by heavy timbers. This jetty system did narrow the river's channel and increased the flow of the current. The faster current swept away the sediment and deepened the mouth of the river. When work was completed in 1879, shipping to New Orleans increased immediately.

AUTOMOBILES AND AIRPLANES

As the largest city in the state, New Orleans showcased a new form of transportation — the automobile. At an amazing race in 1909, the driver set a world record with a speed of 60 miles an hour.

By 1916, more than 9,000 automobiles motored about Louisiana. The increase was due mainly to Henry Ford, who used mass production to reduce the cost of making cars. Ford's Model T automobile cost between $300 and $500, and the buyer had to pay extra for balloon tires and running boards. People who wanted to purchase the Model T could use a new credit method. Making monthly payments on the *install-ment plan* increased consumers' buying power.

The mass production of Henry Ford's Model T changed the transportation system forever.

These new vehicles required new regulations. In 1913, the Bossier Parish police jury passed a law requiring the registration of automobiles. By 1915, the state required automobile licenses, charging a fee of 25 cents for each horsepower.

Another major transportation event took place in New Orleans in 1910, only seven years after the Wright brothers made the first airplane flight at Kitty Hawk, North Carolina. At an "international aviation tournament," one plane climbed to a height of over 7,000 feet and flew a mile in just 57 seconds. The featured event was a race between an automobile and an airplane. The Packard car defeated the airplane. However, the pilot of the plane, John Moisant, was later honored when the New Orleans airport was named for him.

STREETCARS

At the beginning of this era, New Orleans still had horse-drawn streetcars. According to custom, gentlemen paid before sitting down. It was proper for ladies to sit, then pass their money to the nearest man, who gave it to the driver.

In the larger cities, people got around by streetcar. This streetcar (the inspiration for the title of Tennessee Williams' famous play A Streetcar named Desire) *operated in the New Orleans French Quarter.*

By 1889, Shreveport had electric streetcars, called *trolley cars*. Children who rode these trolleys watched with excitement as sparks flew from the lines. Office workers and shoppers welcomed the dependable transportation.

By 1893, the New Orleans and Carrollton Railroad operated electric streetcars, charging a fare of 6 cents. This later became the St. Charles Streetcar, which is still in operation. Soon these electric streetcars traveled all around the city. Consumers Electric Company operated twenty-nine streetcar lines, all but one of which traveled down Canal Street (the main street in New Orleans). The statue of Henry Clay, which had stood on Canal Street for years, had to be removed to make room for all the streetcars to turn.

NEW TOWNS

New industry meant new towns for Louisiana. Lumber towns grew up near the sawmills. Fisher in Sabine Parish stands today like a museum, with its commissary building, tidy houses, and white picket fences. Other towns have disappeared completely, and some have grown into larger towns and cities.

Many of Louisiana's towns were created as the railroads expanded. The layout of the streets in a railroad town was different. The main street ran beside the railroad tracks rather than along the riverfront or the bayou. Towns like Ruston in Lincoln Parish began as railroad towns.

Just as the railroad created new towns, it also killed others. If the railroad bypassed a town, the end was near. During this era when towns were born or died, many parish seats were moved. Some were relocated after a vote in the parish. Sometimes the courthouse records were stolen and moved to another town.

Fisher is a historic treasure. Buildings in this early lumber town include the town hall (top), the depot (above) and the company store (opposite).

Do You Remember?

1. What crop became important in southwest Louisiana in the late 1880s?
2. Where was the first successful oil well in the state?
3. What was the Shed Road?

CROWLEY

One of the many beautiful Victorian homes built in Crowley around the turn of the century.

The earliest towns in Louisiana developed along the waterways, which were the main means of transportation. The coming of the railroad meant that new towns could be built away from the waterways. Often these railroad towns were planned and laid out in a short time. Crowley's story is the story of one of those new railroad towns, and its development parallels Louisiana's twentieth-century changes.

The Duson brothers founded the town in 1887. Cornelius "Curley" Duson was the sheriff of St. Landry Parish. William "Willie" Duson was a real estate developer. The two men visited the area to choose a site for the new town. One version of their visit says the village of Mermentau lost its chance to get the railroad when a local storekeeper refused to sell the Dusons fishing tackle on credit. Regardless, the Dusons chose 174 acres of prairie land on which to build their new town. They paid about 50 cents an acre for the land. The town was named Crowley, after a railroad section foreman. The Dusons had promised to name the town for him if he helped run the railroad tracks into the area.

Once the railroad arrived, the Dusons held a lot sale. Circulars advertised that "good water, good grass and good health overflow." The three-day auction included a free barbecue and games such as roulette and chuck-a-luck. The Dusons attracted plenty of buyers. The first lot sold for $50. The new owners paid half in cash and paid off the rest in a year, with no interest.

Crowley included streets 80 feet wide and avenues 115 feet wide. The streets were numbered and the avenues were lettered. Two avenues were named and intersected to form a circle in the center of town. That circle today contains the Acadia Parish courthouse. The main street of Crowley — Parkerson Avenue — looks like Main Street USA. Small businesses line the four-lane street with a wide median down the center.

Crowley became the parish seat of the new parish of Acadia partly because the Dusons offered to pay $5,000 to help build a courthouse. In a vote in 1887, Crowley won over the town of Rayne by 138 votes. The first courthouse cost $10,000 and, like other buildings of the time, had no running water, bathrooms, or electric lights.

Because the town was built in the 1880s, beautiful old Victorian houses line the early streets. More than forty blocks of these grand structures, which look like wedding cakes, are listed on the National Register of Historic Places. The trees planted when the houses were built now shade the streets with their century-old growth. Crowley is recognized as a, city of trees, because of these beautiful water and live oaks.

Crowley proudly proclaims itself the "Rice Capital of America," and the International Rice Festival in October is a school holiday. The important rice industry is responsible for the highest structures on Crowley's skyline. A seven-story brick bank building was built in 1924, a very modern building for the time and place. Silvery metal rice bins stand alongside the towering rice mills in the business district.

Above: The seven-story First National Bank building in Crowley was considered very modern at the time it was built. *Left:* One of many rice silos in Crowley. Today, about a quarter of all the rice produced in the United States grows within a 50-mile radius of Crowley.

NEW CONVENIENCES

The twentieth century brought new inventions and modern life to Louisiana. Cities and towns were more likely to offer this updated lifestyle. Rural Louisiana continued with life as it had been.

TELEPHONES

The first telephones came to Louisiana's cities in the 1880s. One Bossier Parish man wanted this new invention in his rural home. He received permission to connect his own line to the Shreveport system. His line crossed the Red River, held up by tall cottonwood trees.

Within a decade, telephone companies came to the smaller towns. Donaldsonville had its telephone line installed from New Orleans. One local resident called the telephone a fad that would soon die out. But

within twenty years, there were "speaking telegraphs" and "talking telegraphs" throughout the state.

GASLIGHTS AND ELECTRICITY

It was in New Orleans that kerosene lamps were first replaced by gaslights. The kerosene lamps burned with a smoky light and had to be cleaned regularly. The new gaslights were clean and bright, a marked improvement. Electric lights came to New Orleans in 1887. By 1900, the entire city was lighted by electricity. Consumers Electric Company advised its customers to burn only four light bulbs at a time, at a cost of $1 a month. Burning a fifth bulb would blow the fuse.

The Electric Light and Power Company was formally organized in Donaldsonville in 1896. The company claimed it "could lower the price so that they would soon have its lights in every store and in a great

Modern conveniences came to the big cities first. This view of Canal Street in New Orleans in the early 1880s shows streetcars, gaslights, and telephone poles topped with some of the first electric streetlights.

With Rural Free Delivery, rural Louisianians no longer had to go "to town" to pick up their mail.

number of our private buildings." Crowley and Opelousas built electric light plants in the mid-1890s. The Crowley company gave churches and convents a reduced rate.

By 1916, electric lights had replaced the gaslights in the state's cities and towns. In small towns, the electricity was turned on only at night. Arcadia in Bienville Parish had 24-hour electricity on Wednesday. That was the day set aside to use the new electric irons. Rural Louisiana, however, did not receive electricity until the late 1930s.

MAIL SERVICE

The railroads made mail delivery more dependable. Special delivery was even added by 1885. No longer would rural Louisianians have to go to town to pick up their mail. Mail was delivered to homes on the rural free delivery (RFD) routes. This service became available in Thibodaux, for example, in 1896. The first mail delivery vehicles were horses and wagons.

One of the most important deliveries was the Montgomery Ward or the Sears catalog. These mail-order catalogs soon contained more than 1,000 pages and offered almost any needed item at a price working people could afford. For example, in 1902, the Sears, Roebuck and Company catalog offered a 100-piece set of china for under $5 and a top-of-the-line wood and coal stove for less than $15. No wonder they were called "wish books" by the rural families who ordered their goods.

THE PROGRESSIVE ERA

The goal of improving the quality of life for all Americans was part of the **progressive movement**. As the new century began, reformers examined America. With industrial growth had come larger cities, and urban development led to urban problems. The progressive thinkers recognized the complex political, social, and economic challenges of the twentieth century. These progressives believed government — local, state, and national — was best equipped to deal with these challenges and correct the ills of society. They had faith in the idea of *progress*, the belief that humans could keep improving their society to make it better and better.

Progressives worked to reform society in three main ways. First, they wanted government to fight poverty and improve the living conditions of its citizens. Progressives worked hard to reform prisons, improve working conditions, outlaw alcohol, and extend voting rights to women. Second, they wanted to break up large corporations and regulate business. Third, they wanted voters to have more influence in government.

In Louisiana, the progressives also wanted good government and social justice, but they were more traditional and conservative than the national group. However, even in conservative Louisiana, some of the reforms sought by the progressives were put in place. In 1886, laws were passed regulating the hours that women and children could work. More child labor laws were passed as concern increased.

Each of the early twentieth-century governors introduced some progressive reforms; some governors were more successful than others. W. W. Heard, the first governor of the new century, ended the convict lease system. The next governor, Newton Blanchard, separated youthful offenders from hardened criminals by building a reform school in Monroe.

Blanchard's efforts also improved public education in the state. Education had been neglected because voters would not approve the funding needed for the schools. With Blanchard's support, a new law allowed local school boards to sell bonds. With funds from the sale of these bonds, more than two hundred new schools were built. The number of high schools increased from twenty-six to fifty-three. Governor Blanchard also doubled the state budget for education. He appointed James B. Aswell as the state superintendent of education. Aswell brought qualified teachers to the schools, built new schools, consolidated small country schools, and established a standard high school program. Because of his new programs, Aswell earned the title of "father of modern education in Louisiana."

Governor J. Y. Sanders led the state's first conservation efforts and started a program of road improvement. When Luther Hall was governor, the state started a workers' compensation program (a government insurance program for those killed or injured on the job).

Louisiana's first governor of the twentieth century, Democrat William W. Heard, ended the convict lease system.

WORLD EVENTS

By the end of the nineteenth century, the citizens of Louisiana recognized that the fate of their state was tied to the fate of their country. They accepted their roles as citizens of the United States. Towns and cities sometimes celebrated the Fourth of July, although Confederate Memorial Day (June 3) continued to be an important holiday. This renewed patriotism was challenged by two wars.

THE SPANISH-AMERICAN WAR

At the end of the century, Cuban patriots were fighting a guerrilla war for independence from Spain. In February 1898, the U.S. battleship *Maine* mysteriously exploded in the harbor of Havana, Cuba. Over two hundred American sailors died. Shortly afterward, Congress declared war on Spain, and President William McKinley called for volunteers to drive the Spanish from Cuba. Louisiana responded with two regiments of infantry, three batteries of artillery, and several hundred sailors. A total of about five thousand men from Louisiana served in this war, which lasted only four months. The Second Louisiana Infantry Regiment was among the first American troops to enter Havana. Louisiana lost only one soldier in the Spanish-American War.

The health of Louisiana residents benefited from the studies of yellow fever in Cuba during the war. For the first time, a clear connection was made between mosquitoes and the disease. No longer was the disease blamed on "noxious inhalations from the lakes and bayous." Later work at the Panama Canal provided the knowledge to bring this killer disease under control.

Left: Teddy Roosevelt (center) led the Rough Riders during the Spanish-American War. *Above:* A gigantic "Buy Liberty Bonds" sign hung along New Orleans's Canal Street during World War I. It was the largest sign in the world at the time.

WORLD WAR I

In 1914, war broke out in Europe. The Central Powers, led by Germany and Austria-Hungary, were opposed by the Allied Powers, led by France, Great Britain, and Russia. President Woodrow Wilson declared the United States a neutral nation. In April 1917, however, the United States declared war on Germany because German submarines were sinking passenger ships on the high seas. This war has come to be known as World War I.

During World War I, radio operators trained at an army camp on the Tulane University campus in New Orleans.

As the United States entered another war, Louisiana again supported the action. World War I touched the French connections of many of Louisiana's citizens. At the railroad stations, when Louisiana troops departed for the war, "La Marseillaise" (the French national anthem) was played along with patriotic American songs.

Several military camps were established in the state. A large army camp was located near Pineville, and a camp to train aviators was built in Lake Charles. Shipyards at Madisonville and Slidell built vessels for the United States Navy.

Over 80,000 Louisianians served in the armed forces. Nurses from the Tulane Medical Unit served in Europe. One of the most famous heroes of World War I was Marine Major General John A. LeJeune of Pointe Coupee Parish. He later became the commandant of the Marine Corps, and the famous Marine training camp in North Carolina is named in his honor.

Like the rest of the United States, the people of Louisiana did their part from the home front. Women rolled bandages and knitted sweaters, scarves, mittens, and socks. Families observed "wheatless days" and "meatless days" so that food could be sent to the Allies. Louisianians also supported the war effort by buying some $200 million worth of war bonds.

Louisiana rejoiced in victory along with the rest of the country. At the war's end in November 1918, church bells rang and steam whistles blew. In Shreveport, people celebrated with a two-day bonfire in the middle of Texas Street. Patriotic spirit filled the state.

Do You Remember?

1. When did the first telephone lines come to Louisiana?
2. What did Governor Blanchard do to improve education in Louisiana?
3. How did people at home help in World War I?

SUMMARY

After Reconstruction, the Democrats regained political control of the state. These Bourbon politicians struggled to renew their past as Louisiana approached a new century. The powerful Louisiana Lottery Company influenced both politics and politicians. The constitution of 1879 made the lottery more secure.

All was not right, however. Farmers organized to protect their interests, and labor unions formed to protect the rights of the working classes. From these groups developed a new political party, the Populists. The Republicans and the Populists joined forces in the fusion movement in an unsuccessful effort to gain control of the state.

During this period, Louisiana became more segregated. Jim Crow laws were passed and required separate public facilities for blacks and for whites. Violence and vigilante actions arose from social unrest.

From the poverty left by the Civil War, Louisiana slowly progressed toward the twentieth century. The old ways were being challenged by new ideas and new inventions. The national progressive movement gained strength in Louisiana bringing some political, social, and economic reforms. New prosperity came to Louisiana from industrial growth.

Involvement in the Spanish-American War and World War I reminded Louisiana of its place in the nation. The state joined the rest of the country in this act of American unity.

New Orleans residents were urged to buy war bonds with a military parade down Canal Street during World War I.

CHAPTER · REVIEW

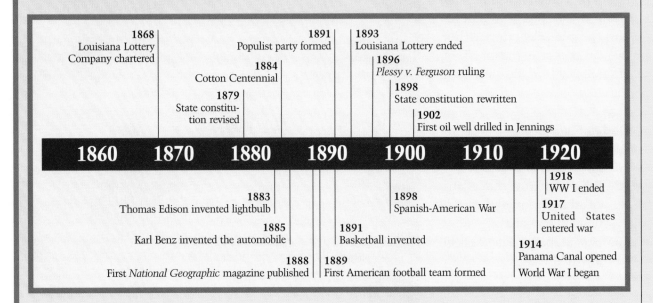

1868
Louisiana Lottery
Company chartered

1891
Populist party formed

1893
Louisiana Lottery ended

1896
Plessy v. Ferguson ruling

1884
Cotton Centennial

1898
State constitution rewritten

1879
State constitution revised

1902
First oil well drilled in Jennings

1860 1870 1880 1890 1900 1910 1920

1883
Thomas Edison invented lightbulb

1898
Spanish-American War

1918
WW I ended

1885
Karl Benz invented the automobile

1891
Basketball invented

1917
United States entered war

1888
First *National Geographic* magazine published

1889
First American football team formed

1914
Panama Canal opened
World War I began

Reviewing People, Places, and Terms

Define, identify, or explain the importance of the following.

1. Bourbons
2. convict lease system
3. disfranchise
4. Farmers' Union
5. fusion movement
6. grandfather clause
7. Jim Crow laws
8. labor union
9. Louisiana Lottery Company
10. noblesse oblige
11. Populist
12. progressive movement
13. reactionary
14. segregation
15. separate-but-equal concept
16. strike

Understanding the Facts

1. How did the lottery influence or control state government?

2. How did the Bourbon Democrats control voting in Louisiana?
3. When did the Louisiana Lottery cease its operations in the state?
4. How did the Creole African Americans react to the state's Jim Crow laws?
5. Why was the U.S. Supreme Court's ruling in *Plessy v. Ferguson* significant?
6. What is a vigilante?
7. What type of work did the leased convicts do?
8. What change in transportation created new towns?
9. How did the Spanish-American War help end the threat of yellow fever?

Developing Critical Thinking

1. Why do you think E. A. Burke was referred to as "the ultimate carpetbagger"?
2. How was the grandfather clause discriminatory?
3. "During the early 1900s, people began to believe that government could become an agent for positive change in society." Do you believe this has proven to be true? Why or why not?

1. Find the following railroad towns on a Louisiana map: Bernice, Bunkie, Crowley, Eunice, and Ruston.
2. Many towns suffered when they were bypassed by the railroads. On a current Louisiana map, check to see whether these nineteenth-century towns still exist: Arizona, Bayou Sara, Bellevue, Grand Coteau, and Vienna.

Special Projects

1. The People's party was considered to be a "third" or minor political party. Prepare a short report on the existence of third parties in our country's history. What issues might be the basis for a third party today?
2. Louisiana towns at the turn of the century proudly displayed their train depot. Having a train depot meant progress. Many railroad depots still exist throughout Louisiana. Locate a railroad depot in or near your town. Describe its appearance and its current use. Research more of the history of this depot. Share your findings with your classmates.

Making Connections

1. What do you think the author's purpose is in this story?
2. Why were the people who lived in the Basin willing to work for the lumber companies?
3. Can you give an example of a recent situation that involved a conflict between the environment and the economy?

Louisiana Lagniappe

- The teddy bear was named for President Theodore Roosevelt after a bear-hunting trip to Louisiana.
- On May 7, 1901, President William McKinley visited New Orleans and attended a special program in his honor held at the Cabildo.

• BUILDING SKILLS: DETECTING BIAS •

Everyone has certain opinions or ideas about certain topics or subjects. For this reason, written material is not always objective (free from the writer's personal opinions). Even though a writer may try hard to be objective, what he or she writes or says may show *bias*, a highly personal and sometimes unreasonable opinion about something or someone. Bias can be either for or against an idea or individual.

To be a good and thoughtful citizen, you need to learn how to detect bias in both written and oral materials from both the past and the present. Asking the following questions may help you.

- When and why was the material written or the statement made?
- Did the writer or speaker use certain phrases for emotional impact or try to play on your emotions rather than present facts?
- Does the writer or speaker tend to show one group as good and the other group as evil?

Try This! Read the following statements and identify any bias you believe exists. Explain why you think bias exists.

MASS MEETING! All good citizens are invited to attend a mass meeting on Saturday, March 14, at 10 o'clock A.M., at Clay statue, to take steps to remedy the failure of justice in the Hennessy case. Come prepared for action.

(A notice in a New Orleans newspaper, March 14, 1901)

Affairs have reached such a crisis that men living in an organized and civilized community finding their laws fruitless and ineffective are forced to protect themselves. When courts fail, the people must act.

(William S. Parkerson speaking to a New Orleans crowd, March 14, 1901)

CHAPTER THIRTEEN

LOUISIANA'S HUEY LONG ERA: POVERTY AND PROGRESS

Evangeline waited for her lover Gabriel who never came . . . But Evangeline is not the only one who has waited here in disappointment. Where are the schools that you have waited for your children to have that have never come? Where are the roads and the highways that you spent your money to build, that are no nearer now than ever before? Where are the institutions to care for the sick and the disabled? Evangeline wept bitter tears in her disappointment. But they lasted through only one lifetime. Your tears in this country, around this oak, have lasted for generations. Give me the chance to dry the tears of those who still weep here.

— Huey Long, at the Evangeline Oak in St. Martinville, 1928

THROUGHOUT THE TWENTIETH CENTURY, conflict between change and tradition has played a major role in the history of Louisiana. In the period after World War I, new ideas and new technology brought real progress to the United States. At the same time, the fear of change caused tension. The politics of Louisiana during that period reflected this friction.

After World War I, many Americans enjoyed a period of prosperity. In the late 1920s, no one expected that progress to end, but they were wrong. The stock market crash in 1929 signaled the worst depression that Louisiana and the rest of the country had ever known.

This statue of Huey Long stands over his grave facing the State Capitol in Baton Rouge, built during his term as governor.

A TIME OF CHANGES

The decade after World War I is often referred to as the "Roaring Twenties" or the Jazz Age. It was a time of rapid change, as if Americans were trying to make up for the time lost during the war.

CULTURAL CHANGES

New Orleans created the music for the Roaring Twenties. Jazz was born on the streets of the city and spread around the world. Brass bands were popular throughout America at the turn of the century. New Orleans bands soon developed their own style as they paraded through the streets. The new music was labeled "jazz," and two famous jazz musicians were Louis Armstrong and Jelly Roll Morton. A popular pastime of the twenties was to ride the steamboats and dance to a jazz band.

That music soon became part of the new radio broadcasts thrilling America. In 1920, the first successful commercial radio station in the United States, KDKA, went on the air in Pittsburgh. Less than two years later, Louisiana had its first radio station — WWL of New Orleans. The station's first broadcast was from Loyola University on March 31, 1922. On that first radio program, the college president began with a commercial asking for donations for a building fund. Then the few radio owners heard a piano composition. WWL still broadcasts from New Orleans. As radios became more common, the broadcasts offered more variety. The continuing dramas, called "soap operas," soon attracted many loyal listeners. Baseball games were vividly described by exciting announcers.

Movies brought another form of entertainment to the twentieth century. The first moving pictures were seen in the state soon after the new century began. In Marksville, "the pictures" or "picture slides" were first shown in a tent pitched on a vacant lot. That type of makeshift theater was also used in other towns and cities. But by 1927, there were fifteen major theaters in New Orleans and fifteen nickelodeon movie houses. The matinees, or afternoon movies, cost 10 cents. The most expensive weekend ticket cost 25 cents.

The first talking movie shown in New Orleans, *The Glorious Betsy*, came to the Tudor Theater in 1928. In 1929, an elaborate new theater in New Orleans, the Saenger, held the premiere of *Evangeline*. That movie, based on the poem by Henry Wadsworth Longfellow, told the story of the Acadian exile. The star of the movie, Delores Del Rio, dressed in a costume described as "Evangeline blue." Store windows soon displayed clothes in the suddenly popular color.

In the 1920s, women's clothing and hair styles changed radically. The women who sported the styles of the Roaring Twenties were called modern or even *flappers*. Short skirts and bobbed hair shocked the older generation. Strict, traditional rules at the Louisiana State Normal School for teachers now seemed very old-fashioned to the students. One young woman was almost expelled from the Natchitoches school because she cut her hair short.

WOMEN'S SUFFRAGE

Women had been very active in the progressive movement, particularly in the prohibition movement. They also formed local clubs to provide charitable aid for their neighbors and to improve the quality of life. For example, a Shreveport club's speaker discussed the need for pure food standards. The Women's Club of Shreveport was responsible for the city's first park, Princess Park.

Opposite: The Fate Marable Band is shown here playing aboard the riverboat S.S. Capital *in 1919. The young Louis Armstrong is the third person from the right.* **Above:** *Jelly Roll Morton was an early jazz pianist and composer. He was born in New Orleans.*

Many women were also involved in the women's suffrage movement, although Louisiana women were generally more conservative about seeking the vote. A few women in Louisiana had spoken out for women's rights when African-American men were granted the vote during Reconstruction. But most Louisiana women of the time did not agree. The *New Orleans Times* gave the general nineteenth-century opinion, "Politics is bad enough for men, without drawing ladies into such an atmosphere of corruption and publicity." In 1914, the Louisiana Federation of Women's Clubs would not even agree to take a stand for women's suffrage.

One early advocate for women's rights in Louisiana was Lavinia Egan from Bienville Parish. She had attended the Baptist college at Mt. Lebanon in Bienville Parish and later studied in Europe. Ahead of her time and place in the South, she asserted her rights at a young age. At a time when other women still rode a horse sidesaddle, she wore pants and sat in a regular saddle. Egan actively participated in the national woman's suffrage efforts and joined other women in Louisiana who wanted the right to vote.

In 1919, the Nineteenth Amendment, which would give women the right to vote, was passed by the U.S. Congress and sent to the states for ratification. In August 1920, Tennessee became the thirty-sixth state to ratify the amendment. Women in Louisiana were able to vote for the first time the following November.

PROHIBITION

There were many people in the country who wanted **prohibition**, forbidding by law the making and selling of alcohol. They blamed society's problems on the excessive use of liquor and believed that banning alcohol would improve American life.

The antiliquor or prohibition movement had started in the late 1800s as part of the early progressive movement. Several organizations formed to work for prohibition; the best known organization was the **Women's Christian Temperance Union**.

In 1917, Congress voted to stop the sale of alcohol. It adopted the Eighteenth Amendment to the U.S. Constitution, which prohibited the manufacture or sale of alcoholic beverages. The amendment was **ratified** (approved) by three-fourths of the states by 1919 and went into effect in 1920. But even before 1920, some parts of Louisiana had made the sale of liquor illegal. A number of towns, parishes, and even wards had held local elections on banning alcohol. Places where it was still

The 'roaring' 1920s brought great changes. You can see that in this view of Canal Street in New Orleans: automobiles are much more common and women's fashions have changed drastically.

Louisiana's coastline made it easy to smuggle illegal whiskey into the state. This fuel truck is being loaded with whiskey in New Orleans.

legal to sell liquor were called "wet," and the places that prohibited liquor were called "dry."

The reaction to prohibition was different in each region of the state. Protestant North Louisiana strongly supported prohibition. The Catholics in South Louisiana did not have the same religious restriction against drinking. People in South Louisiana were, therefore, more open in ignoring the law.

Prohibition created problems throughout Louisiana. Buying illegal liquor was not difficult. Speakeasies, moonshiners, and bootleggers operated throughout the state, from New Orleans to the smallest towns. Speakeasies were illegal bars, where customers had to speak quietly so the police would not hear them. Moonshiners made their own liquor to sell to those who wanted it. Bootleggers sold smuggled liquor; the name came from the practice of hiding flasks of whiskey in their boots. Coastal Louisiana offered these new outlaws the same protection that pirates had always found. Thousands of inlets made it easy to bring in a boat filled with liquor.

POLITICAL CHANGES

Change in society brought change in government. The Bourbons who had controlled the state were replaced by governors who were at least somewhat progressive. John Parker of New Orleans had been one of the state's early advocates of the progressive movement. He had even joined Theodore Roosevelt's Progressive party and had run for governor as its representative in 1916. Parker returned to the Democratic party and was elected governor in 1920.

Governor Parker could not enact all of the progressive changes he envisioned. But he was able to move the state in that direction. He recognized the need for a larger university and moved the campus of LSU to its present location in Baton Rouge.

Another change favored by Parker was a tax on natural resources. For the first time, Louisiana established a **severance tax** on resources taken from the land. The severance tax is based on the idea that removing a resource from the environment means that future generations are deprived of its use. The tax is a fee for using this nonrenewable resource. Parker explained that "those who are getting rich from natural resources of the state owe a debt to this and future generations, as they are removing and destroying resources created by the Almighty . . . never again to be replaced."

Some of the severance tax money went towards improving the roads, with more gravel roads added. Governor J. Y. Sanders had begun the gravel road program, and Governor Parker expanded it. The road construction was done on a pay-as-you-go basis. Because the state could not borrow money to build roads, the road-improvement program was limited.

Governor Parker also faced a problem with the **Ku Klux Klan** during his term. The Klan had been founded in Tennessee in 1865. Originally

When two men who had criticized the Klan were found murdered, Governor Parker worked to ensure that their killers were found and indicted.

Governor J. Y. Sanders (above) began a program to improve the roads before World War I. It was this program that Governor Parker expanded during his term of office.

a social club for Confederate veterans, it quickly evolved into a political force that used violence and intimidation, especially against blacks. The Klan faded in the late 1800s but was revived in the United States after World War I. Terrorism was directed against anyone whose behavior the Klan did not like. Immigrants and minorities were its main targets, with some ugly results. The Ku Klux Klan spread around the country, and violence and lynchings were not limited to the South. States like New York and Ohio reportedly had more than 200,000 members. The Klan even paraded in front of the White House in full regalia (costume).

In Louisiana, the Klan continued to threaten African Americans and commit vigilante actions. A major incident occurred in Morehouse Parish in 1922. Two young white men who had defied the Klan were found tortured and murdered. Governor Parker worked to ensure that the killers were indicted and prosecuted; they were not, however, convicted. Finally, in 1925, Louisiana passed a law that made wearing masks illegal and required members' names to be made known.

THE CONSTITUTION OF 1921

The legal structure of the state government faced more revisions during this period. When John Parker became governor, the state was regulated by the constitution of 1913. That constitution had been written because the state's financial structure needed changes. It also included some ideas of the progressive movement, such as juvenile courts.

But by 1921 there were legal difficulties with the 1913 constitution that required the writing of a new one. The constitution of 1921 is described as the most "legislative" of all the constitutions Louisiana has had. That is, it did not serve as a broad framework for state law but was instead very specific about details. Some of the delegates to the constitutional convention had tried to write a short, clear constitution, but they could not overcome the special interest groups who wanted constitutional protection. Because the constitution was so specific, it required frequent changes that could only be made through amendments. Before the constitution of 1921 was replaced, it had been amended 536 times and was so long it filled five feet of shelf space! (In comparison, the U.S. Constitution, written in 1787, has been amended only twenty-seven times to date.)

The 1921 constitution did include some positive elements. For the first time, the need to protect the environment was recognized. The Railroad Commission, which had been set up to regulate transportation and communication companies, was given more power and became the **Public Service Commission**. It was on the Railroad Commission that Huey Long developed the power that made him governor.

Do You Remember?

1. Where was the first radio station in Louisiana?
2. What did the Nineteenth Amendment change?
3. What were those areas that sold liquor called? What were the areas that banned liquor called?
4. What was the Ku Klux Klan? Against what groups did the Klan operate?

The Ku Klux Klan was not just a force in the South. This march took place in Washington, D. C., in 1926.

HUEY LONG

Who was Huey Long? Even people in other states know he was the governor of Louisiana, and his name is more widely known than any other political figure in Louisiana. Only Charles Lindbergh was photographed more by the journalists of the day.

People who lived in Huey Long's Louisiana were seldom mild in their opinions of him. They either loved him or hated him. Some of the poor considered him a saint. Newspaper notices giving thanks to St. Anthony and St. Jude sometimes added a thanks to Huey Long. In some homes, his picture sat on mantels alongside the religious shrines.

What did this governor do that made him so different and so controversial? He liked to describe himself as one of a kind. When questioned about his methods, he replied, "The end justifies the means." In other words, his use of power would help the people. Some described him as ruthless and power hungry. He controlled all local and state government jobs, and he fired teachers who did not agree with him. People who received state jobs were expected to contribute regularly to his campaign fund. This system was called "the deduct," since money was deducted from state employees' pay. Long made a point of destroying his enemies and was merciless in his personal attacks on his political opponents.

Above: Huey Long, shown here as a teenager, was the seventh in a family of nine children.
Opposite: Huey Long may have provided the best description when he told reporters, "I am suis generis (one of a kind), just leave it at that."

HUEY LONG'S EARLY LIFE

Huey Long's rough road to power in Louisiana began in Winn Parish. He was born near Winnfield on August 30, 1893, a date later honored as a state holiday. The political views of his hometown may have influenced his thinking. Winn Parish was the home of the Populist movement in Louisiana, and in 1912 the Socialist candidate for president got 36 percent of the parish's vote. Long certainly would have heard conversations about the unfair distribution of wealth. However, his father was not a Populist; he led a middle-class life in the community. Long's brothers and sisters resented his later claims of a poor, deprived childhood, which they considered lies to get votes.

From his earliest days, Long was lively and restless. The rule of the day said children should be seen and not heard, but Huey Long ignored this. He gave his opinion whenever he pleased, and he was not reserved with any adults. As a teenager, he went to Baton Rouge to compete in a debate contest. He did not win, but he informed the wife of the superintendent of education that a bunch of professors had cheated him. He also told her that he intended to become the governor and would remember that she had been nice to him.

Huey Long was always described as brilliant, even by his enemies and by the national political leaders who knew him. Although he had

a photographic memory, he was never a good student because he did not concentrate. The year he was supposed to enter the seventh grade he decided to skip that grade. When school started, he just showed up and enrolled himself in eighth grade. He later quit high school before he graduated because of an argument with the school principal. Other students described him as a bossy boy who would not take any role other than the star.

His first jobs were as a traveling salesman, where he learned the art of selling himself to the public. Some of these early sales jobs took him from door to door in the country. His first political strength came from the contacts he made on the road. Later, when he entered politics, he returned to these buyers to ask for their votes.

He met his future wife, Rose, in Shreveport and for a while continued his sales jobs. But his next career move was to enroll in law school at Tulane. Before completing the program, he arranged for a special bar exam just for himself. He said he did not have the time or money to continue classes and was ready to go to work. This incident shows his boldness in going after what he wanted. No one had ever received such special arrangements.

After he passed this test, he returned to Shreveport to practice law. By 1918, he was impatient to start his political career. He had told his wife he planned to be the governor, a U.S. senator, and then the president of the United States. But because of his age (he was only 24), the only statewide office he could hold was on the Railroad Commission (later called the Public Service Commission).

Huey Long intended to use the Commission to gain statewide recognition and power. In his first statewide campaign, Long introduced a new technique — he mailed circulars to the voters. He also borrowed money to buy a car, returning to visit rural residents he had met while a salesman. Winning his election to the Commission, he worked for low utility rates. He also started his lifelong battle with Standard Oil Company, whose pipelines were regulated by the Commission.

By 1923, he was ready to run for governor. Although he did not win, he surprised many politicians with the large number of votes he received. He ran again in 1927. Huey Long prepared for this second race by analyzing his first. He realized that he needed the support of the Acadian Catholic farmers in addition to the Protestant hill farmers. Therefore, he offered his support to Catholic candidates in other races and campaigned on their behalf. In another effort to win South Louisiana votes, he selected a running mate who could campaign in French.

In his first campaign for governor, he had used the new medium of radio to speak to the people of Louisiana. During his second campaign, station KWKH of Shreveport gave Huey free radio time. Another of his campaign techniques was to use trucks with sound systems. He used

This is an early portrait of Huey Long and his wife Rose. Rose completed his U.S. Senate term.

those trucks to travel through rural areas, speaking to voters. He gave over six hundred campaign speeches and mailed out flyers all over the state. Louisiana historian Glenn Jeansonne said Huey Long's campaign promises were different because "the concept of the state government acting like Santa Claus was new to Louisiana, previously it had acted more like Scrooge."

After he was elected governor in 1928, Long worked for such social reforms as improving the roads and providing free school books for children.

HUEY LONG AS GOVERNOR

The strategy worked. In 1928, Huey Long was elected governor. When he won the election, the whirlwind began. The rural people who supported him said, "He hit the ground running and never stopped." Huey Long had big plans for himself and his state.

Positive Steps

Getting the state on the road to progress meant paving the road first —literally. Louisiana was stuck in its muddy roads. Automobiles required better roads, and, by 1930, cars had become common in Louisiana. To get enough money to replace gravel roads with paved roads, however, state law had to be changed. The constitution did not allow the state to borrow money to build roads.

Above: Earl Long, Huey's younger brother, visited state senators one by one to obtain their signed agreement to vote against removal. **Opposite, below:** *The Old Governor's Mansion was built in 1930 during Huey Long's term. It is said that Long wanted to be familiar with the White House when he became president so he had it duplicated in Baton Rouge.* **Opposite, above:** *This is the bedroom of Long's daughter Rose in the Old Governor's Mansion. It can now be seen at the Old State Capitol.*

But Governor Long was able to convince the legislature to change the law and begin the road building. Huey Long's road plan deliberately put a few miles of paved road in each parish so that the people could see how good the road was and demand more. This translated into support for more bond issues and more state spending on roads.

Better roads were just one of Long's campaign promises. By the 1920s, free textbooks were provided to schoolchildren in many other states — but not in Louisiana. Huey Long made free textbooks his crusade. Many of the children in Louisiana attended Catholic schools. In order to get around the issue of using state money for textbooks in church-run schools, Long insisted that the books were for the children individually and not for the schools.

Major opposition to his plan for free textbooks came from Shreveport. The people there believed that giving the books to the church schools was unconstitutional. Also, as Mayor L. E. Thomas said, "This is a rich section of the state. We are not going to be humiliated or disgraced by having it advertised that our children had to be given the books free."

Huey Long's method for handling this opposition is a good example of how he operated. The state owned eighty acres of land that was needed for the new airbase planned for the area. The governor informed Shreveport's leaders that if they were so well off they did not need the textbooks, they did not need the airport either. He would talk about deeding the state land for the airbase to them when they agreed to back his free textbook plan. He later said that he "stomped them into distributing the books."

Other Long programs involved taxes. The poll tax was abolished. The poor supported Huey Long, and he wanted to make sure they could all vote. When the homestead exemption was enacted, property was taxed only on the amount above a certain value. This helped protect a person's home from being seized to cover a tax debt. Huey Long favored a high homestead exemption to protect people from losing their homes during the Great Depression.

Growing Opposition

As Long pushed for his programs, his style offended more and more people. Many people thought his personal crudeness and character were inappropriate for a governor; he seemed to make a point of not being a gentleman. His verbal attacks on critics and opponents were ruthless, and his favorite target was big business. His feud with Standard Oil Company over regulations and taxes became legendary.

Huey Long believed that the profits earned by big business in the state were too high and that big business did not do enough in return. He needed more money to fulfill his promises, and he wanted the business interests to pay for his programs. In 1929, he started an effort to raise the oil severance tax. Standard Oil led the fight against this tax increase.

By this time, Long's opponents had enough backing in the state house of representatives to bring impeachment charges against him. An ugly, bitter political fight followed. The chamber of the house of representatives was a wild scene. One representative walked across the desks to get to the front of the room. He later accused an opponent of throwing a punch and cutting his face. That rival said the man had just run into a fan blade as he ran across the desks.

The house of representatives brought seven charges of impeachment against Governor Long. The impeachment was the ultimate battle of his life. His brother Earl had fought many childhood battles for Huey; once again he stepped in to help. Earl Long visited state senators one by one and obtained their signed agreement to vote against removal from office. This document, called the "Round Robin," was signed by fifteen senators — enough to block the impeachment. Huey Long himself always blamed this incident for his vicious political methods. He said, "I used to get things done by saying 'please.' That didn't work and now I'm a dynamiter. I dynamite 'em out of my path."

"THIS IS HUEY P. LONG SPEAKING"

Huey Long was born into the storytelling tradition. He too became a teller of good stories. This account is written in the language that Long used to appeal to his rural voters.

This is Huey P. Long speaking, ladies an' ge'men. Now before I start my speech, I want each one of you who are listening in to go to the telephone and ring up a half-dozen of your friends. Tell 'em Huey Long is on the air. Tell 'em to tune in, an' stay tuned in. I'll wait till you git through phoning. I'm goin' to tell you things them lyin' newspapers won't tell you. I'm goin' to tell you the God's truth, so help me! This is Huey Long speakin', ladies an' ge'men. Go to your telephone, now, an' call up all your friends. . . .

Well, they're investigatin' me again. They been investigatin' me ever since I was first elected to public office, an' what have they found? Paved roads, free bridges, free textbooks for their own chil-ern — an' it never cost 'em a thin dime! Now, they can't understand that, so they're investigatin' again.

It puts me in mine of a family that I knew once, up in Winn Parish, where I was born an' bred. They were a large family, all boys, an' big strappin' fellers, but — you know — kinda triflin' like. They'd much ruther hunt squir'ls or go fishin' than plant corn or pick cotton. Still an' all, though, they jest had to do some work, or else the grass'd git all the crop, stid o' jist about three-fourths of it.

Now, these boys, they owned a triflin' kind of a little dog — a sort of a fice, or tarrier — somethin' like that. He wasn't worth the powder an' shot it'd

> *"I'm goin' to tell you things them lyin' newspapers won't tell you. I'm goin' to tell you the God's truth, so help me! This is Huey Long speakin', ladies an' ge'men. Go to your telephone, now, an' call up all your friends...."*

take to kill 'im, so they kep' 'im. He thought he was a rabbit-dog, but he wasn't.

Well, one summer, the crop was awfully in the grass. Up in Winn Parish, po' as the land is, it's nothin' short of miraculous how fast the grass an' cuckle-burrs grow, durin' a rainy spell. You got to git up mighty soon in the mornin' to git shet of 'em.

There was a sort of strip o' woods near the cotton patch where the boys was workin', an' this little dog, he was always a-sniffin' an' a-smellin' around, jest investigatin', you know. An' first thing you know, the boys, they'd hear him barkin' up a holler tree, an' they'd say: "Hush! Listen! He's treed a varmint! Come on!"

Then all them eight or ten boys, they'd lay down their hoes, an' they'd hitch the ole clay-bank mule to the rail fence, an' they'd take the ax an' go chop down that tree; but they never found nothin'. The dog was barkin' up the wrong tree — or som'p'n.

But did that discourage that dog? No sir-ee! He'd jest sniff aroun' an' snuff aroun' an' keep on investigatin', till first thing you know, he'd be barkin' up another tree. Seems like he just wouldn't accept defeat! So the boys, they'd lay down their hoes an' stop the plow, an' they'd come an' chop down the tree — an' find nothin'.

An' that kept up all summer. The boys lost their crop, an' they chopped down ever' tree on the place. But . . . They convinced the dog.

Source: Hugh Mercer Blain, ed., *Favorite Huey Long Stories* (Baton Rouge: Otto Claitor, 1937), pp. 11-15.

HUEY LONG AS SENATOR

Long became even more aggressive as he headed toward his political goal. The next step in his planned path to the White House was the U.S. Senate. He ran for the Senate in 1930, after he had been governor for only two years. He won the race, but he refused to take the oath of office or leave the state until he was sure that he still had total control. Lieutenant Governor Paul Cyr had become an enemy because he was too independent. Huey Long did not intend to allow him to take over as governor. Long manipulated the situation so that he could leave Alvin O. King, president of the senate, in charge as the acting governor.

Then he arranged for O. K. Allen to be elected as the new governor. Allen was so widely known as Huey Long's puppet that he was accused of signing anything put in front of him. Earl Long once said that a leaf blew in the window and Allen signed it, because he thought "Huey had sent in another bill." Under Huey Long's control, Allen continued the far-reaching social programs. Charity hospitals provided medical care for the poor. The Louisiana State University (LSU) Medical School was established in New Orleans. The main growth of the campus occurred during this era. New buildings were constructed and funding increased.

Oscar K. Allen was handpicked by Huey Long (standing right, next to Allen) to become the governor in 1932. He continued Long's programs until his death in office in 1936.

The relationship Huey Long had with LSU is complicated. He felt entitled to lead the band, coach the football team, and hire and fire anyone there. This heavy-handed control also led to a censorship incident. In 1934, when the student newspaper at LSU published a story he had tried to **censor** (to remove or suppress), he had the newspaper staff expelled. He commented, "I like students, but this state is putting up the money for that college, and I ain't paying anybody to criticize me."

Long also demonstrated his belief in control of the press by operating his own newspaper, the *Louisiana Progress*, which printed exactly what he wanted it to say. He used cartoons to ridicule his opponents. Their faces were added to buzzards, goats, hogs, and other animals, which were then labeled with insulting nicknames, like "turkey buzzard Walmsley." (T. Semmes Walmsley was the mayor of New Orleans.) The *Louisiana Progress* was even distributed by state workers during their workday.

On the National Stage

In 1932, when Huey Long believed he had total control of the Louisiana government, he finally reported to Washington. There he continued his showy behavior. On his first day in the Senate, he broke the

Huey Long felt entitled to lead the LSU band. Here he is leading the marching band between two drum majors.

rules by smoking a cigar and greeting everyone loudly. He wanted to inform the other senators that the "Kingfish" had arrived. Long had adopted that nickname from the "Amos and Andy" radio show. The Kingfish character was the head of the lodge, the boss of the group.

Long set about acquiring national attention with his economic program. In those depression years, the poor listened eagerly to any voice promising delivery from their misery. Long called his program "Share Our Wealth," and he used as its slogan "Every man a king." The rest of this quotation from William Jennings Bryan was "and no man wears a crown." Huey's critics said he certainly planned for one man to wear the crown — Huey P. Long.

Long's radio broadcasts offered the promise of the American dream. His **Share Our Wealth program** proposed to eliminate poverty by giving every family a minimum income of $5,000 a year, financed by limiting individual incomes to a maximum of $1 million a year. The program would also provide old-age pensions of $30 a month to elderly people who had less than $10,000 in cash.

Long initially supported President Franklin Roosevelt and his New Deal programs. Later he turned against the president and criticized him and his programs in his radio broadcasts.

People living in the nightmare of poverty wanted to believe him. One of his most popular speeches attacked big business. He compared America's wealth to a great barbecue. He accused the richest men in America of taking "85 percent of the grub." The audiences cheered when Long said the greedy could not even use all they had and should share their wealth with everyone.

Long and Roosevelt

This outspoken and radical new senator had arrived in Washington just as the government was battling the depression that began in 1929. Although the two men shared some ideas, the strong personalities of Senator Huey Long and President Franklin D. Roosevelt soon clashed. Long had spent his life making sure no one told him what to do. He did not intend to change this approach just because the other man was the president of the United States.

Huey Long made no secret of his plan to become president, and he even wrote a book called *My First Years in the White House.* Some political analysts say that Long's pressure affected Roosevelt's New Deal programs. (The **New Deal** was the name given to the programs enacted by Congress during President Roosevelt's first two terms to deal with the problems and hardships caused by the Great Depression.) Many historians believe the New Deal programs offered more benefits for the people, including social security and the minimum wage, because so many Americans believed Long's promises of sharing the wealth. Roosevelt once described Huey Long and General Douglas McArthur as the two most dangerous men in America.

HUEY LONG'S LAST DAYS

Despite the excitement of Washington politics and a worthy opponent in President Roosevelt, Huey Long had no intention of allowing Louisiana to function without him. He returned to Baton Rouge frequently, usually directing Governor Allen to call a special session of the legislature. Between August 1934 and September 1935, seven special sessions of the legislature passed 463 bills. These bills gave Long more and more power and added more and more programs to the state government.

In the fall of 1935, Long had several plans to put in effect. He wanted to pass laws giving him control of the New Deal programs in the state. (President Roosevelt had blocked Long's efforts to control this money.) He also wanted the legislature to pass a bill designed to punish a political enemy. The bill would gerrymander Judge Benjamin Pavy's district. (To *gerrymander* means to draw the boundaries of a political district in such a way as to give an advantage to a candidate or political party.) The new judicial district Long envisioned would include mainly Long supporters, a sure way to defeat the judge in the next election.

On a hot September night in 1935, the judge's son-in-law came to the State Capitol. Dr. Carl Weiss was a small, serious-looking man in a white linen suit. Shots blasted in the marble corridor on the first floor. After an encounter that lasted only a few minutes, Dr. Weiss lay dead on the floor, shot more than fifty times. Long's bodyguards had emptied their guns into Weiss's body.

Although he had been shot, Senator Long ran down the corridor, spitting blood and holding his stomach. He was rushed to the then-nearby Lady of the Lake Hospital, where surgery was performed. Huey Long died two days later on September 10.

The shattering events of that night in Baton Rouge still puzzle the world. Questions still have no clear answers. What provoked the incident? Did Dr. Weiss fire the actual shots that hit Huey Long? Was Long hit by bullets from more than one gun? Was the medical care Huey Long received correct?

For more than fifty years, theories and stories about the assassination have circulated. As recently as 1996, a researcher received permission from the Weiss family to exhume (dig up) Carl Weiss's body for study. The researcher, however, was unable to make any new conclusions. The state police also reopened the investigation because some of

Dr. Carl Weiss, the son-in-law of Judge Benjamin Pavy, shot Huey Long on September 8, 1935. Questions about the assassination, however, lingered for years.

More than 175,000 people attended Huey Long's funeral at the State Capitol. Long was buried on the grounds of the State Capitol building.

the evidence, including the gun that Weiss supposedly used, was recovered. The new official investigation concluded that the 1935 investigation was correct. Dr. Carl Weiss fired the bullet that killed Huey Long.

After Huey Long left the scene, his legacy of roads, bridges, hospitals, and free textbooks remained. Two buildings in the capital city tell his story as clearly as anything else he left — the governor's mansion and the Capitol building.

When Huey Long became governor, he did not like the drafty, old governor's mansion. His critics say that he destroyed an antebellum mansion that should have been preserved. He had a crew of inmates from Angola State Prison tear down the old house and build another one on the same site. This property is now maintained by the Foundation for Historical Louisiana.

A LEGACY OF SCANDALS

Huey Long's death left his supporters without a leader. During Long's political career, he had made sure no one became strong enough to challenge his power. After his death, many arguments flared. Finally, Long's supporters agreed on Richard Leche as the candidate for governor. Elected in 1936, he continued most of Long's programs.

Leche did differ from Long in his attitude toward business. Governor Leche created a state Department of Commerce and Industry and showed his support of business by agreeing to a one cent sales tax. Business leaders wanted sales taxes instead of more business taxes; Long had opposed sales taxes because he thought they were not fair to the poor.

Governor Leche did continue Long's programs to help the poor. As he spent more and more money, however, rumors of theft and corruption circulated throughout the state. Newspapers started investigating those reports.

By 1939, Governor Leche had resigned, saying he had health problems. But the federal government soon convicted him of mail fraud. He was sentenced to ten years in the federal penitentiary. He was also accused of making money from oil that was sold without paying the severance tax, but he was not convicted of this. At one point, Leche was reported to have said, "When I took the oath of office, I didn't take any vow of poverty."

Some of the worst scandals involved Louisiana State University. The president, who had been appointed by Huey Long, fled the state with funds belonging to the university. The person in charge of the building programs was also caught in illegal activities. He was accused of taking kickbacks (illegal bribes) for contracts. With the money and stolen building materials, he had built himself a mansion filled with black marble and gold bathroom fixtures.

In addition, illegal slot machines were all over South Louisiana, and many suspected the presence of the Mafia in Louisiana.

Governor Richard Leche is seen leaving the Governor's Mansion with his wife and son following his resignation from office amid rumors of corruption. He was succeeded by Lieutenant Governor Earl Long.

Do You Remember?

1. What was "the deduct"?
2. What was Huey Long's first elected office?
3. What office did Huey Long hold when he was killed?

THE "NEW" STATE CAPITOL

The most famous landmark of Baton Rouge rises near the Mississippi River as a monument to Huey Long. The "new" State Capitol, as many still call it, is just a few blocks upriver from the "old" State Capitol, where the impeachment proceedings against Huey Long took place.

Long had first mentioned the need for a new Capitol building in a 1927 campaign speech. The architects followed Long's suggestion for a tower and designed a "tower type of building with a broad and dignified base."

After great debate over such a huge expense, the legislature finally approved the construction of the Capitol in 1930. A constitutional amendment was required and passed on November 4, 1930. Construction began in the same month and was completed in just over a year.

The 34-story, 450-foot Capitol was dedicated at the inauguration of Governor O. K. Allen on May 16, 1932. Senator Huey Long was in Washington at the time and could not attend the festive ceremony. But today he is buried in the gardens, with his statue facing the building. On September 12, 1935, more than 175,000 people came to see him buried on the grounds of the Capitol he had built.

The building's designers intended to show the state's history, progress, and the "aspirations of the people." They wanted "to express in stone and granite, bronze and marble, and in other enduring materials, the colorful history of this once unbounded dominion, then struggling colony, and now progressive and powerful state."

The art on the base of the building represents the state's resources as well as the struggles and achievements of the people. The designs on the tower symbolize spiritual ideals. The *frieze*, or narrow band of carvings, on the base depicts many scenes from Louisiana history — from the earliest French explorations to the time of the Capitol's con-

Above: "The Pioneers" statue stands to the left of the Capitol entrance. **Opposite, above:** *The Louisiana State Capitol is the tallest capitol building in the United States.* **Opposite, below:** *The steps up to the entrance bear the names of all fifty states.*

struction. Portrait panels of twenty-two important individuals are above the windows. The two large statues at the entrance are called "Pioneers" and "Patriots." The Pioneers statue honors the settlers, and the Patriots statue represents the state's defenders. On the Capitol's tower, huge corner figures represent law, science, philosophy, and art.

Forty-nine steps approach the entrance. The steps welcome visitors from every state and emphasize the interdependence of the United States. Each step is carved with the name of a state, and the states are listed in the order in which they were admitted to the Union. Originally, the top step had only the motto *E Pluribus Unum*. Alaska and Hawaii were added to this step after 1959.

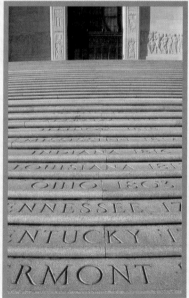

The beautiful gardens surrounding the Capitol were planned with future visitors in mind. More than one hundred boxcar-loads of plants and trees were planted after the building was complete. Larger trees were brought from Avery Island, and camellias were transplanted from plantation gardens.

The central feature of the gardens is the Huey Long monument, which was erected in 1940. The bronze statue portrays Huey Long addressing his supporters. The base of the statue has sculptured representations of his contributions to Louisiana.

THE 1927 FLOOD

Huey Long dominated Louisiana in the 1920s and 1930s. But there were other important events that affected the state during that period.

New Year's Day 1927 was not a day for celebration. Heavy rains and melting winter snow had filled the Mississippi River with rushing water. On January 1, the river reached flood stage in Cairo, Illinois, and the raging water soon announced its possession of the great river valley. Attempts to control the water were broken by the river's force.

The breaks in the levees, called *crevasses*, sent water roaring out over the land. The water that surged across the land also carried roofs of

houses, dead cows, snake-filled tree branches, and almost anything else that had blocked its path. Before the flood ended, more than 70 crevasses had sent flood waters over 16 million acres of land. More than 200 people were killed, and more than 700,000 were left homeless in the Mississippi River Valley.

Armed guards patrolled the levee at places like St. Joseph in Tensas Parish. Some property owners tried to dynamite the levee below their property to save their own land from flooding. The flood waters would rush through any break in the levee, relieving the pressure on the land upriver. After the levee broke at Cabin Teele (about ten miles east of Tallulah in northeast Louisiana), more than 6 million acres were flooded.

The Great 1927 Flood was the worst in the state's history. This locomotive is trying to get through the flood waters at Bayou Sara.

A boat could travel from Vicksburg to Monroe, which lay more than 75 miles from the river.

The flood spread in Louisiana. Pointe Coupee Parish received flood waters from both the Mississippi and the Atchafalaya rivers. Other crevasses in the levees along Bayou des Glaises and the Atchafalaya River brought the flood to the Acadiana region.

U.S. Secretary of War Dwight F. Davis (right) and Secretary of Commerce and future president Herbert Hoover (left) visited one of the tent camps in the devastated Mississippi Valley.

RELIEF EFFORTS

The flood forced more than 275,000 people from their homes in Louisiana. People crowded the levees and the few spots of high ground. They brought along their animals and a few of their most important possessions.

The Red Cross set up refugee camps for the people who were forced from their homes. The Red Cross funded the camps; local citizens provided volunteer labor and supervision. Volunteers came from other states to help. Some of the camps served up to 10,000 people. The refugees were fed, housed in tent cities, and given basic medical care. The camps were located in Iberia and Caldwell parishes, among other places. Boatloads of people and cattle were brought to Baton Rouge and moved to camps in the area.

To keep up the spirits of the people, the Tallulah Orchestra, a group of black musicians, played at the levee. At the Lafayette camp, Cajun fiddlers tempted the refugees to dance for a while.

President Calvin Coolidge did not visit the flooded Mississippi Valley, but he did send Secretary of Commerce Herbert Hoover. Hoover described the flood as "the greatest peacetime disaster in our history." A *National Geographic* writer described his trip on a relief boat as it floated past the treetops in the floodwaters.

FLOOD WATERS NEAR NEW ORLEANS

The city of New Orleans waited nervously as the water headed down the river. Lying below sea level behind levees, the residents feared a tragedy. The city had built even more houses and businesses in the swampy land after the new century began. In 1913, a pump was designed that removed water from the low-lying areas of New Orleans. When the swamp land was drained, the city expanded. A system of pumps and

These refugees at Greaudecore Landing waited anxiously for news of friends and relatives.

canals kept the city dry. If the pumps failed or if water came in faster than the pumps could remove it, the city would become a disaster area. No one was sure what this flood might do to the city built on the swamp.

City government and business leaders in New Orleans decided that the city could be protected from the flood if the water was diverted. The parishes down river would have to take the flood to save the city. Federal officials were persuaded to allow the levee to be dynamited below New Orleans so that the water level would drop. Plaquemines and St. Bernard parishes were flooded, but New Orleans was saved.

THE EFFECTS OF THE FLOOD

The flood of 1927 left that region of Louisiana in ruins; much more of the state was severely damaged. The federal government took action to protect the country from another such disastrous flood. On May 9, 1928, President Coolidge signed legislation that called for spending some $325 million over a period of ten years for flood prevention. The money was to be used to build stronger levees and a flood control structure above New Orleans, which would drain flood waters into Lake Pontchartrain.

THE GREAT DEPRESSION

The flood of 1927 was followed by an even greater disaster—the **Great Depression**. An economic shift shook the world. The United States saw its economy shift from the boom of the Roaring Twenties to a depression that lasted ten years. The stock market crash of October 24, 1929, signaled the change.

During the Great Depression, unemployment reached the highest level the United States had ever measured. By 1937, a government study described the South as the nation's number one economic problem.

*Above: As Franklin Roosevelt campaigned in 1932, he spread a feeling of optimism that times would get better. **Opposite:** Farmers and agricultural workers were already suffering in 1929. The Great Depression made their lives much more difficult. These children playing jacks near Ponchatoula worked as strawberry pickers.*

THE DEPRESSION IN LOUISIANA

Louisiana had only just begun to see economic recovery and growth after the poverty that followed the Civil War. The Great Depression halted all economic growth and brought even more poverty. Much of Louisiana's economy still depended on cotton. But during the Depression, farmers could not make a living selling their cotton crops. The price of cotton, 25 cents a pound in 1929, fell to 5 cents a pound in 1932.

Most residents of rural Louisiana were fairly self-sufficient, a fact that proved useful during the hardships of the Depression. Farmers could at least feed their families by planting gardens instead of money crops. Those who lived in towns and cities had a much harder time. Planting a garden was just not possible for those living on a small lot in town or in a city apartment. Some rural families took in their city relatives to keep them from starving. One resident of Assumption Parish recalled her Depression years: "We did not know where our next meal was coming from and then someone would share from their gardens."

When Franklin D. Roosevelt was elected president in 1932, he took strong steps to help the economy. On March 9, 1933, he ordered a bank holiday. Banks were closed and were not allowed to reopen until they could prove they were sound (financially safe). Until they were approved to reopen, they could only pay out 5 percent of their total deposits in emergency funds. National banks had to be approved to reopen by the United States Comptroller of the Currency. Banks in Louisiana that were chartered by the state had to get approval from the state committee on banking to reopen.

THE NEW DEAL IN LOUISIANA

During the Depression, President Roosevelt urged Congress to pass a series of laws to bring about economic recovery and relieve the suffering of the unemployed. One of the first of these New Deal programs was direct aid for the needy. Federal funds came to the state from the Federal Emergency Relief Administration. For the first time, Louisiana had a statewide program to help the poor — the Unemployment Relief Committee. Before the widespread suffering of the Great Depression brought federal help for the poor, the state had depended on local governments to care for the needy in their areas. The Poor Laws of 1880 and 1916 directed police juries to provide for the poor. Some parishes even maintained a poor house. Now too many people needed help for the local governments to handle.

The federal government also helped by giving groceries to those in need. This was called the *commodity program*. The groceries (commodities) often included coffee, butter, shortening, beans, corn meal, flour, sugar, and rice. Farmers also benefited when their crops were bought to be used as commodities.

These three WPA workers are indexing and filing materials at the Louisiana State Museum in 1940.

Another New Deal program was the **Civilian Conservation Corps** (CCC). This program provided work for single young men between the ages of 18 and 25. They lived in special camps and did physical outdoor labor. In Louisiana, CCC workers did soil conservation work on farms and some road construction.

The CCC camps were located throughout the state. A photograph of the CCC camp in Pleasant Hill in De Soto Parish shows that the young men wore uniforms and lived in barracks. The buildings in the camp included a cafeteria and a library. The camp near Jonesboro was known as CCC Co. 4413, or Camp Colvin, named for the man who donated the land.

Another job program provided work for men with families. This was the **Works Progress Administration**, the WPA. The men, who were paid about $7 a week, built schools, courthouses, parks, and other public buildings.

The new airbase outside Shreveport, Barksdale Field, was also improved by a government work program. The base had been established in 1933 when 20,886 Bossier Parish acres were purchased for $1.5 million. The base is named for a World War I veteran, Lieutenant Eugene Hoy Barksdale. During the 1930s, the WPA paid cotton planters and farmers to grade, plow, harrow, and plant Bermuda grass on 1,400 acres of the base's land to make it flat and green.

Louisiana has other evidence of the variety of work done through the New Deal. The government hired artists to paint murals (large wall paintings) in post offices and federal buildings. When the St.

The Civilian Conservation Corps put thousands of unemployed young men to work on conservation projects.

First Lady Eleanor Roosevelt (center) traveled extensively, serving as her husband's "eyes and ears." This photograph of Mrs. Roosevelt was taken during her 1937 visit to Shreveport. Governor Leche is on the right.

post office, a converted antebellum mansion, was remodeled in 1939, a painting of Evangeline was added above the mantel. The picture shows the Acadian girl quietly sitting on the banks of Bayou Teche. Murals were also painted in the post offices of Eunice and Abbeville. The wall painting in Abbeville is called "The Harvest" and shows a family gathering cotton, sugar cane, and muskrat hides.

Life in the rural South was greatly affected by the Roosevelt plan that brought electricity to farms and other rural areas. The Rural Electrification Administration (REA) paid the cost of extending power lines, which the early electric companies said were too expensive to build and maintain. In addition, the Agricultural Adjustment Administration (AAA) paid farmers not to grow crops. With smaller harvests, crop prices would rise.

The poverty of the Depression years increased Louisiana's health problems. Hunger brought more disease. Reports of malnourished children filled the country, and medical personnel were worried about diseases such as pellagra, which could be prevented with proper diet. Public health nurses worked to establish nutrition programs.

In 1937, Congress passed the National School Lunch Act. One of the new senators who supported this bill was Allen Ellender. Ellender had been an ally of Huey Long in the Louisiana legislature. He served in the U.S. Senate from 1937 until 1972, when he died during his re-election campaign.

The morale of the people of Louisiana was boosted by a visit from First Lady Eleanor Roosevelt. When Mrs. Roosevelt came to Shreveport in March 1937, thousands of people stood on the street to watch her pass. She gave two speeches: "A Typical Day at the White House" and "An Individual's Responsibility to His Community."

Do You Remember?
1. Why did armed guards patrol the levees during the 1927 flood?
2. What was the commodity program?
3. Name three New Deal programs that operated in Louisiana.

SUMMARY

The period after World War I was a time of change. The progressive movement continued to bring about reform, notably prohibition and woman's suffrage.

Change and economic unrest helped elect Huey Long governor of Louisiana in 1928. His campaign promises appealed to those looking for a change. His slogans of "Share Our Wealth" and "Every man a king" made him popular with Louisiana citizens suffering through the depression years. While he was governor and U.S. senator, Long had total control of the state. He aspired to the presidency, but in September 1935 he was assassinated by the son-in-law of a political enemy.

The Great Depression affected Louisiana much as it did the rest of the nation. People struggled to provide their basic needs. Finding work and food became a primary focus. These difficult years created a self-sufficient generation. New Deal programs helped provide some relief.

This rare 1940 color photograph by Marion Post Wolcott shows Cajun children fishing in a bayou near Terrebonne, a Farm Security Administration project.

CHAPTER · REVIEW

1921	1927	1928	1935
New Louisiana constitution written	Major flood on Mississippi	Huey Long elected governor	Huey Long assassinated

1918
Huey Long elected to Railroad Commission

1922
First radio program in state broadcast

1930
Huey Long elected to the U.S. Senate

1915   1920   1925   1930   1935

1927
Charles Lindberg flew solo across the Atlantic

1933
Prohibition repealed

1936
Gone With the Wind released

1928
Penicillin discovered

1932
Amelia Earhart was first woman to fly solo across the Atlantic

1920
Prohibition went into effect
Nineteenth Amendment ratified

1929
Stock market crash
Great Depression began

1931
"Star Spangled Banner" became national anthem

Reviewing People, Places, and Terms

Define, identify, or explain the importance of each of the following.

1. censor
2. Civilian Conservation Corps
3. Great Depression
4. Ku Klux Klan
5. Huey Long
6. New Deal
7. prohibition
8. Public Service Commission
9. ratify
10. severance tax
11. Share Our Wealth program
12. Dr. Carl Weiss
13. Women's Christian Temperance Union
14. Works Progress Administration

Understanding the Facts

1. What new music spread from New Orleans during the Roaring Twenties?
2. What was the goal of the early women's clubs?
3. How did people ignore the prohibition law?
4. What items are subject to a severance tax?
5. How did Louisiana lawmakers try to stop the Ku Klux Klan?
6. Why is it said that the constitution in 1921 is the most "legislative" of all the constitutions?
7. Over what issue did Huey Long and the city of Shreveport disagree?
8. How did the Great Depression contribute to the popularity of Huey Long?
9. What positive changes did Huey Long bring to Louisiana?
10. How was New Orleans saved from the 1927 flood?
11. What New Deal programs helped Louisiana during the Depression years?

Developing Critical Thinking

1. Why do you suppose some women opposed the Nineteenth Amendment?
2. How did Huey Long's early job as a traveling salesman help him in his political career?
3. How was Huey Long a political threat to Franklin D. Roosevelt?

1. In 1927, the Mississippi River flooded as far west as Baldwin, Bastrop, Grayson, Harrisonburg, Marksville, Lafayette, Monroe, New Iberia, and Washington. Locate and mark these towns on a map of Louisiana. Choose three of the towns and determine their distance from the Mississippi River.

2. Many people responded with help after the disastrous flood of 1927. Today, many government and volunteer agencies help in case of disaster. Make a list of the relief agencies that exist in your community.

Special Projects

1. Interview someone who can remember a New Deal program in Louisiana. Ask the person to tell you about the program. What did it do and who participated?

2. The WPA employed artists to draw murals in government buildings depicting local life. If this program were to be revived, what would you put in a mural today showing life in your local community?

Making Connections

1. Huey Long used the old country expression "Barking up the wrong tree" to develop his story. What point was he trying to make?

2. People often tell stories to help them make a point. What stories have you heard someone tell to teach a lesson or give the person's point of view?

3. Identify a current political conflict in which this story might apply.

Louisiana Lagniappe

• The Washington, D.C., firm that had constructed the Lincoln Memorial and the National Cathedral won the contract to build the State Capitol.

• Trappers in Louisiana supplied pelts for the fur coats worn by the flappers.

• The Orpheum, built in 1921, was the first movie palace in New Orleans.

• BUILDING SKILLS: RESEARCHING TOPICS •

Researching topics is just one part of a historian's work. Historians are much like detectives looking for clues and possible solutions to questions or mysteries. The historian knows that a library is often a researcher's best friend.

As a student, you often have assignments that require you to find information in a library. When you visit a library for research, there are specific places to look for information. Your key aids in the library are the card catalogue (either paper or electronic) and the *Reader's Guide to Periodic Literature*.

Visit your school library or media center and find information on the following subjects:

• The Bonus Army
• The Public Works Administration
• The National Industrial Recovery Administration

These three topics have to do with the Great Depression and the New Deal. For each of these topics, find one reference in each of the following sources: encyclopedia, periodical, biographic or historical dictionary, and general history book.

Once you locate your sources, list the name of the book or periodical, making sure to include all the information you need for a bibliography: the title of each book or article, the author, publisher, and the date of publication. This list will help you find the information again if necessary. After completing this task, think about these questions:

• Are there sources in your library that emphasize Louisiana history or give information on the state? Does your library have a "Louisiana Collection"?

• In which of the categories above was it most difficult to locate the information you needed? Why do you think it was difficult?

CHAPTER FOURTEEN

LOUISIANA'S WORLD WAR II ERA: PATRIOTISM AND PROSPERITY

The birds were singing as I listened carefully for signs of Japanese or other human life. I know the sounds of the swamps in Louisiana well, and it's no different anywhere else. If the birds are singing, all is well.
— Recollections of Marine Captain Jefferson J. Deblanc of Lockport hiding on the Japanese-held island of Kolobangara in World War II

WORLD WAR II ENDED the Great Depression in the United States because of the demand for war materials and supplies. This economic change also brought Louisiana out of the struggle of the Depression years. People left the farms to join the armed forces and to seek new jobs in the cities.

Louisiana citizens served their country well during World War II. By the war's end, almost 275,000 Louisianians had served in the military. Others worked in the factories that made the war supplies.

You can visit the U.S.S. Kidd, a World War II destroyer, in Baton Rouge.

In the 1930s, Germany under Adolf Hitler tried to take over Europe. At the same time, the Japanese were expanding in Asia. When Hitler attacked Poland in 1939, World War II broke out in Europe.

Although President Roosevelt had proclaimed America's neutrality in 1939, he watched with alarm as Japan, Italy, and Germany carved up the world. The president looked for ways to help Great Britain, France, and their allies. The Allies' need for materials and supplies brought the United States out of the Great Depression.

PREPARING FOR WAR

As the situation in Europe grew more threatening, the United States passed the first peace-time draft law on September 16, 1940. The military began to prepare American troops for possible fighting in Europe. Two major military training exercises or "mock wars" were held in Louisiana. The state offered the right climate and rural areas with few people to disturb. The people of Louisiana followed these maneuvers with great interest.

The first maneuvers started in August 1941. The United States's Third Army was divided into two groups — the Red Army and the Blue Army.

The Red Army was headquartered at Mansfield in DeSoto Parish; Vernon Parish served as the headquarters for the Blue Army. The two armies carried out their mock battles over 30,000 square miles of Louisiana land.

After the Blue Army won, another mock war took place. This time, the Blue Army group faced the Second Army. Headquarters for the two armies were Winnfield in Winn Parish and Alexandria in Rapides Parish.

These training exercises brought thousands of soldiers to Louisiana. The men and their equipment filled the rural areas of northern and central Louisiana. Part of the Army came with cavalry horses; others had the new two-man Jeeps. After the Louisiana war games, the Army determined that horses would no longer be used in battle. The new equipment was more efficient.

The experience the men gained during these exercises was credited with saving thousands of American lives during the real fighting. General Dwight Eisenhower and General George Patton, two of America's most famous World War II commanders, directed the operation.

By the end of the war, Louisiana was the site of five military training camps and ten flying fields. Barksdale Field, which had been established in Bossier Parish in the 1930s, became an important training center. It continued its military importance after World War II and now serves as the headquarters for the United States 8th Air Force. Other flying fields became local airports after the war ended.

Opposite: This photograph shows Adolf Hitler in a triumphant motorcade following the fall of Paris. Above: This tank alongside a column of cavalry during the Louisiana war games was a sign that horses in battle would soon be obsolete.

PEARL HARBOR

In 1941, Japan decided to invade the Dutch East Indies (now Indonesia) and seize that country's oil, which Japan badly needed. The only force that could stop the Japanese was the U.S. Navy stationed at Hawaii. The Japanese made a surprise attack on the fleet at Pearl Harbor on December 7, 1941, causing great damage. On December 8, the United States declared war on Japan and entered World War II. A few days later, Germany and Italy declared war on the United States.

The people of Louisiana heard the news of Pearl Harbor on their radios on Sunday afternoon. Some of them were in their cars, others were in restaurants eating lunch. A Bienville Parish woman recalled, "I was standing at my kitchen sink washing dishes when the news came over the radio." People who had just left church returned to pray for their country.

LOUISIANA IN WORLD WAR II

Once the United States entered the war, the country prepared for possible attack. In the week following the bombing, special security measures were taken at Barksdale Field. In the Caddo-Bossier area, bridges, city water supplies, and the nearby defense plants were put under extra guard to protect them from **sabotage** (deliberate damage or destruction).

Efforts to protect the country included the civil defense organization. Older men who could not go to war watched for enemy planes and enforced the rules for **blackouts**. During blackouts, cities had to be completely dark at night so that enemy planes could not locate them if there were an air raid. New Orleans, Shreveport, and other Louisiana cities held practice air raid blackouts regularly. Loud air raid sirens announced the blackouts.

Above: *On December 7, 1941, Japanese warplanes attacked the U.S. naval base at Pearl Harbor on the Hawaii island of Oahu.* **Left:** *Louisiana citizens served in all branches of the U.S. armed forces during World War II.*

During the war, Louisiana citizens served their country well. Louisiana's first hero of the war was a famous pilot who led his "Flying Tigers" in air battles against the Japanese. General Claire Lee Chennault from Waterproof in Tensas Parish named his flying team after the Louisiana State University athletic team. The P-40 and P-51 airplanes were painted with the frightening eyes and teeth of a shark.

By the war's end, some 274,000 people from Louisiana had served in the military. The list of casualties has over 4,000 names. National cemeteries in Louisiana are the burial sites for some of those who died during the war.

THE HOME FRONT

The location of New Orleans and the available labor supply made the city a vital shipbuilding center during World War II. One New Orleans shipbuilder, Andrew Jackson Higgins, developed the largest shipbuilding plant in the world. The United States Navy sent his ships across the English Channel and to the beaches of Africa and the Mediterranean Sea.

Several defense plants were built in Louisiana. A large shell-loading plant was built in Webster Parish. One interesting wartime industry was the dehydration plants set up to provide food for the soldiers. (The dehydration process removes the moisture from food.) An egg dehydration plant was located in Ruston.

Many Louisianans worked in the factories that made war supplies. World War II brought even more women into the work force than World War I had done. Women filled jobs formerly held by men who had gone off to war. Businesses throughout Louisiana trained women for these jobs. For example, Andress Motor Company in Shreveport trained women as automobile mechanics.

This World War II magazine advertisement shows the Higgins troop landing boat.

"We took the Beaches with Higgins Boats"

"Without the boats that Higgins is manufacturing the Combined Operations Command could not exist."
—LORD MOUNTBATTEN

PT-254

AFRICA! SOLOMONS! CHANNEL! NEW GUINEA! ATTU! SICILY! SALERNO!

"These Higgins boats are so tough they land directly on rocky beaches, unload troops, tanks and equipment dry-shod, retracting themselves by their own power. They're plenty fast in assault, can turn on a dime to zig-zag away from trouble, and I never saw one capsize."

HIGGINS BOATS designed and built for the United Nations were described thus by veterans of Guadalcanal and Africa, who also said, in official records, that these boats were the "Best in the World." This praise comes from men who manned them under fire—from men whose lives often depended upon these boats' unusual maneuverability, stamina and trouble-free operation.

Today Higgins plants are engaged the clock around in manufacturing boats, planes and other products to meet the swiftly changing needs of nations at war. It is this ability to change—to pioneer—to anticipate tomorrow's needs—that makes "Higgins" a name to watch.

Higgins INDUSTRIES INCORPORATED

NEW ORLEANS HUB OF THE AMERICAS

BOATS • ENGINES • AIRPLANES • WOOD ALLOYS

BUY MORE WAR BONDS To Help Pay For The Ever-decreasing Cost That Mass Production Makes Possible

Because of the country's war needs, it became necessary to **ration** (limit the consumption of) civilian goods. Rationing boards were established in each state. One of the first items rationed was tires. As a result, bicycles were soon in short supply. Sugar, coffee, canned fruits and vegetables, butter, and meat were later added to the ration list. As they did during World War I, the citizens of Louisiana observed "meatless" days.

Shoe rationing began with three pairs per person per year, then dropped to only one pair before the war ended. Families used shoe rations for their children; as a result, many adults could not replace worn shoes even if they had the money. One young Bossier Parish bride was given shoe coupons by her friends so she could have new shoes for her wedding.

Most families also repeated the World War I practice of planting a garden for their use. The gardens were called **victory gardens**. Across the country, such gardens supplied over 40 percent of America's fresh vegetables

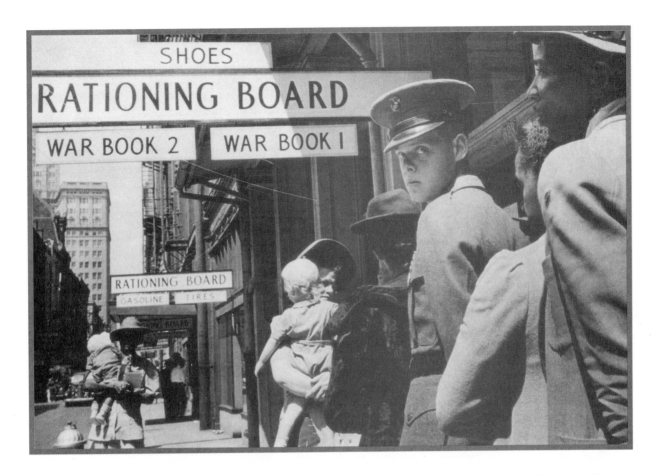

during the war. The military also planted victory gardens. The largest covered 250 acres at Barksdale Field and supplied the mess halls there.

Children in Louisiana also joined in the war effort. Boy Scouts delivered blackout booklets. High school boys made balsa wood airplane models, which were used in civil defense training. Schools collected scrap metal, rubber, and scrap paper. The scrap drives became competitive, and school yards were piled high with scrap metal. In New Orleans, Jesuit High beat Warren Easton High by collecting more scrap metal.

People showed their patriotism and support for American troops in many ways. A star on a lapel pin or on a banner hung in a window indicated a son or husband away in the service. Patriotic signs were everywhere. A huge seven-story flag hung on Canal Street in New Orleans.

Communities in Louisiana provided a place for entertainment and relaxation for the soldiers stationed nearby. These **United Service Organizations**, or USOs as they were called, were intended to provide a "home away from home" for those serving in the military. Veterans of World War II have fond memories of dancing with the young ladies of the area. The music known as the "Big Band sound" was the favorite dance music. The first USO building in the nation was built in DeRidder in Beauregard Parish. This USO was built to serve the soldiers from

Because of the shortage of consumer goods, rationing often resulted in long lines.

This USO Club in New Orleans, like many others, provided a place for military personnel to rest and relax.

nearby Camp Polk (now Fort Polk) and was completed just twenty-four hours before the USO in Galveston, Texas.

A number of POW (prisoner of war) camps were located in wartime Louisiana. Lincoln, Rapides, and West Baton Rouge parishes were just three of the sites for the camps. The German prisoners held in West Baton Rouge Parish were used as laborers during the sugar cane harvest.

THE END OF THE WAR

In 1945, Louisiana celebrated the news of the war's end. Strangers hugged on Canal Street in New Orleans and on Third Street in Baton Rouge. Workers dropped confetti from the windows of businesses in the downtown districts. The churches filled with people saying prayers of thanks. The *Shreveport Times* reported, "The people of Shreveport celebrated V-E Day with tears and laughter, in prayer and gratitude, in silence and sorrow."

The returning soldiers needed jobs and housing. In 1944, Congress passed the Servicemen's Readjustment Act, popularly referred to as the "G.I. Bill," to help returning veterans. The legislation provided unemployment and education allowances and home, farm, and business loans for millions of World War II veterans. Soldiers received unemployment pay of $20 a week for 52 weeks, setting up what many called the "52-20 Club." Many of Louisiana's former soldiers headed to school.

The end of the war brought back some of the celebrations that had stopped during the war. Mardi Gras was not celebrated in New Orleans from 1941 to 1945. Now everyone wanted to make up for the lost years of fun.

Do You Remember?
1. Where is the 8th Air Force of the United States headquartered?
2. What was the purpose of the civil defense organization?
3. How did children help the war effort?

Left: This seven-story American flag on Canal Street was one way New Orleans residents showed their patriotism. *Above:* General Claire Lee Chennault of Waterproof, Louisiana, led the famed "Flying Tigers" during World War II.

Huey Long's death in 1935 did not end his influence on Louisiana. State politics continued to be divided into pro-Long and anti-Long factions. The anti-Long faction included those who opposed Long's ideas of government programs and those who believed Huey Long and his followers were guilty of abuse of power and corruption. Some politicians joined the anti-Long faction because they wanted to be on the winning side.

Governor Sam Houston Jones, who took office in 1940, established the civil service system for state workers.

Those politicians sometimes switched to the pro-Long side when it looked like that side would win.

The struggles between the pro-Long and anti-Long factions continued throughout the 1940s. The anti-Long faction won the 1940 election when Sam Jones beat Earl Long in the governor's race. Jimmie Davis, another anti-Long candidate, was elected in 1944 to continue the reforms. The pro-Longs did not win back the governor's office until 1948.

SAM JONES

Sam Jones had served as an assistant district attorney in Calcasieu Parish. A veteran of World War I, he was an active member of the Louisiana American Legion. This organization for war veterans supported his campaign for governor. The voters liked Jones because he was not part of the "political crowd" in state government.

Jones's main campaign promise was to bring honesty to state government. After his election, he stopped Huey Long's "deduct" system. State workers were no longer expected to make political contributions. Jones also took steps to end voter fraud by making voter registration lists available to the public. This was done to keep the names of dead people off the voting lists.

Governor Jones's goal was an efficient state government. He reorganized state departments in a more businesslike way. Companies who wished to work on state projects had to submit competitive bids. A *bid* is an offer to pay a certain price, in this case an offer to complete the state project at a certain price. The lowest bidder is usually awarded the job.

Governor Jones provided job protection for state workers by establishing a **civil service system**. Before civil service, state workers lost their jobs every time a new governor was elected. That system, known as *patronage* or the *spoils system*, rewarded people with government jobs for helping a candidate win. Under the civil service system, workers take tests for government jobs and cannot be fired for their political views or party affiliations. Jones, however, made sure that Long supporters did not get the protected jobs. He delayed the start of the civil service system until the Long people were fired and the Jones people hired.

Jones was a reformer, but he did not try to restrict the social programs Huey Long had established. In fact, he increased the amount of old-age pensions and added more children to the free school-lunch program. Education received more funds, and capital improvements continued, which meant more roads, bridges, and hospitals for the state.

All this was possible because state revenue had increased with the economic prosperity brought on by World War II. The war helped the United States recover from the Great Depression, and Louisiana recovered along with the rest of the country. When Sam Jones's term ended, he left the state a budget surplus.

JIMMIE DAVIS

In 1944, the people of Louisiana elected James H. "Jimmie" Davis as governor. Davis had first been elected as a city official in Shreveport and then served on the Public Service Commission. Because this board helped consumers, most members of the board became very popular throughout the state.

The story of Jimmie Davis began in the hills of North Louisiana, in Jackson Parish. He was the son of a sharecropper, one of eleven children. He described his childhood as one of poverty and hard work in a loving country family. He put himself through college, becoming a history teacher and earning a master's degree. One of the ways he earned money for his education was to sing on the street corners in Alexandria. His voice and his guitar playing later provided him with a career in country music and the movies.

Davis had already made money as an entertainer when he ran for governor. Some people said that was a good reason to elect him; he didn't need to steal from the state! Davis's campaign slogan was "peace and

Governor Jimmie Davis was a well-known country music singer. Here he is seen performing at a governors' conference dinner in Miami in 1946.

The four-poster bed of Governor Jimmie Davis is on display at the Old State Capitol. The quilt hanging over the end of the bed was made by Davis's mother from his old ties.

harmony," and his campaign style reflected that. He campaigned by speaking only briefly and then singing with his band. The campaign crowds liked the free entertainment.

As governor, Davis served Louisiana during World War II. Public attention was focused on the war and on the federal government in Washington, D.C. During the war years, the state government was not expected to do much. Even so, Davis was sometimes accused of being out of the state too much, taking care of his show business career.

The economy of the war years brought more money to the state. The charity hospital system added a new hospital in Shreveport. State workers were, for the first time, protected with a retirement system. Because he was a former teacher, Davis directed state money towards improving education. Many new buildings were constructed at the state colleges and universities.

Davis had promised the voters a balanced budget, and, with the economic war boom, he had no trouble keeping that promise. The budget surplus he inherited when he became governor was even larger when he left. In 1948, the state surplus had grown to $48 million. Jimmie Davis also left the state without scandal. Many people considered this a relief after the bad national publicity Louisiana had received in the 1930s.

Davis continued his musical career after he left the governor's office. He sang and starred in a Hollywood movie made about his term as governor. In 1972, he was made a member of the Country Music Hall of Fame. The song that he wrote, "You Are My Sunshine," is one of the most recorded songs in history; it has even been recorded in Japanese. It is also one of Louisiana's two state songs.

Do You Remember?

1. What was Governor Sam Jones's main campaign promise?
2. Which Louisiana governor is a member of the Country Music Hall of Fame?
3. What song written by Jimmie Davis is the state song?

POST-WAR POLITICS

One member of the Long family had not given up his political ambitions. Earl Long had been blocked from power first by his brother and then by the disputes among his brother's followers. Earl Long's big chance came in 1948, when he was elected governor.

On the national scene, a group of southern Democrats left the party to oppose President Truman's re-election in 1948. They formed a third political party, the States' Rights Democratic party. These **Dixiecrats**, as they were called, opposed Truman's stand on racial issues. The Dixiecrats nominated J. Strom Thurmond, the governor of North Carolina, for president. In the November election, Thurmond won in Louisiana. Earl Long, however, disagreed with the Dixiecrats' desertion of the Democratic party and with their political views.

EARL LONG

The relationship between Huey and Earl Long was as complex as the brothers themselves.

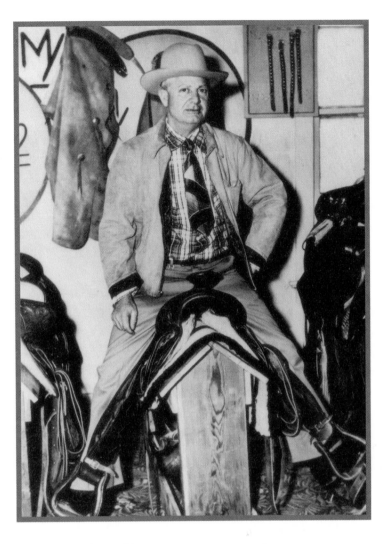

Governor Earl Long on a shopping spree in New Mexico. He bought twelve of these Western saddles.

When Earl stepped into Huey's sales position, Huey charged him a fee to take over the route. At times during Huey Long's career, Earl helped "save Huey's hide," as he would say. At other times, he opposed Huey. On one occasion, Earl even testified in Congress against his brother.

Many people who knew both Huey and Earl Long said they liked Earl more, and he was considered the better one-on-one politician. Huey Long used politics as a means to power. Earl Long loved politics and campaigning. He had a true concern for the poor, believing "the fortunate should assist the unfortunate, the strong should assist the weak, and the rich should assist the poor."

Earl Long had been lieutenant governor under Richard Leche. When Leche resigned in 1939, Earl completed his term as governor. He intended to have the job again. Earl ran for governor in 1940 but was defeated by Sam Jones, losing in forty-one parishes. But in 1948, he defeated Sam Jones in sixty-two of the sixty-four parishes. He was on his way to the Capitol that Huey built.

This photograph shows Earl Long being sworn in as governor for the first time, following the resignation of Governor Leche.

Earl Long's campaign style was colorful. He sent sound trucks out ahead, telling the people he would soon arrive and give away hams and bacon before his speech. Some people came for the giveaways; others came to hear his humorous and rough attacks on his opponents.

The Winn Parish farm Earl Long called his "pea patch" was his favorite place. He did engage in a little campaign trickery about his peas. He knew people liked the idea of getting peas grown at his farm. He would buy peas at one campaign stop and give them out at the next, saying they were from the pea patch. He proudly called himself a country boy and proved it by wearing overalls on the farm. This love for his rural roots was not a campaign tactic, as Huey's had been.

When Earl Long was elected governor, he invited the country folk to his inauguration. He served hot dogs and buttermilk to the crowd that attended. The kegs of beer were hidden from the teetotalers (those who do not drink alcohol).

As governor, Earl Long pushed for more spending on social programs (government programs intended to improve the quality of life for its citizens). The good economy provided revenues for the state. Long used those revenues to increase spending on health, welfare, education, and highways. African-American teachers had filed a lawsuit to require equal pay for white and African-American teachers, and it was during Long's term as governor that the pay for black teachers was raised. The state even gave the veterans of World War II a bonus of $1,000.

Soon, however, more money was needed to continue the programs Long wanted. He saw to it that the sales tax, the gasoline tax, and the severance tax were raised to provide the needed funds.

Earl Long intended to reward his friends and punish his enemies, in the Long political style. He persuaded the legislature to eliminate the civil service system. State jobs were once again subject to political pressure. Long carefully controlled membership on state boards, and he used the power of the governor's office to interfere with local government. For example, he pushed through legislation that changed the composition of the city government of New Orleans.

ROBERT KENNON

The governor elected in 1952 to follow Earl Long was his opposite in political style. Robert Kennon had been elected mayor of his hometown of Minden in Webster Parish. At twenty-three years of age, he was the youngest mayor in the United States. He later served as a district attorney and a state supreme court justice before he ran for governor.

Governor Kennon described his style of government as the "civics book approach." He intended to follow the rules for good government. Efficiency and reform were his goals. To eliminate voter fraud, Kennon introduced voting machines. The machines were intended to count votes accurately and fairly.

Governor Robert Kennon introduced many reforms during his term in office.

Kennon convinced the legislature to restore the civil service system to protect government workers from political firings. In addition, the legislature strengthened the civil service regulations and revised the law to require a two-thirds vote of the legislature to change civil service. These moves made it much more difficult for future governors to do away with the system. Governor Kennon also got rid of "deadhead jobs," jobs filled by people who did little or no work but who had received the jobs as a reward.

One of the major legislative changes during the Kennon years was a constitutional amendment making it harder to raise taxes. The amendment required that issues involving taxes be approved by a two-thirds vote of the legislature. To help ensure that state agencies operated fairly, without politics, the governor appointed special committees. These committees were called *blue ribbon boards* because of their highly qualified members.

The governor also fought gambling in the state. Gambling in South Louisiana was wide open, with slot machines in many restaurants.

Congressional hearings headed by Senator Estes Kefauver revealed the influence of organized crime in Louisiana. Kennon pushed for an investigation. The state police, under the direction of Francis C. Grevemberg, raided gambling places and seized gambling equipment.

During Kennon's term, the harsh conditions and brutal treatment of prisoners at the state penitentiary at Angola received national coverage. The governor ordered an investigation and changes. Guidelines for the prison were established, and the pay for guards was increased to attract more qualified people.

New Orleans benefited from Governor Kennon's reform program. The city government had been used as a political football by the Longs. When Huey Long decided the city government was too powerful, he used the state government to take away much of the city's authority. Earl Long had continued this control. Governor Kennon extended home rule to the city government of New Orleans, ending state interference.

THE RETURN OF EARL LONG

In the 1956 governor's race, the voters turned away from the reform movement and back to Earl Long. Long's opponent in the election was the popular reform mayor of New Orleans, deLesseps Morrison. Long campaigned by ridiculing his opponent's name and his expensive suits. Long said he would stick to his country roots and not wear those fancy tailored clothes. He said "on ole' Earl, those clothes would look like socks on a rooster."

Earl Long had enjoyed his first term as governor. His second term was not as easy. He could not add more government programs without increasing taxes, and a new law made increasing taxes almost impossible. He was able, however, to increase spending on his social programs because state revenues were increasing.

Governor Long stayed fairly low key for the first part of the term, but in 1959, he lost control in a very public setting — during a speech to the legislature. For two hours he yelled and screamed at the legislature, naming names as he issued his insults. His behavior was so extreme that no one heard his message.

The governor was angry because the segregationists (those who believe in keeping the races separate) were removing black voters from the registration list. Earl Long had encouraged blacks to register and vote. In fact, the number of black voters had increased from under 10,000 to more than 100,000 during his second term. Long's social programs benefited the poor blacks in Louisiana, and he wanted their votes. The segregationists, however, did not approve of his actions. The legislature passed a law stating that any two people could challenge a person's voter registration. The segregationists were using the law to remove blacks from the voting rolls. It was this activity that so angered Earl Long.

deLesseps Morrison, Earl Long's opponent in the 1956 gubernatorial election, was mayor of New Orleans four times. He ran for governor unsuccessfully three times.

His behavior continued to be so unpredictable that his wife and his nephew, Russell Long, had him committed to a mental hospital in Galveston, Texas. After a few weeks, he was transferred to the East Louisiana State Hospital in Mandeville. Once there, he fired the director, which he claimed he had the right to do as governor. He then appointed a new director, who released him.

Next, he set out on a wild trip across the country, receiving huge media attention. When he got tired of reporters, he put a pillow case over his head. His picture made the front page of newspapers around the nation.

There have been several possible explanations for Long's behavior, but, like his brother Huey, Earl Long had always had some eccentric habits. It was as if those behaviors had become much more intense during this period. Stories of his binge buying had entertained people long before his hospitalization. One of his favorite shopping spots was Schwegmann's in New Orleans. He bought the specials then gave them away. Politicians chuckled about judges and legislators being required to go in to buy sacks of potatoes so that Long could load up his car with sale items.

This photograph was taken in El Paso during Governor Earl Long's "wild" trip across country. The man on the right is David Bell, Louisiana Commissioner for Veterans Affairs, who arrived in El Paso ahead of Long.

The interesting relationship between the Longs and the voters of Louisiana is illustrated by what happened after Earl Long's crisis period. He could not run for governor again in 1960, because at that time the constitution did not allow a governor to serve two consecutive terms. He decided to run for Congress in his home district. On the day of the election, he had a heart attack. He refused to go to the hospital because he said the people would not vote for him if they knew he was sick. After the polls closed, he went to the hospital. He died a few days later knowing he had won his last election.

Do You Remember?

1. What was Earl Long's relationship to Huey Long?
2. Why did Governor Kennon refer to his view of government as the "civics book approach"?
3. How did the segregationists remove blacks from the voting rolls in the late 1950s?

POST-WAR CHANGES

The period following World War II was a time of rapid and remarkable change, both in the United States and in Louisiana.

THE ECONOMY

During the 1940s and 1950s, Louisiana's economy shifted from agriculture to industry. Agricultural jobs disappeared when machines replaced laborers on the farms. Farm workers moved to towns and cities to work or left the state to find jobs. African-American farm workers in particular migrated to northern cities like Detroit where they could find factory jobs, less discrimination, and a different lifestyle. By the 1950s, the majority of Louisiana's population was urban.

The postwar period saw even more growth in Louisiana's oil industry. An exciting new opportunity was born when the Kerr-McGee Corporation successfully drilled for oil in the Gulf of Mexico in 1947. In addition, the chemical plants that were the newest development of Louisiana's petroleum industry began locating along the Mississippi River between Baton Rouge and New Orleans. New jobs with higher wages changed the lifestyle of many who lived in the area.

Money began pouring into the state from oil leases on state land. This money led to a dispute between Louisiana and the federal government over the oil extracted from the floor of the Gulf of Mexico. The federal government laid claim to the land — and its valuable oil deposits — that was three miles or more off the coast. Louisiana considered this too close and said the 3-mile limit would deprive the state of its fair share of the oil royalties. Oil companies pay **royalties** to landowners when oil is extracted from the land.

President Truman offered a settlement that would have given the state the royalties within the 3-mile limit plus 37.5 percent of the royalties received beyond the limit. However, neither Governor Kennon nor Governor Long considered the federal offer to be enough. The dispute became a lawsuit that was not settled until the 1980s.

The economic growth after World War II also led to the growth of labor unions. Governor Kennon and others believed that labor unions had become too powerful in Louisiana. They argued that the state's economy suffered since new businesses did not want to come to Louisiana because of the strong labor movement here.

In 1954 the legislature passed a **right-to-work law**, a law that allows workers to get and keep jobs without having to join a union. Union members and Governor Earl Long worked to have the legislature repeal the law, which it did in 1956. After 1956, a labor union could negotiate a contract with a business that called for a *closed shop* (workers had to belong to the union to get the job), a *union shop* (workers had to

Above: President Harry Truman, who took office on the death of Franklin Roosevelt, offered a proposal to settle the dispute over offshore oil royalties. Louisiana's governors, however, turned it down. **Opposite:** *Geologists working for Kerr-McGee are seen here exploring for oil in the Gulf of Mexico in 1947.*

THE GARDEN IN THE FOREST

The beautiful formal gardens at Hodges Gardens in Sabine Parish include staggered gardens.

The nation's largest privately operated botanical park and wildlife refuge lies in the hills of Louisiana, near the western border. The 4,700 acres of Hodges Gardens include formal gardens, greenhouses, natural scenic overlooks, picnic grounds, a 225-acre artificial lake, an outdoor theater, and a wildlife refuge. Its beauty is enjoyed by both nearby residents and visitors from around the world.

A. J. Hodges had made his money in the oil and forestry industries, but he also realized the importance of conserving the beauty of Louisiana. One of Louisiana's most important conservationists, Hodges funded a reforestation program and forest genetics research.

He owned some land in Sabine Parish on which there was an abandoned stone quarry. Hodges turned the quarry into a beautiful garden. Waterfalls, streams, and pools now fill the ravines and gullies where the rock was extracted. A popular tourist attraction, the multilevel garden offers year-round interest. Every season offers new color and changing beauty. In the spring, a magnificent display of azaleas fills the quarry. In the forested areas, pine trees and natural plants shelter wild deer in winter.

An island in the lake features a monument to the Louisiana Purchase. A huge terrazzo (stone chips set in concrete) map of the United States shows the area acquired by the purchase. Flags portray the history of our state.

Hodges Gardens, opened in 1956, is owned and operated by the nonprofit Hodges Foundation. The garden is the site of concerts and

festivals throughout the year. The best known is the Easter Sunrise Service, featuring the Centenary College Choir from Shreveport. Thousands of visitors come to the "garden in the forest" for this annual event.

Louisiana has other beautiful public gardens. The Gardens of the American Rose Center in Shreveport is the national headquarters of the American Rose Society. It is also a research facility, and the garden features fields of experimental roses. In Monroe, Elsong Gardens is noted for its seasonal themes and showcases a walled town garden. In Hammond, Zemurray Gardens features 150 acres of azaleas.

Top: The 225-acre lake is at the heart of Hodges Gardens.
Above: This Halloween display welcomes visitors at hte main entrance. *Left:* There are three formal rose gardens at Hodges Gardens.

join the union once they got the job), or an *agency shop* (all workers had to pay union dues regardless of whether they actually belonged to the union).

CULTURAL CHANGES

It was during the post-war period that television began to change the culture of America. The state's first television stations included New Orleans station WDSU and station WAFB in Baton Rouge. On December 18, 1948, people in New Orleans excitedly filled the Municipal Auditorium to watch their first television broadcast. By the 1950s, this new invention had reached many homes in Louisiana. Families soon gathered around the television set in the evening to watch comedies like "I Love Lucy," game shows like "What's My Line," and the popular western "Gunsmoke."

Another cultural change shocked the older generation in the 1950s. Rock and roll music became the soundtrack of teenage life. Louisiana

Above: Elvis Presley returned to Louisiana to film King Creole.
Right: New Orleans-born Antoine "Fats" Domino was a popular rock-and-roll musician.

jazz and blues music provided the background from which rock and roll was created. Some of the early performers, such as Fats Domino, recorded their new music in New Orleans.

Elvis Presley, the most famous of the new musicians, thrilled young Louisiana audiences before he became nationally famous. He appeared on the "Louisiana Hayride," a country music radio show, in Shreveport in 1954. Soon, teenagers from all over North Louisiana flocked to hear Elvis at the "Hayride." The girls screamed and squealed, shocking the regular fans of country music at the show. On August 28, 1956, New Orleans teenagers flocked to the Municipal Auditorium to hear Elvis sing. The music critic of the *Times-Picayune* reported, "He sang 'Blue Suede Shoes' and 'Heartbreak Hotel' with what passes for a voice." Elvis returned to New Orleans in 1958 to film the movie *King Creole*.

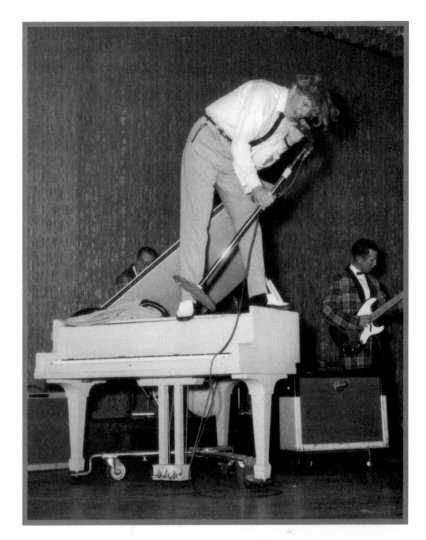

THE COLD WAR IN LOUISIANA

While some people in Louisiana focused on the new social changes after World War II, others turned their attention to world tensions. The relationship between the United States and the Soviet Union grew strained as the two nations negotiated after World War II. The hostility was called the **Cold War** because it was mainly fought with words and diplomacy.

The fear of the spread of communism through Soviet aggression provoked American reaction. The United States formed a number of military alliances hoping to contain communism. Tensions from the Cold War led to actual fighting in Korea in 1950. Some World War II veterans returned to fight in that war, and they were joined by younger soldiers. Louisiana families again waited anxiously for word from the war zone. The Korean War ended in 1953, but the conflict between communism and capitalism continued. An arms race developed between the Soviet Union and the United States, and fear of the atomic bomb threatened world peace.

Jerry Lee Lewis was born in Ferriday in North Louisiana. He has always been a showman. This photograph was taken at a live performance in 1958.

THE POLIO EPIDEMIC

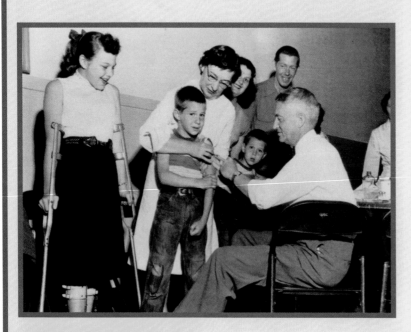

In 1951, a polio epidemic struck Shreveport. Polio, or poliomyelitis, is caused by a virus that attacks the nervous system, which in turn paralyzes muscles. When respiratory muscles are paralyzed, the result can be death. The 1951 Shreveport epidemic involved 250 cases, with more than 150 cases reported during the month of August alone. That number would have been equal to about 9,000 people in New York City at that time.

In 1921, Franklin D. Roosevelt, who later became president, contracted polio. His legs were paralyzed, and he could walk only by using leg braces and crutches. In 1938, Roosevelt founded the organization that would later become the March of Dimes. Schoolchildren were asked to contribute dimes to fund research for this crippling disease.

Scientists at Harvard found a way to grow large quantities of the polio virus, the first step toward producing antibodies. Dr. Jonas E. Salk was the first to develop a vaccine using an inactive virus. In 1954, Salk's polio vaccine was field-tested and found to be effective. Mass innoculations began soon afterward.

At the same time, a Russian immigrant named Albert B. Sabin developed an oral vaccine containing live viruses. Sabin's oral vaccine was successfully tested in 1957. These two vaccines are responsible for virtually eliminating the scourge of polio from children in the United States and most of the developed world.

Health officials urged parents to immunize their children once the vaccine became available. The Louisiana representative for the National Foundation for Infantile Paralysis, F. Owen Grace, said, "We hope that parents wake up and protect their children and themselves by using the vaccine now. Tomorrow may be too late." Protection from this disease is now part of the routine immunizations required for all children before they enter school.

Top: A San Diego boy receives a polio shot while his sister, a polio victim, looks on. ***Above:*** *Dr. Jonas Salk developed the vaccine.*

Military bases and oil refineries in Louisiana were considered prime targets. State and local governments prepared for possible attack. Evacuation plans were developed for Louisiana's major cities. Practice evacuation drills were even held in some Louisiana schools. Buildings were designated as "fallout shelters," where people could go in case of an atomic attack.

The Civil Defense Office encouraged Louisiana citizens to build their own fallout shelters. Architects provided do-it-yourself plans and explained how individuals could build a shelter for $300 in about two weeks. People in North Louisiana were warned that Barksdale Air Force Base might be bombed. They were advised to build bomb shelters with one-foot-thick concrete walls and three feet of earth covering the roof.

Newspapers carried mock headlines such as "Shreveport 'Destroyed' in Civil Defense Tests" (Shreveport *Times*) and "Who's Afraid? Not We!" (Baton Rouge *Morning Advocate*). The *Morning Advocate* printed an enhanced photograph of the State Capitol being blown up. In spite of this publicity, most people did not build fallout or bomb shelters. Preparing for an atomic attack seemed futile.

Do You Remember?

1. In the 1950s, was the majority of Louisiana's population rural or urban?
2. What industry developed along the Mississippi River between Baton Rouge and New Orleans?
3. On what radio show did Elvis Presley appear?

Thousands of American troops participated in the Korean War in the early 1950s.

SUMMARY

In 1941, Louisiana and the United States found themselves involved in World War II. The war brought the state and the nation out of the Great Depression. Military camps were built around the state, and mock wars held in rural areas of the state helped prepare American soldiers for battle. Over 274,000 people from Louisiana served in the war. After the war, soldiers returned to Louisiana to resume their former lives. Many enrolled in the universities. Others found jobs in the booming oil industry.

Economic recovery encouraged Louisiana's people in the 1940s and 1950s. Anti-Long governors, such as Sam Jones, Jimmie Davis, and Robert Kennon, brought new ideas to Louisiana's government. The civil service system brought job security to state workers. Improvements in education, roads, and hospitals were encouraging changes after the bleak years of the Depression.

Earl Long served two different terms as governor of Louisiana during the postwar period. His colorful personality and campaign style appealed to many.

CHAPTER · REVIEW

1940	1941	1944			1952		

1940
Sam Jones elected governor

1941
Mock wars held in Louisiana

1944
Jimmie Davis elected governor

1947
First offshore oil well drilled in Gulf of Mexico

1948
Earl Long elected governor

1952
Robert Kennon elected governor

1956
Earl Long elected governor

1940	**1950**	**1960**

1950
Korean War began

1948
State of Israel founded

1954
Ernest Hemingway won Nobel Prize for literature

1947
Jackie Robinson became first black to play major league baseball

1941
Pearl Harbor attacked

U.S. entered WW II

1945
President Roosevelt died
Harry S Truman became president
World War II ended

1939
World War II began in Europe

Reviewing People, Places, and Terms

Define, identify, or explain the importance of the following.

1. blackout
2. civil service system
3. Cold War
4. Dixiecrats
5. Sam Jones
6. Earl Long
7. Pearl Harbor
8. ration
9. right-to-work law
10. royalty
11. sabotage
12. United Service Organizations
13. victory garden

Understanding the Facts

1. Why was Louisiana the site of so many training exercises just before World War II?

2. What event finally led the United States to enter World War II?

3. How many Louisianians served in the armed forces during World War II?

4. Name three items that were rationed during World War II.

5. What was the name of the system in which people received government jobs in return for helping a candidate get elected?

6. Why did Earl Long eliminate the civil service system once he was elected governor?

7. Name three reforms put through by Governor Kennon.

8. Why did Earl Long get angry at the legislature in 1959?

9. Why did agricultural jobs decrease after World War II?

10. Explain the differences among a closed shop, a union shop, and an agency shop.

11. What is a fallout shelter?

Developing Critical Thinking

1. Why was rationing necessary in the United States during the war years?
2. Why do you think some people favor the right-to-work law and some people oppose it?
3. Do you believe that television has changed American life? If so, how?

Using Your Skills

1. Locate Tokyo, Japan; Rome, Italy; Berlin, Germany; and Moscow, Russia on a world map or globe. What are the coordinates (longitude and latitude) of these cities? Which is closest to your town?
2. In which parishes are the following military bases located: Barksdale Air Force Base and Fort Polk?

Special Projects

1. Louisiana was the site of a number of training camps and bases during World War II. Use various resources to determine which military base was located in your parish or was located closest to your parish. Prepare a report on how this land is used today. Include photographs or sketches if possible.
2. Andrew Jackson Higgins developed a profitable shipbuilding industry in New Orleans during World War II. Access resources at your library, your local chamber of commerce, or the Internet to identify 3-5 industries in your area. Prepare a chart telling when they started and how they were affected by the war.

Making Connections

1. Other major diseases that have had an impact on Louisiana include yellow fever, cholera, diphtheria, tuberculosis, and influenza. Research to find out which of these diseases are still considered a threat and which have been eliminated in Louisiana.
2. One of the efforts to stop polio in Louisiana involved the spraying of a pesticide, DDT. Interview someone who remembers the polio epidemics of the postwar period. What precautions did people take then?

• BUILDING SKILLS: RECOGNIZING PROPAGANDA •

The use of propaganda to persuade people to make certain decisions has been a part of political life since political parties were organized. What we sometimes forget is that these same techniques are used in advertising today. Some of the more common techniques include the following.

Bandwagon approach. You've probably used this technique on your parents to try to convince them to let you do something or go somewhere because "everybody else is." You hope your parents will think it's all right since other parents are allowing their sons and daughters to go.

Testimonials. With this technique, a well-known person, such as an athlete or a movie star, describes how great a particular product is or explains why you should vote for a particular political candidate. This is an attempt to *transfer* the honor, respect, or good feeling we feel about one individual to another.

Repetition. Watch television one evening and you'll see that a short commercial is often repeated several times during a particular show. Advertisers hope that if you see the message often enough, you'll remember it.

Cause-effect relationships. A misleading cause-effect relationship is often used to persuade. "Twenty students who used Computer X to write their history reports got an A." The advertiser is trying to convince you that those twenty students only got an A because they used Computer X.

Try This! Write an ad for a newspaper or television station for a product or a political candidate using one or more of the above techniques.

We Don't Buy Where We Can't Work

CHAPTER FIFTEEN

LOUISIANA'S CIVIL RIGHTS ERA: CHALLENGE AND CHANGE

. . . ending segregation . . . will require the utmost patience, understanding, generosity, and forbearance from all of us.
— Judge J. Skelly Wright, federal judge in New Orleans, 1960

IN 1954, THE U.S. SUPREME COURT changed the direction of Louisiana. Segregation, the separation of the races, was ruled unconstitutional. This history-making decision was the result of the **Brown v. Board of Education of Topeka** lawsuit. Until that twentieth-century court case, the highest legal authority in the United States had protected segregation.

In 1896, the U.S. Supreme Court had upheld a Louisiana law that required separate railroad cars for blacks and for whites. In this ruling in the *Plessy v. Ferguson* case, the Court said that a person's constitutional rights did not include protection from social discrimination. The ruling made segregation legal in the United States and established the separate-but-equal concept. The *Brown* ruling reversed the *Plessy* decision.

In the *Brown* case, the Supreme Court considered the issue of segregation and declared that inequality existed throughout the country. The schools for African-American children were not equal to the schools for white children. The Court went further with its opinion, stating that, even if the school facilities were exactly the same, segregation still deprived African Americans of equal rights. The Court's ruling stated that separate facilities were unconstitutional because they violated the basic rights provided by the U.S. Constitution.

In April 1965, CORE protesters, led by national director James Farmer (right), held a march in Bogalusa.

Whites had long operated in a system that benefited them and deprived blacks. Most white southerners did not consider this unjust or racist. (*Racism* is a belief in the natural superiority of one race.) Segregation was just the unquestioned way of life. The white community and the black community lived parallel lives that crossed only under unspoken but rigid rules.

The signs of segregation were seen everywhere. Some were literal. Water fountains were marked "White only." African Americans had to use the rear entrance to movie theaters and sit in the segregated balcony marked "Colored." Restaurants for whites did not serve African Americans. In stores, all of the white customers were waited on before a black person could buy anything. Other signs of segregation were more subtle. Job opportunities were limited for African Americans. The educational system directed black children toward manual labor instead of professional jobs.

Throughout the segregated South, voices from the black community began to rise in protest. Many of those voices belonged to black veter-

Jubilant attorneys capture a historical moment on the steps of the United States Supreme Court after the high court rules in their favor in Brown v. Board of Education, *ending school segregation. Left to right, George Hayes, Thurgood Marshall, and James Nabrit, Jr. Which of these attorneys went on to become a Supreme Court justice?*

ans. They had fought for the United States in World War II, and now they wanted their full rights as citizens. The country had followed the *Plessy v. Ferguson* separate-but-equal ruling in name only. Life was separate but not equal. Blacks were tired of poor schools and all the restrictions of segregation.

In the *Brown* decision, Louisiana's black citizens saw the opportunity to end their treatment as second-class citizens. The changes ahead would end generations of discrimination. Equal treatment had been declared the only American way.

RESISTANCE TO CHANGE

To the white community, segregation was the way of life. As a result, the *Brown* decision brought a fear of change and uncertainty about the future. Some whites formed **Citizens' Councils** to support segregation. This group, however, used propaganda rather than the violence so often used by the Ku Klux Klan. (**Propaganda** is ideas, facts, or rumors spread to help a cause or to hurt an opposing cause.) The Louisiana Citizens' Council was led by state senator Willie Rainach from Claiborne Parish. Another segregationist leader was Leander Perez, who was known as "the boss of Plaquemines Parish."

Perez and others described desegregation as a communist plot. In the 1950s and 1960s, the communist powers were a real world threat, and some people accepted the argument linking desegregation and communism. Earl Long, however, ridiculed the idea. He warned Perez that he was foolish to try to fight the federal government. "You might as well give up. The feds have the atom bomb." Long meant that the strength and power of the United States government would back the change to a desegregated society.

In 1959, Jimmie Davis again ran for governor, campaigning as a strong segregationist to appeal to voters. As governor, Davis faced a state filled with racial unrest. The states' rights argument, first heard before the Civil War, was discussed again in the South. Louisiana's legislature argued that the state had the right to enforce segregation. It passed a law declaring the *Brown* decision null and void in Louisiana. This was called the **interposition** act; that is, the state legislature was interposing (placing) itself between the federal government and the people.

Fire fighters used firehoses in an attempt to break up a protest against desegregation in front of the New Orleans City Hall in late 1960.

ORGANIZING FOR CIVIL RIGHTS

The black community faced this strong opposition. One of the most important black organizations seeking equal rights for African Americans was the **National Association for the Advancement of Colored People** (NAACP), which had been organized nationally in 1909. The first Louisiana chapter of the NAACP was formed in New Orleans in 1915. The organization had supported the *Brown v. Board of Education* case. Now its members struggled to change Louisiana's segregated schools.

A longtime leader of the Louisiana NAACP was A. P. Turead of New Orleans. One of the first African-American lawyers in the state, he fought for equal rights long before the civil rights movement of the 1960s. His Creole family had lived in Louisiana for generations. Turead graduated from the Howard University Law School, then returned to Louisiana to begin his court battles.

In 1952, Turead had filed a lawsuit to enable a black student to enter a formerly all-white school in New Orleans. This occurred two years before the U.S. Supreme Court made its ruling in the *Brown v. Board of Education of Topeka* case. The New Orleans case, however, had to wait until the Court made its ruling in the *Brown* case.

NEW ORLEANS SCHOOL CRISIS

The schools for black children in New Orleans were overcrowded and run-down. At first, the parents pushed for improvements to the schools, willing to keep the separate schools if they could be made equal to white schools. These requests were ignored by the whites in power.

New Orleans then became the battleground in the struggle over desegregation in Louisiana. Because of the *Brown* decision, segregated schools were now unconstitutional. In 1956, a federal judge ordered the Orleans Parish School Board to submit a desegregation plan. The long, ugly battle to desegregate the schools of New Orleans began.

The school board refused and appealed the decision. The state legislature reacted by passing a law to take control of the New Orleans school system and other local school boards. The law allowed the governor to take over any school system that was ordered to integrate. (**Integration** refers to opening facilities to people of all races or ethnic groups without restrictions.) Other new laws declared that integrated schools would not be accredited (officially recognized) by the state. The legislature also established a Joint Committee on Segregation, headed by Willie Rainach. Reacting to pressure, the committee tried to block changes.

In 1960, the federal judge imposed his own desegregation plan. Four 6-year-old girls led the way to change. Their path was not easy. One little girl, Ruby Bridges, was the only black child sent to William Frantz Elementary School. The school was located in a poor neighborhood that had both a white housing project and a black housing project. (A *housing project* provides publicly funded housing for low-income families.) The white parents felt very threatened by the change and resented the fact that schools in wealthier neighborhoods were not part of the desegregation plan.

A crowd of mostly women gathered to scream at the little girl in the starched white dress. Federal marshals escorted Ruby Bridges to school each day to protect her from the mob. White children assigned to her first-grade class did not attend school all year. Ruby and her teacher spent the days alone.

The entire state watched the situation in New Orleans, which was not resolved for more than a year. The worldwide publicity the city received was mostly negative. Finally, local leaders realized that the city's economy was being affected. The rest of the country did not want to do business with this conflict-filled city. Business leaders urged New Orleans citizens to accept the changes and move forward.

Opposite, above: For more than forty years, A. P. Turead of New Orleans led the struggle for civil rights for blacks in Louisiana.
Opposite, below: Desegregation of the New Orleans school system did not go smoothly. In this November 1960 photo, white parents and students at the William Frantz Elementary School protested the assignment of Ruby Bridges to the school.
Above: Black first grade students, accompanied by their mothers, register at Lafayette School in New Orleans in 1962.

PUBLIC PROTESTS AND DEMONSTRATIONS

The conflicts did not end with the settlement of the New Orleans school crisis. African Americans in Louisiana wanted an end to segregation. Their protests became louder when changes did not come. Stores

In July 1965, A. Z. Young read a statement in Governor McKeithen's office announcing a 30-day cooling-off period in the Bogalusa protests.

that refused to employ black workers were boycotted. A **boycott** is a refusal to deal with a person, store, or organization until certain conditions are met. Public transportation was also boycotted until black riders were no longer forced to sit in the back of the bus.

Downtown stores had always refused to serve blacks at their lunch counters. African Americans began to stage **sit-ins** as a protest. Groups of mostly young people would sit at the counter, requesting service.

The Washington Parish town of Bogalusa filled with unrest during this period. The town had been established as a lumber town, and the mill continued to be the largest employer. The town was still a segregated community; the civil rights of African Americans were largely ignored.

Civil rights groups demanded better mill jobs for black workers and pushed to end inequality throughout the community. The Congress of Racial Equality (CORE), a national civil rights group, organized the protests in Bogalusa. The group's members were younger and more militant (aggressive) than the NAACP. Violence erupted.

Governor John McKeithen realized he had to take action to prevent riots. He met with leaders of both sides and managed to bring about a

compromise. He then appointed a statewide biracial committee to continue the efforts started in Bogalusa. In 1967, when A. Z. Young, a leader of the Bogalusa protests, led a march from Bogalusa to Baton Rouge, the governor protected the marchers with the State Police and the National Guard.

Protests such as these in Louisiana and across the South brought results. The U.S. Congress passed the **Civil Rights Act of 1964**, which ended segregation by prohibiting discrimination in public facilities and in employment. The 1965 **Voting Rights Act** outlawed all literacy tests and poll taxes and sent registrars into the southern states to register black voters. The number of blacks registered to vote increased greatly.

A. Z. Young (center) leads a march in August 1967 from Bogalusa to Baton Rouge. Marchers were protected by the Louisiana National Guard.

Do You Remember?
1. What 1954 history-making decision by the U.S. Supreme Court changed segregation in the United States?
2. Give two examples of the segregation that existed in Louisiana in the 1960s.
3. Where was the first Louisiana chapter of the NAACP started?

POLITICS IN THE CIVIL RIGHTS ERA

The 1960s and 1970s were turbulent years for Louisiana and the rest of the southern states. Desegregation brought conflict to Louisiana and threatened to overshadow almost everything else. In spite of the difficult times, the state's governors led the state toward progress in other ways.

*Above: Criticized when it was first built, the Sunshine Bridge is now recognized as an economic asset. **Opposite:** Jimmie Davis again entertained a meeting of governors—this time at the 1961 Southern Governors' Conference in Nashville.*

JIMMIE DAVIS

Jimmie Davis had first served as governor during World War II. In 1959, he campaigned on the accomplishments of his first term. He talked about harmony and unity, and his campaign slogan was "Jimmie Davis never raised your taxes." But low taxes would not solve the problems or ease the turmoil facing the state in the 1960s.

Governor Davis planned several projects to benefit Louisiana's future. One of those projects was a new bridge across the Mississippi River between Baton Rouge and New Orleans. When the bridge was built, it connected cane fields on one side of the river to cane fields on the other side. Critics claimed it was a waste of state money. Today that bridge connects industry on both sides of the river. Named the "Sunshine Bridge" after Davis's song "You Are My Sunshine," it is now recognized as an economic asset.

Other construction projects completed during Davis's term were the Toledo Bend Dam and the present governor's mansion. The dam and reservoir at Toledo Bend provide electricity and recreation for both Louisiana and Texas. The elaborate plantation-style governor's mansion includes eighteen bathrooms, a fact often mentioned by the critics who thought the old mansion was quite adequate.

The quality of state government was improved with a written code of ethics. The **code of ethics** described the rules or standards by which state business should be conducted. Another move toward better government was the addition of a legislative auditor to formally examine state spending.

One scandal during Governor Davis's term led to another improvement. The so-called Baker Bank scandal involved the investment of state funds. A bank in the town of Baker in East Baton Rouge Parish received state funds for deposit. The state accounts that were set up benefited the bank rather than the state. After that information was made public, the legislature passed laws to require the proper investment of idle state funds (money not immediately needed to pay expenses).

THE ASSASSINATION OF PRESIDENT JOHN F. KENNEDY

On the morning of November 22, 1963, President and Mrs. Kennedy and Vice President and Mrs. Johnson flew to Dallas:. The president and vice president, as was customary, in separate planes. At the Dallas Airport, President and Mrs. Kennedy joined Texas Governor John Connally, Jr., to begin the fateful drive into the city.

"Ask not what your country can do for you — ask what you can do for your country." This is the most-remembered line from the inaugural address of President John F. Kennedy in January 1961. The young and charming president served only two years before he was assassinated. President Kennedy was riding in a motorcade in Dallas, Texas, on November 22, 1963, when he was shot. Dallas police arrested 24-year-old Lee Harvey Oswald and charged him with murdering the president. The tragedy became even more bizarre when Oswald was shot and killed two days later by Jack Ruby. Oswald was being moved to another jail, and television cameras were on hand to broadcast the move. The cameras caught Oswald's murder and transmitted it live to viewers.

Americans immediately began to search for an explanation for the president's assassination. Earl Warren, the chief justice of the Supreme

Court, led the investigation. The Warren Commission concluded that Oswald had acted alone and that there had been no conspiracy to murder the president. Some people did not agree with this conclusion.

One person who believed there had been a conspiracy to kill the president was Jim Garrison, the district attorney of Orleans Parish. Garrison claimed that the group of conspirators included people who lived in New Orleans. In March 1967, District Attorney Garrison indicted New Orleans businessman Clay Shaw, accusing him of plotting to kill President Kennedy. The Shaw trial in 1969 ended with a jury verdict of not guilty. But even today the questions continue.

*Left: Lee Harvey Oswald was arrested by the Dallas police and charged with killing the president. He was being moved to another jail when he himself was killed. **Top:** Jim Garrison believed that there was a conspiracy to kill President Kennedy. **Above:** Clay Shaw was acquitted of the charge of plotting to kill the president.*

JOHN MCKEITHEN

John McKeithen took over the governor's office in 1964. McKeithen described himself as a country lawyer from Columbia in Caldwell Parish. He was the first candidate to use television effectively. He ended each television ad by repeating his campaign slogan — "Won't you 'hep' me?" — in his North Louisiana drawl.

This skilled campaigner learned about Louisiana politics from Earl Long. McKeithen had been a floor leader in the legislature during Earl Long's last term. McKeithen shared some of the Longs' social views,

Above: *In the 1964 governor's race, John McKeithen was one of ten candidates in the Democratic primary.* **Right:** *As governor, McKeithen supported reform measures and worked hard to improve the state's economy.*

but what he did not copy was their dictatorlike behavior. During the McKeithen years, the legislature was much more independent than the Longs would have ever allowed.

Governor McKeithen too brought progress to state government. Governmental reforms included strengthening the state ethics commission, which is responsible for protecting the citizens from unethical behavior by state officials. He established a central purchasing system for state government, which was much more efficient.

Governor McKeithen also worked hard to improve the state's economy. Businesses came to Louisiana because the governor traveled around the country promoting the state. The importance of tourism to the state's economy was recognized. Advertisements invited people to come to Louisiana, and a separate state agency was established to promote tourism.

John McKeithen was a popular governor and the first in the twentieth century to succeed himself, due to an amendment to the Louisiana Constitution.

John McKeithen was so popular during his first term that many people wanted him to continue as governor. At the time, however, the Louisiana constitution did not allow the governor to run for re-election. In 1966, the voters approved a constitutional amendment to change this restriction.

The voters gave McKeithen 80 percent of the votes in the 1967 governor's race. Despite this strong vote of confidence, Governor McKeithen soon ran into problems in his second term. The expensive Superdome project and labor problems brought criticism. The Superdome in New Orleans was projected to cost $31.5 million, but it ended up costing more than ten times that amount — $362 million.

Strong labor unions in Louisiana clashed with business interests. Increasing violence brought negative publicity to the state. In 1967, *Life* magazine ran a series of articles linking the state's labor problems to organized crime. The magazine reported that Carlos Marcello, described as a "Mob boss," had too much influence in Louisiana. Governor McKeithen traveled to New York to meet with the magazine's editors about those claims. State investigations, however, did not result in any indictments.

SUPERDOME

Above: *The Superdome draws visitors to New Orleans for sports events, concerts, and conventions.* **Opposite, above and below:** *New Orleans and the Superdome hosted the 1988 Republican National Convention, at which George Bush and Dan Quayle (above, left to right) became the standard-bearers for their party.*

Today, the Superdome appears on the landscape of New Orleans looking like a huge round space ship. In the 1960s, a New Orleans businessman, Dave Dixon, convinced Governor John McKeithen that Louisiana needed a stadium that would compete with Houston's Astrodome. He argued that a stadium would bring in more tourists, conventions, and professional sports. Governor McKeithen liked the idea, which fit in with his economic goals for the state. The governor then convinced the legislature to pass a bill establishing the Louisiana Stadium and Exposition District. The voters overwhelmingly approved the necessary constitutional amendment for the district.

As the project developed, so did controversy. Both the size and the cost of the Superdome were more than voters had expected. Over $165 million in taxes were required to pay for the building. Opponents of the project organized, but in the end, nothing could stop the project.

Architect Curtis said the Superdome should be "Large enough to house the most spectacular extravaganza and small enough to accommodate a poetry reading." The architect used new computer technology to finish the plans, and the building itself took four years to complete. Hundreds of construction workers filled the site each day. The swampy soil required more than two thousand pilings. The 10-inch pilings had to go down 165 feet to find stable rock.

The Superdome opened in 1975. The people of Louisiana were very proud of the amazing structure, which is big enough to house the Astrodome under its roof. On the opening day, the billboard read "Welcome to Tomorrow." Even the *New York Times* seemed impressed: "The Louisiana Superdome will make all other stadiums in existence as obsolete as Rome's Colosseum."

The Superdome covers 13 acres. It is tall enough for a 26-story building to fit inside and contains 125 million cubic feet of space. The air conditioning that had become common in Louisiana by the 1970s made possible the stadium's controlled environment. The system in the building uses 9,000 tons of air conditioning equipment to keep the interior at a comfortable 72 degrees.

The Superdome contains 52 meeting halls, 2 restaurants, 68 hot dog stands, 40 party rooms, 132 box suites, 32 escalators, and 10 elevators. The scoreboards are 88 feet tall and were among the first computerized scoreboards ever used. Almost 75,000 people can be seated for football games.

The list of major events held in the Superdome since it opened is wide-ranging. In 1987, Pope John Paul II held a youth rally there when he visited New Orleans. The Republican National Convention was held at the Superdome in 1988. Concert goers have seen the Rolling Stones and Whitney Houston. The Superdome provides a great setting for the Super Bowl. Other sporting events held there include the Bayou Classic, the annual football game between Southern University and Grambling College, and the Sugar Bowl. The NCAA basketball Final Four games have also been played here.

Edwin Edwards was a popular governor during his first term and was re-elected in 1975.

EDWIN EDWARDS

The Voting Rights Act of 1965 finally enforced the constitutional right of African Americans to vote. For the first time, no obstacles kept them from voting. Long lines at the polls included many first-time voters who were more than sixty-five years old. This new group of voters changed Louisiana's elections. Now, candidates courted black voters instead of promising to keep them from voting. In 1971, Edwin Edwards was the first twentieth century governor to be elected with the support of the African-American community.

Edwards also had the strong backing of another group of Louisianians. Despite his English-sounding name, Edwards is a Cajun from Marksville in Avoyelles Parish. After graduating from LSU Law School, he moved to Crowley in Acadia Parish. Edwards reached his Cajun constituency by speaking to them in French.

Governor Edwards began his first term with a broad base of support. He appointed a number of blacks and women to high-level state jobs. These two groups had not been included in positions of power before. He also emphasized social programs. More money was spent on charity hospitals, providing care for the poor. Welfare benefits were increased. Vocational schools, parks, and tourism also benefited.

An increase and a change in severance taxes brought more money into the state treasury. The tax on crude oil was increased by 30 percent, and the natural gas tax was raised 50 percent. In addition, the severance tax was now based on the value of the resource instead of on the volume or amount removed. Before this change, tax revenues did not increase if the price of oil or gas went up. The rising price of oil in the 1970s meant that Louisiana received much more money from the severance tax. The state benefited even more when the federal government deregulated oil. This **deregulation** removed a number of federal rules and restrictions from the oil industry. The change brought more money to the industry and to the state of Louisiana.

In 1975, Governor Edwards was re-elected with strong Democratic support. The social programs of his first term made him a popular candidate. The people were satisfied because the Louisiana economy was strong.

Several government reforms were enacted during his second term. One law required that all government meetings, involving both elected and appointed groups, be public. This is called the **sunshine law** because the idea is to open the meetings to the light of day. Another law was passed to stop people from holding more than one government office or job.

In the 1950s, the legislature had briefly enacted a right-to-work law. In 1977, two powerful groups again lined up on either side of the issue. The American Federation of Labor-Congress of Industrial Organizations (AFL-CIO), a labor union led by Victor Bussie, lobbied to keep union protection for workers. The Louisiana Association of Business and Industry (LABI) argued that the unions were pushing wages too high and hurting the economy. The labor violence of the late 1960s and early 1970s led the legislature to again pass a right-to-work law. Soon afterward, the labor unions lost much of their power in Louisiana.

Governor Edwards's second term also brought him problems. Scandal developed around the governor, who was beginning to be described as a sharp politician but a playboy. In 1980, charges were brought against Charles Roemer, the appointed head of the Edwards administration. Roemer was accused of mismanagement of the state employees' insurance fund. The FBI sting operation that caught the participants was called "Brilab."

In 1971, Edwin Edwards campaigned on a promise to rewrite the state's constitution. He kept that promise, and the constitutional convention convened in 1973.

THE 1974 CONSTITUTION

Louisiana needed a new constitution. The 1921 constitution had been amended many times and was thousands of pages long. One critic had described it as a "patchwork of deals . . . containing endless trivia." Edwin Edwards had campaigned in 1971 for a new constitution. He said, "The present constitution is an impediment to progress. We need a new constitution to get our state moving in a new direction."

A constitutional convention met in Baton Rouge in 1973. The delegates included 105 who were elected and 27 who were appointed by the governor. The new constitution they developed was a vast improvement over the previous constitution. Even so, the delegates could not agree to eliminate some of the details. Governor Edwards told them when they finished that if they had stopped after the completion of the bill of rights and the three articles on the executive, the legislative, and the judicial branches, they would have had a "beautiful document."

The 1974 constitution includes a strong **bill of rights**, which guarantees basic rights. For example, Article 1, Section 3 establishes the right to individual dignity. It provides that "no law shall discriminate against a person because of race or religious ideas, beliefs, or affiliations." It goes on to say that laws cannot discriminate because of birth, age, sex, culture, physical conditions, or political ideas or affiliations.

The delegates included civil service protection in the document to make sure government workers would not lose their jobs for political reasons. At the same time, they planned a more efficient government bureaucracy. Limits were placed on the governor's powers. The state's power to tax also had more limits.

Environmental protection was added to this constitution after a national movement brought attention to Louisiana's environmental problems. Education had been an area of conflict throughout the 1960s. The shift from segregated schools presented challenges for the governing bodies in charge of education. The new constitution streamlined these boards to make them more efficient.

The constitution had been written by delegates directly elected by the people. Then, for the first time since the constitution of 1879, the people voted directly to ratify the constitution.

Do You Remember?
1. What was Jimmie Davis's campaign slogan in 1959?
2. What new campaign technique did John McKeithen use in the 1963 governor's race?
3. How did Edwin Edwards reach his Cajun constituency?
4. What is a bill of rights?

POLITICAL AND SOCIAL CHANGES

The activism of the 1960s brought political and social change. Even in conservative Louisiana, changes took place. The voices demanding to be heard could not be ignored.

WOMEN'S RIGHTS

The emphasis on civil rights in the 1960s brought attention to the rights of women. In 1964, Governor McKeithen appointed a Commission on the Status of Women to study women's rights and opportunities. He stated, "The full realization of the rights and potentials of women is of vital importance to the advancement of our state." The group's report included a recommendation that Louisiana laws concerning voting, holding public office, serving on a jury, and owning property be revised to be uniform (the same) for both men and women. At the time, women were called to serve on juries only if they had specifically signed up to be considered.

More women were elected to public office as the women's rights movement brought attention to the lack of women in these positions. Louisiana had elected women to public office before the 1960s. The first woman to be elected to a statewide office was Lucille May Grace, who was elected as the register of the State Land Office in 1931. She succeeded her father in the position. In 1936, after her husband's death, Doris Holland was appointed to finish his term as a state senator. She then ran for a seat in the state house of representatives and served there until 1948.

The first woman to be elected to the Louisiana senate was Virginia Shehee. She was elected in 1976 from a Caddo Parish district. Louisiana also sent a woman to Congress in the 1970s. When Congressman

Corinne "Lindy" Boggs was the first woman elected to Congress from Louisiana. She filled the seat held by her husband Hale, who was killed in an Alaska plane crash in1972. Lindy Boggs served nine terms in the U.S. House of Representatives.

Ernest Morial celebrates his election as mayor of New Orleans in 1977. He was the first African American elected to that office. In 1967, he had been the first African American to be elected to the legislature since the end of Reconstuction.

Hale Boggs from New Orleans died in a plane crash in Alaska, his wife was elected to take his place. Lindy Boggs served the district for eighteen years and became a popular and powerful member of Congress.

Changes in attitudes about the role of women finally ended a state law known as the "head and master law." This law made the husband the head and master of his household. One interpretation of the law required the man to take care of his family. The law was also used against wives because a husband could mortgage or sell the family home without her knowledge.

AFRICAN-AMERICAN ELECTED OFFICIALS

In 1965, the U.S. Supreme Court issued a decision in the *Baker v. Carr* case. In the ruling, the Court stated that voting districts must be fairly based on population. Voting districts had to be reapportioned. After those changes, African Americans had a voice in Louisiana elections. Since the 1970s, more African Americans have been elected to local and state offices.

The first African American to be elected to the legislature in the twentieth century was Ernest Morial from New Orleans. He was elected in 1967 and served until he became a judge. His seat was then held by the first African-American woman in the state legislature, Dorothy Mae Taylor. Morial went on to be elected the first African-American mayor of New Orleans in 1977. Marc Morial, his son, was elected mayor of New Orleans in 1994.

SUBURBAN GROWTH

The **interstate highway** system began with an act of Congress in 1956. These multilane, limited-access highways were planned to cover America from coast to coast. The two east-west highways that pass through Louisiana were begun during the 1960s. By 1976, Louisiana had more than five hundred miles of interstate highways. The elevated highway crossing the Atchafalaya Basin was an engineering marvel.

The interstate system brought changes to the landscape and the lifestyle of Louisiana. The small towns that were bypassed by the new highways soon declined. New businesses developed near the access ramps of the new interstates. Fast-food restaurants enticed travelers to stop for a quick meal. Cities changed as the highways crowded out old businesses and neighborhoods.

The interstates fed the growth of the suburbs. American cities developed **suburbs**, neighborhoods on the outer edges of cities, after World War II. When the soldiers returned from the war, they married and bought homes in the new subdivisions. The G.I. Bill helped finance that growth.

The I-10 bridge across the Atchafalaya Swamp received design awards even before it opened in March 1973.

Air conditioning and television antennas signaled the new technology available to suburban homeowners. New appliances such as dishwashers and clothes dryers changed the lifestyle of Louisiana's families. Shopping malls replaced downtown shopping districts and served as gathering places.

The conflict over integration in the city schools also added people to the suburbs. After the *Brown* ruling, the federal court had issued a second ruling known as *Brown II*. The justices stated that desegregation must be carried out "with all deliberate speed." At first, this was interpreted as allowing freedom of choice; students could request a transfer to a school where the majority of students were of another race. When this approach brought little progress toward desegregation, a new plan was introduced.

Desegregation in school districts was to be achieved through **busing**. That is, schoolchildren could be transported to a school out of their neighborhood to create schools that were racially "balanced." *White flight*

was the result. White parents moved their families to the suburbs to avoid the busing, and private schools were established in many parishes in Louisiana.

The changes of the 1960s and 1970s also included a new lifestyle for young Americans. Although most of the young people in Louisiana were not "hippies," evidence of the new culture could be seen in the state. In Jackson Square in New Orleans, tie-dyed clothing, bare feet, and long hair were common sights. The adults of the 1960s and 1970s were even more upset by this cultural change than they had been about the rock and roll of the 1950s. The conflict between the older generation and the younger generation centered around the Vietnam War. Fathers who were veterans of World War II were angry and disappointed that their sons wanted to dodge the draft instead of serving their country.

As American soldiers slogged through the rice paddies of Vietnam, the nation was dividing over America's involvement in the war.

VIETNAM

In the 1960s, the world turned its attention to a small area of southeast Asia. Vietnam was a divided nation, with North Vietnam controlled by the communists. Because the United States became more and more concerned about the growing threat and expansion of communism, Presidents Eisenhower and Kennedy sent military advisors to South Vietnam. The advisors were replaced with troops, and, by 1968, there were almost 600,000 Americans serving there.

Young soldiers from all over America were sent to Fort Polk in Vernon Parish for army training. The increase in population improved the economy of both Vernon and Beauregard parishes during this period.

People in Louisiana were generally more supportive of the war because there were so many military bases in the state. Children at a Baton Rouge elementary school wrote letters to the father of one of their third-grade classmates. His reply described Vietnam as looking much like the area between Baton Rouge and New Orleans. He also explained the war to the children: "War is so terrible that I doubt if anybody wins because the price is so high. But our forces are defeating the Viet Cong most every time we can find them, and I believe we will defeat them, though I am afraid it will be a long and hard war."

The *Shreveport Times* sent a special monthly Ark-La-Tex newsletter to three thousand troops serving in Vietnam. News briefs kept the soldiers up to date on life at home. Three army specialists from North Louisiana wanted a Louisiana state flag to fly in Vietnam. The *Shreveport Times* sent them a flag, which they flew proudly over their barracks. "We are proud to be from a state whose citizens are so civic minded. Of course, this spirit of patriotism and civic action is as old in Louisiana as the state itself. Many people gain honor in many and varied ways, but we know of no greater way than to say 'We are from Louisiana.' "

Local communities honored their citizens involved in the military in various ways. The New Iberia newspaper informed the town that Daniel Holmes, a local young man serving in the Navy, had been selected from among eight thousand men to be honored as "Sailor of the Month." In Lake Charles, the Young Men's Business Club built a tower as a memorial to peace.

Local support was also organized by the Red Cross. In Baton Rouge, the group sponsored "Christmas in Vietnam" by having local women make drawstring cloth bags. Residents could pick up a bag and fill it with military-approved personal items. The bags were sent to Vietnam for several years.

Student protests, however, became louder as the war continued. A group of several hundred Louisiana State University students marched three miles from the campus to the old State Capitol. This protest followed the deaths of four college students at Kent State University in Ohio. The LSU students protested the use of U.S. military troops on unruly campuses. They wanted to "commemorate the deaths of our fellow students who were murdered." The rally was closed with the National Anthem, but many students refused to sing.

College students across the country joined in an antiwar moratorium on October 15, 1969. In Louisiana, this event was generally

The initial philosophical differences which grew from the Vietnam War gave way to anger, violence, demonstrations and the burning of draft cards and flags. On October 21, 1967, 50,000 anti-war demonstrators gathered around the Lincoln Memorial in Washington, D.C. Soon demonstrators stormed the Pentagon across the Potomac, clashing with military police.

President Lyndon Johnson (top) gradually increased the number of American troops in Vietnam. Because of the growing opposition to the war, Johnson did not seek re-election in 1968. During the 1968 election, Richard Nixon (above) declared he had a plan for ending the war. The last American combat troops did not leave Vietnam until 1972.

peaceful and uneventful. At LSU and Tulane University, crosses were planted to symbolize the war dead. The antiwar groups at most Louisiana campuses were a small part of the student body. At Northeast Louisiana University in Monroe, where enrollment was about 7,000, only about 300 students attended the rally. At Nicholls State in Thibodaux, the demonstration was canceled, and more than 2,000 students wore buttons that said "I am proud I am an American."

Some young Americans supported the war effort. More than one thousand students from Loyola University in New Orleans sent President Lyndon Johnson a petition supporting the war. College students in the Shreveport area organized the Young Americans for Freedom group in 1966. Students from Louisiana Tech and from Centenary College led the group supporting the war. They described the protests as "irresponsible mutterings" and urged students to support the United States.

LOUISIANA CELEBRATES THE BICENTENNIAL

By 1976, the mood in the country had changed. Louisiana joined the nation in celebrating the Bicentennial of the Declaration of Independence. In every parish, bicentennial committees presented the local area's role in the two-hundred-year-old United States. Only Massachusetts had more communities involved in bicentennial programs than Louisiana.

An interest in local history and landmarks developed from the bicentennial effort. The United States Bicentennial Commission provided grants to local groups. Towns and cities around the state planned local projects. Baker restored an early twentieth-century home. St. Tammany Parish made a video on the history of the parish. Students at Southeastern Louisiana University were involved in an oral history project. The 1907 town hall in Slidell was renovated to become a museum. Beauregard Parish had a festival, and Bossier City painted an outdoor mural.

Louisianians were very interested in the national wagon train. Each state had one or more wagons, which traveled to Valley Forge, Pennsylvania, for July 4, 1976. Louisiana sent three wagons — a Conestoga, a prairie schooner, and a chuckwagon. The wagons left Shreveport, traveled through the state, and headed north on the Natchez Trace. Louisiana had not been a state in 1776, but the citizens of 1976 proudly celebrated the Bicentennial.

Do You Remember?
1. What was the "head and master law"?
2. What are suburbs?
3. What is "white flight"?

SUMMARY

Life for many in Louisiana during the 1960s and 1970s was challenging. Issues of segregation and civil rights forced people to reconsider values and standards that had been a part of their lives for generations. Schools became one of the first battlegrounds in this fight.

The U.S. Supreme Court decision in *Brown v. Board of Education of Topeka* addressed the inequality that existed in schools throughout the United States. For Louisiana, this meant change was inevitable. Desegregation started in New Orleans with protests and boycotts. Lawmakers developed plans to keep segregation. Efforts by organizations such as the NAACP were met with resistance. Boycotts, demonstrations, and marches characterized the frustrations felt by the African-American community.

Governor Jimmie Davis walked a careful path among angry legislators, federal laws, and African-American groups. His accomplishments include the Sunshine Bridge, the Toledo Bend Dam, and a code of ethics for state government.

Davis's successor, John McKeithen, also faced racial unrest. McKeithen appointed a statewide biracial committee to bring the groups together and ease the tensions. He also struggled with labor problems and allegations of organized crime in Louisiana.

Edwin Edwards became governor in 1972. This popular Cajun from Crowley campaigned for social programs and for a new constitution. Other laws passed during his two terms changed the way government operated and how labor unions operated in the state.

Political and social changes brought more opportunities for women and minorities. For the first time in Louisiana's history, African Americans held legislative positions. The development of the interstate highway system led to other changes, such as the growth of suburbs. With U.S. involvement in Vietnam, Louisiana was once again the site of numerous training facilities.

The whole nation celebrated the Bicentennial in 1976. These July 4th fireworks are over Liberty Hall in Philadephia. Only Massachusetts had more communities involved in bicentennial programs than Louisiana.

CHAPTER · REVIEW

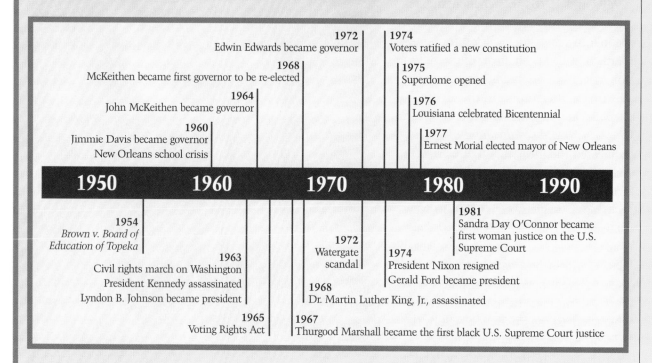

1972
Edwin Edwards became governor

1968
McKeithen became first governor to be re-elected

1964
John McKeithen became governor

1960
Jimmie Davis became governor
New Orleans school crisis

1974
Voters ratified a new constitution

1975
Superdome opened

1976
Louisiana celebrated Bicentennial

1977
Ernest Morial elected mayor of New Orleans

| 1950 | 1960 | 1970 | 1980 | 1990 |

1954
Brown v. Board of Education of Topeka

1963
Civil rights march on Washington
President Kennedy assassinated
Lyndon B. Johnson became president

1965
Voting Rights Act

1972
Watergate scandal

1968
Dr. Martin Luther King, Jr., assassinated

1967
Thurgood Marshall became the first black U.S. Supreme Court justice

1974
President Nixon resigned
Gerald Ford became president

1981
Sandra Day O'Connor became first woman justice on the U.S. Supreme Court

Reviewing People, Places, and Terms

Define, identify, and explain the importance of each of the following.

1. bill of rights
2. boycott
3. *Brown v. Board of Education of Topeka*
4. busing
5. Citizens' Council
6. Civil Rights Act of 1964
7. code of ethics
8. deregulation
9. integration
10. interposition
11. interstate highways
12. NAACP
13. propaganda
14. sit-in
15. suburbs
16. sunshine law
17. Voting Rights Act

Understanding the Facts

1. How did the Louisiana legislature react to the court-ordered desegregation of New Orleans schools?
2. Why did business leaders in New Orleans urge residents to accept school desegregation?
3. Name two accomplishments of Governor Davis during his 1960-1964 term of office.
4. How was Governor McKeithen able to run for re-election?
5. What changes in the severance tax led to increased revenues for the state?
6. What was the significance of the U.S. Supreme Court's ruling in *Baker v. Carr*?
7. How did the interstate highways change life in Louisiana?

Developing Critical Thinking

1. In your opinion, do some groups today still experience discrimination? Explain.

2. Tax money was used to build the Superdome. But the Superdome has also created almost $4.6 billion of spending in New Orleans. Do you think building the Superdome was a wise use of state funds? Should this money have come from private investors?

Using Your Skills

1. Compile a list of the civil rights granted to citizens in the U.S. Constitution and in the state constitution. How do the two lists overlap? What are the differences?
2. Trace the path of the Louisiana Bicentennial wagon train through the state on a map. The order of the towns visited was: Shreveport, Stonewall, Mansfield, Pleasant Hill, Marthaville, Natchitoches, Montgomery, Colfax, Alexandria, Pineville, LeCompte, Bunkie, Ville Platte, Eunice, Crowley, Lafayette, Youngsville, New Iberia, Breaux Bridge, Butte LaRose, Krotz Springs, Erwinville, Port Allen, Baker, Baton Rouge, Denham Springs, Port Vincent, Gonzales, Lutcher, Norco, Metairie, New Orleans, and Slidell.

Special Projects

1. What do you think life was like for teenagers in the 1960s or 1970s? Make a list of clothes, music, movies, television, and fads that you associate with either decade. Next, interview an adult who was a teenager during that period. Write an essay comparing and contrasting your assumptions with the information from your interview.
2. How has the interstate highway system affected life in your area? Interview several adults to get their opinions about change in your community. Make a list of businesses that closed or moved because of the interstate.

Making Connections

1. Americans who were old enough to remember November 22, 1963, can describe in detail how they learned of the death of President Kennedy. Ask at least one person how he or she heard the news. Write up the interview in a question-and-answer format.
2. Make a poster or collage expressing the meaning behind President Kennedy's quote.

• BUILDING SKILLS: CONDUCTING INTERVIEWS •

Interviewing people who lived Louisiana's history brings interest and information to our study of state history. When conducting an interview, follow the steps below to ensure that you get the information you want or need.

1. Before you schedule the interview, call or visit the person to get permission for the interview.
2. Plan and then write out the questions you will ask. You might start with *who*, *what*, and *where* questions.
3. Either write or tape-record the person's answers, after first asking and receiving permission to do so.
4. When you are finished, thank the person for the information.
5. Soon after the interview, go over your notes or listen to the tape recording. You may remember another point that was not included.

Try This! Many people make contributions at the local level but never receive national or statewide acclaim for their efforts. Interview relatives or other responsible adults who have lived in your area for some time. Ask them for information about local citizens who have made contributions of note. Record the names and achievements of those individuals. Be sure to find out the essential information about the individual's achievements (time period, motives, obstacles faced, people who benefited, and so on). Bring the information to class to share.

CHAPTER SIXTEEN

LOUISIANA'S CONTEMPORARY ERA: PROBLEMS AND PROSPECTS

The romantic and historic past, the bustling, industrial present, and the boundless future are happily combined in Modern Louisiana.
— Edwin A. Davis, noted Louisiana historian

TODAY IN LOUISIANA, Anthony heads for soccer practice in Covington, while in Plain Dealing Alice goes to the gym for basketball practice. Taylor surfs the Web at the library in Shreveport, while Laura babysits her preschool neighbors in Castor. Sam and his dad load their gear for a canoe trip on Alligator Bayou. In Webster Parish, Hays cleans the bream he caught in the pond. Elsewhere in the state, Chip heads for the golf course, and Jason meets his friends at the video arcade. Lizzie saddles her horse for a short ride, and Sophie goes to the mall.

Young people in Louisiana share the interests and dreams of all American young people. At the same time, the unique culture and special environment of Louisiana still shape their way of life. Their story of Louisiana connects yesterday, today, and tomorrow.

Contemporary New Orleans is a study in contrasts. These modern office towers exist not far from the lacy balconies of the Vieux Carré.

THE LOUISIANA ECONOMY

An economic crisis hit Louisiana during the 1980s. In the 1970s and early 1980s, the **Organization of Petroleum Exporting Countries** (OPEC) and non-OPEC oil producers succeeded in forcing the price of crude oil up to record amounts. From a price of $1-$2 per barrel in 1970, oil prices skyrocketed to $12 a barrel in 1975 and $40 a barrel in 1981. The severance tax on the oil produced in Louisiana added millions of dollars to state revenues.

But the oil boom turned into an oil bust. The high oil prices were an economic hardship on oil-importing countries and led to a worldwide recession. (A **recession** is a temporary downturn in economic activity or prosperity.) With the recession, demand for oil decreased. Energy conservation and improved technology also decreased the demand for oil. In addition, new sources of oil in the North Sea and Alaska and overproduction, especially by the non-OPEC countries, soon resulted in an oil surplus. Oil prices began to decline sharply. The price of a barrel of oil dropped so low that drilling was no longer profitable. Drilling in Louisiana halted, and unused oil field equipment was stacked in vacant lots.

Oil prices dictated the health of Louisiana's economy . With declining oil prices, the economy suffered. Businesses failed, and a record number of bankruptcies were filed. **Bankruptcy** is a legal judgment that a person or organization cannot pay its debts and its financial affairs must be administered to pay off those debts. During the 1980s, Louisiana had the highest unemployment in the nation. The population actually declined as people moved to other states to find work. The future seemed bleak.

The severance tax income that had kept the state budget balanced dropped drastically. Instead of having plenty of money for pet projects and new programs, the state now had trouble meeting its basic budget requirements. At the same time, the federal funding that had supported many programs was also reduced. With the loss of tax income, the governors and the legislature faced financial trouble. The state budget faced cuts. Funding for education was cut, with colleges and universities especially hard hit. Maintenance for roads and state buildings suffered from the loss of funds. Many state parks were closed during this budget crisis.

Low oil prices continued throughout the 1980s. The state's economy started to improve in the early 1990s. One boost came from the Persian Gulf War of 1991. That conflict, which began when Iraq invaded Kuwait, led to a rise in oil prices.

Another economic problem involved Texaco. Louisiana's attorney general, William Guste, claimed that the huge oil company owed royalties to the state. The legal battle was finally settled in 1994, with an agreement that Texaco pay the state $250 million and spend $152.2 million for more drilling on state-owned lands.

THE 1984 NEW ORLEANS WORLD'S FAIR

In 1884, New Orleans hosted the World's Industrial and Cotton Centennial Exposition. In the 1970s when the state's economy was booming, planning a 1984 world's fair seemed like a good idea. The state could celebrate the one-hundredth anniversary of the earlier exposition. New Orleans attracted many tourists, and the fair was expected to bring even more people to the state. Planning for the event involved private and public funding. The official title of the fair describes its theme — *The World of Rivers: Fresh Water as a Source of Life*.

But by the time the Louisiana World Exposition opened in May 1984, the state's economy was struggling. Although more than 7 million people visited the fair, more than 11 million visitors were needed to meet expenses. Officials gave free tickets to schoolchildren to increase attendance. Those visitors who did attend complimented the event. A favorite attraction for the children was the Kiddie Car Wash, designed to cool them in the sweltering summer heat.

The state and the city eventually provided financial assistance to cover the costs. That bailout was controversial because at the time state revenues had dropped. Today, that investment has proved to be a long-term, positive benefit for the New Orleans economy. The exhibit hall constructed for the fair has been converted into a convention center. The Riverwalk, now enclosed as a shopping and dining center, allows visitors to enjoy a close view of the Mississippi River. Shops and art galleries fill the nearby warehouse district.

More than 7 million people attended the 1984 New Orleans World Exposition.

POLITICAL TRENDS

Politics in Louisiana changed in the 1980s. The growth of the Republican party pushed the state toward a two-party system. Before this period, most of the state's voters were registered as Democrats. Political battles took place within the Democratic party rather than between the two parties.

The first sign of developing Republican strength was the candidacy of Republican Charlton Lyons in the 1963 governor's race. The number of registered Republicans was not enough to be a real threat to the Democratic control, but statewide advertising promoted the Republican candidate and brought attention to the party.

But in 1972, Louisiana sent a Republican to Congress, something that had not happened since Reconstruction. David Treen was elected to represent his Jefferson Parish district in Washington. In the Congressional election of 1974, Henson Moore of Baton Rouge became the second Republican Congressman from Louisiana.

The growing strength of the Republican party was due in part to the 1973 open primary law. Voters could cast their ballots for candidates from any political party. Many registered Democrats voted for Republican candidates. This was not what the Democrats in power had intended when they changed the system.

LOUISIANA IN CONGRESS

The growth of the Republican party in Louisiana is reflected in the state's Congressional delegation. The 1996 election sent five Republicans and two Democrats to the House of Representatives.

The Democratic party, however, has continued to hold both of Louisiana's seats in the U.S. Senate. Russell Long, the son of Huey Long, went to Washington as a Louisiana senator in 1948, when he was only thirty years old. By the time he retired in 1986, Russell Long had become a powerful and influential senator. John Breaux of Crowley was elected in 1986 to fill the seat held by Long. Louisiana's other long-time senator was J. Bennett Johnston from Shreveport, who was first elected in 1972. At one time, he served as the chairman of the Senate Energy

Top: *Russell Long was a U.S. senator for almost forty years.* **Above:** *Senator J. Bennett Johnston from Shreveport.*

and Natural Resources Committee. Johnston's 1996 retirement opened the door for another change.

Mary Landrieu made history by becoming the first woman to be elected as a U.S. Senator from Louisiana. The daughter of a former mayor of New Orleans, Landrieu was just twenty-three when she was elected to her first political office in the Louisiana house of representatives. In the election of 1996, Landrieu defeated Republican Woody Jenkins.

A long-time conservative politician, Jenkins had also served in the Louisiana house. Jenkins challenged the election results and pushed for an investigation. He claimed that there was vote buying and accused the gambling interests in New Orleans of influencing the election. The Senate investigated his claims and then declared Landrieu the official winner.

GRASSROOTS POLITICAL MOVEMENTS

In the early 1980s, ordinary citizens also became involved in government and lobbied for legislative change. **Mothers Against Drunk Driving** (MADD) forced the state to focus on the very high number of accidents and deaths caused by drunk drivers. MADD convinced the legislature to increase the penalties for DWI (driving while under the influence).

At about the same time, a group of state legislators led the effort to enact a law requiring Louisiana schools to teach the Biblical account of creation. The supporters of this idea called it the Creation Science Bill. Opponents said the law was a religious opinion rather than a scientific theory, and they asked Governor David Treen to veto the bill. However, after the state legislature passed it, the governor signed the bill into law. Opponents appealed in court, and the U.S. Supreme Court said the law was unconstitutional because it required teaching religion in school.

Do You Remember?
1. What caused the oil surplus in the 1980s?
2. What was the theme of the 1984 world's fair in New Orleans?
3. What laws did the MADD lobby affect?

Mary Landrieu (top) was the first woman elected U.S. senator from Louisiana, defeating Republican Woody Jenkins (above).

The political trends of the 1980s and 1990s are reflected in the men chosen by the state's voters as their governors.

In 1979, David Treen of Jefferson Parish was the first Republican elected governor of Louisiana in the twentieth century.

DAVID TREEN

By 1979, Louisiana's Republican party was ready to elect a governor. David Treen won that election and became the state's first Republican governor in the twentieth century. Nationally in 1980, voters elected Republican Ronald Reagan as president.

Treen had first run for the governor's office in 1971, but he was defeated by Edwin Edwards. After serving two consecutive terms, Edwards could not run in 1979. This opened the door for a new governor.

The 1979 governor's race was hard fought. The election was so bitter among the Democrats that several of them endorsed Treen rather than the Democrat in the runoff. Once elected, Governor Treen wanted to build alliances with the opposing factions. He appointed several Democrats to cabinet positions.

At the beginning of Treen's term, the state was still receiving a great deal of money from oil severance taxes. Because of this, the governor encouraged the legislature to cut the state's income tax as a benefit for voters. At the same time, the governor and the legislature increased the budget and added new programs. When the price of oil — and the severance taxes collected by the state— dropped, funding the budget became much more difficult.

To raise additional revenues, Governor Treen favored a special tax on the companies that operated in the wetlands. Called the Coastal Wetlands Environmental Levy (CWEL), the tax was intended not only to raise needed monies but also to help protect the fragile environment. However, the governor could not get enough legislative support to pass his tax plan. Without the money from the proposed tax, the governor struggled to meet the state's basic financial needs.

Governor Treen had a difficult term as governor. The economic problems made those years hard for Louisiana. He was criticized for his bailout of the 1984 world's fair in New Orleans at a time when state revenues were dropping. Also, Treen's leadership style was described as too low key. Critics said he was not available to the people. Louisiana expected its governor to be a public figure, seen frequently around the state.

EDWIN EDWARDS

Because of these problems, the voters chose to return Edwin Edwards to the governor's office in 1983. For the beginning of his third term, Edwards arranged quite a show. Versailles, the palace of King Louis XIV of France, heard talk about Louisiana in the eighteenth century, when it was a French colony. In the twentieth century, conversation about Louisiana again filled Versailles for one unusual night. The state's Cajun governor took his supporters on an extravagant fund-raiser to the elegant structure outside Paris, where they had dinner. The trip cost contributors $10,000 each. More than six hundred people went on the trip. Some were reporters and legislators, who were allowed to travel at cost.

However, attention soon shifted from the excitement of the trip to new problems. By February 1985, the U.S. attorney had indicted (formally accused) Edwards and seven others for wrongdoing regarding hospital and nursing home permits. The first trial resulted in a *hung jury*; that is, the jurors could not agree on a verdict. In the second trial, Edwards was acquitted (found not guilty).

In his third term, Edwards also faced serious economic problems. The low price of oil meant the state's economy still struggled. Edwards's style, however, seemed more suited to the easy years than to this time of crisis.

CHARLES "BUDDY" ROEMER

The problems Edwards faced brought out a long list of opponents in the 1987 gubernatorial election. In the first primary, Edwards did not get the most votes; he received only 28 percent of the votes. The list was headed by Charles E. "Buddy" Roemer III who received 33 percent of the votes cast. Because he was the incumbent, Edwards had expected to receive the most votes. When he did not, Edwards dropped out of the race entirely.

This meant that Roemer became the governor without a runoff election. Buddy Roemer had been considered an unlikely winner when he entered the race. The other candidates began with more statewide name recognition. Roemer had served Louisiana as a congressman from the Shreveport district.

Roemer campaigned as an outsider who would bring change. He promised reform, and his supporters labeled his campaign the "Roemer Revolution." Although Roemer was a Harvard graduate, his speeches referred

Controversial Governor Edwin Edwards answers reporters' questions outside the federal courthouse on the first day of his 1985 trial, which ended in a hung jury. Edwards was acquitted following a second trial.

When he was inaugurated governor in 1988 (above), Charles "Buddy" Roemer of Bossier Parish faced serious problems with the state budget.

more often to his boyhood on a Bossier Parish farm. He received a big boost when most of the major newspapers of the state endorsed him.

As governor, Roemer faced major budget problems. Decreased state revenues made it hard to operate state government, and the new governor faced a huge budget deficit. The governor and the legislature established a new system that allowed the state to borrow money. This Louisiana Recovery District was praised by some as a way to save the state's finances and criticized by others as poor management.

Governor Roemer also had plans to totally change state taxes. While the state does have a personal income tax and a property tax, Louisiana gets most of its revenue from taxes on businesses and from the sales tax. (Other states get more of their revenue from property taxes.) The governor wanted to shift some of the tax burden off businesses by increasing personal income taxes and allowing local governments to increase property taxes. Governor Roemer proposed that the amount allowed for the homestead exemption from property taxes be lowered. However, the governor soon discovered that Louisiana's residents preferred to keep their property taxes low and the homestead exemption untouched. His tax reform plan failed to get the support needed.

Another reform plan was more successful. Governor Roemer established the position of state **inspector general** to uncover fraud and waste in government. To fill the position, he appointed Bill Lynch, who had been an investigative reporter for the *Times-Picayune*. Citizens were able to report suspected fraud to Lynch, who investigated and then forwarded his findings to the governor.

Another Roemer program focused on education. The governor believed that evaluating teachers would improve Louisiana's educational future. He increased teacher pay and developed a plan for intense teacher evaluation.

One of Governor Roemer's actions surprised the state. He had been a long-time Democrat who spoke of his admiration for President Kennedy. In the middle of his term, he announced that he was changing to the Republican party. He also was criticized by supporters who said he was not consistent with his positions.

THE RETURN OF EDWIN EDWARDS

The next gubernatorial primary election saw Edwin Edwards receive the highest number of votes for the governor's office; David Duke from Metairie was second, and incumbent Governor Roemer was third. The runoff election, then, was a race between Edwards and Duke. This election drew national attention because of the controversy surrounding David Duke.

In the 1970s, Duke often spoke at the LSU Free Speech Alley. In those speeches, he blamed Jews and blacks for America's problems. Later Duke was a leader in the Ku Klux Klan but was careful to say that he did not advocate violence. By 1989, he had toned down his speeches and was elected to the state legislature from Jefferson Parish. He continued to say that whites were being unfairly treated because blacks were given too many special rights. In 1990, he ran an unsuccessful but strong race for the U.S. Senate against J. Bennett Johnston. By 1991, Duke decided to run for governor of Louisiana.

The runoff election attracted media attention from around the world. Reporters uncovered and published more information about Duke's beliefs and his past speeches and activities. Influential people in business began to speak out, concerned about the backlash the state could experience if a person who was so openly racist became governor. Even though Edwards had lost some of his earlier support, many people urged his election. The idea of David Duke being governor frightened many Louisiana citizens, both black and white.

As a result, in 1992 Edwin Edwards became governor for the fourth time, the only person since statehood to hold the office for so many terms. During this Edwards term, there was a dramatic increase in state spending on Medicaid programs. **Medicaid** is a program that provides health care for the poor, partly funded by the federal government and partly by the state.

The 1991 gubernatorial election was between Edwin Edwards and David Duke (above). The campaign drew national attention because of Duke's racist background.

THE PERSIAN GULF WAR

One legacy of the Vietnam War was a reluctance to get involved in foreign wars. That changed in 1991 when Iraqi dictator Saddam Hussein's army invaded neighboring Kuwait. Although some felt that the Gulf War was more about protecting America's oil supply than liberating Kuwait, troops around the nation got a rousing welcome home.

Conflict in the Middle East led the United States into the Persian Gulf War in 1990. Iraqi dictator Saddam Hussein invaded Kuwait in an attempt to expand his power. This invasion violated Kuwait's sovereignty and threatened the Mideast oil supply.

The United Nations called on Hussein to withdraw from Kuwait, but he refused. U.S. President George Bush imposed economic sanctions (penalties) against Iraq and sent diplomats to try to resolve the crisis. When those efforts failed, President Bush ordered reserve military units to report for duty and sent U.S. troops to the Middle East in preparation for possible conflict. This military action became known as "Desert Storm."

As U.S. bombers reached Iraqi air space, the president's press secretary announced, "The liberation of Kuwait has begun." The first planes were B-52 bombers from Barksdale Air Force Base in Bossier Parish. The 14,000-mile flight took thirty-five hours, and the planes refueled in the air four times.

The number of U.S. troops sent to the Persian Gulf region reached 500,000. Many members of the Army Reserves left their civilian jobs in Louisiana to serve in this war. Louisiana sent several specialized groups, including medical and transportation companies. Although the war was over in six weeks, many of the troops spent a much longer time in the Middle East.

Louisiana was also affected by the war in another way. Oil prices rose in the United States. With the oil price slump ended, Louisiana's economy improved.

Governor Edwards's fourth term was not without controversy. Federal investigations revealed that some people were submitting improper Medicaid charges. In addition, concern about state-sponsored gambling increased. The governor surprised the state when he announced he would not run for office again.

MURPHY J. "MIKE" FOSTER

In 1896, Louisiana voters elected Murphy Foster as governor. One hundred years later, in 1996, another Murphy Foster, the grandson of the first, took the governor's oath of office. This Murphy Foster, who prefers to be called "Mike," is a Republican. He had announced his change to the Republican party before he entered the race. His grandfather had led the conservative Democrats against the challenge of the Republicans and the Populists. The earlier Murphy Foster might be surprised at the party of his grandson, but he would not disapprove of his conservative views.

Mike Foster described himself as a conservative businessman and promised to run the state the same way. His opponent, Cleo Fields, was the first African-American candidate to reach the gubernatorial runoff election in the twentieth century. Fields had been a member of Congress before he ran for governor. Both candidates promised not to campaign on race but to debate the issues. Foster campaigned as a conservative and Fields as a liberal. Political observers said that once again the state had eliminated the moderate candidates in the center, leaving only the right and the left of the political spectrum.

As governor, Foster benefited from a strong economy. The national economy and the oil industry had improved since the 1980s, and growth in other industries had helped move Louisiana away from its

Republican Murphy (Mike) Foster celebrates his victory in the 1996 governor's race.

total dependence on oil. Louisiana's economic growth provided a good climate for Foster's programs. He approached problems with a direct no-nonsense style and frequently said that the state should be run like a business.

Governor Foster appointed a very young man to head the important Department of Health and Hospitals. Bobby Jindal was a graduate of Baton Rouge High School who went on to become a Brown University graduate and a Rhodes Scholar. At age twenty-four, Jindal faced a budget crisis that threatened health care and Medicaid. He soon earned praise for the changes that headed the program in the right direction. Jindal's reforms saved the state millions of dollars. In 1998, he was selected to head a Medicare improvement program in Washington, D.C. **Medicare** is a federal government program that pays for medical care for people sixty-five and over.

Governor Foster also directed his attention to other insurance programs. Voters were concerned about the high cost of insurance. Louisiana has an elected commissioner of insurance; two previous insurance commissioners had been convicted of taking bribes. The public demanded reforms and expected closer supervision of insurance regulations. The voters had also begun to complain about the high rates of automobile insurance. The 1997 legislature voted to raise the driving age from fifteen to sixteen to help bring down the insurance rates.

An earlier effort to make the highways safer and reduce insurance costs had required the state to raise the legal age for buying alcohol from eighteen to twenty-one. The National Minimum Drinking Age Law, signed into law by President Reagan in 1984, required states to adopt the law or lose federal highway funds. The Louisiana legislature adopted that law in 1986.

Governor Mike Foster and his wife Alice are seen here at home, posing with the governor's collection of duck decoys.

Do You Remember?

1. Which governor provided funds to help rescue the 1984 world's fair?
2. Where did Edwin Edwards take his supporters after his election?
3. What was Governor Roemer's plan to stop government fraud and waste?
4. What grandfather and grandson have both served as governors of Louisiana?

GAMBLING

In 1991, Louisiana became one of a growing number of states to use a lottery to raise money for the state. However, unlike the private corrupt lottery of the nineteenth century, this lottery is operated by the state under close regulation.

Once the lottery was established, the legislature began to approve other forms of gambling. It approved video poker machines and riverboat casinos in 1991. The riverboat casinos in Lake Charles, Shreveport, and Bossier City attract large crowds from nearby Texas. New hotels and other related businesses have been built near the casinos. The legislature then approved a land-based casino in New Orleans. Controversy developed when the gambling company opened a temporary casino and then claimed bankruptcy.

In 1996, Louisiana voters faced local option decisions on gambling in their parishes. That is, voters in each parish could decide to end any form of gambling or all gambling in the parish. Many parishes voted to make video poker illegal. Many experts consider video poker to be the most addictive form of gambling. Parishes that voted for video poker argued in favor of the economic benefits.

But state-sponsored gambling has brought problems along with a new revenue source. There have been scandals involving influence peddling by state officials and bribery of state officials. Citizens continue to debate the issue of gambling.

The Casino Rouge in Baton Rouge is just one of the riverboat casinos anchored in the Mississippi River.

ENVIRONMENTAL ISSUES

After years of neglect, Louisiana's environment is receiving attention. For years, the benefits of industrial development overshadowed concerns about the environment. Today, however, more and more citizens are urging the state to enforce federal and state environmental laws. The state must find a balance between economic development and environmental protection, especially as environmental problems become more obvious.

A recent environmental controversy centered on plans for a new PVC (polyvinyl chloride) plant in St. James Parish. Some residents favored the economic growth, while others said their neighborhood was unfairly chosen. Some critics say that poor communities get industries

that others do not want in their neighborhood. The small community of Grand Bois in Lafourche Parish received national coverage in 1997 over an oil field waste disposal dump. This situation is part of a national problem. Congressional legislation on hazardous waste exempted oil field waste from the strict controls of the federal Environmental Protection Agency (EPA).

Congress has taken action to help clean up some hazardous waste sites in Louisiana and in other states. A "Superfund" was established by a 1980 act of Congress. The chemical and petroleum industries are taxed to pay for the work. Louisiana has many sites on the program's cleanup list. The cleanup is supervised by the EPA and the state Department of Environmental Quality (DEQ).

Stricter regulations now control hazardous waste. The risks involved in transporting dangerous chemicals on the state's highways and waterways trouble environmentalists. A barge accident on the Mississippi River in 1997 sent a chemical cloud over Baton Rouge for days. Hundreds of nearby residents were evacuated until the area was safe.

Scientists are also studying the effects of polluted air and water on the residents of Louisiana. Water supplies are tested frequently for dangerous pollutants. Air quality is tested to ensure that ozone levels do not get too high. Fish from a number of rivers and lakes are tested for the presence of dangerous chemicals such as mercury.

The state is also concerned with saving the coastal wetlands. More than 80 percent of the total wetlands loss in the United States takes place along Louisiana's Gulf Coast. Louisiana has lost between 25 and 40 square miles of marsh a year for several decades. With the encouragement of Senator John Breaux, Congress passed legislation in 1990 to save the wetlands. The Coastal Wetlands Planning, Protection and Restoration Act (CWPPRA) provides federal funds for wetlands projects each year. Louisiana receives over $35 million for work that will help stop the loss.

A partnership between public and private agencies was formed to help save the environment. The Louisiana Natural Heritage Program was established in 1986 by the DEQ and the Nature Conservancy to identify significant natural habitats.

Senator John Breaux (above, right, with President Ronald Reagan) encouraged Congress to pass legislation to protect Louisiana's coastal wetlands, like these in Cameron Parish (top).

EDUCATION

Today, Louisiana has turned its attention to education for all citizens. Public education developed slowly in Louisiana because the first schools were private and Roman Catholic. Other early private schools were called *beneficiary schools*, which were partly supported by state funds. The Louisiana Constitution of 1845 called for a public school system, but the legislature provided little money to support the schools.

The Civil War slowed the development of education even

more. It was during the Reconstruction years that efforts were begun to provide public education for African Americans. After Reconstruction, Louisiana's schools developed into a segregated system that lasted well into the 1960s. That system deprived many children of an adequate education. With the end to segregation, more problems developed as schools adjusted to the changes.

The end of segregation was marked by the opening of the New Orleans branch of LSU in 1958. LSUNO (now the University of New Orleans) was opened to all students regardless of their race. Today, a consent decree outlines a plan for cooperation between the formerly one-race colleges and universities.

The limitations of poorly educated citizens affect everyone. For many years, people could make a living without much education. But twenty-first-century life requires more. A healthy economy needs educated workers, and economic diversity requires a work force with new skills. **Technology** (the practical use of scientific knowledge, especially in business and industry) is also driving the need for a better educated work force. People need training for the jobs of the future. Expanded vocational and technical education has become a new priority, and the state is establishing new community colleges and vocational schools to meet this need.

The Department of Education and other state and private organizations are cooperating to develop a comprehensive plan for education. A major effort to improve education at all levels began in 1986 when a special trust fund was established for education projects. The money for the trust fund was the result of federal legislation settling a dispute over offshore oil revenues. The fund is generally referred to as **8g**, which was the number of the amendment in the federal law. Each year,

Top: Today, 8g funds are being used to improve the state's schools. Northwood High School is one example. **Above:** *Technical and vocational schools, such as this one near Houma, provide important work skills to Louisiana residents.*

interest from the trust fund provides the money for between five hundred and eight hundred projects to improve education. Several recent projects have funded technology improvements in schools.

METROPOLITAN AREAS

Baton Rouge is just one of the cities in Louisiana that is revitalizing its downtown area.

During the 1980s, the economic recession led to a loss of population in Louisiana's cities. An improved economy in the 1990s has brought changes to Louisiana's metropolitan areas. The recovery can be seen in new businesses and new buildings.

A new north-south interstate highway has also brought North and South Louisiana together economically. Interstate 49 was finally completed in the mid-1990s after years of construction. Until I-49 was opened, most of the trip from Shreveport and Baton Rouge was made on two-lane highways, which were slow and dangerous. With the new interstate, travel between North and South Louisiana became much easier.

However, Louisiana's cities — large and small — struggle with the urban problems found in other cities across the United States. Louisiana's large inner cities face crime and poverty. Drug use and violence now affect all regions of the state.

Increased crime has increased the number of prisoners. New prisons have been built, including some that are operated by private companies. The state prisons in Allen and Winn parishes are part of this privatization of government services.

The move toward private involvement in community services can also be seen in urban renewal programs, intended to improve metropolitan life. The public and private cooperation is resulting in innovative ideas for revitalizing downtown areas. For example, in Baton Rouge the Mid-City Redevelopment Alliance has assisted residents in the inner city with home improvements. The Alliance has also encouraged businesses to return to the area. These efforts reflect a growing awareness of the need to improve the quality of life for everyone in Louisiana.

Do You Remember?
1. When did the current Louisiana Lottery begin?
2. What organizations supervise the cleanup of toxic waste sites in Louisiana?
3. How did the opening of LSUNO show progress for Louisiana?
4. What parts of Louisiana does I-49 connect?

QUALITY OF LIFE

A good quality of life allows Louisiana's young people to fulfill their dreams and reach their goals. *Culture* is the word used most often to describe the elements that measure the quality of life. Some of these cultural elements are art, literature, music, sports, and architecture.

Cultural elements in Louisiana continue to reveal the unique past of the state. The heritage of the many blended cultures is still strong. The result is an interesting mix of human activity.

THE ARTS

The arts are celebrated in formal and informal ways around the state. Art galleries and museums display important works of well-known artists, past and present. For example, the New Orleans Museum of Art was built in 1910 with a donation from a wealthy sugar planter. Much of the history of art in Louisiana can be learned from studying the exhibits there.

One famous Louisiana artist is a folk (or primitive) artist. Clementine Hunter was a self-taught artist who painted scenes of her days on Melrose Plantation in Natchitoches Parish. In strong, bright colors, Hunter depicted details in the daily lives of her neighbors. Hunter's simple but powerful expressions are prized by collectors throughout the world.

Photography is art as well as technology. Photographers record the Louisiana we all see, while showing us images through the artist's eye.

Top: This painting of a baptism is by folk artist Clementine Hunter of Melrose Plantation.
Above: The New Orleans Museum of Art displays many paintings by Louisiana artists.

Phillip Gould records the people and the landscape of South Louisiana. Neil Johnson has offered scenes of North Louisiana, as well as a photographic story of the state. In his nature photography and writings, C. C. Lockwood of Baton Rouge shares with readers his outdoor adventures in the Atchafalaya Basin and other exciting locations. Debbie Fleming Caffrey takes moody, evocative black and white photographs of Louisiana's people and places.

Sculpture is the art medium that is the means of expression for two well-known Louisiana artists. Some of Frank Hayden's outdoor works depict the history of Louisiana. Clyde Connell has created huge wood carvings in her studio near Lake Bistineau.

The music that accompanies life in Louisiana is varied. Music of the past and present combine to enrich Louisiana's culture. Young people are learning the old songs and techniques and showing a renewed interest in their cultural inheritance. Beginning musicians study jazz piano, blues harmonica, and Cajun fiddle. Other Louisiana music lovers, young and old, enjoy more recent forms of music. Rap music has spread in popularity, and reggae has been adapted from the Caribbean culture.

Symphony orchestras and opera were first heard in New Orleans when Louisiana was still a colony. Today, these classical forms of music are still enjoyed around the state.

The colonial culture also fostered the beginning of theater in Louisiana. For years, one theater in New Orleans presented plays in French, while the "American" theater offered the English-language version. Theater today includes professional acting companies as well as community groups of interested amateurs. Broadway touring companies provide another theatrical experience. Two beautifully restored theaters, the Strand in Shreveport and the Saenger in New Orleans, provide the proper setting for the big musicals and dramas from the New York stage.

LITERATURE

The art of the written word has described Louisiana since the journals of the explorers. Early well-known writers featured the culture and history of Louisiana. George Washington Cable reported life as he saw it, receiving criticism from his nineteenth-century contemporaries and praise for his honesty by later readers. Other nineteenth-century writers include Grace King, who wrote historical accounts, and Kate Chopin, whose fiction is considered ahead of its time.

More recent Louisiana writers have also received national prizes and recognition. Francis Parkinson Keyes wrote historic fiction set in Louisiana, and Lillian Hellman was a twentieth-century playwright. The Pulitzer prize has been awarded to these twentieth-century Louisiana writers: Oliver La Farge, Shirley Ann Grau, Robert Penn Warren, John

Kennedy Toole, and historian T. Harry Williams. Two of the most renowned twentieth-century writers are Walker Percy of Covington and Ernest Gaines of Pointe Coupee Parish. Percy's novels are considered literary masterpieces, and Gaines is noted for his writing about African-American experiences in Louisiana.

SPORTS

The climate of Louisiana makes outdoor sports a popular activity. One of the state's regions has even been called "Sportsman's Paradise."

Today, organized sports are available to anyone who wants to participate. Children and adults enjoy the fun and competition. Soccer has become a popular activity for both boys and girls in many towns and cities. In addition, high school and college sports are no longer mainly for boys. The federal Title IX regulations have opened up many more sports opportunities for girls.

All of the state's college teams attract loyal fans. The Louisiana Tech women's basketball team, the LSU baseball team, and the Southern University football team are among the championship teams that attract huge crowds.

Professional football attracts sell-out crowds to cheer on the New Orleans Saints in the Superdome. Professional hockey teams have added an interesting sport to this southern state. Lafayette was the first Louisiana city to welcome this sport, and the Ice Gators attract large crowds to their games. Shreveport and Baton Rouge also have ice hockey teams. Louisiana loves sports, and ice hockey now attracts enthusiastic fans.

Above: *St. Francisville's Grace Episcopal Church, built in 1858, is just one Louisiana landmark on the National Register of Historic Places.* **Left:** *The Pointe Coupee girls' volleyball team rides the ferry to a game.*

HISTORIC PRESERVATION AND MAIN STREET

All over Louisiana, old buildings tell stories of the state's past. After years of neglect, many of these buildings are getting new attention. Entire communities are joining together to save these landmarks. The state Division of Historic Preservation works to encourage these efforts. Private nonprofit organizations such as the Foundation for Historical Louisiana also support these efforts.

STATE PARKS

Top: *Winter Quarters State Commemorative Area at Newellton.* **Above:** *Sailing at Cypremort Point State Park on the Gulf Coast.*

For less than the price of a movie ticket, you can visit one of Louisiana's wonderful state parks. The state park system is operated by the Department of Culture, Recreation and Tourism. Visitors from around the world hike and camp in the parks. Local residents can return again and again to enjoy the natural environment.

The beauty of Louisiana is on display at the parks. Tall pine trees whisper overhead near Lake Claiborne. Spanish moss and live oaks set the scene at Lake Fausse Pointe. If you want to see every kind of tree native to Louisiana, go hiking at the State Arboretum at Ville Platte.

Lakes and bayous attract visitors for fishing and boating at many of the parks. Bass boats, canoes, bateaus, pirogues, racing boats, and sail boats are all found at one or another of the state parks. At the Grand Isle State Park, you can climb a lookout tower to see the ships in the Gulf of Mexico.

Some of the state parks are called commemorative areas. These are locations with special historical importance. The Audubon State Commemorative Area near St. Francisville features Oakley Plantation, the home where John J. Audubon stayed while he painted Louisiana birds. Further north, in Newellton, is Winter Quarters. This restored ante-

bellum home was the country home of a wealthy Natchez, Mississippi, plantation owner whose lands were on the Louisiana side of the river. Los Adaes is the site of a colonial Spanish fort established to keep the French from entering Spanish Texas. Archaeologists study the area to learn more about Louisiana's colonial history. As you walk on the grounds, you can imagine that long-ago life in the wilderness.

Interpretive programs at the commemorative sites provide more of the history of the sites. People in costume take you back in time to learn more about the past. You can participate in activities that are no longer part of everyday life in Louisiana.

You will have even more parks and commemorative areas to visit in the future. The state's long-range plan includes new parks on the Tickfaw River and in Tunica Hills. Watson Brake Mounds are a recently discovered prehistoric Indian site that will be protected by the state.

Top: The beautiful gardens at Audubon State Commemorative Area. ***Above:*** *A swamp in Sam Houston Jones State Park near Lake Charles.*

*Both Houma (above) and
Natchitoches (opposite, below)
have been designated as Main
Street towns. These and the
other Main Street towns have
restored many of their downtown historic buildings.*

The National Register of Historic Places is a list of important historical sites. Louisiana has more than a thousand listings on the National Register. The sites range from a railroad depot in DeQuincy in
Calcasieu Parish, to the Bank of Grand Cane in DeSoto Parish, to the
Rose Theater in Bastrop in Morehouse Parish. Other listings include
houses, schools, jails, businesses, public libraries, and churches.

The people who have always loved the old places because of their
history are now joined in preservation work by people who see an eco-
nomic benefit to the community. A new state program, called Main
Street, is working with these groups to save the downtown districts of
Louisiana's small towns. Some of these communities enhance their
downtown areas by restoring the brick streets of the past. The Main
Street program is a partnership between public and private organiza-
tions and applies to towns that have a population of fewer than 50,000.
Some of the Main Street towns are Abbeville, Amite, Columbus,
Covington, Denham Springs, DeRidder, Franklin, Hammond,

Houma, Jennings, Minden, Morgan City, Natchitoches, New Iberia, Opelousas, Plaquemine, Pontchatoula, Ruston, St. Francisville, St. Martinville, Springhill, Vivian, Winnfield, and Winnsboro.

Do You Remember?

1. What word is used to describe elements that measure the quality of life?
2. What is the focus of Ernest Gaines's writings?

SUMMARY

The last two decades of the twentieth century reflect the problems of life in contemporary Louisiana and point toward the positive prospects for the new century. One major problem plaguing Louisiana during this time has been the economy. In the 1980s, changes in the price of oil shut down oil fields and left many without jobs. Without a strong economic base, state government struggled to provide the needed programs for its citizens. Even the 1984 world's fair faced financial problems. Low atten-

dance placed another hardship on state finances.

Political trends have swung the Louisiana pendulum toward the Republican party, reflected by the 1979 election of Republican David Treen as governor. The terms of Governors Treen, Edwards, and Roemer were all difficult because of the poor economy. In 1992, Edwin Edwards returned for a fourth term as governor. He served the state longer than any other Louisiana governor. By 1996, the economy in the United States and in Louisiana had improved. Mike Foster, a Republican businessman, took advantage of this economic growth and instituted new state programs.

Legalized gambling has brought more money to the state as well as problems. New concerns for the environment have led to increased protection. Louisiana's long-term education problems continue to be discussed, with new plans being implemented. Metropolitan areas struggle with problems of crime as they experience economic growth. The complexity of life in Louisiana offers challenges for today and tomorrow.

CHAPTER · REVIEW

```
1979
David Treen elected first Republican governor
since Reconstruction
        1986                    1987
Education trust fund established    Buddy Roemer
        1984                    elected governor
        Louisiana World
        Exposition
```

```
1991
Edwin Edwards won fourth term as governor
State lottery started
                    1995
                    Mike Foster elected governor
                    1996
                    Mary Landreau elected
                    to U.S. Senate
```

1980   1990   2000

```
1980
Ronald Reagan
elected president
        1986
        Space shuttle Challenger
        exploded, killing seven

        1987
Pope John Paul II visited New Orleans
```

```
1991
Persian Gulf War
                1996
1989            Summer Olympics held
Berlin Wall torn down    in Atlanta, Georgia

1988
Republican National Convention met in New Orleans
```

Reviewing People, Places, and Terms

Define, identify, or explain the importance of each of the following.

1. 8g
2. bankruptcy
3. inspector general
4. Medicaid
5. Medicare
6. MADD
7. OPEC
8. recession
9. technology

Understanding the Facts

1. What caused Louisiana oil prices to drop in the early 1980s?
2. Why did the 1984 world's fair have financial problems?
3. Explain this statement: "The growth of the Republican party pushed the state toward a two-party system."
4. Who was the first Republican elected to Congress since Reconstruction?

5. Why was Governor Roemer's tax reform plan unsuccessful?
6. Why was David Duke a controversial candidate for governor?
7. What was so remarkable about the 1991 election of Edwin Edwards?
8. What is the Superfund?
9. Name three of the elements that define "culture."

Developing Critical Thinking

1. The following bumper sticker was spotted in Lafayette during the oil slump: "Will the last person to leave Lafayette please turn out the lights?" What does this imply about the economy of Lafayette during this period? What do you know about Lafayette that would explain why it was so hard hit by a drop in the price of oil?
2. How is a recession different from a depression?
3. Senator Russell Long described most people's attitude about taxes this way, "Don't tax me and don't tax thee, tax the man behind the tree." What did he mean? Do you agree that this describes most people's attitudes about taxes?

4. Privatization is a move to have private companies operate services formerly done by government. Some of Louisiana's prisons are now privatized. Make a list of five reasons for and five reasons against the privatization of Louisiana's prison system.

Using Your Skills

1. During the Persian Gulf War, planes flew from Barksdale Air Force Base to Saudi Arabia. If these planes traveled 14,000 miles in 35 hours, how many miles per hour did they travel? If they refueled four times, about how many hours did they fly before their first refueling?
2. Using a Louisiana highway map, locate the parish of each of the Main Street towns listed in this chapter. Then locate and label each town on a map of Louisiana's parishes.

Special Projects

1. Draw an editorial cartoon supporting the laws against drunk driving.
2. Congress is studying the possibility of adding another north-south interstate highway in the state. Which other Louisiana metropolitan areas need to be linked? Study a map to choose a route through the state for this new highway. With a partner, draw a map showing your proposed route. What present interstate highways might your new interstate connect?
3. Use your computer to find recent environmental information on Louisiana. Visit the Department of Environmental Quality Web site to discover current projects. Make a report of your findings to share with your class.

Making Connections

1. What part did the world supply of oil play in the Persian Gulf War?
2. How did the Persian Gulf War help Louisiana's economy?

Louisiana Lagniappe

* Governor Foster's home in St. Mary Parish is named Oak Lawn and once belonged to Alexander Porter, a wealthy Irish planter. This antebellum home is open for tours.
* The U.S. Navy has a submarine christened the *Louisiana*. This is the fourth vessel named for the state during the history of the U.S. Navy.

• BUILDING SKILLS: VISITING STATE PARKS •

You have the following task: For your vacation you want to visit as many of the state parks and commemorative sites as you can. However, you have two limits on your plans: time and money. As a result, you can travel no more than 550 miles round trip on your vacation; you cannot go over your mileage limit.

Use a list of the state parks and a state highway map to help you design your route. You may wish to choose a traveling companion to keep you company and to help in planning. Begin your trip from your starting point (your town or school). Visit as many sites as possible until you have used your allotted mileage. Remember to include the mileage needed to return home.

Present your vacation trip to the class by marking your route on a map. After completing your plan, answer the following questions.

1. What parks and historic sites did you include on your trip?
2. Will you visit all the parks and historic sites you want to see?
3. How did your starting point limit the number of sites you could include?
4. Why do you think the state chose to make the sites you visited into state parks?
5. Is there a local site that you would like to see developed into a state park? Why do you think it would make a good park?

STATE SYMBOLS

BIRD
Eastern Brown Pelican

COLORS
Blue, White, and Gold

CRUSTACEAN
Crawfish

DOG
Catahoula Leopard Dog

DRINK
Milk

FLOWER
Magnolia

FOSSIL
Petrified Palmwood

FRUIT
Tomato, Canteloupe

GEMSTONE
Agate

INSECT
Honeybee

MARCH SONG
"Louisiana, My Home Sweet Home"

MOTTO
Union, Justice, and Confidence

NICKNAMES
Bayou State, Pelican State, Sugar State

REPTILE
Alligator

SONGS
"Give Me Louisiana," "You Are My Sunshine," and "Song of Louisiana"

TREE
Bald Cypress

LOUISIANA GOVERNORS

FRENCH PERIOD

Governor	Term of Office
Pierre le Moyne, Sieur d'Iberville	1699
Sieur de Sauvole (died in office)	1699 - 1701
Jean Baptiste le Moyne, Sieur de Bienville	1701 - 1713
Antoine de le Mother Sieur de Cadillac	1713 - 1716
Jean Baptiste le Moyne, Sieur de Bienville	1716 - 1717
Jean Michiele, Siegneur de Lepinay	1717 - 1718
Jean Baptiste le Moyne, Sieur de Bienville	1718 - 1724
Pierre Duguém Sieur de Boisbriant	1724 - 1725
Etienne de Perier	1725 - 1733
Jean Baptiste le Moyne, Sieur de Bienville	1733 - 1743
Pierre Francois deRigaud, Marquis de Vaudreuil	1743 - 1753
Louis Billouart, Chevalier de Kerlerec	1753 - 1763
Jean Jacques Blaise d' Abbadie (died in office)	1763 - 1765
Charles Philippe Aubry	1765 - 1769

SPANISH PERIOD

Governor	Term of Office
Antonio de Ulloa	1766 - 1768
Alejandro O'Reilly	1769
y Amezaga Luis de Unzaga	1769 - 1777
Bernardo de Gálvez	1777 - 1785
Esteban Miro	1785 - 1791
Francisco Louis Hector, Baron de Carondelet	1791 - 1797
Manuel Gayoso de Lemos (died in office)	1797 - 1799
Francisco Bouligny	1799
Sebastian, Marquis de Casa Calvo	1799 - 1801
Juan Manuel de Salcedo	1801 - 1803

TRANSITIONAL PERIOD

Governor	Term of Office
Pierre Clement de Laussat	1803

TERRITORIAL PERIOD

Governor	Term of Office
William C. C. Claiborne	1803 - 1812

STATE PERIOD

Governor	Term of Office
William C. C. Claiborne	1812 - 1816
Jacques Philippe Villeré	1816 - 1820
Thomas Bolling Robertson (resigned)	1820 - 1824
Henry Schuyler Thibodaux	1824
Henry Johnson	1824 - 1828
Pierre Derbigny (died in office)	1828 - 1829
Armand Beauvais	1829 - 1830
Jacques Dupre	1830 - 1831
André Bienvenu Roman	1831 - 1835
Edward Douglass White	1835 - 1839
André Bienvenu Roman	1839 - 1843
Alexander Mouton	1843 - 1846
Isaac Johnson	1846 - 1850
Joseph Marshall Walker	1850 - 1853
Paul Octave Hebert	1853 - 1856
Robert Charles Wickliffe	1856 - 1860
Thomas Overton Moore	1860 - 1864
George F. Shepley (military governor)	1862 - 1864
Henry Watkins Allen (Confederate governor)	1864 - 1865
Michael Hahn	1864 - 1865
James Madison Wells	1865 - 1867
Benjamin Flanders	1867 - 1868
Joshua Baker	1868
Henry Clay Warmoth	1868 - 1872
P. B. S. Pinchback	1872 - 1873

John McEnery (elected, but ruled out) 1873

William Pitt Kellogg (declared) .... 1873 - 1877

Francis T. Nicholls .... 1877 - 1880

Louis Alfred Wiltz (died in office) .... 1880 - 1881

Samuel Douglas McEnery .... 1881 - 1888

Francis T. Nicholls .... 1888 - 1892

Murphy James Foster .... 1892 - 1900

William Wright Heard .... 1900 - 1904

Newton Crain Blanchard .... 1904 - 1908

Jaren Young Sanders .... 1908 - 1912

Luther Egbert Hall .... 1912 - 1916

Ruffin G. Pleasant .... 1916 - 1920

John M. Parker .... 1920 - 1924

Henry L. Fuqua (died in office) .... 1924 - 1926

Oramel H. Simpson .... 1926 - 1928

Huey P. Long (resigned) .... 1928 - 1932

Alvin O. King 1932

Oscar K. Allen (died in office) .... 1932 - 1936

James A. Noe 1936

Richard W. Leche (resigned) .... 1936 - 1939

Earl K. Long .... 1939 - 1940

Sam H. Jones .... 1940 - 1944

Jimmie H. Davis .... 1944 - 1948

Earl K. Long .... 1948 - 1952

Robert F. Kennon .... 1952 - 1956

Earl K. Long .... 1956 - 1960

Jimmie H. Davis .... 1960 - 1964

John J. McKeithen .... 1964 - 1972

Edwin W. Edwards .... 1972 - 1980

David Treen .... 1980 - 1984

Edwin W. Edwards .... 1984 - 1988

Charles Roemer III .... 1988 - 1992

Edwin W. Edwards .... 1992 - 1996

Murphy J. Foster .... 1996 -

LOUISIANA PARISHES

Parish	Date Founded	Parish Seat
Acadia	1886	Crowley
Allen	1912	Oberlin
Ascension	1807	Donaldsonville
Assumption	1807	Napoleonville
Avoyelles	1807	Marksville
Beauregard	1912	DeRidder
Bienville	1848	Arcadia
Bossier	1843	Benton
Caddo	1838	Shreveport
Calcasieu	1840	Lake Charles
Caldwell	1838	Columbia
Cameron	1870	Cameron
Catahoula	1808	Harrisonburg
Claiborne	1828	Homer
Concordia	1807	Vidalia
DeSoto	1843	Mansfield
East Baton Rouge	1810	Baton Rouge
East Carroll	1877	Lake Providence
East Feliciana	1824	Clinton
Evangeline	1910	Ville Platte
Franklin	1843	Winnsboro
Grant	1869	Colfax
Iberia	1868	New Iberia
Iberville	1807	Plaquemine
Jackson	1845	Jonesboro
Jefferson	1825	Gretna
Jefferson Davis	1912	Jennings
Lafayette	1823	Lafayette
Lafourche	1807	Thibodaux
LaSalle	1908	Jena

Lincoln	1873	Ruston
Livingston	1832	Livingston
Madison	1838	Tallulah
Morehouse	1844	Bastrop
Natchitoches	1807	Natchitoches
Orleans	1807	New Orleans
Ouachita	1807	Monroe
Plaquemines	1807	Pointe-a-la-Hache
Pointe Coupee	1807	New Roads
Rapides	1807	Alexandria
Red River	1871	Coushatta
Richland	1868	Rayville
Sabine	1843	Many
St. Bernard	1807	Chalmette
St. Charles	1807	Hahnville
St. Helena	1810	Greensburg
St. James	1807	Convent
St. John the Baptist	1807	Edgard
St. Landry	1807	Opelousas
St. Martin	1807	St. Martinville
St. Mary	1811	Franklin
St. Tammany	1810	Covington
Tangipahoa	1869	Amite
Tensas	1843	St. Joseph
Terrebonne	1822	Houma
Union	1839	Farmerville
Vermilion	1844	Abbeville
Vernon	1871	Leesville
Washington	1819	Franklinton
Webster	1871	Minden
West Baton Rouge	1807	Port Allen
West Carroll	1877	Oak Grove
West Feliciana	1824	St. Francisville
Winn	1852	Winnfield

GLOSSARY

A

abolitionist one who wanted to free the slaves (10)

Acadians French Canadians or descendents of French Canadians who migrated to Louisiana from Acadia (now Nova Scotia) in the eighteenth century (1)

agribusiness farming as a large-scale business operation (3)

agriculture farming (5)

alluvial soil soil that has been deposited by a river (2)

ally a person or country that cooperates with others on some projects (7)

amendment an addition or correction to a document, particularly a constitution (4)

anarchy an absence of government or a state of lawlessness (11)

ancestors those people from whom one is descended (5)

Anglos those with an English-speaking heritage (1)

annex to add territory to an already existing governmental unit, such as city, state, or nation (8)

antebellum the period before the Civil War (9)

archaeologist a scientist who studies the items left behind by ancient peoples to determine how they lived (5)

artifact an item left behind by ancient people and studied by archaeologists to determine how they lived; examples include bits of stone, bone, pottery, tools, cave paintings, weavings, skeletons, items buried with the dead, leftover trash (5)

atlatl a handle with weights used by prehistoric people to throw spears with more force and for farther distances (5)

attorney general the primary legal officer for the state (4)

B

Bailey's dam a wing dam built by Union forces in 1864 in order to raise the water level in the Red River so that Union gunboats could sail downriver (10)

bankruptcy a legal judgment that a person or organization connot pay its debts and its financial affairs must be administered to pay off those debts (16)

barrier island a sea island that protects the wetlands, estuaries, and bays from the direct impact of ocean waves (2)

barter trading goods and services without money (3)

bayou usually, a small and sluggish creek; may also be miles long and deep enough for navigation (2)

bicameral describes a legislative body made up of two houses (4)

bill a proposed law (4)

bill of rights a section of the state constitution that guarantees basic rights (15)

biological resources plants and animals; also called *flora* (plants) and *fauna* (animals) (3)

Black Code a series of laws passed by the legislature after the Civil War that restricted the freedmen's actions, movement, and conduct and that required the freedmen to sign one-year labor contracts (11)

blackout a period when a city had to be completely dark at night so that enemy planes could not locate it during an air raid (14)

blockade to use naval forces to isolate a seaport and prevent any ships from entering or leaving the port (8)

blues (the) a music style based on black folk music, especially on the chants of the black workers on the plantations; characterized by wavering "blue notes" (1)

bond a document that serves as proof of a long-term debt; the bondholder receives interest at set times and the original investment is returned at the end of a certain number of years (4)

bounty a one-time reward (10)

Bourbons the name given to those Redeemer-Democrats who held political power in Louisiana in the late 1800s; they supported states' rights and white supremacy and did not see the need for change (12)

boycott a refusal to deal with a person, store, or organization, usually to show disapproval or to force the acceptance of certain conditions (15)

Brown v. Board of Education of Topeka the 1954 U.S. Supreme Court case that resulted in the ruling that segregation was unconstitutional (15)

budget a plan for receiving and spending money (4)

busing transporting students to schools out of their neighborhoods in order to create racially balanced schools (15)

C

Cabildo the governing body of Louisiana while it was a Spanish colony; the Cabildo made legal decisions, set policy for the colony, and advised the governor (7)

calumet a peace pipe (5)

campaign a military plan with a specific goal (10)

canal a manmade waterway that connects other bodies of water, such as Louisiana's rivers and bayous (9)

capital the seat of government for a state or nation (8)

capital resources the money and property (factories, tools, bridges, machines, and so on) that are used to produce goods and services (3)

carpetbagger the term applied to a northern white who moved into the South to help carry out Congress's Reconstruction plan after the Civil War (11)

cartography mapmaking (2)

cash crop a crop that is raised to make a profit (6)

casket girls young women who came to Louisiana in 1728 to become wives of the settlers; the young women brought their trousseaus in a casket, or barrel-like chest (6)

caucus a group of legislators with specific interests who join together to promote bills that help their common goals (4)

censor to remove or suppress (13)

census an official count of the population conducted every ten years (4)

Citizen's Council an organization formed after the *Brown* decision to support segregation (15)

civil laws laws that deal with the relationships among individual citizens (4)

Civil Rights Act of 1964 a federal law that ended segregation by prohibiting discrimination in public facilities and in employment (15)

civil service system an employment system where workers take tests for government jobs and cannot be fired for their political views or party affiliations (14)

Civilian Conservation Corps a New Deal program that provided work for single young men between the ages of 18 and 25; the young men did soil conservation work and some road construction (13)

clan a group of people who believe themselves related by blood (5)

climate the average weather of an area over a long period of time, such as 25-30 years (2)

code of ethics a written description of the rules or standards under which an organization or profession should operate (15)

Code Noir a set of laws governing the conduct of the slaves during the French colonial period (6)

Cold War term used to describe the strained relationship between the United States and the Soviet Union after World War II; this "war" was mainly fought with words and diplomacy (14)

colony a group of people who settle in a distant land but who are still under the control of their native land (6)

compromise a way to settle disagreements in which each side gives way a little on its demands (9)

Compromise of 1850 legislation passed by Congress by which California was admitted as a free state, part of Texas was given to New Mexico, the slave trade was banned in the District of Columbia, the fugitive slave law was strengthened, and the issue of whether slavery would be permitted in New Mexico and Utah would be determined by a vote of the people living in those territories (10)

Confederate States of America the name of the government formed by the southern states when they seceded from the Union in the early 1860s (10)

confederation an entire group of related allies (5)

Confiscation Act legislation passed by the U.S. Congress in July 1862 that enabled Union forces to seize the property of rebels (10)

conscription a draft; compulsory enrollment for military service (10)

conservation the careful management of a natural resource to prevent its destruction (2)

constituents the people represented by an elected official (4)

constitution a document that sets up the broad organization of a government, or any other organization, and the rules under which it will operate; grants power to the government to act in the interest of the people but includes limits to protect the rights of the state's citizens (4)

consumer one who buys or uses goods or services (3)

contract a formal, written agreement (11)

convict lease system a method to earn money for the state by leasing convicts to private businesses; the convicts built bridges, levees, roads, and railroads and worked and lived under terrible conditions (12)

credit the ability to buy something now and pay for the item over a period of time (11)

Creoles those African-French people who were born in the Louisiana colony instead of in Europe or Africa (1)

criminal laws those laws intended to protect society from the wrongdoing of an individual (4)

cultural anthropologist a scientist who studies human cultures (1)

cultural diffusion the spreading of one's own culture (1)

culture a group's way of life and its own view of itself and other groups; elements of a culture include religion, music, food, clothing, language, architecture, art, literature, games, and sports (1)

D

deficit a situation that occurs when expenditures are more than revenues (4)

Department of Environmental Quality (DEQ) the Louisiana government agency charged with protecting the environment and maintaining it for future generations (3)

depression a severe, continued downturn in the economy where sales and prices drop, manufacturing decreases, businesses close, banks fail, and people lose their jobs (9)

deregulation the removal of federal rules and restrictions from an industry (15)

diplomat one who is skilled in dealing with others (8)

discrimination any actions that deny people their rights because of prejudice (9)

disfranchise to take the right to vote away from a person or group (12)

Dixiecrats members of the States' Rights Democratic party, a group of southern Democrats who left the party to oppose President Truman's re-election in 1948 because they objected to Truman's stand on racial issues (14)

E

8g refers to the education trust fund established in 1986 with funds from the settlement of the dispute over offshore oil revenues (16)

economy a community's system of producing, distributing, and consuming goods and services (3)

ecosystem a community of organisms — plants, animals, bacteria, and so on — and its environment that function as a unit in nature (2)

elevation the height of a place above sea level (2)

Emancipation Proclamation the 1863 proclamation by which President Abraham Lincoln freed the slaves in the Confederate states (10)

environment surroundings (2)

Environmental Protection Agency (EPA) the federal government agency charged with protecting the environment and maintaining it for future generations (3)

erosion the gradual wearing away of the land by the action of wind or water (3)

estuary the place where the river meets the sea; the mouth of a large river where its flow is affected by the tides (2)

ethnic group a group of people who have strong feelings of belonging and who share common traditions, beliefs, and patterns of living that include language, religion, customs, and cuisine (1)

executive branch that branch of government responsible for enforcing the laws of the state; also operates the state government and administers state services (4)

expedition a journey for a specific purpose, such as exploration (6)

exports goods sent out of the country for sale or sold to another country (9)

F

faction a small group with common goals within a larger group (9)

factor a commercial agent who provides financial and business assistance to clients (9)

fais-do-do a Cajun dance; French for "go to sleep" (1)

famine an extreme shortage of food (9)

Farmers' Union a farmers' organization started in 1888; the Union urged members to work together to keep their costs down (12)

Frasch process a technique, developed by Dr. Herman Frasch, of using superheated steam to melt underground sulphur and force it to the surface (3)

fraud deliberate deception for unfair or unlawful gain (11)

free people of color those of African heritage who were free during the years of slavery; *gens de couleur libre* (1); those of mixed blood; in early New Orleans, referred also to former slaves who had purchased their freedom (8)

freedmen former slaves (11)

Freedmen's Bureau a federal government agency established in 1865 to provide food, shelter, education, health care, and employment for former slaves in the South (11)

French and Indian War the name given to the conflict that took place in North America between France and Great Britain between 1754 and 1760; so named because the majority of Indian tribes sided with the French against the British (7)

fusion movement the name given to the cooperation of the Republicans and Populists in the late 1890s in an attempt to defeat the Democrats (12)

G

geography the study of the earth's natural features, climate, resources, and population (2)

goods physical items such as food, clothing, cars, and homes (3)

gospel music church music that blends elements of folk music, spirituals, hymns, and popular music (1)

governor the chief executive officer of the state; head of the executive branch (4)

grandfather clause a clause in the 1898 state constitution that, to register to vote, excused a person from proving he owned property and could read and write if he had been able to vote on January 1, 1867; the clause virtually disfranchised blacks (12)

Great Depression the depression that began in 1929 with the stock market crash and lasted into the 1940s (13)

guerrilla a member of a small military group that harasses the enemy (10)

gumbo a traditional Louisiana dish; a hearty Creole soup made of seafood, chicken, okra, and other vegetables (1)

H

hardwood a broadleaf, deciduous tree that sheds its leaves in winter (2)

heritage the values and traditions handed down from previous generations (5)

home rule the power of political subdivisions to govern themselves; local self-government (4)

human resources the people who supply the labor to produce goods and provide services (3)

hurricane a severe windstorm that originates over tropical ocean waters and whose wind speeds are at least 74 mph; hurricane winds rotate around an *eye* and get their energy from the warm, moist air (2)

I

immigrant one who moves into a new country in order to settle there (9)

immunity natural resistance to disease (5)

impeachment the process of bringing charges of wrongdoing against a public official while that official is still in office (4)

imports goods brought into a country to sell (7)

impressment the practice of forcing sailors into service against their will (8)

inspector general a position in the executive branch of state government concerned with uncovering fraud and waste in government (16)

integration the process of opening facilities to people of all races or ethnic groups without restrictions (15)

interdependence the concept that businesses and industries in an economy rely on each other and on other economies to succeed (3)

internal improvements roads, bridges, canals, and other transportation needs (9)

interposition the idea that the state legislature could place itself between the federal government and the people; a part of the states' rights argument (15)

interstate highways multilane, limited-access highways that extend through more than one state and are therefore part of the federal highway system (15)

Isleños Canary Islanders or those descended from Canary Islanders who were brought to Louisiana when it was a Spanish colony (1)

J

jambalaya a basic Spanish-Cajun dish made with rice and some other ingredient such as ham, shrimp, sausage, or chicken (1)

jazz a kind of music with strong rhythms and much syncopation (accents in unexpected places), often improvised; jazz was born in New Orleans (1)

Jim Crow laws laws that restricted the freedom of African Americans and required separate but equal public facilities for whites and for blacks (12)

judicial branch that branch of government that consists of the courts (4)

jury a group of citizens chosen to hear evidence on a legal case and to make a decision based on the evidence presented (4)

K

Knights of the White Camellia a secret organization that operated in Louisiana during military Reconstruction and that used threats and physical violence to keep the freedmen from voting or to force them to vote for Democratic candidates (11)

Ku Klux Klan a secret, racist organization that used violence and intimidation against those, especially immigrants and minorities, whose behavior or actions it did not like (13)

L

labor union an organization of workers formed to improve wages, benefits, and working conditions for workers (12)

land grant a parcel of land given to the directors of the Company of the West under the condition that they bring settlers to the colony (6)

latitude a system of imaginary lines that measure a location's distance north or south of the equator; also called *parallels* (2)

legislative branch that branch of government that is the law-making body (4)

lieutenant governor the official in the executive branch second in command to the governor (4)

lignite the lowest-quality coal; a soft, brownish-black coal that, because of its high water content, burns poorly (3)

lobbying the process of trying to influence a legislator about a proposed law (4)

longitude a system of imaginary lines that run from the North Pole to the South Pole and measure how far east or west a location is from the Prime Meridian, the arbitrary starting point at Greenwich, England; also called *meridians* (2)

Louisiana Lottery Company a private company that operated a lottery in Louisiana during the late 1800s; the lottery company held a great deal of political power because of the contributions it made to politicians (12)

Louisiana Purchase the 1803 purchase from France of over 600 million acres of land in North America for $15 million (8)

lowland South the Louisiana culture that developed in the low-lying lands along the rivers on which plantations were established (1)

M

map a document that shows the direction from one place to another and indicates the distance between those locations (2)

Mardi Gras "Fat Tuesday," the day before Ash Wednesday; the period before Lent celebrated with parties, balls, street dances, and parades (1)

marsh a wet, treeless prairie covered with water and grasses (2)

mastodon a prehistoric elephant like animal (5)

Medicaid a program that provides health care for the poor, partly funded by the federal government and partly by the state (16)

Medicare a federal government program that pays for medical care for people over 65; funded by employee payroll deductions and a matching employer tax (16)

mercantilism an economic policy under which a government strictly controlled its resources and its markets in order to acquire wealth (gold and silver), which the government used to build up its military forces and become even more powerful; the government worked to have a "favorable balance of trade"; colonies were expected to provide the raw materials needed for manufacturing *and* ready markets for the mother country's products (3)

midden a garbage mound left by prehistoric people (5)

militia a military force composed mainly of citizen-soldiers (7)

mineral resources inorganic substances that occur naturally in the earth; examples of mineral resources include oil, natural gas, salt, sulphur, and lignite (3)

Mississippi Bubble the collapse of the French investment company, the Company of the West (6)

Missouri Compromise the 1820 agreement by Congress that Missouri would enter the Union as a slave state and Maine as a free state and slavery would not be allowed in any states formed north of a line even with Missouri's southern border (10)

Mothers Against Drunk Driving (MADD) an organization that lobbied the state to change laws to increase the penalties for DWI (16)

mounds raised areas created by prehistoric peoples and thought to be used for ceremonial and burial purposes (5)

N

National Association for the Advancement of Colored People (NAACP) an organization formed in 1909 to work for equal rights for African Americans (15)

natural resources a gift of nature, part of the natural environment; includes the air, the soil, water, and minerals (3)

navigable describes water that is deep enough for safe travel by boat, canoe, pirogue, or skiff (2)

neutral not taking sides in a disagreement (7)

New Deal the name given to the programs enacted by Congress during President Franklin D. Roosevelt's first two terms to deal with the problems and hardships caused by the Great Depression (13)

noblesse oblige the belief that a person who has wealth and position should help those who do not (12)

nomad a wanderer (5)

nonrenewable refers to natural resources not replaced by nature once they are extracted from the environment (3)

Northwest Passage a water route that early Europeans believed went through the North American continent to Asia (6)

nutria a water rodent that eats the vegetation protecting the freshwater marsh, allowing salt water to move in (2)

O

open primary an election in which all candidates compete for a position regardless of political party; voters can choose any candidate also regardless of political party (4)

Organization of Petroleum Exporting Countries (OPEC) an international organization founded in 1960 to coordinate the petroleum policies and prices of its member states (16)

P

parish a political subdivision within the state (2)

pirogue a dugout made by Native Americans and the French; cypress logs were partially burned and the burned section scraped out (5)

plantation a large estate or farm (6)

police jury the form of government used in most of Louisiana's parishes; has five to fifteen elected members (4)

political alliance several groups of people joined together to support a political cause or candidate (4)

Populist a member of the People's party (12)

precipitation any form of water — liquid or solid — that falls from the atmosphere and reaches the ground (2)

president of the senate the official elected by the members of the state senate to preside over its sessions (4)

privateer a privately owned ship that was armed and, with the backing of a government, expected to capture the ships of the government's enemies (8)

producer the person or organization that makes or provides goods or services (3)

progressive movement a series of movements whose members believed that government was best equipped to correct the ills of society; progressives wanted government to fight poverty and improve the living conditions of citizens, to break up large corporations and regulate business, and to ensure that voters had more influence in government (12)

prohibition forbidding by law the making and selling of alcoholic beverages (13)

propaganda ideas, facts, or rumors spread to help a cause or to hurt an opposing cause (15)

proprietorship a system that gave an individual a charter (or contract) to operate a colony as a business (6)

Protestant a Christian non-Catholic (1)

Public Service Commission a state commission whose job it was to regulate transportation and communication companies; originally called the Railroad Commission (13)

pulpwood smaller, softer trees (mostly pine) that are shredded into pulp to be made into paper (3)

R

radical one who holds extremist views or wants drastic changes (11)

ratify to approve or make valid (13)

ration to limit the consumption of scarce resources or supplies (14)

reactionary one who strongly opposes progress (12)

reapportionment the process of redrawing the boundaries of legislative districts in order to achieve relatively equal populations (4)

rebellion open resistance to authority (7)

recession a temporary downturn in economic activity or prosperity (16)

Reconstruction the steps taken to restore the southern states to the Union and to rebuild the South after the Civil War (11)

region an area defined by similar features, which usually include common climate, landforms, and economic or recreational opportunities (1)

relief the difference between the highest and lowest elevation in a given area (2)

renewable refers to biological resources that replenish themselves in time (3)

right of deposit during the Spanish colonial period, the ability to store ("deposit") goods in warehouses in New Orleans before loading them onto ocean-going ships (7)

right-to-work law a law that allows workers to get and keep jobs without having to join a union (14)

royalty a payment made to land owners when oil is extracted from the land (14)

rural countrylike (1)

S

sabotage deliberate damage or destruction (14)

salt dome a formation of layers of rock that have folded upward, rising above the surface of the marsh; contains valuable minerals such as salt, petroleum, and sulphur (2)

scalawag the term applied to a native white southerner who supported the Republican party during Reconstruction (11)

scarcity the concept that there are not enough resources (natural, human, and capital) available to satisfy all needs and wants; as a result, choices must be made (3)

secession the withdrawal of a state from the Union (10)

secretary of state the chief election officer and keeper of the state's official records (4)

segregation public and social separation of the races (12)

separate-but-equal concept the concept resulting from the U.S. Supreme Court ruling in *Plessy v. Ferguson* that permitted states to pass laws that made it legal to have separate public facilities for whites and blacks (12)

services the work people do for others for a fee; examples include medical treatment, education, equipment and car repairs, haircuts, and concerts (3)

severance tax a tax on the resources taken from the land (13)

Share Our Wealth program: Huey Long's economic program that would have eliminated poverty by giving every family a minimum income; the program also called for providing an old-age pension to elderly people (13)

sharecropping an agricultural system that developed in the South after the Civil War where a planter provided the land, the tools, and a cabin and the workers labored all year in return for a share of the profit when the crop was sold (11)

siege a situation that occurs when armed forces try to capture a fortified fort or town by surrounding it and preventing any supplies from reaching it (7)

sit-in a demonstration where a person or group enters a facility and refuses to leave until they are recognized or their demands are met (15)

slave a person who is bound to a life of service to others and who is considered property (6)

smuggling illegal trade (3)

speaker of the house the official elected by the members of the Louisiana house of representatives to preside over its sessions (4)

specie gold or silver (6)

speculator one who buys items (such as land) hoping they will increase in value and, when sold, provide a profit (6)

spirituals the sacred folk songs of African Americans (1)

states' rights the principle that the rights and responsibilities of the states should take precedence over the rights and responsibilities of the federal government (10)

strike a labor union tactic where workers refuse to work, usually over some grievance, until their demands and are heard and addressed (12)

suburbs neighborhoods on the outer edges of cities (15)

suffrage the right to vote (9)

sunshine law a law that requires all government meetings, involving both elected and appointed groups, be public (15)

Superior Council a group existing during the French colonial period that was in charge of judicial matters and was presided over by the commissary commissioner (6)

Superport an offshore port in the Gulf of Mexico that was constructed to handle extremely deep ships; serves primarily the offshore oil industry and Louisiana's oil refineries (3)

surplus a situation that occurs when revenues are more than expenditures (4)

surveyor one who measures and marks off boundary lines to establish land ownership (7)

swamp a seasonally flooded forest (2)

T

tariff a tax on imports designed to keep out foreign competition (9)

taxes amounts charged citizens by their governments (federal, state, and local) to pay for services provided (4)

technology the practical use of scientific knowledge, especially in business and industry (16)

temple mound a mound built by prehistoric Indians and used for religious ceremonies (5)

topography physical features of the land (2)

tornado a severe and unpredictable windstorm characterized by a funnel-shaped cloud; wind speeds, which move counterclockwise around a low pressure center, may reach as high as 500 mph (2)

totem a tribal symbol; an animal, plant, or natural object serving as a symbol of a clan or family (5)

treason the crime of trying to overthrow the government of one's state or country (7)

treasurer the custodian of the state's money (4)

treaty a formal agreement between two or more nations (5)

tribe a group of people who share a common ancestry, language, name, and way of living (5)

tutor a private teacher (9)

U

Unionist a person who supported the Union during the entire Civil War period (11)

United Service Organizations USOs; organizations intended to provide a home-away-from-home for those serving in the military (14)

upland South the hill country of North Louisiana plus the neighboring states of Mississippi, Alabama, and Georgia (1)

urban of or like the city (1)

V

veto to refuse to approve legislation (4)

victory garden a garden planted by civilians during World War II to provide fresh vegetables (14)

Voting Rights Act a federal law passed in 1965 that outlawed literacy tests and poll taxes and that sent registrars into the southern states to register black voters (15)

W

weather the immediate conditions of the Earth's atmosphere: temperature, precipitation, and wind (2)

wetlands swamps, marsh, and other areas that have a natural supply of water and are covered or soaked with water at least part of the year (2)

White League an organization established in 1874 by the Redeemer-Democrats to restore political power to the prewar white Democrats (11)

wolds raised uplands and ridges in the Hills region (2)

Women's Christian Temperance Union an organization that worked to stop the sale of alcoholic beverages (13)

Works Progress Administration a New Deal program that provided work for men with families; the men built schools, courthouses, parks, and other public buildings; the WPA also hired artists to paint murals on public buildings and writers to compile county information (13)

writ of habeas corpus a court document requiring that a person being held be brought before the court to determine if that person is being held lawfully (9)

Z

zydeco the music of French-speaking African Americans of South Louisiana; the song is sung in French and musical accompaniment includes an accordion and the rub board (1)

INDEX

The purpose of the index is to help you locate information quickly. The index contains references to not only text but also photographs, maps, and other illustrations. A page number with an **m** before it indicates a map; a page number with a **p** before it indicates a photograph, painting, or other type of illustration.

Isleños, 41, 245, **p**245

J

Jackson, 280-281, **p**280, **p**281
Jackson, Andrew, 280, **p**285, 286, 288, 312, 314
Jackson Parish, 419, 497, 574
Jackson Square, 240, 288, 357, 536
jambalaya, 16
Jayhawkers, 370, 390
jazz, 2, 450
Jefferson Davis Parish, 574
Jefferson Island, 72, **p**72
Jefferson Parish, 89, 148, 149-150, 546, 574
Jefferson, Thomas, 151, 265, 266, 274, 275, 278
Jena, 180, 574
Jena Band of Choctaw, 180
Jenkins, Woody, 547, **p**547
Jennings, 37, 102, 428, **p**428, 567, 574
jetties, 431-432, **p**431
Jewish community, 339
Jim Crow laws, 418
Jindal, Bobby, 554
Johnson, Andrew, 386, **p**386
Johnson, Henry, 312, 572
Johnson, Isaac, 572
Johnson, Neil, 560
Johnston, J. Bennett, 546-547, **p**546, 551
Joliet, Louis, 196, **p**196
Jones, Sam, 496-497, **p**496, 499, 573
Jonesboro, 574
Jonesville, 481
judges, 141
judicial branch, 140-142
jury, 141-142

K

Kansas-Nebraska Act, 347
Kellogg, William Pitt, 392, **p**392, 393, 573
Kennedy, John F., 524, **p**524
Kennon, Robert F., 501-502, **p**501, 504, 573
Kerlerec, Louis Billouart, Chevalier de, 225, **p**225, 571
Keyes, Francis Parkinson, 561
King, Alvin O., 466, 573
King, Grace, 561
Kisatchie National Forest, 78-79

Kisatchie Wold, 76
Knights of the White Camellia, 392
Know-Nothings, 314
Korean War, 509, **p**511
Ku Klux Klan, 455-456, **p**457, 551

L

L'Ouverture, Toussant, 265, **p**265
La Salle, René Robert Cavelier, Sieur de, 172, 197-198, **p**197, **p**198, 199
labor,
    child, 441
    freedmen, 388, 420-421
    Knights of Labor, 421
    right-to-work laws, 504, 531, 532
    unions, 421, 504, 527, 531-532
    See also slaves.
La Farge, Oliver, 561
Lafayette, 8, 19, 31, 476, 519, 562, 574
Lafayette, Marquis de, 312
Lafayette Parish, 574
Lafitte, Jean, 284, **p**284, 286
Lafourche Parish, 30, 148, 173, 574
Lake Bistineau, **p**58-59, 60
Lake Borgne, 59, 286
Lake Bruin, 60, **p**60
Lake Charles, 59, 444, 537, 555, 574
Lake Chicot, 59
Lake Claiborne, 59, **p**76-77, 564
Lake D'Arbonne, 59
Lake Fausse Point, 564
Lake Maurepas, 59
Lake Peigneur, 72, **p**72
Lake Pontchartrain, 59, 213, 332, 352, 477
Lake Providence, 574
Lake St. Joseph, **p**60
lakes, **m**51, 59-61
land grants, 214, 272
land regions, *see* natural regions.
Landrieu, Mary, 547, **p**547
language, 2
Larto Lake, 60
LaSalle Parish, 574
latitude, 48
Laura Plantation, **p**324-325
Laussat, Pierre Clément de, 572

N

Nacogdoches Wold, 76
Napoleon Bonaparte, 128, **p**129, 264, **p**264, 265, 267, **p**269
Napoleonic Code, 128
Napoleonville, 574
Nast, Thomas, 135
Natchez Indians, 167, 168-169, 182, 186, 191, 218-219, 222
Natchez Uprising, 218-219
Natchitoches, 12, 17, 294, 364, 567, **p**567, 575
  during Spanish colonial period, 243, 251, 256
  establishment of colony, 206-211, **p**210-211
Natchitoches Parish, 5, 13, 290, 575
National Association for the Advancement of Colored People (NAACP), 518
National Grange, 415
National Guard, 131-132
Native Americans, 42, 157-193, 307
  and early explorers, 166, 203
  Chickasaw War, 220-224
  culture, 166, 182-191
  federal recognition of, 170
  in American Revolution, 180
  land cessions, 177, 180
  language families, 167, **m**167
  Natchez Massacre, 218-219
  prehistoric cultures, 158-165
  relations with British, 222, 223
  relations with French, 203, 206, 218-219, 220-224
  trade with, 170, 184
  See also specific tribes.
Native Guards, 373-374, **p**374
natural gas, 104, 429
Natural Levee area, 65, 67
natural regions, 63-77, **m**63, **m**64
  Hills, 76-77
  Marsh, 70-73
  Mississippi Floodplain, 65-67
  Red River Valley, 74-75
  Terraces, 68-69
natural resources, 94, 101-113, 143
  biological, 108-113
  conservation of, 88-89
  forests, 108, 424
  minerals, 102-107, 428-429

  natural gas, 104, 429
  oil, 102, 428
  salt, 104
  sulphur, 106-107
  tax on, 455
  water, 50-53, 56-62, 101
navigable, 50
Neo Indians, 161-165
neutral, 248
Neville Brothers, 6
New Basin Canal, 331
New Biloxi, **p**214-215
New Deal, 468, 469, 478-482
New Iberia, 8, 71, 244, 257, **p**399, 537, 567, 574
New Orleans, 2, 5, 15, 19, 34, 97, **p**123, 128, 269, 275, 279, 349, 394, 396, 400, 401, 403, 406, 409, 419, 423, 433, 439, **p**439, 450, 451, **p**452-453, 490, **p**490, 492, 493, **p**494, 508, 509, 522, 525, 527, 534, 545, 555, 575
  and 1927 flood, 476-477
  and civil rights movement, **p**517, 518-519,
  and cultural elements, 559, **p**559, 562
  and politics, 314, 315
  antebellum, **p**300-301, 302-303, 305, 318, 319, 331, 332, 333, 338, 340
  architecture of, 254, 275
  as capital, 283, 312
  during French colonial period, 225, 227, 265, 267
  during Spanish colonial period, 234, 237, 239, 240, 248, 251, **m**252, 253, 256, 257, **p**259
  founding, 213-214
  geography, 63, 67, 86, **m**266
  government of, 149, 314, 501, 502
  in Civil War, 350, 351, 354, 356-357, **p**356-357, 372, **p**372, 374, 375-376
  port of, 292, 203, 318, **p**318-319, 333, 432
  race riot, 389
  in War of 1812, 286
New Orleans Picayune, 334, 349, 389
New Roads, 19, 37, 575
Newellton, 564
newspapers, 257, 334, 372, 467
Nicholls, Francis T., 397, 413-414, **p**414, 573
Nicholls State University, 538
Nineteenth Amendment, to U.S. Constitution, 452
noblesse oblige, 413

ACKNOWLEDGEMENTS

SURVEY PARTICIPANTS: The following teachers of Louisiana History participated in a survey as we developed plans for *Louisiana: The History of an American State*.

Albarado, Lori — Livaudais Junior High, Jefferson Parish
Atkins, Cynethia — Keithville School, Caddo Parish
Bairnsfather, Bryan — Archbishop Shaw High School, Jefferson Parish
Besse, Gil — Morgan City Junior High, St. Mary Parish
Brice, Madge — Glenbrook School, Webster Parish
Champagne, Rita — Bethany Christian School, East Baton Rouge Parish
Fontenot, Julia — Sacred Heart Elementary, Evangeline Parish
Gilliland, Anna M. — West Monroe Junior High, Ouachita Parish
Graham, Atonia — Walker Junior High, Livingston Parish
Hankins, Lisa — Lake Castle School, Orleans Parish
Haynes, Cynthia — Haynesville Junior High, Clairborne Parish
Helton, James A. — Christ the King Parish School, Jefferson Parish
Heurtin, Sherry C. — J. B. Martin Middle, St. Charles Parish
Jackson, Joann — Hollywood Middle, Caddo Parish
Jackson, Leonard — East Iberville Jr./Sr. High, Iberville Parish
Jackson, Paul — Routhwood Elementary, Tensas Parish
Kittler, Ann Frances — Christ the King School, Bossier Parish
Koerner, Paula — St. Joseph Catholic School, Caddo Parish
Landreneau, Janis — Evangeline Parish School Board, Evangeline Parish
Landry, Cary, — Fisher School, Jefferson Parish
LeBlanc, Rose — Gueydan High, Vermilion Parish
Lewis, Kristen A. — Saint Mark's Cathedral School, Caddo Parish
Martin, Barbara — St. Pius X, Orleans Parish
Martin, Nick — St. Louise DeMarillac School, St. Bernard Parish
Masson, Terryl — St. Louis King of France, Jefferson Parish
Matherne, Ronald P. — Lacache Middle School, Terrebonne Parish
Milliken, Jeannie — Huntington School, Concordia Parish
Moore, Martha P. — William Pitcher Jr. High, St. Tammany Parish
Olivier, Patsy — Church Point Middle School, Acadia Parish
Pratt, Harry, D. A. — Holy Savior Menard Central High School, Rapides Parish
Ross, Marie D. — St. Cecilia, Lafayette Parish
Shanz, Dale Beglis — LeBlanc Middle School, Calcasieu Parish
Smith, Donette — Ridgewood Middle School, Caddo Parish
Stahl, Rosemary — St. Mark, St. Bernard Parish
Stelly, Pamela — J. I. Watson Middle, Calcasieu Parish
Strother, Kristy — Florien High School, Sabine Parish
Swayze, Pam — Harrisonburg Elementary, Catahoula Parish
Tyler, Rhonda M. — Brame Junior High, Rapides Parish
Vance, Jerry — Reeves High School, Allen Parish
Veazey, Sheryl M. — Pecan Island High School, Vermilion Parish
Vickers, Jimmy R. — Jena Junior High, LaSalle Parish
Wilson, Adrian L. — Sherwood Middle School, East Baton Rouge Parish
Wilson, Holly R. — Broadmoor Middle School, East Baton Rouge Parish
Wilson, Vicki — Mangham Junior High, Richland Parish
Zoska, Raymond — Atonement Lutheran School, Jefferson Parish

Fleming Caffrey. 152-153 (both) Debbie Fleming Caffrey. **CHAPTER FIVE:** 156 -157 Debbie Fleming Caffrey. 159 Pinson Mounds State Archeological Area, TN. 160-161 (both) Pinson Mounds State Archeological Area, TN. 162-163 (both) Robin McDonald. 164-165 (all) Robin McDonald. 166 UASC. 168-169 Robin McDonald. 170 Peabody Museum, Harvard University. 171 Robin McDonald. 172 Debbie Fleming Caffrey. 173 LOT. 174-175 Debbie Fleming Caffrey. 176 Debbie Fleming Caffrey. 177 Robin McDonald. 178-179 (all) Debbie Fleming Caffrey. 180-181 (both) Joslyn Art Museum, Omaha, Nebraska. 182 Smithsonian Institution. 183 Peabody Museum, Harvard University. 184 Smithsonian Institution. 185 Peabody Museum, Harvard University. 186 Smithsonian Institution. 187 Peabody Museum, Harvard University. 188-189 Peabody Museum, Harvard University. 190-191 UASC. **CHAPTER SIX:** 194-195 Robin McDonald. 196 HNOC. 197 (left) LC; (right) HNOC. 198 LC. 199 HNOC. 200 HNOC. 201 New Orleans Museum of Art. 202 Museum of the City of Mobile. 203 Robin McDonald. 204 Museum of the City of Mobile. 205 Museum of Versailles. 206-207 (both) Robin McDonald. 208 (above) LOT; (below) Robin McDonald. 208-209 Robin McDonald. 209 (below) Robin McDonald. 210-211 (all) Robin McDonald. 212 LOT. 213 HNOC. 214-215 USAC. 215 (right) Corbis/Bettmann. 216 (top) LC; (above) HNOC. 217 HNOC. 218-219 (both) Smithsonian Institution. 220 Robin McDonald. 221 HNOC. 222-223 Peabody Museum, Harvard University. 224-225 (both) HNOC. 226-227 Robin McDonald. **CHAPTER SEVEN:** 230-231 Robin McDonald. 232 Washington and Lee University. 233 Wisconsin Historical Society. 235 LC. 236-237 HNOC. 238 HNOC. 239 LC. 240 LSM. 241 HNOC. 242-243 Robin McDonald. 244 HNOC. 245 Isleños Center, St. Bernard. 246-247 (both) Debbie Fleming Caffrey. 248 LC. 249 HNOC. 250 HNOC. 251 LSM. 252 HNOC. 253 LSM. 254-255 (both) Robin McDonald. 256 Corbis/Bettmann. 257 HNOC. 258-259 (all) LSM. **CHAPTER EIGHT:** 262-263 LSM. 264 LC. 265 LC. 266 (all) HNOC. 267 (both) LC. 268-269 HNOC. 271 LSM. 272 HNOC. 273 LSM. 274-275 HNOC. 275 (right) Robin McDonald. 276-277 (all) Robin McDonald. 278 (above) LC; (below) LSM. 279 LC. 280-281 (all) Robin McDonald. 282 LSM. 283 HNOC. 284 LSM. 285 HNOC. 286-287 HNOC. 288-289 (both) HNOC. 290-291 (all) Robin McDonald. 292 HNOC. 293 Louisiana State University Museum of Art. 294 HNOC. 295 Robin McDonald. 296 Robin McDonald. 297 LC. **CHAPTER NINE:** 300-301 HNOC. 302-303 (both) LSM. 304-305 LSM. 306 (left) Robin McDonald; (right) LOT. 307 New Orleans Museum of Art. 308 HNOC. 309 LC. 310 (both) HNOC. 311 Robin McDonald. 312-313 Robin McDonald. 314 LC. 315 LSM. 316-317 (all) Robin McDonald. 318-319 HNOC. 320-321 Louisiana State University Museum of Art. 321 (right) Robin McDonald. 322-323 (all) Robin McDonald. 324-325 (all) Robin McDonald. 326 HNOC. 327 LSM. 328-329 Robin McDonald. 329 (right) HNOC. 330-331 HNOC. 333 HNOC. 334 (above) HNOC; (below) Robin McDonald. 335 Debbie Fleming Caffrey. 336 Robin McDonald. 337 (top) Collection of Robin McDonald; (below left) Robin McDonald; (below right) Kentucky Historical Society. 338 LSM. 339 Robin McDonald. 340 (above) Robin McDonald; (below) New Orleans Museum of Art. 341 HNOC. **CHAPTER TEN:** 344-345 Robin McDonald. 347 LC. 348 LC. 350 (above) HNOC; (below) LSM. 350-351 LSM. 351 (above right) Robin McDonald. 352 *Battles and Leaders of the Civil War.* 353 LSM. 354-355 HNOC. 356 (below) HNOC. 356-357 HNOC. 357 (below right) *Battles and Leaders of the Civil War.* 358 (above left) *Battles and Leaders of the Civil War.* 358-359 Louisiana State University Museum of Art. 360

Kurz and Allison. 361 Louisiana State University Museum of Art. 362-363 Louisiana State University Museum of Art. 363 (below right) LOT. 364-365 (both) LSM. 366 (above) LOT; (below, left and right) Robin McDonald. 368-369 (all) LC. 370 *Battles and Leaders of the Civil War.* 371 U.S. Army Military History Institute. 372 LSM. 373 *Harper's History of the Civil War.* 374 LSM. 375 (above) University of North Carolina at Chapel Hill; (below) UASC. 376 (left) *Harper's History of the Civil War;* (right) Tulane University. 377 HNOC. 378 (left) LC; (right) Robin McDonald. 379 LC. **CHAPTER ELEVEN:** 382-383 Robin McDonald. 384 HNOC. 385 Corbis/Bettmann. 386 Tennessee State Museum. 387 HNOC. 388 (above) HNOC; (below) LSM. 389 *Harper's History of the Civil War.* 390-391 (both) HNOC. 392-393 (both) HNOC. 394 LC. 395 LSM. 396 HNOC. 397 LC. 398 HNOC. 399 LSM. 400 HNOC. 400-401 Art Resource/Musée d'Orsay, Paris. 402-403 (both) LSM. 404-405 (all) Robin McDonald. 406-407 (both) LSM. **CHAPTER TWELVE:** 410-411 LSM. 413 LSM. 414-415 (both) HNOC. 416-417 (both) LC. 418-419 LC. 420 HNOC. 421 (both) Robin McDonald. 422-423 HNOC. 423 (below right) LSM. 424-425 (both) LSM. 426 LOT. 428 (above) LOT; (below) HNOC. 429 HNOC. 430 LOT. 431 (above) HNOC; (below) LSM. 432 -433 (both) HNOC. 434-435 (all) Robin McDonald. 436-437 (all) Debbie Fleming Caffrey. 438-439 HNOC. 440-441 (both) HNOC. 442-443 (both) LC. 444-445 (both) HNOC. **CHAPTER THIRTEEN:** 448-449 Robin McDonald. 450 LC. 451 HNOC. 452-453 HNOC. 454 UPI/Corbis/Bettmann. 455 HNOC. 456 OSC. 457 LC. 458 OSC. 459 UPI/Corbis/Bettmann. 460-461 (both) OSC. 462 HNOC. 463 (both) Robin McDonald. 465 UPI/Corbis/Bettmann. 466 HNOC. 467 OSC. 468-469 (both) UPI/Corbis/Bettmann. 470 OSC. 471 UPI/Corbis/Bettmann. 472-473 (all) Robin McDonald. 474-475 UPI/Corbis/Bettmann. 476-477 (both) UPI/Corbis/Bettmann. 478 Atlanta Historical Society. 479 LC. 480 LSM. 481 LC. 482 HNOC. 483 LC. **CHAPTER FOURTEEN:** 486-487 Robin McDonald. 488 LC. 489 HNOC. 490 (below left) HNOC. 490-491 UPI/Corbis/Bettmann. 492 HNOC. 493 LC. 494-495 (all) HNOC. 496 HNOC. 497 UPI/Corbis/Bettmann. 498 Robin McDonald. 499 UPI/Corbis/Bettmann. 500 HNOC. 501 OSC. 502 HNOC. 503 (UPI/Corbis/Bettmann. 504 LC. 505 HNOC. 506 -507 (all) Robin McDonald. 508-509 (all) UPI/Corbis/Bettmann. 510-511 (all) UPI/Corbis/Bettmann. **CHAPTER FIFTEEN:** 514-515 Robin McDonald. 516-517 (both) UPI/Corbis/Bettmann. 518-519 (all) UPI/Corbis/Bettmann. 520-521 (all) UPI/Corbis/Bettmann. 522 Robin McDonald. 523 UPI/Corbis/Bettmann. 524-525 (all) UPI/Corbis/Bettmann. 526-527 (all) OSC. 528 Robin McDonald. 529 (both) UPI/Corbis/Bettmann. 530-531 Debbie Fleming Caffrey. 532 HNOC. 533 UPI/Corbis/Bettmann. 534 UPI/Corbis/Bettmann. 535 Debbie Fleming Caffrey. 536-537 (both) LC. 538 (both) LC. 539 UPI/Corbis/Bettmann. **CHAPTER SIXTEEN:** 542-543 Robin McDonald. LC. 545 UPI/Corbis/Bettmann. 546 (both) UPI/Corbis/Bettmann. 547 (both) OSC. 548 OSC. 549 UPI/Corbis/Bettmann. 550-551 (both) UPI/Corbis/Bettmann. 552 *Atlanta Journal & Constitution.* 553 UPI/Corbis/Bettmann. 554 Debbie Fleming Caffrey. 555 Robin McDonald. 556 (above) Debbie Fleming Caffrey; (below) UPI/Corbis/Bettmann. 557 (both) Robin McDonald. 558 Robin McDonald. 559 (above) Rodger Houston Ogden Collection, New Orleans; (below) Robin McDonald. 560 Debbie Fleming Caffrey. 561 (above) HNOC; (below) UPI/Corbis/Bettmann. 562-563 (both) Robin McDonald. 564 (above) Robin McDonald; (below) LOT. 565 (above) Robin McDonald; (below) LOT. 566-567 (both) Robin McDonald. **APPENDIX ONE:** 570 LOT.